Contemplative Learning and Inquiry across Disciplines

Contemplative Learning and Inquiry across Disciplines

Edited by

Olen Gunnlaugson

Edward W. Sarath

Charles Scott

Heesoon Bai

Published by State University of New York Press, Albany

Printed in the United States of America

For information, contact State University of New York Press, Albany, NY
www.sunypress.edu

Production by Jenn Bennett
Marketing by Kate McDonnell

Library of Congress Cataloging-in-Publication Data

Contemplative learning and inquiry across disciplines / edited by Olen Gunnlaugson, Edward W. Sarath, Charles Scott, and Heesoon Bai.
pages cm
Includes bibliographical references and index.
ISBN 978-1-4384-5239-5 (hc : alk. paper) 978-1-4384-5240-1 (pb : alk. paper)
1. Education—Moral and ethical aspects. 2. Interdisciplinary approach in education. 3. Mind and body. 4. Contemplation. I. Gunnlaugson, Olen, editor of compilation.

LC268.C775 2014
370.11'4—dc23 2013030148

10 9 8 7 6 5 4 3 2 1

Contents

PART II
DOMAIN SPECIFIC PERSPECTIVES

PART III
CONTEMPLATING CHANGE: INDIVIDUAL AND COLLECTIVE TRANSFORMATION IN CONTEMPLATIVE EDUCATION ENVIRONMENTS

An Introduction to Contemplative Learning and Inquiry across Disciplines

Olen Gunnlaugson, Edward W. Sarath, Charles Scott, and Heesoon Bai

Background of Contemplative Perspectives

We are delighted that the long awaited academic window for writing this book has finally opened! The good news is that contemplative approaches to higher education are beginning to emerge across a wide cross section of disciplines and fields from the work of scholar-practitioners who are pushing the boundaries of traditional theories and practices of post-secondary instruction and learning. As well, scholar-practitioners are finding ways in which long-established contemplative theories and practices can optimally fit into or be shaped by existing academic disciplines. This is not entirely surprising. Thinkers such as Pierre Hadot (1995) and Michel Foucault (2001) have noted the convergence and divergence of contemplative and academic traditions in the past; Foucault and many others have extensively documented the "Cartesian moment," a turn in the history of Western thought where contemplative practices, as part of care of the self in context of community and cosmos were divorced from academic pursuits. While contemplative practices have been foundational to wisdom traditions throughout various cultural periods, more recently these practices are being reexamined across different context(s) of learning, particularly in mainstream North American institutions of higher education. Many scholars are finding it increasingly necessary to incorporate the rigors of contemplative practice within academic contexts, discovering that contemplative process and method is well equipped to enhance, deepen, and broaden academic thought and praxis across disciplines. As well, as the essays in this volume make clear, contemplative practices help focus the mind, offer the dispassionately reflective capacities of mindfulness, reduce stress, create and uncover meaning, insight and wisdom, as well as facilitate awareness of both inner and outer worlds and our fruitful engagements in them. Among the most significant contributions is that these practices help students and instructors deepen their awareness of and engagement with self, others, and the world.

In the past decade, several academic conferences and a growing educational literature have focused on contemplative approaches to instruction, learning, and knowing. As an example, the following conferences in recent years have either exclusively focused on or featured presentations about contemplative approaches to instruction and learning: Contemplative Pedagogy in Higher Education (Amherst College, May 2003), Contemplative Practices and Education: Making Peace in Ourselves and in the World (Teachers College, 2005), Uncovering the Heart of Higher Education (San Francisco, 2007), Mindful Learners: The Uses of Contemplative Practice in the Classroom (CUNY, 2006), Creativity, Consciousness, and the Academy: Bridging Interior and Exterior Realms of Teaching, Learning, and Research (University of Michigan, 2006), Developmental Issues in Contemplative Education (Garrison Institute, 2008), The Contemplative Heart of Higher Education, First Annual Association for Contemplative Mind in Higher Education (Amherst College, Massachusetts, 2009), and The Contemplative Academy, Second Annual Association for Contemplative Mind in Higher Education Conference (Amherst College, 2010).

In addition to institutions that were founded upon contemplative principles, such as the California Institute for Integral Studies, JFK University, Maharishi University, and Naropa University, all of which are accredited up through the graduate level, mainstream institutions such as Brown University and the University of Michigan have implemented contemplative curricula. The Rocky Mountain Contemplative Higher Education Network based in Colorado offers programs for academics interested in contemplative approaches to education as does the Center for Contemplative Mind in Society (CCMS) in Massachusetts, which has hosted annual contemplative retreats for contemplative curriculum development and issued over 130 individual fellowships for U.S. academics across North American campuses to develop courses that employ contemplative practices and more recently monthly Webinars. The creation by the CCMS of the Association for Contemplative Mind in Higher Education provided a national network to further promote this work. Finally, *Teachers College Record* (September, 2006) devoted an entire issue to the topic of contemplative education, and journal articles on contemplative approaches to instruction have appeared in other academic journals.[1] This research represents an acknowledgment that scholars wish to include and are including contemplative practices and the study of contemplation as legitimate elements in a number of academic disciplines beyond the confines of humanities and religious studies.

Traditionally, contemplatives were masterful at observing their experience, capable also of observing and interpreting signs and patterns distilled from contemplative engagement in the natural world. What signs are we reading in this current burgeoning interest and activity around contemplative ways of knowing in the academy? How are we *reading the world* and in turn, interpreting one another differently from a sustained engagement with the subtle phenomena of perception and consciousness? How might contemplative practice, both traditionally and re-conceived, address the hunger and search for re-balancing the pervasive modern habits of production and consumption without sufficient awareness of its psycho-social-environmental impacts—all habit structures in which our North American culture has been mired? How might traditionally conceived notions of contemplative practitioners engage more fully with the academic and surrounding communities, ecologies, and more-than-human worlds—in turn inspiring new ethics of engagement and activism?

We read the above-mentioned proliferation of contemplative approaches to studies, instruction, and learning in higher education as a poignant sign that the current life-world situation of our time is one that needs to regain a measure of dynamic balance, wisdom, and intelligence capable of embodying sustaining and sustainable alternative courses for the future. Our current academic world, characterized by increasing complexity, connectedness, and change, is increasingly asking for curricular and pedagogical approaches that effectively address these realities. Meanwhile, we note from personal teaching experience in the academy and the research literature (Astin, 2004; Astin, Astin, & Lindholm, 2010; Bai, Scott, & Donald, 2009; Lindholm, 2007; Palmer & Zajonc, 2010) that scholar-practitioners and students are looking for meaning, are interested in spiritual issues, and are looking for effective means and opportunities to explore these within their academic pursuits. Moreover, in pursuit of broadening epistemic boundaries and new knowledge, the academic community is finding contemplative approaches useful in this endeavor.

Yet in spite of the above-mentioned developments and issues, a peer-reviewed volume of current scholar-practitioners' accounts of contemplative learning and inquiry has not yet been published, until now. As we originally shared with our invited authors, we interpret this omission as an occasion and call for this book. Given what we feel is a growing collectively held view that contemplative approaches to learning and teaching will contribute significantly to the field of higher education at large, we have envisioned this book as a response to the timely need for providing an overview of the current landscape of contemplative instruction, pedagogy, and curriculum from the perspectives of leading researchers and practitioners across departments and institutions in North America.

This volume brings together a range of contemplative academic voices that draw upon diverse contexts. Our intention is to raise awareness of the applicability of contemplative studies as a watershed field, capable of informing, enriching, and sustaining the many disciplines and instructional contexts that comprise the field of higher education. In effect, this book will be the first to comprehensively map out current academic voices and perspectives on contemplative approaches to learning and inquiry through featured writings on the details, experiences, challenges, and promise of contemplative approaches. Additionally, this book explores key theoretical aspects of contemplative learning, outlining current approaches and blind spots within various contexts and the emerging field as a whole.

We anticipate the primary readership of this book will be faculty across disciplines, teacher educators, researchers, students, consultants, and others with an interest in contemplative approaches to higher education. We also hope the book will act as a resource that will serve university educators and teachers looking for innovative and comprehensive solutions to challenges they face. Finally, we look forward to this book being adopted for curricula relating to innovative approaches to higher education.

Characteristics of Contemplative Learning and Inquiry

To date, scholar-practitioners have taken inspiration for the investigation of contemplation from the world wisdom traditions (Buddhist, Vedantic, Taoist, Quaker, Christian, Sufi, ancient Greek, etc.) as well as perspectives in new branches of scientific thought (i.e., neurophenomenology, cognitive science, etc.), social sciences and the humanities (positive psychology, perennial philosophy, art studies, environmental studies, ethics and moral education), business (learning organizations, leadership studies), among others—each advocating approaches to teaching and learning that affirm the significance of cultivating individual and collective forms of enhanced intelligence, wisdom and well being with our students through contemplative ways of knowing.

To the extent that most if not all higher educational settings have at least an implicit or tacit contemplative dimension, we begin with the foundational assumption that any course can be taught with a contemplative orientation. Whether in the form of aspiring to hold the creative tensions of multiple perspectives or polarities in a conversation from a place of equanimity; sitting a few minutes in engaged silence with one's class, supporting, enacting, and drawing from the intersubjective field of learning; listening from and being the relationship with one's students; engaging in contemplative practices with one's students before, during, and after class; occasioning situations that attend to the class subject in relation to the dynamics of our richly dimensioned inner lives (cognitively, somatically, aesthetically, emotionally, spiritually) and outer world, contemplative approaches to teaching and learning are informed by the needs for wholeness, integration, interrelatedness, completion, and unity.

In working toward transforming disengaged forms of academic analysis and disenchanted and instrumental habits of mind and life, the project of cultivating contemplative capacities of presence, discernment, and equanimity with one's students, colleagues, and communities becomes a significant offering for our time. At the same time, we might inquire into the distinguishing features or capacities of contemplative inquiry and what commonalities or differences might exist for engagement across academic disciplines. Several contemplative capacities or features have been noted by scholars: focused, nonconceptual attention; a witnessing mindfulness; presencing; suspension of assumptions and judgments; discernment; a broader or deeper sense of connection with others and one's surroundings and a concomitant expanded sense of self; empathy and compassion; respect; intimacy; an increased sense of wholeness and integration; a deeper sense of engagement and participation.

Emerging from this range of considerations is what might be called a transdisciplinary praxis of contemplation: an integration of the theoretical understandings of contemplation and its roles in a (post)modern, secular, and pluralistic society and the experimental, experiential practice of contemplative methodologies developed out the rigorous and scholarly interplay of various historical contemplative traditions, contemporary scientific research, the arts and humanities, health sciences, and organizational management and leadership. It seems reasonable that addressing the usefulness and issues of contemplative education in a transdisciplinary fashion allows for broader and more diverse epistemic perspectives; at the same time, a transdisciplinary approach offers greater possibilities for enriching the field of contemplative education. We already have a growing body of literature to support new and varied tributaries, such as the ones mentioned above. With time, these will add significantly to the common watershed of contemplative theory and practice, creating both a comprehensive knowledge base in theory and a diverse set of practices that can respond to changing circumstances and evolving needs not previously present or known, connecting the lived realities of our students and communities in ways that meaningfully address real and current issues. The academy in its diversity can contribute much to and advance a field once held to be the province of the wisdom traditions and monastic orders. This collection of essays allows us to identify common needs and challenges, as well as the diverse perspectives and approaches which can allow us to develop meaningful and responsive curricular and pedagogical practices in contemplative education.

Among the important contributions we seek to make in this volume to the evolution of this praxis is an enlivened self-critical sensibility, whereby this still-young field reflects on its patterns, tendencies, assumptions, and hidden ideologies that, over time, may inhibit progress. The fact that many key questions that contemplative educators have wrestled with from the inception of this movement remain as elusive as ever underscores this need.

What exactly does—or perhaps more aptly given the wide range of activities that might be deemed contemplative—does not, constitute contemplative practice? To what degree, if any, are contemplative forms of knowing different, connected to, or emergent from somatic, sensory, rational, and emotional ways of knowing? How are contemplative forms of learning a part of transformative learning? Who is qualified to teach these practices? What curricular and pedagogical approaches are best suited to a comprehensive understanding and practice of contemplation? If contemplative practices are to be integrated in credit-bearing coursework, how are they to be assessed? Is the effectiveness of contemplative practice compromised when these methodologies are extricated from the traditions in which they have originated and evolved and adapted to academic classrooms? Contemplative practices have traditionally been situated within spiritual and moral philosophies—how necessary is such an integration? Are we prepared to accept and respond to with possibly powerful and sudden transformations or disruptions—positive or negative, physical, psychological, or existential-spiritual—which contemplative practices might bring.

While it is neither the intention nor within the scope of this volume to articulate definitive responses to all of these questions, we believe the extent to which they are acknowledged within this collection of essays represents significant strides forward in the contemplative education conversation. We are also happy to see in the following pages what might be reasonably characterized as a newfound depth in this conversation, marked by the intersection of intellectual rigor, spiritual richness, and pedagogical innovation—all of which are essential to the integrity and progress of the field. That, moreover, within this paradigm-expanding thrust sophisticated work is being done in the intersubjective dimension—arguably a new dimension of contemplative studies—adds to our enthusiasm for the project. Such a praxis of contemplative education serves in helping students develop, through contemplative practices, a deeper awareness of self, others, and the world, and through that a deeper sense of purpose, place, and connection with others, as well as surrounding communities, ecologies, and greater cosmos.

Overview of the Book

This book offers an overview of the current landscape of contemplative instruction, pedagogy, and curriculum from a variety of perspectives across disciplines. Our hope is that this book will act as a resource to serve a broader range of university instructors looking for contemplative solutions to the teaching and learning challenges we face.

Part I: Contemplative Studies: A New Academic Discipline

In this opening section, we examine a wide cross section of the work being done in the field as well as the benefits and challenges that accompany the introduction of this field into the academy. Arthur Zajonc begins by situating contemplative education within the largely objective/exterior orientation of the conventional academy. Deborah Orr fills an important gap in delineating philosophical underpinnings for this work from the perspectives of several contemplative traditions. Mara Adelman brings us back to the day-to-day realities of many students and faculty, often characterized by a morass of turbulence and information overload, and illustrates the practical benefits that contemplative methodologies offer to these challenges. John Miller reminds us that it is nothing less than the innermost being of our students that is being touched by this kind of pedagogy. David Lee Kaiser and Saratid Sakulku offer an interesting comparison between U.S. and Thai perspectives and approaches to contemplative learning and teaching. Harold Roth closes this section with a pedagogical framework he has evolved over many years of working with contemplative methodologies in the classroom.

Part I: Domain Specific Perspectives

In this section, we encounter the perspectives of contemplative educators who approach this domain through the lens of particular fields of study. David Kahane shares insights from his work with students in a political science class and how contemplative practices both bring to awareness tendencies to remain oblivious to, as well as enliven compassion for, the suffering of distant strangers. Elise Young approaches history from a contemplative vantage point, drawing from Buddhist and African traditions to show the process of historicizing to be a kind of contemplative pathway. Daniel Barbezat uses contemplative practices in his economics teaching to help students become more aware of prevailing patterns that mediate desire and fulfillment. Nancy Waring chronicles the integration of mindfulness practice with conventional academic discourse in an innovative class she has created and reflects on the further curricular inroads that have been opened up from this work at her institution. David Levy recounts his experience in an information technology class, where in addition to silent, sitting meditation, he devises an innovative, contemplative approach to the process of email. Finally, Alfred Kasniak shares insights into contemplative experience and pedagogy from the perspective of cognitive sciences.

Part III: Contemplating Change: Individual and Collective Transformation in Contemplative Education Environments

In this section, we encounter a variety of perspectives on the transformative nature of this work, which we will see manifests not only in the experience of individuals on the contemplative path but also on collective scales. Diana Denton provides a candid portrayal of resistance to the furthering of this work from academic colleagues, and also articulates capacities for transforming this resistance into openings for expansive levels of feeling and understanding. John Baugher similarly explores the capacity for negative emotions to be transformed into positive experiences and pathways for individual and collective growth. Daniel Vokey reminds us of the potential for compromising the depth inherent in the contemplative domain as we introduce contemplative education into an academic world that is not predicated on interior growth. Richard Brown invites us to consider the transformative spaces and moments that arise in contemplative teaching and how they may be harnessed by mindful, creative educators for profound growth. Heesoon Bai, Avraham Cohen, Tom Culham, Sean Park, Shahar Rabi, Charles Scott, and Saskia Tait provide personalized reflections on various dimensions of contemplative experience and development, with reflections into the underlying nature of experience and reality—notably the *Dao*-field as an overarching stratum of consciousness, as posited in Daoism and many contemplative lineages—that are not commonly broached in academic contemplative discourse. In so doing, they set the stage for a consideration of possible new vistas for the field in the final section of the book.

Part IV: New Frontiers of Contemplative Learning and Instruction

Having considered a range of perspectives and approaches to contemplative education that might reasonably be characterized as normative in nature, the question naturally arises—what might the future evolution of the field entail? In this section, several possible responses to this question begin to come into view, common to all of which is an interest in the intersubjective realm. If, as is customary in contemplative education circles, conventional education might be viewed as third-person-oriented due to its exterior/objective emphasis, with contemplative practices bringing into the mix a first-person, interior/subjective dimension, the intersubjective domain deals with second-person, interactive, relational experience and development. Within the second-person realm, furthermore, the notion of a collective, field aspect of consciousness that may be enlivened in various types of interaction poses important ramifications not only for new classroom instructional approaches, but connections between the higher educational world and investigations into the non-dual nature of human consciousness and reality. Inasmuch as the notions of underlying interconnectedness and non-duality are posited by most of the world's wisdom traditions, this facet might be seen as a catalyst for deepening grounding between particular disciplines and the contemplative traditions that inform and inspire them but which in actuality often occupy the periphery of thinking and practice. It is one thing to engage in contemplative practice with the primary intentions of stress release and perhaps sharpening of cognitive faculties. It is quite another for contemplative instruction to be driven by a deeper non-dual relational understanding of learning and teaching.

At the same time, the second-person perspective—particularly when construed as "writ large" to also include cutting-edge contemporary developments in intersubjective interaction—may feed back insights to these traditional ideas, thus exemplifying aspects of an "integral" approach in which age-old precepts and new explorations coexist and coevolve.

Within this expansive perspective, Olen Gunnlaugson delineates three approaches to intersubjectivity and their ramifications for a new vision of leadership. Charles Scott draws from the work of Martin Buber and other contemplative sources important insights for pedagogical application of intersubjective approaches. Joanne Gozawa characterizes intersubjectivity in terms of an overarching "environment" that includes not only individuals but broader dimensions, physical and non-physical (e.g., archetypal influences), of an educational space. Edward W. Sarath, examining contemplative education through an integral lens, views the second-person, intersubjective domain as a key gateway to an entirely new educational worldview that both sheds critical light on the current contemplative project and suggests openings for future progress in the field. The final contribution is a conversation about intersubjectivity and the dynamics of collective fields between editor Olen Gunnlaugson and Chris Bache, author of *The Living Classroom: Teaching and Collective Consciousness* and *Dark Night, Early Dawn: Steps to a Deep Ecology of Mind.*

Closing Reflections

It is difficult to imagine a more compelling response to the legacy of appeals for educational reform that—particularly in light of the circumstances of today's world—are issued with an ever-increasing crescendo than the integration of contemplative study and practice in the higher education. Our hope is that this collection of essays at once serves as a summing up and, indeed, a celebration of the accomplishments made so far. Our intent is that the book establishes criteria by which further strides are to be measured, and that it also provides a glimpse of future possibilities that will be pursued by those contemplative scholar-practitioners who are positioned, inclined, and equipped as groundbreakers. The sheer volume of activity in this emerging field being pursued, the groundswell of interest in the current generation of students, the conductivity of the field toward first-rate scholarship as well as cutting-edge pedagogical innovation: these are signs that the field of contemplative studies in higher education is here to stay. What remains to be seen is what forms and directions the discipline takes as it evolves, and the extent to which growth is, on one hand, confined to horizontal expansion of the prevailing contemplative studies paradigm as opposed to, on the other, vertical transformation in which it becomes grounded in entirely new underpinnings.

While our inclination is to promote thinking and discourse that favors the second of these, it has been our distinct pleasure and honor to have had a chance to play a part in the evolution of this project in its early stages. No work is closer to the heart of what education is ideally all about.

We would like to express our appreciation for all the support and diligent work of the editorial staff at SUNY Press. Thanks to Nancy Ellegate who shepherded the book through the various stages of production and the editorial and marketing team she coordinated: Our thanks to Jenn Bennett and Kate McDonnell of SUNY Press, and Sue Morreale and Sharon Green at Partners Composition.

Dedication

We dedicate this book to those intrepid and daring souls who, in exploring the rich landscape of contemplative practice in their work and lives, have called and are currently calling into question and parting company with a whole range of educational conventions that have unwittingly compromised or marginalized the human journey of learning, growing, healing, and evolving course of development. Without your humanizing visions and wisdom, none of this project could have been possible.

Note

1. Other journals include the *American Journal of Education*, *Educational Theory*, *Journal of Transformative Education*, *Educational Leadership*, *Educational Insights*,

Paideusis, Journal of Philosophy of Education, Journal of Humanistic Psychology, Liberal Education, Innovative Higher Education, English Journal, Journal of Cognitive Affective Learning, Educational Psychologist, Social Work Education, New Directions for Community Colleges, New Directions for Teaching & Learning, Encounter, Reflective Practice, Music Educators Journal, Canadian Journal of Environmental Education, Trumpeter, and *International Journal of Lifelong Education* among others.

References

Astin, A. (2004). Why spirituality deserves a central place in liberal education. *Liberal Education, 90*(2), 34–41.

Astin, A., Astin, H., & Lindholm, J. (2010). Cultivating the spirit: How college can enhance students' inner lives. San Francisco: Jossey-Bass.

Bai, H., Scott, C., & Donald, B. (2009). Contemplative pedagogy and revitalization of teacher education. *Alberta Journal of Educational Research, 55*(3), 319–334.

Foucault, M. (2001). *The hermeneutics of the subject: Lectures at the Collège de France, 1981–1982* (F. Gros, Ed.; G. Burchell, Trans.). New York: Picador.

Hadot, P. (1995). *Philosophy as a way of life: Spiritual exercises from Socrates to Foucault.* Oxford: Blackwell.

Lindholm, J. A. (2007). Spirituality and the academy: Reintegrating our lives and the lives of our students. *About Campus, 12*(4), 10–17.

Palmer, P., & Zajonc, A. (2010). The heart of higher education: A call to renewal. San Francisco: Jossey-Bass.

Wilber, K. (2001). *Eye to eye: The quest for the new paradigm* (3rd ed.). Boston: Shambhala.

Zajonc, A. (2006). Love and knowledge: Recovering the heart of learning through contemplation. *Teachers College Record, 108*(9), 1742–1759.

Part I

Contemplative Studies

A New Academic Discipline

1

Contemplative Pedagogy in Higher Education

Toward a More Reflective Academy

Arthur Zajonc

There is no logical path leading to these laws [of nature], but only intuition, supported by sympathetic understanding of experience.

—Albert Einstein (cited in Miller, 1996, p. 369)

The colleges and universities of the world evidence the profound commitment we have to our future. What more can one want from an educational institution than a great faculty, terrific facilities, and a brilliant student body? Isn't this a bit of heaven? As you walk around campus, remind yourself that all these big buildings, the faculty, staff, and many billions of dollars annually—all this is directed toward something totally invisible, the minds of those student attending. The cultivation of the human being is the single *raison d'être* for this investment. So what could be the problem, why are faculty at countless schools occupied with questions of general education, pedagogy, and curriculum? What could possibly be wrong in paradise?

Problems in Paradise

Are the critics of American universities right when they say, as Harvard College's former dean Harry Lewis emphatically states, "Harvard and our other great universities lost sight of the essential purpose of undergraduate education." They are neglecting the central task of helping students "learn who they are, to search for a larger purpose for their lives, and to leave college as better human beings" (Lewis, 2007, p. xv). Echoing Lewis's sentiments, former Yale Law School dean Anthony Kronman argues in his book *Education's End* that the true purpose of higher education has been lost, namely, a deep exploration concerning "what life is for."

> A college or university is not just a place for the transmission of knowledge but a forum for the exploration of life's mystery and meaning through the careful but critical reading of the great works of literary and philosophical imagination. (Kronman, 2007, p. 6)

Stanley Fish in his recent *New York Times* op-ed, writes for many when he laments the monetization of higher education that measures education's "value" purely in terms of financial return on investment. And in a 2009 *New York Times* op-ed, the President of Harvard University, Drew Gilpin Faust, wrote about "The University's Crisis of Purpose" (Sept. 1, 2009):

> But even as we as a nation have embraced education as critical to economic growth and opportunity, we should remember that colleges and universities are about a great deal more than measurable utility. Unlike perhaps any other institutions in the world, they embrace the long view and nurture the kind of critical perspectives that look far beyond the present. . . . As a nation, we need to ask more than this [utility] from our universities. Higher learning can offer individuals and societies a depth and breadth of vision absent from the inevitably myopic present. Human beings need meaning, understanding and perspective as well as jobs. The question should not be whether we can afford to believe in such purposes in these times, but whether we can afford not to.

Each of these leaders in higher education points beyond utility and financial gain to a larger mission that higher education has and should continue to embrace. Depth, breadth, meaning, understanding, and perspective are the words used. What is the task of the university? To instruct in a discipline, surely. But beyond this, what? The author and poet (and English professor) Wendell Berry (1987) sums it up this way in his essay "The Loss of the University":

> The thing being made in a university is humanity. . . . [W]hat universities . . . are *mandated* to make or to help to make is human beings in the fullest sense of those words—not just trained workers or knowledgeable citizens but responsible heirs and members

> of human culture. . . . Underlying the idea of a university—the bringing together, the combining into one, of all the disciplines—is the idea that good work and good citizenship are the inevitable by-products of the making of a good—that is, a fully developed—human being. (p. 77)

This is a formidable mandate: the making of the human being. To begin with, what is the image we have of the human being these days? Who sits before us in the classroom, or works beside us at the lab bench? What does it mean to be human? This image informs our approach to teaching and learning either consciously or unconsciously. In my view we suffer today from a profoundly impoverished image of the human being and of our world. We have a diminished and inadequate ontology. What is needed is a truer, multidimensional understanding of the human being that will in turn lead to a comparably rich, multidimensional education. Only then can we hope that, through the collaborative effort of teachers and learners, we might, as Wendell Berry puts it, "make human beings in the fullest sense of those words." I want to explore with you some of the lost or neglected "dimensions" of ourselves and of higher education. Only when we knit together the multiple strands of learning and teaching will we have an education that addresses the depth, breath and meaning dimensions of life.

The Several Dimensions of Higher Education

Space is multidimensional (three-dimensional, if we leave aside relativity and string theory). Our learning, too, is multidimensional. Before turning to the role of contemplative pedagogy explicitly, I need to set the stage considering the importance of breadth in integrative education.

As an undergraduate, one is asked early in one's studies to declare a major area of disciplinary concentration: physics, English, neuroscience, French, and so on. This is a first axis or straight-line highway put down through the vast territory of learning. The full mastery of a single area of human knowledge or endeavor is of signal importance. One eventually comes to stand at the shoreline that separates what is understood and what is not. It is the province of discovery, innovation, and the new. But is mastery of a single domain really enough?

Ever since Diderot and D'Alembert codified the map of knowledge in their eighteenth-century *Encyclopédie*, universities around the world have adopted the divisions they made with the consequence that thousands of colleges and universities offer an essentially identical set of disciplinary concentrations. Lines are drawn by the dominant power (in this case the leaders of the French Enlightenment) and centuries later we are still living with that legacy. Did Diderot and D'Alembert get it right? Should there be any lines at all? Should the axes through the intellectual landscape be more like meandering creeks or twisted footpaths than linear highways? Are we constrained to walk one path only?

Wendell Berry remarked that the idea of the university is "the bringing together, the combining into one, of all the disciplines." Interdisciplinary teaching and research bring individuals together from diverse disciplines to tackle problems using multiple lines of inquiry and expertise. Yet simple juxtaposition of different views is no guarantee of a genuine synthesis or creative insight. For that to occur, the community of discourse must be internalized so it can live within a single person with sufficient intensity to overcome the mind's inertia, its resistance to change. The whole is then reflected in the individual, and in such measure that it can become an active force that liberates and animates.

When Albert Einstein was an obscure young clerk at the Berne patent office in Switzerland, he joined up with two new friends and together they created the tiny *Akademie Olympia*. Einstein had recently completed his studies in physics at the ETH (Eidgenössische Technische Hochschule) in Zurich (the MIT of Switzerland). His friends Solovine and Habicht were not scientists but students of philosophy and mathematics, respectively. Over the three years that their little academy existed, from 1902 to 1905, the group read and debated such books as Hume's *Treatise of Human Nature*, Spinoza's *Ethics,* Mill's *A System of Logic*, Mach's *Analysis of Sensations*, Poincaré's *Science and Hypotheses*, and Cervantes' *Don Quixote.* They hiked the magnificent Berner Oberland, in the evenings Einstein entertained them with his violin, they would eat what they could afford (i.e., not much), and they talked; above all, they talked. Einstein's breadth of thought was greatly extended by the intensive, wide-ranging, intellectual intercourse he had with Solovine and Habicht. In looking back on the *Olympia Academy,* Solovine said, "Our material situation was far from being brilliant; but, in spite of that, what enthusiasm we had, what a passion for the things that really mattered" (cited in Clark, 1984, p. 80). And Einstein noted similarly, "We had a wonderful time in those days in Berne in our cheerful 'Academy,' which was less childish than those respectable ones which I later got to know only too well" (American Institute of Physics, 2004).

Einstein appeared out of nowhere in 1905, the year the Academy ended, when he published four landmark papers, including his discovery of special relativity and his equation $E = mc^2$. He would later remark on the importance of Ernst Mach, David Hume, Henri Poincaré, and other authors read in the

Academy, for his accomplishments during that astonishing year of creativity. Through his friends and their intensive conversations, he had succeeded in integrating into his own thinking the breadth of thought these giants offered, their critical stance, and divergent views, and Einstein was deeply helped thereby. Of Ernst Mach, for example, Einstein would write, "I see Mach's greatness in his incorruptible skepticism and independence . . ." (Clark, 1984, p. 80), an independence that appealed to Einstein's own personality. The Academy offered a community of ardent intellectual conversation that animated Einstein and opened him to fresh notions of what space, time, matter, energy, and light really were. The consequent revolution wrought by Einstein has still not been fully appreciated.

Contrast Einstein's experience with our curricular strategies for ensuring breadth of study. The juxtaposition of one course next to the other, as is common with distribution requirements, is not in my view, a satisfactory way of addressing the issue of breadth. We need models of engagement much more like the Olympia Academy than a sushi menu. Who would you invite to an incandescent conversation on science, art, philosophy, social justice, environmentalism . . . ? With whom would you hike the Sierras, and what books would you have in your backpack? Broaden yourself by engaging difference. The observations and thoughts of others are doors that open onto rooms whose existence you may never have imagined. Those others include the voices of great thinkers and artist of the past, as well as your contemporaries. Treated in this way, we can internalize the breadth of our world and civilization, and are the richer for it.

As rich as interdisciplinary study and research can be, it fails to integrate the "vertical" dimensions of human experience and inquiry, of human aspiration and action. It's as if one were content with the geometry of Flatland, blithely unaware of a missing dimension to space. Higher education should include both labors of ascent (*anodos*) and descent (*kathodos*), as well as the complementary modalities of *vita contemplativa* and the *vita activa*, which comprise the largely neglected vertical dimension to education whose absence is so lamented by Lewis and Kronman, among others. What are the distinguishing features of the vertical dimension, why are they significant, and how does one integrate them into higher education? Here I believe we find a special role for contemplative pedagogy in higher education.

True insight requires the student or researcher leave the constraining cave of everyday conventional thought in order to see more clearly and by a new light. One labors not only to understand but to create, for here is the place of the new. While we cannot engineer creativity or manufacture insight, we can ask after the conditions, practices, and capacities that support innovation and insight. The conditions for creativity are several, but three of the most important are the ability to engage with paradox or contradiction, to sustain that engagement over long periods of time, and to nurture the moment of insight so as to bring it into a lucid mathematical form. In the genesis of both the special and general theories of relativity, we witness a classic instance of these three conditions and their relation to the contemplative and reflective dimensions of research.

Einstein tells us that the sought for "principle [of relativity] resulted from a paradox upon which I had already hit at the age of sixteen" (in Schilpp, 1949, p. 49). Thus, ten years before discovering the principle of relativity, he began to think about pursuing a beam of light at the speed of light. He wondered: What would a light wave look like in such a situation? Could he catch up with light, rendering it stationary? But that would be in direct conflict with the recently established theory of electromagnetism by James Clerk Maxwell. This was the contradiction he contemplated for the next ten years and that led to his discovery of special relativity.

The general theory of relativity was likewise born of a paradox, what Einstein called the "happiest thought" ("der glücklichste Gedanke meines Lebens") of his life. Sitting in his chair in 1907 at the Bern patent office, he suddenly wondered how he could distinguish between himself sitting in his chair in the gravitational attraction of the earth, and being accelerated up. As he pondered the two situations, it seemed like the two different situations would be indistinguishable experimentally. Billions of people sit in chairs every day without having this thought! Or, consider the opposite situation. If he, Einstein, were to fall off a tall building, gravity would literally disappear as far as all experimental effects could determine (at least until he hit the ground!). This has become enshrined as the "equivalence principle" in physics: that is, gravity and acceleration are "equivalent." But it would not be until 1916, nine years later, that he would find a way to complete his general theory of relativity. The circumstances of his final resolution to the problem are remarkable and valuable to us in our considerations of higher education in support of the creative act.

At a 1931 dinner party in Charlie Chaplin's Beverly Hills residence, Albert Einstein's wife Elsa gave the following report on the days in 1916 prior to Albert Einstein's discovery (see Jammer, 1999, p. 56). Elsa's story is recounted by Chaplin in his autobiography.

> The Doctor came down in his dressing gown as usual for breakfast but he hardly touched a thing. I thought something was wrong, so I asked what was troubling him. "Darling," he said, "I have a wonderful idea." And after drinking his coffee, he went to the piano

and started playing. Now and again he would stop, making a few notes then repeat: "I've got a wonderful idea, a marvelous idea!" I said: "Then for goodness' sake tell me what it is, don't keep me in suspense." He said: "It's difficult, I still have to work it out."

She told me he continued playing the piano and making notes for about half an hour, then went upstairs to his study, telling her that he did not wish to be disturbed, and remained there for two weeks. "Each day I sent him up his meals," she said, "and in the evening he would walk a little for exercise, then return to his work again. Eventually," she said, "he came down from his study looking very pale. 'That's it,' he told me, wearily putting two sheets of paper on the table. And that was his theory of relativity." (Chaplin, 1964, pp. 346–347)

Sustained Voluntary Attention

In these accounts of Einstein's acts of creative genius, we can discern three aspects which I would suggest we can cultivate in ourselves and in our students through contemplative exercises. The first is the capacity for *sustained voluntary attention*. That is, one strengthens the ability to direct one's attention to a topic, thought, object, or question of one's choosing, and sustains that attention for long periods of time. The founder of scientific psychology, William James, wrote in *Principles of Psychology* (1890),

> The faculty of voluntarily bringing back a wandering attention, over and over again, is the very root of judgment, character, and will. . . . An education which should improve this faculty would be *the* education *par excellence*. But it is easier to define this ideal than to give practical directions for bringing it about. (p. 424)

Indeed, our attention does wander over and over again. And William James was right in his assessment that "the education which should improve this faculty would be the education *par excellence*." The challenge of giving practical directions for the cultivation of attention is one that many professors have taken up in recent years. They have been making use of the contemplative exercises of mindfulness on a simple object (for example, a paper clip) or process (for example, the breath) as a means of strengthening attention. In recent years, neuroscience research has convincingly demonstrated that contemplative practice of this kind can enhance attention.[1] Improved attention is of obvious value in all academic contexts, and for life more generally, and so well worth including in our pedagogy starting at least in the high school years and extending on into college (Zajonc, 2009).[2]

Since 1997 the academic program of the Center for Contemplative Mind in Society (www.contemplativemind.org) has been working with many hundreds of professors and university administrators, developing the field of contemplative pedagogy. Each year through conferences, summer programs, retreats, and online resources, the Center has supported faculty in making their curricula and pedagogical methods more reflective and contemplative. In collaboration with the American Council of Learned Societies, the Center has awarded 158 Contemplative Practice Fellowships to professors in every type of academic institution. Recently the Center has founded the Association for Contemplative Mind in Higher Education (www.acmhe.org). This is a professional association which allows colleagues from colleges and universities around the world to interact with each other and share their writings and ideas. The Center also commissioned a review of the research into contemplative pedagogy relevant to higher education (Shapiro, Brown, & Astin, 2011).

Nearly every area of higher and professional education is now being taught with contemplative exercises for the training of attention from poetry to biology, from medicine to law. There is a fast-growing appreciation of contemplative pedagogy that makes extensive use of secular contemplative exercises for stress reduction (Shapiro, Schwartz, & Bonner, 1998), for general capacity building (such as strengthening attention or cultivating emotional balance), as well as subject-oriented practices designed for a particular class. For example, the contemplative art of "beholding" in art history and compassion practices that shift game theoretical outcomes in an economics class are both being taught at Amherst College (see, for example, Daniel Barbezat's essay in this volume). An interesting recent example of the uses of mindfulness training has arisen within the context of leadership and leadership education. The Vice President for Public Responsibility and Deputy General Counsel at General Mills Janice Marturano has been offering mindfulness as part of a leadership training course for some time.[3] Following her 7-week course, Mindful Leadership@Work, (with some 40+ respondents) she recently surveyed participants pre- and post-course asking:

- I am able to be fully attentive to a conversation.
- Pre-course: 26%, Post-course: 77%
- I am able to make time on most days to prioritize my work.
- Pre-course: 17%, Post-course: 54%

- I am able to notice when my attention has been pulled away and redirect it to the present.
- Pre-course: 23%, Post-course: 67%

Along this line, faculty conversations and some efforts at integration of the contemplative in leadership education have begun among a group of Boston area educators meeting at Harvard University.

Sustaining Contradictions

In addition to sustained voluntary attention, Einstein was able to productively engage paradox and contradiction. Recognizing the value of these, Niels Bohr once remarked, "How wonderful that we have met with a paradox. Now we have some hope of making progress" (in Moore, 1966, p. 196). We normally avoid paradox, but like a Zen master working with a koan, Einstein sought out contradictions and worked with them for years until finally they resolved themselves. Importantly, the resolution was only possible at a higher level than that of the paradox itself. If we are limited, for example, to classical notions of space, time, and matter, the paradoxes that lay at the root of Einstein's theory of relativity persist. Only by fundamentally reconceiving the very nature of these fundamental aspects of reality do the paradoxes resolve, but only if we are willing and able to make profound psychological and ontology changes to our worldview. To make such profound ontological shifts requires an extraordinary freedom of thought, one where the conventional patterns and habits of thinking are broken and replaced by a new and more fluid conception of reality. The contemplative traditions have long maintained that the exercises they have developed are designed for exactly this purpose, that is, to free the mind from is habitual and mistaken conception of the world and the Self. Contemplative exercises are now being adapted and used in completely secular settings in thousands of classrooms to this end.

To be concrete, in the case of relativity, we learn for example that the lengths of moving objects are foreshortened, that moving clocks run slow, and that the notion of "now," that is, simultaneity, is different for different states of motion. As a consequence, the notion of *primary qualities* such as length and mass, as properties inherent to things themselves—a view which has been common view since Galileo, Descartes, Locke, and Newton—is undermined by Einstein's theory of relativity. In the language of David Bohm (1965), objects and their interactions have been replaced by events and processes (p. 148). Analytical meditation works with a sequence of thoughts that leads to an insight of the type encapsulated by Bohm. One then pauses to dwell on such insights, allowing them to sink in, to be fully appreciated (Dalai Lama & Hopkins, 2006). One moves in this way between what are called "analytical meditation" and "calm abiding."

Cultivating attention usually begins on a single simple object, be it a paper clip or the breath. Strengthening concentration is certainly a good thing, valuable in every subject area. However, sustaining attention in the absence of easy clarity, which is the situation of paradox or contradiction, requires another level of contemplative engagement. To these two stages is added a third, that of *contemplative insight or knowing*. In the account given by Einstein's wife of the discovery of general relativity, we see Einstein *holding open* the time of creativity by playing the piano or, in other instances, his beloved violin, followed by an intensive period during which the elusive ideas are cast into equations and words.

The contemplative practice of open receptivity is well-known and has been the subject of research in the emerging area of contemplative neuroscience. Lutz, Slagter, Dunne, and Davidson (2008) at the University of Wisconsin in Madison have made a careful study of the contrasting contemplative states of *focused attention* and *open monitoring*. I view the capacity for open monitoring as important for the creative dimension of research and scholarship (Zajonc, 2006).

Conditions for Creativity and Insight

Scholars of creativity and insight distinguish four phases (Sternberg & Davidson, 1995). The first is *mental preparation*, which consists in confronting the paradox or contradiction at the root of the problem in a serious and sustained way. The second phase is *incubation*, during which time one moves between active struggle with the problem and disengagement. The third phase is *illumination,* at which moment a flash of insight appears, one that must be grounded or held. In his discovery of quaternions, for example, the mathematician William Rowan Hamilton was walking across the Broom Bridge in Dublin with his wife. Suddenly a problem he had long studied was solved. Knowing how elusive such solutions can be, Hamilton carved the crucial identity into the wooden railing of the bridge with his penknife. The final fourth phase is *verification.* After all, insights can be mistaken.

In a 1904 essay, Poincaré was aware of these stages and drew special attention to the means by which we see the new. He wrote, "It is by logic we prove, it is by intuition we invent." In 1908, he concluded that "logic, therefore, remains barren unless fertilized by intuition." He added: "To make geometry, or to make any science, something else than pure logic is necessary. To designate the something else we have no word other than *intuition*" (in Miller, 1996, pp. 351–353). Albert Einstein would say it this way, "There is no logical path leading to these laws [of nature], but only intuition, supported by sympathetic understanding of experience" (p. 369). The historian of science Arthur Miller recognized that only Albert Einstein was willing to undertake the labors of ascent required to resolve the conflict between mechanics and electrodynamics. "Einstein, alone, was willing to *redefine* the concept of intuition to a level of abstraction higher than in the mechanics and electrodynamics of 1905" (p. 373).

While discovery always contained in it elements of genius and grace, higher education can nonetheless prepare the ground and provide the conditions for creativity and insight. For example, contemplative exercises come in two types. The first strengthens concentration on a single simple object or later on paradox, but a complementary exercise schools "open awareness." In open awareness one releases the object of concentration from the mind and sustains a lucid yet undirected, receptive mental state. The movement between concentrated attention and open awareness is much like the required movement between the two phases of mental preparation and incubation described above. By practicing this pair of contemplative exercises, student or researcher becomes accustomed to the inner cognitive movement or rhythm of attention required for creative insights. It is a pedagogy for creativity.

The Descent

Insights are barren unless you can make them real. It may take two weeks in isolation to find the means of expressing what you have seen intuitively in an instant, as was the case for Einstein's general theory of relativity. When Hamilton discovered quaternions he immediately realized that the next few years would be spent in working out the implications.

Parallel with his work in physics, Einstein was a lifelong advocate for peace, and viewed the cultivation of ever-widening compassion as one of humanity's greatest tasks. In the language of the Stoics, Einstein was committed to expanding "his circles of affection" and so treated those around him as he would his own family and kin.[4] Einstein also saw this as the high aspiration of humanity.

> The human being is a part of a whole, called by us "the universe," a limited part in space and time. He experiences himself his thoughts feelings as something separated from the rest . . . a kind of optical

> delusion of his consciousness. This delusion is a kind of prison for us, restricting us to our personal desires and to affection for a few people nearest to us. Our task must be to free ourselves from this prison by widening our circle of compassion to embrace all living creatures and the whole of nature in its beauty. (cited in Calaprice, 2005, p. 206)[5]

A college education is as much about embodying what we learn as it is about the learning itself. How is it we make what we know fruitful for others? Our students seek to wed knowledge with action, insight with ideals. The rise of centers for community engagement and service learning on countless campuses is testimony to students' interest and commitment to "making it real." In a recent conversation with a Gates scholar at Amherst College, I learned how each week for the last three years the student tutored those who, like him, grew up destitute and with little understanding of English. He plans on going on to become a physician; others will take up teaching, law, or business. In every vocation, moral issues will arise. How can we prepare our students for them?

In a recent gathering on leadership and the contemplative aspects of leadership education, Sandra Sucher of the Harvard Business School spoke eloquently concerning the course she teaches on Moral Leadership, a Harvard course initiated by the legendary teacher and activist Robert Coles. Through the case study method students are placed on the horns of a moral dilemma. The financial realities of the case press forcefully in one direction, while ethical and perhaps even legal considerations point in a very different direction. When presented vividly, which is to say *experientially*, the struggle of students to discern the right way forward can be very real. What becomes completely clear is that leading a business, which many of Sucher's students will ultimately do, entails far more that financial analysis or people skills. If we pause to consider the deep foundations of vocation, we find that personal character and moral discernment are of enormous importance. Whatever we can do as educators to support the development of character and discernment among future business leaders will be an investment that repays society handsomely in the form of a trustworthy business community, something whose value has never been more evident than today. Is the practice of medicine, law, government service, teaching, scientific research . . . any different? Do they not also rest on the same moral foundations?

The contemplative practice known as "loving kindness" is a powerful way of expanding our "circles of affection," or in Einstein's words, "widening our circle of compassion to embrace all living creatures and the whole of nature in its beauty." In this exercise one practices sending generosity to three persons who represent a class of those we know: close mentors or friends, strangers, those with whom we have difficulty.[6]

If ethics forms the foundation for right action in one's disciplinary or vocational field, then it seems to me that the aspiration toward an ideal is the star high above by which students (and their teachers) seek to orient their lives. The aspiration to lead lives of meaning, purpose, and commitment is not passé. According to recent research by the Higher Education Research Institute at UCLA, half of students entering college declare that "to find my purpose in life" is a very important reason for attending college, and the percentage rises to 80 percent if one includes those who say it is a least a "somewhat important" reason (Astin, Astin, & Lindholm, 2011). The same research finds that some two-thirds of new students feel that it is very important that college help them in finding a purpose in life. These data confirm that students arrive on campus hoping their teachers and courses will help them to find purpose, enhance self-understanding, and develop personal values. As Lewis and Kronman state, too often as faculty we avoid these issues and fail to meet students' expectations, whose hopes I think are fully legitimate.

An Integrative Education

An integrative education is, as said at the outset, multidimensional. It includes the breadth of multiple perspectives and disciplines, but in a way that is not limited to simple juxtaposition Instead, it proceeds in a manner that incorporates the varied perspectives of the literature and our colleagues into our own view. We live not only our original view, but the multiple views of others, synthesizing them. In the geometry of integrative education, this forms the broad horizontal plane of our public inquiry and discourse. To be complete, however, we need to include in our education a crucial vertical axis, one that allows for both ascent and descent. The ascent takes place through varied forms of contemplative practice. We learn to sustain our attention even in the face of paradox and contradiction with profound equanimity, and when insight arises, we know how to draw it steadily to us, finding the language and concepts that will allow it an active life. We may make use of analytical meditation and calm abiding. The final dimension of an integrative education is that of moral or altruistic action supported by compassion practices. Insight can remain barren or even harmful (think of Einstein's $E = mc^2$ and the atom bomb), without an adequate moral foundation or ideals by which to lead a life.

The broad horizon of knowledge available in our colleges, universities, and professional schools will thus be joined to the cultivation of students' capacities for attention and emotional balance, and to a contemplative epistemology that leads to insight and a moral commitment to action guided by one's ideals. Contemplative pedagogy will become, in my view, an essential component of a truly integrative education and will lead to a more reflective academy that responds to Wendell Berry's ideal of the university as a place committed to aiding in the full development of the whole human being.

Notes

1. For further information see Richard Davidson's Center for Investigating Healthy Minds, <http://www.investigatinghealthyminds.org/>. Clifford Saron at the UC Davis Center for Mind and Brain, the Shamatha Project, <http://mindbrain.ucdavis.edu/labs/Saron/shamatha-project>, and B. Alan Wallace, Santa Barbara Institute, <http://www.sbinstitute.com/research.html>.

2. See also The Association for Contemplative Mind in Higher Education, <www.acmhe.org>.

3. Janice Marturano, The Center for Mindful Leadership, <http://www.umassmed.edu/cfm/mindfulleadership/index.aspx>.

4. See Hierocles (100 AD), as drawn from Stobaeus (4.671,7-673,11): "Each of us is, as it were, entirely encompassed by many circles, some smaller, others larger, the latter enclosing the former on the basis of their different and unequal dispositions relative to each other. . . ."

5. Letter of 1950, as quoted in *The New York Times* (29 March 1972) and *The New York Post* (28 November 1972). This is the version in *The New Quotable Einstein* by Alice Calaprice.

6. For instruction in this practice see: <http://www.contemplativemind.org/practices/subnav/kindness.htm>.

References

American Institute of Physics. (2004). *"Academy" members Konrad Habricht, Maurice Solovine, and Einstein.* Retrieved from <http://www.aip.org/history/einstein/ae12.htm>.

Arthur Z. (2009). *Meditation as contemplative inquiry.* Great Barrington, MA: Lindisfarne Press.

Astin, A., Astin, H. S., & Lindholm, J. A. (2011). *Cultivating the spirit: How college can enhance students' inner lives.* San Francisco: Jossey-Bass.

Berry, W. (1987). The loss of the university. *Home Economics.* San Francisco: North Point Press.

Bohm, D. (1965). *The special theory of relativity.* New York: W. A. Benjamin.

Dalai Lama, & Hopkins, Jy. (2006). *How to see yourself as you really are*. New York: Simon and Schuster.

Calaprice, A. (2005). *The new quotable Einstein*. Princeton, NJ: Princeton University Press.

Chaplin, C. (1964). *My autobiography*. London: Bodley Head.

Clark, R. W. (1984). *Einstein: The life and times*. New York: HarperCollins.

James, W. (1890). *Principles of psychology, vol. 1*. New York: Holt and Co.

Jammer, M. (1999). *Einstein and religion*. Princeton, NJ: Princeton University Press.

Kronman, A. (2007). *Education's end: Why our colleges and universities have given up on the meaning of life*. New Haven, CT: Yale University Press.

Lewis, H. (2007). *Excellence without a soul: How a great university forgot education*. New York: PublicAffairs (Perseus Books).

Lutz, A., Slagter, H., Donne, J., & Davidson, R. (2008). Attention regulation and monitoring in meditation. *Trends in Cognitive Science, 12*(4), 163–169.

Miller, A. I. (1996). *Insights of genius*. New York: Springer-Verlag.

Schilpp, P. A. (1949). *Albert Einstein: Philosopher-scientist (Library of Living Philosophers, Vol. VII)*. LaSalle, IL: Open Court Publishing.

Shapiro, S., Brown, K., & Astin, J. (2011). Toward the Integration of meditation into higher education: A review of research evidence. *Teachers College Record, 113*(3), 493–528.

Shapiro, S., Schwartz, G., & Bonner, G. (1998). Effects of mindfulness-based stress reduction on medical and pre-medical students. *Journal of Behavioral Medicine, 21*, 581–599.

Sternberg, R. J., & Davidson, J. E. (1995). *The nature of insight*. Cambridge, MA: MIT Press.

Zajonc, A. (2006). Love and knowledge: Recovering the heart of learning through contemplation. *Teachers College Record, 108*(9), 1742–1759.

2

A Philosophical Framework for Contemplative Education

Deborah Orr

Introduction

As the Introduction to this volume and the papers it contains show, there is a growing interest in classroom uses of contemplative education that is supported by a rapidly expanding practical and theoretical literature. Contemplative education is a wide-ranging term that encompasses the use of practices drawn from traditions around the world. Currently there is a substantial and growing interest in classroom uses of Classical Yoga, most frequently with a strong focus on the third of its eight limbs, the practice of asana or postures (see Hartranft, 2003; Iyengar, 1991), as well as Buddhist meditation techniques drawn from the many schools of Buddhism which have themselves evolved from the Hindu yoga tradition.

While the meditational dimension of asana practice is increasingly being stressed by teachers and researchers of Classical Yoga (Boccio, 2004), space prevents me from developing this area here; I can merely make a few references to it in what follows. In my own work teaching in an academic context, in addition to the use of Classical Yoga and its philosophy (Hartranft, 2003; Iyengar, 1991; Whicher, 1997, 1998) I draw heavily on Buddhist meditation practices. I have found that, as a philosopher teaching in a Humanities Department and with a focus on challenging oppressive discourses, mindfulness practices are a rich resource for my work. However, both my personal experiences as well as conversations with colleagues who have begun to employ the techniques of Yoga and Buddhist Vipassana/insight/mindfulness meditation (I will use the term "mindfulness" throughout unless I am referring specifically to the Vipassana school) have told me of experiences that are quite similar to ones I have had. On the one hand, there is the belief that these are specifically religious practices. Unfortunately, space prevents me from fully addressing this important area, however in this work these practices and their philosophy are presented with no specific religious component (see Kabat-Zinn, 1994). On the other hand, there is a skeptical attitude grounded in the belief that these practices have more to do with how the student feels than with learning the content and procedures that have held pride of place in the educational field. One may encounter such attitudes as, "Well, relaxing and learning to focus may be useful for the student, but academic learning is another thing entirely," or "Emptying the mind is okay but students have to learn to think!"

In this chapter I address the second set of beliefs by arguing that it is mistaken in fundamental ways. To do this I will bring three main voices into conversation. First is that of Nagarjuna, the circa-first-century-BCE-to-first-century-CE Indian founder of the Madhyamika school of Buddhism. His major work, *Mūlamadhyamakakārikā* (*MMK*), is accepted as their philosophical framework by all major Buddhist schools (Gomez, 1976; Walser, 2005): Theravada, which is the source of the mindfulness practices most popular in the West; Mahayana, to which Nagarjuna belonged; and Vajrayana, now identified with Tibet. Focusing on his concept of language-games, the mature-period work of the twentieth-century Western linguistic philosopher, Wittgenstein, will help to develop the point that while Nagarjuna's work was specifically developed to deal the sorts of intellectual confusions that were to be found not only in the time and place of the historical Buddha, but in students and the general population of the contemporary West, the mindfulness practices that it grounds address all levels of the student's experience; cognitive, emotional, spiritual, behavioral. Finally, the work of the thirteenth-century Japanese founder of the Soto Zen school, Dogen, on forms of thought will also contribute to the development of this argument. Thus the argument of this chapter is that mindfulness practices provide the educator with a powerful set of tools with which to address the oppressive discourses and hidden curricula of contemporary education and, more broadly, culture.

Why Nagarjuna and Wittgenstein Matter

The linguistic philosophy of Nagarjuna shares close affinities with that of the twentieth-century Western philosopher Ludwig Wittgenstein, and I will draw on Wittgenstein's work of the period from *Philosophical Investigations* (1968) onward both to throw light on Nagarjuna's work and to stress that Nagarjuna's concerns and the results of his philosophical investigations are compatible with mainstream Western work. A conversation between Nagarjuna and Wittgenstein is especially useful for this chapter because, while Nagarjuna drew on commonplace concepts, which are important to Buddhist discourse in order to draw out the implications of the positions—especially their essentialism, reificationism, and nihilism—that dominated both philosophy and ordinary discourse in both his day and our own, Wittgenstein, whose work is in agreement both methodologically and in terms of his findings with Nagarjuna's, gives us a closely detailed picture of the ways in which language is woven into and consequently affects all aspects of human life.

While Nagarjuna drew in broad strokes and Wittgenstein provides minute detail of language use, both of them were, avowedly and in practice, concerned with identifying misuses of language, both in theoretical and everyday discourses. They both believed that their work is important since these misuses of language are potent sources of the confusions, delusions, and suffering (*dukkha*, as this is understood in both Yoga and Buddhism) that humans undergo and so their philosophical therapy, by working with these illnesses of the understanding, can have a salutary effect. Importantly, as we will see, for neither of them is language simply a cognitive matter, rather it is interwoven with, and so helps to structure and develop, the totality of human experience. Thus, working with the understanding can have a broader existential and experiential effect that goes well beyond simply changing one's mind about something. At the same time, it also works on a conceptual level to provide a framework that overcomes the limitations not only of dualistic worldviews but also of the extremes of materialism and radical constructionism.

It is the close attention to language and the effects concepts have on the full range of human experience (cognitive, emotional, somatic, and relational) that I argue makes mindfulness such a powerful tool for education. It can not only help one to abandon dysfunctional concepts and discourses, for instance, those of racism, sexism, and homophobia, but it can also help loosen the hold of habitual and conditioned responses to any sort of material—a poem, a social or political idea (Orr, 2007), a solution to a problem—and so open up a space for the emergence of new, creative responses to a wide range of academic material. Having said that, it is important to notice that the piecemeal treatment of specific areas of the understanding, which is appropriate for classroom use, is very far from the full force of what meditation might achieve. The thirteenth-century Japanese Master Dogen has said, "There is no gap between practice and enlightenment or zazen [sitting meditation] and daily life" (1976, p. 47). At the same time, paradoxically, there *is* a profound difference, and dedicated practice is necessary to realize it. That difference lies in the existential experience of the practitioner. Dogen holds that we are already enlightened because that is our natural state, but still the dedicated practice is necessary in order to have "the body and mind fall away" (p. 46), that is, to drop attachments to problematic linguistic structures along with their experiential dimensions that form our lives. At this point the practitioner is no longer in thrall to the dualistic and objectifying thinking which characterizes most uses of "body" and "mind." I argue below that it is precisely by overcoming the manifestations of dualism and objectification in one's life that makes meditation "work" in an academic context, but this does not mean that our students will become Buddhas by taking our courses. They may, however, achieve a somewhat more mature, equanimous, and caring experience in their own lives (Kabat Zinn, 1994). Thus, as Charles Scott has pointed out to me, with this our students may take that "first step on the journey of a thousand miles." Let us turn now to a closer examination of the work of Nagarjuna and Wittgenstein.

Conceptual Grammar and *Sunyata*

On the most general level, both Nagarjuna and Wittgenstein were concerned with mapping what Wittgenstein calls "conceptual grammar." Conceptual grammar provides a linguistic topographical map by charting the legitimate uses of language in language-games; it is these uses that have "sense." Wittgenstein calls statements descriptive of conceptual grammar "senseless" in that they serve merely to point to the limits of valid use while not actually using the concepts being mapped in their home language-games. These limits include not only the relationships between words, for example, "all bachelors are unmarried men"—but also between words and human life and human lived experience: "I shall also call the whole, consisting of language and the actions into which it is woven, a 'language-game'" (1968, §7). So, the uses of language within established language-games have "sense," descriptive uses are "senseless," and illicit, e.g., metaphysical, uses are "nonsense." Thus, to the extent to which they both eschew advancing theses of their own, and both were adamant on this point, the texts of both Wittgenstein and Nagarjuna are "senseless" in this technical sense. Their usefulness lies in making us aware of the limits or boundaries of concepts and thus more able to identify and resist "nonsense."

The work of Nagarjuna and Wittgenstein is stylistically similar in that both proceeded by responding to problematic positions advanced by an interlocutor and thus it is important, and sometimes difficult, to identify which "voice" is speaking in their works. The interlocutor's problems that they sought to debunk arose from illicit, or nonsensical, uses of language, and both were especially concerned with those that sought to give a word a metaphysical or reified use that it lacks in the language-games in which it has sense. While new language-games are invented all the time, concepts do not necessarily retain all or any of their previous sense when moved to a new game; and one potent source of confusion is the belief that they do. Wittgenstein was also especially concerned with the ways in which language can mislead by projecting pictures that mislead us. For instance, "sensations are private" (1968, §248) is a "senseless" statement of a rule of a language-game that creates an image of an inner space or container for sensations[1], but this misleads us when we take it as a picture of "how things really are." Wittgenstein writes, "A *picture* held us captive. And we could not get outside it, for it lay in our language and language seemed to repeat it to us inexorably" (1968, §115). The confusions will be further complicated if we overlook that most language is not used to name things and thus does not have sense by designating non-linguistic elements; rather, it is fundamentally a form of communication grounded in the fact that the human form of life is relational (1968, §23, 244; Taylor, 1980). Against these sorts of confusions both philosophers employ the argumentative technique of *reductio ad absurdum* to take the interlocutor's position seriously and then draw out the sorts of conclusions it leads to, although these conclusions are often not ones that are acknowledged by the interlocutor. The patent absurdity of these conclusions serves to debunk the position that is being investigated and this in turn should begin to persuade those who hold it to abandon it. Thus Wittgenstein says, "What *we* do is to bring words back from their metaphysical to their everyday use" (1968, §116).

A final aspect of similarity between them, which I will foreground here is that, while both philosophers are at pains to point out that *all* they are doing is investigating language and not advancing theories of their own, they both believed that this investigation could have radical consequences in people's lives. Approximately twenty centuries after Nagarjuna, Wittgenstein believed that we not only misunderstand our language, we do so in ways that create in us "diseases of the understanding," which can infect both individuals and cultures (see especially Wittgenstein, 1980, passim). In a passage that resonates strikingly with Buddhist thought, Wittgenstein says, "Man can regard all evil within himself as delusion" (1980, p. 67).

This is a position with which Nagarjuna would agree, although he would go further in analyzing that "disease" or illness (*dukkha*) from which we suffer into the traditional three poisons: delusion or ignorance, craving or attachment, and anger. *Avidya*, translated as delusion or ignorance, is both a source and a form of suffering in Buddhist thought and in its mother tradition, Hinduism. In explaining the "causes of suffering," Patanjali says in his *Yoga Sutra* (2:4): "Not seeing things as they are is the field where the other causes of suffering [egoism, attachment, aversion and clinging to life] germinate . . ." (Hartranft, 2003, p. xx). For instance, we tend to reify our self, or perhaps the soul or mind or ego as a part of our self, and thereby endow our self with a tacit substantiality and immortality. As well, usually without even thinking about it, we *act as if* we are entirely separate and distinct from others and from the rest of our world; that is, we objectify our self.

Contemporary Western culture encourages forms of hyper-individualism (Taylor, 1989; Stone, 1984) and nuances these with categories of social differentiation such as sex (Laqueur, 1992), race, class, and many others, and thus hyper-individualism is a primary form *avidya* takes for modern Westerners. On the cognitive level the problem of identifying with these categories is twofold: most fundamentally it is sourced in dualistic thinking, the radical separation of the self from all else, and by this the self is objectified and set against all else. Second, it involves the reification of the self and identification with that falsely reified self. Both of these moves involve ignorance (*avidya*) as they contravene the conceptual grammar of "self," which Nagarjuna designates as emptiness or non-substantiality (*sunyata*), and interdependence or dependant arising (*pratityasamutpada*). Further, the assumption of immortality, which seems a "natural" outcome of the suppression of *sunyata* and *pratityasamutpada,* is in contradiction with *anitya*, the impermanence or transitoriness of all things, which follows from *sunyata* and *pratityasamutpada*. The implication of rejecting *anitya* is stasis and the denial of the very possibility of human life which involves coming into existence, change, and passing away. Let us look a little more closely at a few of Nagarjuna's arguments to clarify these concepts.

The Significance of *Sunyata*, *Pratityasamutpada*, and *Anitya*

As we have noted, conceptual grammar shows us what can and cannot be said with sense and Nagarjuna is clear from the opening verse of his *Mūlamadhyamakakārikā* that this is what he is concerned with:

> [1] Neither from itself nor [2] from another,
> [3] Nor from both,
> [4] Nor without a cause,
> Does anything whatever, anywhere arise. (*MMK* 1:1, in Garfield, 1995)

This is not to assert a metaphysical position regarding cause and effect; rather, it shows what cannot be said with sense and so Nagarjuna's use of these words is itself senseless: his words delineate conceptual grammar and thereby attack metaphysical uses. What is at issue here is not only important for understanding ordinary uses of these words but also understanding the centrality of the notion of dependant arising (*pratityasamutpada*) to Buddhist thought. As is typical throughout this work, Nagarjuna considers the logical possibilities if "cause" and "effect" are taken as names of extra-linguistic reality that are characterized by inherent existence (*svabhava*) and reduces each possibility to absurdity. I will follow Kasulis's (1981) discussion in summarizing the argument condensed in this passage. If [1] cause and effect are identical, nothing arises and since these terms call for change, this is absurd; if [2] they are completely different there can be no continuity for the cause is "causing" something that is nonexistent and this is absurd; if [3] the cause and effect are both identical and not identical there is a contradiction; if [4] then there is also absurdity in that this holds that relating cause and effect is a category mistake—that is, that we can not relate these terms in ordinary language-games (1981, pp. 20–21; see also *MKK* 1:7). In his discussion of Nagarjuna's similar treatment of the concepts of time, Kasulis clearly states what is at stake, "If these terms refer to nonlinguistic bits of reality . . . there can be no possible connection among those bits . . . and without those interconnections the terms themselves are meaningless . . . it is absurd to think of [those terms] as having any extralinguistic reality" (p. 19). But these terms *are* meaningful, they have their sense within the language-games we play with them, although there they do not function as names that designate bits of inherently existing (*svabhava*) extra-linguistic reality as metaphysics would have it.

The arguments Nagarjuna makes in *Mūlamadhyamakakārikā* show that all positions arguing for the existence of eternal, self-subsisting (*svabhava*) entities (central to Western essentialist/reificationist[2] theories (Garfield 1990, 1995) as well as many everyday assumptions, especially about the self) are incoherent. Against the ontology of self-subsisting or reified things, Nagarjuna argues for the emptiness (*sunyata*) of all things, which, most simply put, is the rejection of essentialized metaphysical and ontological positions on the ground of incoherence. His work undertakes to show that concepts so used lack sense; in Wittgenstein's terminology, they are nonsense. In this he is not only rejecting the possibility of a transcendent Platonic realm and its modern descendants, as exemplified by the Cartesian *cogito,* but also materialist positions such as those exemplified by Hobbes (1851/1958) and often connected with both empirical science and with theories of persons as "isolated social atoms." The concept of *pratityasamutpada* (interdependence or dependent co-arising) is a reminder that language and our experience of the world function in an interdependent, relational manner, in Wittgenstein's term, in language-games.

Sunyata, or emptiness, is a rejection of metaphysical uses of language whether these occur in the theories of philosophers, theologians, scientists, or other theorists, or in the everyday assumptions and discourse of people as they go about their daily lives. However, Nagarjuna is not advancing any theory to the effect that things "don't really exist" although he, and Buddhism generally, are often misinterpreted to be doing so (Abe, 1985). Like other words, "exist" has sense within language-games. The implication of *pratityasamutpada* is that we and the things in our world do "really" exist, in the ordinary sense(s) of the word "exist," just not in the (metaphysical or reified) way we often tend to think that it they do.

In his commentary, Jay Garfield (1990, 1995) notes that Nagarjuna is working within the framework of Buddhist thought and investigating its central concepts—cause and effect, the Four Noble Truths, nirvana, the Buddha, and so on—and that fundamental to this investigation is explaining *pratityasamutpada*. "This term denotes the nexus between phenomena in virtue of which events depend on other events, composites depend on their parts, and so forth" (1995, p. 91). What Nagarjuna is doing here is exploring the conceptual grammar of these terms, and that grammar, the language of ordinary discourse, organizes the phenomenal world in ways that make sense for us. Wittgenstein's use of language-games as an analytic tool also makes this point by revealing the multitude of ways in which words relate to all aspects of human experience: cognitive, emotional, somatic, and relational. Wittgenstein maintains that the purpose of his work is to destroy metaphysical "houses of cards [nonsense]" (1968 §118), and this so that we can build houses fit for human habitation. Thus, the comprehension of *sunyata, pratityasamutpada*, and *anitya* bring us to a more clear-sighted understanding of everyday experience by debunking the *avidya*, or ignorance of the true nature of things, to which we are prone.

> MMK 24 develops the relationship between the realm of sense and that of nonsense. The first 6 verses of MMK 24 (Garfield, 1995) state the position of an interlocutor who would understand Nagarjuna as rejecting the everyday existence of things by the use of the concept *sunyata*. But Nagarjuna argues that the position of his interlocutor result in nihilism, and further that it is this that harms him. (*MMK* 24:7; see also see also *MMK* 24:11 and 24:15)

Nagarjuna follows *MMK* 24:7 with a passage that encapsulates the crux of his entire work:

> The Buddha's teaching of the Dharma
> Is based on two truths:
> A truth of worldly convention
> And an ultimate truth. (*MMK* 24:8)

This may appear to contradict the interpretation of his work that I have been outlining by positing an "ultimate truth" distinct from "worldly convention," but it does not do so. The "truth of worldly convention" is what is expressed in the language used by linguistic communities, that is, in language-games. These can vary greatly in structure amongst communities as, for example, comparative work on Western and Chinese cultures has shown (Hall and Ames, 1995; Nisbett, 2003). But whatever the language, because of the nature of language, on careful analysis it can be shown to be *sunyata* and so Nagarjuna's work can be widely applied.

Since the work that Nagarjuna is doing is work on language, it cannot be used to advance theses about "things themselves," nor can the concept of *sunyata* be reified or turned into a theory. He is explicit about this point in *MMK* 22:11, saying that *sunyata* and its negation are only used nominally. The boundaries (*koti*) of the "truth of worldly convention" and the "ultimate truth" of *MMK* 24:8, are isomorphic since the language of emptiness and non-emptiness is only being used to delineate conceptual boundaries. These terms are senseless and so do not name "things," extra-linguistic bits of or spaces in reality; they simply delineate the boundaries of sense. Thus there is no "truth" beyond the realm of here-and-now in the sense of there being some other level of reality that we can access. Or, as another contemporary philosopher put it, "The ultimate truth is that there is no ultimate truth" (Siderits, cited in Garfield, 1995, p. 91, fn. 7); all things are empty (*sunyata*).

Thus we see that throughout *MMK* 24 Nagarjuna not only rejects nihilism and reificationism, he also is explicit in locating emptiness and dependent arising in the world of everyday language and experience. If these are denied, then the totality of ordinary life is rendered impossible. The "middle way" he seeks lies between these two extremes (*MMK* 22:11).

This understanding of *MMK* 24 throws light on the meaning of *MMK* 25:19–20 and brings out their significance for human life. In these verses Nagarjuna asserts the identical boundaries (*koti*) of cyclical existence or *samsara*, which refers to the life of *dukkha* or suffering, and *nirvana* or the liberated life. He says, "There is not the slightest difference, Between cyclical existence [*samsara*] and *nirvana*" (19), "Whatever is the limit [*koti*] of *nirvana*, That is the limit [*koti*] of cyclic existence [*samsara*]" (20). This seems a paradoxical statement since surely these two have been understood as radically different; and the very point of Buddhist teaching, including the work of Nagarjuna, is to show the way out of *samsara*, which is characterized by *dukkha*, and into *nirvana* or liberation from suffering. One key to resolving the paradox is to bear in mind the central role of linguistic investigation in Nagarjuna's work. That is how the "ultimate truth," that all is *sunyata*, or, put another way, that we cannot transgress the boundaries of our language and still make sense, was demonstrated. The "truths of worldly convention" have to do with the here-and-now, with the phenomenal world, including its human inhabitants, and the language we use as we live in it. That language was created by us to meet our needs in the here-and-now. Thus this phrase also points directly to language and the conventions of its use and, since Wittgenstein has shown that language has sense in the context of language-games—that is, in the context of human life—it points to human life and experience as well. This focus on human life is the second key to understanding the paradox for it is here that the difference is to be found. The person who has, so to speak, moved from *samsara* and into *nirvana* is not someone who has moved to or had access to a different realm but rather one who has changed in their understanding by overcoming *avidya*, which, as we have seen, refers to the ignorance or confusion about the true nature of things. That is, this person is different on an *experiential* level; it is not simply that they have *decided* that it is wrong to reify the self, that it is logical nonsense to do so, but they *live* this difference, this non-reified self. As Jay Garfield (1995) has put it, "Nirvana is only samara experienced as a Buddha experiences it. It is the person who enters nirvana, but as a state of being, not as a place to be" (p. 333). "It is a way of being here" (p. 332).

Getting to Thinking Beyond Thinking and Nonthinking

Although Garfield's statement refers to experiencing reality "as a Buddha experiences it," obviously I am not going to suggest that schools at any level be turned into quasi-monasteries designed to turn out Buddhas, were that even possible! Importantly, one of the great pedagogic strengths of mindfulness is that it cannot be used to indoctrinate or manipulate students, the success of the process is up to each of them. However, exploring an example of what is involved in becoming a Buddha is useful for helping us hone in on some of those aspects that can be adapted to classroom use. In a useful comparison of psychotherapy and Buddhism, David Loy (1992) explores what is most fundamentally at issue. Loy argues that at the deepest existential level the problem we all face is not sexual repression as Freud had it, nor even the realization that we will one day die as others have held. In fact, it is not strictly speaking a psychological problem at all, although it often manifests as psychological symptoms; it is more correctly understood as a spiritual problem. Rather than providing psychotherapy, "Buddhism analyzes the sense-of-self into sets of impersonal mental and physical phenomena, whose interaction creates the illusion of *self*-consciousness, i.e., that consciousness is the attribute of a [reified] *self*" (1992, p. 152). It is this illusory nature of the self that *sunyata* uncovers, the void or groundlessness at the heart of our existence. While we may never consciously have the thought of this void, it is something we intuit and try to come to terms with by creating a ground for our self which is our very self, a reified, solid, and independent, but illusory, self. This is, "The quest to deny one's groundlessness by becoming one's own ground: the ground (socially conditioned and maintained but nonetheless illusory) we know as being an independent person" (p. 152). The Buddha, then, is one who has overcome this fear of a void or groundlessness at the heart of existence and has the living experience of *sunyata* and *pratityasamutpada*. As Loy concludes, "By accepting and yielding to that groundlessness, I can discover that I have always been grounded, not as a self-contained being but as one manifestation of a web of relationships which encompasses everything" (p. 176). But the move from the experience of *samsara* to the experience of *pratityasamutpada* (interconnectedness) is not a direct leap, it is a process. It is within that process that we can analytically identify steps that can have a role in teaching at all levels.

Masao Abe (1985) uses the well-known discourse given by the Chinese master Ch'ing-yuan Wei-hsin to make two major points about Buddhism and becoming a Buddha. The first stresses the fundamental importance of intellectual development. "Although intellectual understanding cannot be a substitute for Zen's awakening, practice without a proper and legitimate form of intellectual understanding is often misleading . . . practice without learning is apt to be blind" (p. 4). This speaks directly to the misperception often raised against the use of meditation in the academic context, that Zen and other forms of meditation are "anti-intellectualism" or "cheap intuitionism" (p. 3). While a full-fledged study of Nagarjuna is not necessary for all of our students, it is important and fundamental to meditation that it be about *something*, very often one's thoughts, but also the emotions, somatic experiences, and relationships that connect with them. This is what is foregrounded by Wittgenstein's concept of language-games (1968 passim) and Nagarjuna's "truths of worldly convention" (*MMK* 24:8); our concepts are an integral part of the rest of our experience and students can benefit greatly by having an understanding of their relationships. My proposal is that the thoughts students meditate on in the classroom can be deliberately chosen for their relevance to their course of study. For instance, sexist or racist discourse can be meditated on *along with the emotions and somatic experiences that go with it,* and in that process revealed to be impermanent. Because of their experience of impermanence on all levels, students may begin to break their attachment to the subject language-game and thus achieve a deeper level of learning (Forbes 2002; Orr 2002, 2005, 2007, 2009).[3]

The second main point that Abe (1985) makes is that the movement from *samsara* to *nirvana* is a process which involves overcoming the forms of *avidya* that Nagarjuna's work is concerned with, especially reification and objectification of the self, and more broadly these as they construct *samsara* in its totality. Ch'ing-yuan Wei-hsin's short discourse is as follows:

> Thirty years ago, before I began the study of Zen, I said, 'Mountains are mountains, waters are waters.'
>
> After I got an insight into the truth of Zen through the instruction of a good master, I said, 'Mountains are not mountains, waters are not waters.'
>
> But now, having attained the abode of final rest [Awakening or Nirvana], I say, 'Mountains are really mountains, waters are really waters.' (1985, p. 4)

The instructions for meditation given by Dogen in his "A Universal Recommendation for Zazen" (1976) is one of the best-known statements about achieving Garfield's "way of being here" and, therefore, I will use it to elucidate Abe's second point. After describing how to sit in meditation (zazen), Dogen instructs the student to "Think of nonthinking. How is this done? By thinking beyond thinking and nonthinking" (p. 46). Kasulis (1981) points out that the Japanese terms Dogen uses for "thinking," "nonthinking," and "thinking beyond thinking and nonthinking" are traditional terms used in Zen dialogues.[4] Let us clarify these and so move toward a clearer sense of Dogen's instructions and their relationship to Ch'ing-yuan Wei-hsin's discourse. In what follows I will treat "thinking," "nonthinking," and "thinking beyond thinking and nonthinking" as stages for the sake of the discussion. Dogen (1976) would object to that characterization, in part because he rejects a distinction between "practice" and "enlightenment" (p. 45), or that "zazen is step-by-step mediation" (p. 46); at the same time, he stresses the importance of practice and is clearly making a distinction here which we need to understand.

In Dogen's instructions "thinking" refers to cognition contaminated by *avidya*. As in Loy's (1992) discussion, for instance, we reify and objectify a concept of self to which we are attached to the point of identifying with it: "I *am* that reified self." We also do this more broadly with things in the world through dualistic thinking; we understand them as radically separate from our self, and so we understand mountains and rivers as separate entities in the world in the sense that Nagarjuna critiqued. Meditation practice must confront and defeat this sort of "thinking" as it results in the logically absurd positions of stasis and nihilism that Nagarjuna revealed. Being attached to them is delusional and thus negatively affects our lived experience.

In his discussion of the second stage, nonthinking, Kasulis (1981) uses the example of someone being kept awake by his or her thoughts and worries and so trying to get to sleep by attempting to "not-think." They may roll over, take a deep breath, and resolve not to think at all. Thus, "not-thinking" is essentially a negating attitude toward all the mental acts of "thinking" (pp. 73–74). As Kasulis describes it, this comes closest to what is often wrongly understood as the blissed out or empty-minded state of meditation. In relating this to the second stage in Ch'ing-yuan Wei-hsin's discourse, Abe points out that this is the stage of realizing that "everything is empty." Here one may be tempted to fall into nihilism and assert, for instance, that "nothing really exists," mountains are no longer mountains as they were understood in stage one and so they do not really exist at all, for these are the only options dualistic thinking gives us, to exist or not to exist. Here we can also see that at the root of this is a more fundamental dualism, that between "thinking" and "not-thinking." And so, Abe argues, "Emptiness must empty itself" (1985, p. 8).

"Thinking beyond thinking and nonthinking" is distinct from both of these. Kazulis maintains that, ". . . in its assuming *no* intentional attitude whatsoever . . . it neither affirms nor denies, accepts nor rejects, believes nor disbelieves. In fact it does not objectify either implicitly or explicitly" (1981, p. 75). He calls this "prereflective" and holds that "the without-thinking act supplies the raw material out of which the later reflective, thinking act develops" (pp. 75–76). This is correct as far as it goes, but we must not be misled into interpreting Kasulis's notion of "prereflective" to mean a return to a childish state. We need a fuller understanding of what Dogen had in mind.

Thinking Beyond Thinking and Nonthinking

I have previously argued that Buddhism affirms a different way of experiencing and that this involves addressing misperceptions that are sourced in part in linguistic misunderstandings. For Nagarjuna, and for Wittgenstein in the West, these involve misunderstanding about the self. A special focus on Wittgenstein's work was the Western dominant discourse's radical distinction between mind, and thus cognition/thinking, and the rest of human being. He argued that this dualistic distinction leads first to solipsism and ultimately reduces language to nonsense (1968, passim). Rather, as he showed throughout his mature work, language functions in language-games and these involve nonlinguistic and relational experience in a myriad of ways. Thus Wittgenstein undercuts the radical separation of mind from body, emotion, and relationship that has dominated Western discourse since the time of ancient Greek culture. However, the separation of mind and body that has dominated in the West has not been a predominant part of Japanese or Chinese culture[5] and it is with this observation that we can gain a fuller picture of Dogen's notion of "Thinking beyond thinking and nonthinking."

The Japanese and Chinese words that are sometime translated into English simply as "mind" (*xin* in Chinese, *shin* in Japanese) have a much broader meaning. Berling (1992) points out that the Chinese word for heart, *xin*, "stands for both the physical heart and the cognitive center of the person (the brain), along with all of the psyche" and so she argues that it should be translated "mind-and-heart" (fn. 37). Hall and Ames (1995) translate it as "heart-and-mind" and quote Mencius, in a passage that resonates with Dogen's view, that "It is not the case that only those of superior character have this heart-and-mind (*xin*); all people have it. Those of superior character are simply able to avoid loosing it" (p. 192). Thus, this gives us a more holistic concept of the person, which has clear affinities with that found in Wittgenstein's work, and of "thinking," *xin*, which, while it involves cognition, is not limited to it. More broadly it involves, in Garfield's words, a "way of being here."

The Japanese concept of *shin* carries the same implications as *xin* in Chinese (Abe, 1985, passim; Yuasa, 1987, passim). Yuasa points out that the phrase *shinjin ichinyo*, which can be translated as "the oneness of body-mind," was first used to characterize the Zen experience by Eisai, who is considered the founder of Japanese Zen.[6] But this phrase is not limited in Japanese culture to meditation practice: it is to be found in activities as diverse as *No theater* and martial arts training. In an interesting analogy, he observes that in the West athletes are trained to coordinate mind and body although most non-athletes are not. Today, sports training "in the zone," the training for which involves the use of meditation techniques, is commonplace in the West although it is not considered to have effects beyond enhancing athletic performance (see, however, Forbes, 2002). Yuasa continues,

> In contrast, in the East, physical training that is not accompanied by the training of the mind as well is regarded an aberration, for the mind and body cannot be essentially separated. Consequently, the Eastern martial arts have been regarded since ancient times as an outward-moving form of meditation. (p. 24)

With this in mind, we can see that for Dogen "thinking beyond thinking and nonthinking," does not imply a purely nonlinguistic experience, one where thinking simply drops out, although it may well be that in some instances. Rather it is, as he says elsewhere, "to cut off the function of discriminating consciousness and turn away from the road of intellectual understanding" (in Yuho, 1976, p. 57); that is, to bring an immediacy to experience uncontaminated by *avidya*. In a sense, the use of *all* language must return to that "primitive" form that Wittgenstein also pointed to, before a child has learned to theorize or has imbibed the preconceptions and distortions of her or his culture. In doing this, the way one is in the world is changed.

It is clear that neither Dogen nor Buddhist thought generally advises eschewing language or thought. Buddhist literature is replete with the *sayings* of the masters, from the historical Buddha to Nagarjuna and onward, and, as we have seen, Ch'ing-yuan Wei-hsin *says* after his awakening that, "Mountains are really mountains, waters are really waters." He uses language but without the deluded consciousness that characterizes his *samsaric* experience; he does not project that reified and objectified grid onto himself or onto the rest of reality. That the awakened mind was for everyday use is stressed by Dogen not just in principle but also in practical advice, such as his *Instructions for the Cook* (2001). The cook is the second most important person in the Zen monastery, after the abbot, and in his advice Dogen stresses throughout the importance of working with "a sincere mind" when preparing even the most simple ingredients; "do not regard them with ordinary [deluded] eyes, or think of them with ordinary [deluded] emotions" (p. 24). As Nagarjuna was at pains to show, the boundaries (*koti*) of *samsara* and *nirvana* are the same and most certainly *samsara* includes thought and language, but so does *nirvana*. And so it is our relationship with our words and the ways in which this colors our lived experience that is at issue for Dogen; and it is on that level, on the level of cognition which involves reification, objectification, and attachment to the things so construed, that meditation practice has a role in teaching and learning.

Jon Kabat-Zinn (1994) is one of the best-known Western teachers of Vipassana or mindfulness meditation. "Mindfulness," he says, "means paying attention in a particular way: on purpose, in the present moment, and non-judgmentally" (p. 4). He explains that this practice is simple but not easy (pp. 8–10). Each of the elements of mindfulness can present challenges. In fact, paying attention, being in the moment, in itself is something that many find difficult unless it is done for the purpose of enjoyment or escapism (chatting or texting with friends, watching television, etc.); otherwise, keeping focused for even a short period of time can be difficult. However, doing so "on purpose" can open the door to introducing a wide range of material to the practice. Mindfulness stresses paying attention not only to cognitive content but also to emotions and somatic experiences and if, for instance, one is dealing with racism, the student can meditate on words with racist uses, such as black and white, and observe the experience of each on these levels (Orr, 2005, 2005, 2009). Or one can do this with a passage from a text, a visual image, or any other material. A lot of the effectiveness of this practice comes from becoming aware of the transitoriness (*anitya*) of experience. As one sees that the discomfort experienced while meditating on a racial category comes and goes (*anitya*) then, over time, one may be able to overcome it entirely simply by letting it extinguish of its own accord. This will contribute to the non-judgemental attitude that Kabat-Zinn recommends; while the concepts are still in one's lexicon they have been shorn of their power to delude. It will also begin to open the door to generating new responses or ways of approaching questions, problems, texts, one's life. Without a mindful approach, no matter how fully convinced a student may be of a position or idea contrary to their habitual way of thinking, its noncognitive dimensions may remain to color future understanding and experience.

Conclusion

Mindfulness practice thus can begin to break down, not only on a cognitive level but more fully on an experiential level, many of the preconceptions and conditioned responses that stand in the way of learning and creativity. This is important for any learning that seeks to bring about change and especially for pedagogy that involves challenging oppressive or even simply outmoded discourses. This is of special significance as we struggle with the oftentimes exclusionary and rigid worldview of the modern era. I have argued that Nagarjuna's work on *sunyata* and *pratityasamutpada* along with Wittgenstein's on language-games provides a framework for understanding mindfulness practice as described by teachers from Dogen to Jon Kabat-Zinn. This practice can contribute to the revisioning necessary to meet contemporary demands for effective social and political action by providing us with a way to understand ourselves not as the "isolated social atoms" of much contemporary social, political, and moral discourse but as essentially and intimately connected with others (Orr, 2007). Extended beyond the domain of human interpersonal issues, their work can radically reconfigure our understanding of reality and of our place in this vast and complex web. In the words of Dogen,

> To study the Buddha way is to study the self. To study the self is to forget the self. To forget the self is to be actualized by myriad things. When actualized by myriad things, your body and mind as well as the bodies and minds of others drop away. No trace of realization remains, and this no-trace continues endlessly.[7] (Dogen, in Tanahashi, p. 70)

Or, in David's Loy's (2008) more contemporary words, "Understood properly, taking care of the earth's rainforests is like me taking care of my own leg" (p. 109).

Notes

1. This is one source of the "problems of other minds" (how do we *know* other people aren't automata? We don't, but we don't doubt it either. A remark on the conceptual grammar of "know"), and the "private language problem" (how can we *know* what sensations words mean? We don't know that either), which Wittgenstein addressed in *Philosophical Investigations.*

2. Garfield (1990, fn. 10) uses the term "everyday metaphysics" as the "fallacy" of the "person-on-the-street" who, roughly put, tends to reify nouns. Although it also can be misleading, I prefer the term "reification" or "everyday reification" as "everyday metaphysics" makes the problem we are trying to identify and address seem much more intellectual and theoretical than it is. Wittgenstein (1969) argued in *On Certainty* that a "world picture," not a metaphysical theory, organizes much of not only one's intellectual orientation but one's lived experience. This complex concept covers both the broad "view of things" of a culture or specific group, as well as those aspects specific to individuals within cultures and groups. The main point for our concerns is that a world picture is on one level a cultural inheritance, but on a second, more fundamental level is sourced in the way human beings live in their world. That is, on the second, lived, level much of it is never even articulated by the "person-on-the-street," let alone critically investigated, unless an occasion for doing so arises (Orr, 1989). Nevertheless, culture and social practices may lead one to live *as if* certain aspects of one's world-picture reflected an objective, reified reality, for instance those aspects of the world-picture that support sexism, racism, homophobia, and many others (see Orr, 2002, 2005). Of what we might call the upper, more cultural, level of the world-picture, Wittgenstein (1969) says, "That is to say, the *questions* that we raise and our *doubts* depend on the fact that some propositions are exempt from doubt, are as it were like hinges on which those turn" (p. 341). And of the deeper, lived, level: "Does a child believe that milk exists? Or does it know that milk exists? Does a cat know that a mouse exists?" (p. 478). "My *life* consists in my being content to accept many things" (1969, p. 344). Some of the things that one is "content to accept" logically may not be amenable to proof: for instance, as Wittgenstein argues at length in *Philosophical Investigations*, the existence of other people. This is the level of logical "bedrock" about which he says,

> I want to regard man here as an animal; as a primitive being to which one grants instinct but not ratiocination. As a creature in a primitive state. Any logic good enough for primitive means of communication needs no apology from us. Language did not emerge from some kind of ratiocination. (1969, p. 475)

However, on the upper level, our concept of persons may be nuanced by cultural ideology (lived out as attitudes) that we have also never questioned, perhaps never even specifically acknowledged, but which are open to question and refutation, e.g., the attitudes underlying racism or sexism or homophobia. It is at this level that mindfulness practice can challenge oppressive discourses.

3. For those who are looking for an introduction to key ideas in Nagarjuna's work for classroom use, there are also very good introductory texts written for the non-specialist, such as David Loy's *Money, Sex, War, Karma* (2008) and the Dalai Lama's *Essence of the Heart Sutra* (Gyatso, 2002). Loy is a highly esteemed Buddhist scholar of the middle way and his book is authoritative enough for me to use in one of my university courses, yet is clearly and simply written.

4. In his discussion Kasulis uses "thinking," "not-thinking," and "without-thinking" for the three categories (pp. 71–86). I find Kasulis's third term, "without-thinking," potentially misleading as it seems to play into the anti-intellectualism view of meditation that I have rejected and which he quite explicitly rejects as well (p. 74).

5. In their anthology of world philosophy, Solomon and Higgins (1993) provide a useful introduction to the wide variety to be found in philosophical traditions, including notions of personhood. See also Berling (1992) and Hall and Ames (1995).

6. The word "Zen" in Japanese derives from the Chinese "Ch'an," which in turn comes from the Sanskrit work "Dhyana," which is the seventh limb of Classical Yoga and means meditation. Thus, "Zen" means meditation.

7. Both Tanahashi's (1985) translation using the word "actualized" and those of others who use "to be *one* with myriad [or 'all'] things" have merit. The sense of this passage becomes clearer in Tanahashi's Introduction where he discusses Dogen's poem "On Zen Practice," which uses the metaphor of the reflection of the moon on water which breaks into many droplets. Tanahashi comments that, "For Dogen, meditation practice implies this sort of mutual permeation between an individual's "light" and the activities of all things. Although one person's practice is part of the practice of all awakened beings, each individual practice is indispensable, as it actualizes and completes everyone's activity as a Buddha" (p. 13, see also the discussion on pp. 14–15 "Realm of 'All is Nonseparate'").

References

Abe, M., & W. R. LaFleur (Eds.). (1985). *Zen and western thought.* Honolulu, HI: University of Hawai'i Press.

Berling, J. (1992). Embodying philosophy: Some preliminary reflections from a Chinese perspective. In Frank Reynolds & David Tracy (Eds.), *Discourse and practice* (pp. 233–260). Albany, NY: State University of New York Press.

Boccio, F. J. (2004). *Mindfulness yoga: The awakened union of breath, body, and mind.* Boston: Wisdom Publications.

Dogen (1976). A Universal Recommendation for Zazen (Fukan Zazen-gi). In Yuho Yokio & Daizen Victoria (Eds.), *Zen master Dogen: An introduction with selected writings* (pp. 45–47). New York and Tokyo: Weatherhill.

Dogen (2001). *Instructions for the cook.* In Jisho Warner, Shohaku Okumura, John McRae, and Taigen Dan Leighton (Eds.), *Nothing is hidden: Essays on Zen master Dogen's instructions for the cook* (Griffith Foulk, Trans.) (pp. 21–40). New York, Tokyo: Weatherhill,

Forbes, D. (2004). *Boyz 2 Buddhas: Counseling urban high school male athletes in the zone.* New York: Peter Lang.

Garfield, J. L. (1990). Epoche and sunyata: Skepticism east and west. *Philosophy East and West, 40*(3), 285–307.

Garfield, J. L. (1995). *The fundamental wisdom of the middle way: Nagarjuna's mūlamadhyamakakārikā.* New York and London: Oxford University Press. (Cited as *MMK* in the essay.)

Gomez, L. O. (1976). Proto-Madhyamika in the Pali canon. *Philosophy East and West, 26*(2), 137–165.

Gyatso, T. (2002). *Essence of the heart sutra.* Boston: Wisdom Publications.

Hall, D. L., & Ames, R. T. (1995). *Anticipating China: Thinking through the narratives of Chinese and Western culture.* Albany, NY: State University of New York Press.

Hartranft, C. (2003). *The yoga-sutra of Patanjali: A new translation with commentary.* Boston and London: Shambhala.

Hobbes, T. (1851/1958). *Leviathan, parts one and two.* New York: The Bobbs-Merrill Company.

Iyengar, B. K. S. (1991). *Light on yoga.* Hammersmith, London: Thorsons.

Kabat-Zinn, J. (1994). *Wherever you go, there you are.* New York: Hyperion.

Kasulis, T. P. (1981). *Zen action zen person.* Honolulu, HI: University Press of Hawai'i.

Laqueur, T. (1990). *Making sex: Body and gender from the Greeks to Freud.* Cambridge, MA: Harvard University Press.

Loy, D. (1992). Avoiding the void: The *lack* of self in psychotherapy and Buddhism. *The Journal of Transpersonal Psychology, 24*(2), 151–180.

Loy, D. R. (2008). *Money, Sex, war, karma: Notes for a Buddhist revolution.* Boston: Wisdom Publications.

Nisbett, R. E. (2003). *The geography of thought: How Asians and Westerners think differently . . . and why.* New York: The Free Press.

Orr, D. (1989). Did Wittgenstein have a theory of hinge propositions? *Philosophical Investigations, 12*(2), 134–153.

Orr, D. (2002).The uses of mindfulness in anti-oppressive pedagogies: Philosophy and praxis. *Canadian Journal of Education, 27*(2) 247–267.

Orr, D. (2005). Minding the soul in education: Conceptualizing and teaching the whole person. In Jack Miller (Ed.), *Holistic learning: Breaking new ground* (pp. 87–99). Albany, NY: State University of New York.

Orr, D. (2007). The mind/body paradigm crisis and a new paradigm for feminism. In Deborah Orr, Dianna Taylor, Linda Lopez McAlister (Eds.), *Feminist Politics: Identity, Difference, and Agency* (pp. 15–39). Lanham, MD: Rowman & Littlefield Publishers.

Solomon, R. C., & Higgins, K. M. (Eds.). (1993). *From Africa to Zen: an invitation to world philosophy.* Lanham, MD: Rowman & Littlefield.

Stone, L. (1984). *The family, sex and marriage in England 1500–1800* (Abridged ed.). Harmondsworth, Middlesex, UK: Penguin Books.

Tannahashi, K. (1985). *Moon in a dewdrop: Writings of Zen master Dogen*. San Francisco: North Point Press.

Taylor, C. (1980). Theories of meaning. *Proceedings of the British Academy, 66*, 283–327.

Taylor, C. (1989). *Sources of the self: The making of modern identity*. Cambridge, MA: Harvard University Press.

Walser, J. (2005). *Nagarjuna in context: Mahayana Buddhism and early Indian culture*. New York: Columbia University Press.

Whicher, I. Nirodha (1997). Yoga praxis and the transformation of the mind. *Journal of Indian Philosophy, 25*(1), 1–66.

Whicher, I. (1998). *The integrity of the yoga darsana: A reconsideration of classical yoga*. Albany, NY: State University of New York Press.

Wittgenstein, L. (1968). *Philosophical Investigations* (G. E. M. Anscombe, Trans.). Oxford: Basil Blackwell.

Wittgenstein, L. (1969). *On Certainty* (G. E. M. Anscombe & G. H. von Wright, Eds.; Denis Paul and G. E. M. Anscombe, Trans.). New York: Harper Torchbooks.

Wittgenstein, L. (1980). *Culture and Value* (G. H. von Wright, Ed.; Heikki Nyman, Denis Paul, & G. E. M. Anscombe, Trans.). Chicago: University of Chicago Press.

Yuasa, Y., Shigenori, N., & Kasulis, T. (1987). *The Body: Toward an Eastern Mind-Body Theory*. Albany, NY: State University of New York Press.

Yuho, Y., & Victoria, D. (1976). *Zen master Dogen: An introduction with selected writings*. New York and Tokyo: Weatherhill.

3

Kindred Spirits in Teaching Contemplative Practice

Distraction, Solitude, and Simplicity

Mara Adelman

> We are born to interruption—it is attention we must cultivate.
>
> —Paraphrase of Jackson, *Distracted*, 2008, p. 79

> Deciding what to pay attention to for this hour, day, week, or year, much less a lifetime, is a peculiarly human predicament, and your quality of life largely depends on how you handle it.
>
> —Gallagher, 2009, p. 11

Topics essential to understanding contemplation are like kindred spirits that can move us beyond preaching to the choir. Secular, everyday issues that are highly relevant to the teaching of contemplative practices can broaden its appeal. Given the frenetic pace of our students' lives, examining and critiquing the status quo may offer insights, even inspiration, to furthering their mindfulness practice. This chapter outlines how the topics of distraction, solitude, and voluntary simplicity (herein referred to as "simplicity") and related subtopics can complement our understanding and experience of contemplative practice. This chapter also highlights a course entitled "Restorative Solitude" (Adelman, 2009) and a faculty workshop entitled "The Elephant in our Living Room: Distraction in Students Personal and Academic Lives" (Adelman, 2010). In both of these programs, contemplative practices, including meditative and reflective practices, were used throughout, often with insightful outcomes.

Given the onslaught of "attention capitalism" where attention is up for sale (for example, pop-ups, hyperlinks, streaming advertising), it is critical that we understand contemplative practices as an antidote to the notion that our capacity to focus is now a valued commodity, reframed as the "attention economy" a "currency" or "asset" with "value" (Davenport & Beck, 2001). Contemplative practices are embedded within the larger social context, and the commoditization of attention demands scrutiny. Themes of distraction, solitude and simplicity provide starting points for examining this cultural backdrop.

Rationale

It is not uncommon to hear faculty bemoan students' hectic lives and their attachment to screens like babies to mammary glands—and then within minutes speak of the busyness of their own lives. Herein the term "screens" will be used to describe all technological devices, including computers, portables, phones, television, and so on, including techno-usage such as phoning, emailing, texting, and Internet searching. Academic climates, like most institutional climates, exalt the busy life. We reward it.

Since we assume that we live in a culture of busyness, hyper-schedules, and tech-saturated, time-compressed encounters, we often do not speak about the elephant in the living room. These taken-for-granted assumptions about life fuel tacit understandings of the unsustainable. In part, this chapter argues that we need to name the elephant, critique it, unpack it, and engage our students in critical reflection. The cultural wash of busyness and techno-saturation is so pervasive that it remains unchecked and unexamined. Like Thoreau's move to Walden Pond, when we examine these kindred spirits, we too move to the outskirts of town to reflect and ponder.

Dialectical Perspective

The dialectical perspective is grounded in the notion that we need to examine contrary perspectives that appear as opposites but, in fact, vacillate in nature. Like a tightrope, these "oppositions" are held in tension and only momentarily resolved. In our everyday lives, we often move in tension between various opposing states of being. For example, couples often negotiate the dialectic of dependence and independence, such as the amount of time spent together or apart.

> Contradictions and dialectical tensions are central features of a dialectical analysis. . . . Motion, activity, and change are thus fundamental properties of social life in a dialectical perspective, and the present state of any relationship is considered an incessant achievement. (Rawlins, 1992, p. 7)

The ways in which our reality is constructed are highly relevant to embedding contemplative practices into our intellectual and popular climate. A major perspective in explaining how we perceive reality is the concept of the "social construction of reality" that privileges communication (including mass media) as the major channel for creating shared meaning. However, Braman (2007) argues for a "contemplative construction of reality"—including the importance of silence, solitude, and contemplative practices by which a person comes to know the world. This contemplative construction of reality happens "within the individual and within the broader natural environment that includes but goes beyond the human . . ." (p. 284). Contemplative practice shapes our communicative competence: "Silence brings us to our selves, to possibilities of knowledge, to awareness of what is around us, and to a sense of what it is meaningful to speak or not to speak" (p. 291). Dialectically, social and contemplative practices can oscillate, feeding into each other, as a cycle of activity and respite; a pulse for everyday life.

Central to the contemplative construction of reality is the dialectic of engagement versus disengagement (Koch, 1994). In contemplative practice, as in solitude, we intentionally disengage from the public eye, and move inward. However, normative social pressures often make this movement difficult. Culturally, the dialectical tension emphasizes engagement, coupling, and other-oriented states of connection that are magnified in our highly saturated, mediated communicative culture. This saturation is compounded by normative pressures, such as professional and social demands to stay perpetually connected and responsive. It is no wonder that students often struggle with disengagement.

The dialectical perspective is helpful for students as they foster their own contemplative practices, especially as they deal with competing demands and attempts to cope with technological engagement. This perspective emphasizes the contextual and mutable nature of relationships; the tensions inherent in the course of daily life. Murphy (1971), who writes on the dialectics of social life, reminds us that

> The definition of a phenomenon does not lie in an inner quality that endures and gives substance to the phenomenon; it derives from its boundaries or limits, the parameters beyond which it becomes

> something else. . . . Things are continually pushing against their opposites, the latter reacting as contradiction, and in going beyond these oppositions go beyond themselves into a new state. (p. 96)

This chapter posits three dialectal tensions:

Distraction: Distraction–Attention
Solitude: Engagement–Disengagement
Simplicity: Consumption–Simplicity

Rather than casting these as polar opposites, it is the "tensions" or "betweenness" (to evoke Buber) that we often grapple with.

Distraction

. . . between distraction and attention

> Welcome to the attention economy, in which the new scarcest resource isn't ideas or even talent, but attention itself.
>
> —Davenport & Beck, 2001, front jacket flap

The twenty-first century may well be characterized as the age of "solitude loss." We are wired as never before and distracted to death. Two decades ago, Gergen (1991) coined the phrase "social saturation" to address the state of being perpetually on-call to our social worlds, resulting in what he termed the "multiphrenic personality." Currently, "acceleration" and "distraction" describe our communicative climate amidst technological and social demands. Long before technology and multi-tasking eroded our attention, we were skimmers, scanners, and skippers of information. As early as 1982, a *New York Times* website article drew attention to this problem:

> THEY [emphasis in original] are everywhere—people who have the ability to read, but never look between the covers of a book, seldom glance beyond the headlines of a newspaper and search only for the pictures in magazines. Their reading centers around the bare essentials: road signs, labels on food packages, television listings and product instructions. The name that some social scientists have given to such people is "aliterates," [sic] those who know how to read, but won't. . . . (Maeroff, 1982)

Ironically, alliteracy skills are refined in graduate school; skimming abstracts and speed reading lengthy books often resulting in surface rather than deep understanding. The irony of this habit becomes evident when skimming articles on mindfulness.

Mindfulness is the antithesis of distraction. In *Distracted*, Jackson provides compelling evidence for the interplay between efficiency in our increasingly compressed lives (for example, multi-tasking, hyper-scheduling, Taylorism) and chaos, fragmentation, and loss of discourse.

Sherry Turkle, an MIT professor who has been writing for decades on the downside of our preoccupation with technology, argues that we inhabit a liminal state, a "betwixt and between" the virtual and real. She charts the isolation of being hyper-connected: "Online, we easily find 'company' but are exhausted by the pressures of performance. We enjoy continual connection but rarely have each other's full attention. We can have instant audiences but flatten out what we say to each other in new reductive genres of abbreviation (Turkle, 2011, p. 280). With regard to our interactions, Turkle cleverly describes the ever frequent stop-and-go of our face-to-face conversations due to techno-interruptions, rendering us all "plauseable" and she concludes that ultimately we are not engaged by the ". . . ties that bind. But . . . the ties that preoccupy" (p. 280). Like the sailors on the Odyssey, we succumb to the Sirens.

In our world of gadgets, life is stranger than fiction, especially in our attachment to the screens. A newly minted term bantered on various websites is "nomophobia" a mental feeling of inadequacy due to lack of (or loss) of mobile phone contact. Although postings about nomophobia humorously comment that people actually panic, have a loss of self-esteem, or feel depressed if they are without their mobile phones, my students don't find this funny. They confess that they would be "lost" without their cellphones and they experience not only anxiety, but actual fear of being "stranded" or deprived of a critical call or social opportunity. It is fascinating how cellphones have redefined an "emergency" and "fear," part of the growing post 9/11 cultural ambience. Like Linus in the Peanuts cartoon, who carries his signature blanket, the cellphone is the new transitional object. Tethered to their phones, within a ring away from parents and friends, students are in the situation where the phone becomes the new panopticon, their personal surveillance system (chosen or enforced), always within reach, always to be viewed, photographed, and pursued.

Technology reshapes our experience of time and self. As never before, time management takes on a renewed urgency. I recall when my daily calendar was divided into days, then hours, then 20 minute segments, and now 10. This time compression contributes to the constant sense of fragmentation and stress in daily life. Even interruption science and interruption rights, both growing areas in academic and marketing research, suggest the value placed on focusing.

Jackson reminds us that *attention = memory*. As our short-term and long-term memory become eroded with perpetual "multi-tasking" and "task switching," the costs are significant. "If attention makes us human, then long-term memory makes each of us an individual. Without it, we are faceless, hence our morbid fascination with amnesia of all kinds" (p. 94). Food, sex, work, relationships, and life in general are portable, fluid, shifting realities.

Historically, concerns for distraction and the significance of solitude were deeply rooted in American culture. Calls to return-to-nature (Thoreau) and appealing religious solitude (Merton, 1958) were offered as remedies to frantic, shallow lives. We were encouraged to live life "deliberatively." Solitude has a long history among contemplatives (for example, the Desert Fathers), up to its contemporary version: the rapid growth of personal, physical, and religious retreats (see Retreatfinder.com). If "the world is too much with us," today we can simply retreat from the world.

Among students, addressing the topic of distraction can be a rather charged discussion, and often gratifying. Students comment that they resent when course syllabi and discussions around students' use of technology begins to sound autocratic and patronizing. More than ever, their worlds are immersed in the digital age, and a Luddite mentality can come across as overly ideological and out-of-touch. Conversely, they appear to welcome frank discussions regarding a professor's "ground rules" and their colleagues' comfort zones.

To celebrate collegiality, I often use the metaphor of "lost conversations" to refer to the loss of meaningful, sometimes fleeting conversations that sustain everyday life, such as spontaneous interpersonal (IRL) meetings with professors on the sidewalk or in a cafe, students gossiping during class breaks, rituals of greeting and saying good-bye. I share with them that when students are glued to their screens/earphones/phones, I do not engage them, much less say "Hi." This is a lost conversation. Students commented that this metaphor makes them feel they are losing out on their education. I reply, "You are."

Solitude

. . . between engagement and disengagement

> There are days when solitude is a heady wine that intoxicates you with freedom. . . .
>
> —Colette (1966)

The notion of solitude is predominately associated with physical isolation, far from the madding crowd. Rather than treat solitude as simply a physical separation, Koch (1994) argues for a more psychological withdrawal, a state of "engaged disengagement."

> . . . the most promising place to look for the core of solitude is in the realm of social disengagement . . . solitude is, most ultimately, simply an experiential world in which other people are absent. . . . Other people may be physically present, provided that our minds are disengaged from them. (p. 15)

He expands on the quality of this experience, as a reflective, highly present state, freely chosen.

So what are the benefits of solitude for our lives? Koch (1994), Long and Averill (2003), and later Barbour (2004), in their analyses of solitude in autobiographical writing, identify various "virtues" of solitude in everyday life. The following is a melding of these virtues that speak to the far-reaching benefits of solitude, including:

(1) Freedom: refers to physical movement, thought, and imagination free from social constraints, the "letting-go," disinhibition, and sense of abandonment in the absence of others;

(2) Attunement to self or "self-formation": reclaiming one's voice; recollecting a sense of self, the deeper and authentic self. Koch (1994) notes that the ". . . final test of self-understanding achieved in dialogue is its durability in solitude; disengaged from all others, fully attending to my own feelings, does the explanation still satisfy?" (p. 115). It is often in the quiet that we reclaim our moral good and glimpse deeply into our personhood.

(3) Attunement to nature: extraordinary connection to the natural world. Three distinct experiences: i) clear, undistracted, sensitized perception, enhanced observation, ii) symbolic perception (a kind of anthropomorphizing of nature; life-as-an-ant), and iii) fusion/interfusion, loss of barriers between self and nature; flowing into nature. For example, moments when we are moved by nature's grandeur and we experience a sense of awe, mystery, smallness, an egoless state, often spiritual for some;

(4) Reflective perspective: reflective life-assessments; memory, past experiences. "Called variously 'contemplation' or 'enlightenment,' it is described as a kind of beholding or gazing which arises beyond the limits of willful rational inquiry" (Koch, p. 129). Contemplation allows those moments for epiphanies, the "ah-ha!" and also for creative insights, original thought, and the synthesis of ideas;

(5) Creativity: Koch summarizes Cobb's earlier work (1977) based on the autobiographies of 300 geniuses, where "she found that a powerful solitary revelation in childhood played an important role in their creative lives" (p. 133). Barbour (2004) elaborates on Storr's (1998) contention that the capacity to be alone is crucial to the creative process (p. 147), the time alone needed for gestation and creation of ideas and engagement in various art forms (for example, music, art, writing);

(6) Healing: response to loss, trauma, or suffering—people sequestered to heal physical or psychic wounds. Solitude can provide "regenerative power," a time alone to grieve, find meaning in loss. Furthermore, drained and depleted by social interactions, in solitude we can gain perspective, see cycles of life and death, focus on "other" nonhuman activities—such as a house, garden, or animals.

Critical to understanding solitude's role for contemplative practices is the notion of voluntary versus involuntary solitude. The conflation of voluntary solitude with involuntary states is common. Koch refers to these involuntary states as "near relations," including loneliness, isolation, privacy, and alienation. This assumed conflation is so prevalent, that I felt compelled to label my course "Restorative Solitude."

Many of us frequently and subconsciously associate solitude with loneliness, which is a very specific emotion, a longing. In the first scholarly work on loneliness, the authors noted that the stigma of loneliness was so great that few scholars would touch the subject (Peplau & Perlman, 1982). Koch argues that unlike the specificity of negative emotion in loneliness, solitude is not attached to a particular mood. The consequence of this conceptual sloppiness is that solitude gets stigmatized. Turkle (2011) concludes her work on technology and connectedness, paradoxically called *Alone Together*, with a reclaiming of solitude, "My own study of the networked life has left me thinking . . . about solitude—the kind that refreshes and restores. Loneliness is failed solitude. To experience solitude you must be able to summon yourself by yourself; otherwise, you will only know how to be lonely" (p. 288).

People also associate solitude with the study of theology, hermits, and spiritual quests. This latter association becomes the iconic vision of solitude as the grand, extreme, or intensely religious quest—for example, *Seven Years in Tibet*, Thoreau and Walden Pond, Moses in the desert, Tenzin Palmo and the cave. Koch (1994) argues that this romanticized version raises the solitude bar too high for most of us. As a result, our everyday efforts at sporadic attainment may appear puny, but are nonetheless significant.

As early as 1936, Petroff reminded us that solitude is a process that he calls "solitarization": ". . . to draw away from others objectively and subjectively, to exclude others or to be excluded by others. It is the process of becoming solitary" (p. 2). Although we may physically "exclude ourselves," the monkey mind that wildly chases ideas and images, and the residual relationships that occupy our thoughts, often interfere with disengagement. Thus, helping students with quieting the mind is part of this solitarization.

The following are some of the issues that often emerge from lectures and class discussions on solitude that are relevant to teaching contemplative practice:

Silence: The cacophony of everyday noise is so intense that we rarely experience the luxury of silence, yet without it, we never feel quiet within ourselves. Koch (1994) argues that silence and solitude mutually inform each other, deepening the journey. Similarly in our contemplative practice, the beauty of contemplative practices, especially eating meditation, is the silence that envelopes the action and facilitates mindfulness. In *Pursuit of Silence*, Prochnik (2010a) unpacks his lifelong search of silence, its significance in life, and the ever-growing intrusion of noise.

Nature: Koch (1994) speaks to the quality of solitude in nature, whereby one experiences a "fusion/interfusion: the loss of the sense of barriers between oneself and nature, the sense of flowing out into it as it simultaneously flows through oneself" (p. 118). When the fusion is great enough we sustain a sense of awe (Louv, 2005). Imagine life without awe? In his book, *Last Child in the Woods*, Louv speaks about nature deficit disorder, which is not only about the disassociation and diminishment of children's links to nature, but also their incapacity to fuse, experience wonder, and be still. In my courses, students reminisce about their lost childhoods, wandering for hours, lost in nature—in contrast to now, where they experience increasing fear to be alone in parks or wilderness (the "stranger danger" fear).

Boredom: I mention this subtheme, as it is a pervasive reaction when students discuss distraction, solitude, and contemplative practice. Nietzsche (1974) is quoted as saying, "To ward off boredom at any cost is vulgar" (p. 108). Oddly enough, students found discussion of boredom compelling and helpful, so I expanded this topic as part of the course lectures and readings. Even Bertrand Russell (1930) thought boredom is essential: ". . . one of the things that ought to be taught to the young" (p. 52). Students fear the lack of optimal stimulation, ennui, or boredom in solitude. They confess that even if a ping of boredom is felt, they instantly move to their "screens"—doomed to constant stimulation. Herein there is no space for "down time" to seize moments for reflection and rejuvenation, for creativity and epiphanies that in the words of Walter Benjamin, "hatches the egg of experience." Trunnell, White, Cedarquist, and Braza (1996) advocate for mindfulness education in helping students commune with nature as a means for reducing boredom.

Flow: Undoubtedly, the ultimate "high" from full attention is captured in Csikszentmihalyi's (1990) notion of "flow." He defines flow as when ". . . the information that keeps coming into awareness is congruent with goals, psychic energy flows effortlessly . . ." (p. 39). Flow consists of those rare moments when we become "one" with our engaged activity, one-with-the-rock (rock climbing), one-with-the-moment (meditation). "The mark of a person who is in control of consciousness is the ability to focus attention at will, to be oblivious to distractions, to concentrate for as long as it takes to achieve a goal . . ." (p. 31). In this prophetic book, the author writes that the major culprit for attention and the potential psychic energy is "psychic disorder"—that is, information that conflicts with existing intentions, or distracts us from carrying them out (read as techno-distractions). Clearly, moments of flow can emerge in reading or playing video games—a state of total absorption. Granted, flow can be experienced with others, such as in playing sports or performing in a string quartet. However, the cultivation of a skill and the full attention required for many flow experiences are often achieved alone, without social distractions.

While Csikszentmihalyi goes on to identify factors that give rise to optimal experience (for example, relationship of task to one's competency), students quickly grasp the experience, advantages, and joy of flow. Often in class discussions on flow, students' speech becomes more passionate and animated, as though the very concept optimizes energy. Sadly, while they yearn for more moments of flow, there is a recognition of its loss.

Simplicity

. . . between consumption and simplicity

> There is great happiness in not wanting, in not being something, in not going somewhere.
>
> —Krishnamurti, 1967, p. 23

In an age of sustainability, a call for material simplicity is fashionable. Today, thrift stores are chic. However, simplicity is also a state of mind, a paring of the extraneous, the bare essentials (or in Buddhist thought, "bare attention"). In his famous comedic riff about "stuff," George Carlin (1981) reminds us about our possessiveness around stuff and how it expands, but that ultimately, ". . . all you need in life, is a little place for your stuff." Fascination with stuff is evident in the recent publications and reality shows on hoarding, a phenomenon that has spurned endless self-help books and is now officially labeled as a disease. Similarly, articles and advice columns on uncluttering or organizing are the staples in any popular self-help or home magazine. Over-scheduling is also part of stuff. Stress reduction seminars advocate for simplifying your life so you can smell the roses.

If contemplative practice is part of the sustainable self, then its complement is the voluntary simplicity movement. This movement was rooted in the ground-breaking book by Elgin (1981), and it then morphed into a larger sustainability movement. Contemplative practices and sustainability in the form of voluntary simplicity are complementary for several reasons. First, "making time"—getting to the essence, living a reflective life—with intention and deliberation are Thoreauvian themes inherent in both the contemplative and simplicity literatures. They have long been kindred spirits, even symbiotic. Practically speaking, it is difficult to carve out a significant contemplative practice in a cluttered and harried life. As our calendars become increasingly compressed, our anxiety expands. Second, in writing about consumption, Brown and Kasser (2005) found mindfulness to be helpful: "Instead, a mindful consideration of one's inner states and behavior along with a set of values oriented more towards intrinsic than extrinsic aims appear to simultaneously benefit both individual and ecological well-being" (p. 361). Third, consumption is both material and ubiquitous. As a visible practice, as we make efforts to simplify, we reinforce mindfulness and conscious sustainability, rewriting Madonna's "material girl."

Case Study: Restorative Solitude

Recent scholarly overviews (Jackson, 2008) and commentaries (Deresiewicz, 2009) point to the "end of solitude" and the ways distraction erodes attention and subsequently affects our sense of stability and change. "Restorative Solitude" is a quarter-long course offered by the Department of Communication at Seattle University. As a communication scholar, I was intrigued by the questions, "How does solitude inform the quality of our discourse and our relationships? What is the quality of our life and conversations without opportunities for reflection, originality, epiphanies?" The syllabus, assignments, and resources can be found on the course website, solitudecourse.com.

This course revolves around three themes: contemplative practices, solitude, and simplicity. Within these themes, topics include virtual and IRL relationships, involuntary solitude, creativity, technology, distraction, boredom, faith, consumption, and other emergent interests. Assignments are designed to engage students in critical and analytical thinking, reflection, contemplative, and experiential learning. Perhaps the most practical assignment in this course is the two-part series on media logging and media liberation. Logging requires the students to record all media/screen usage for one week, recording feelings and activity before, during, and after engagement. At the end, they are asked to summarize the time spent in various activities and key themes that emerged regarding their feelings.

Liberation requires a full 24-hour period (introductory course), or four-day (Restorative Solitude course) disengagement from all media/screen activity, except what is required for work and school. Originally I had proposed a week for media liberation; however, students balked at this requirement. Since the spirit of the assignment was more important than the time spent disengaged, I asked them what they could commit. Answers have varied each quarter from three to four days. One student wrote:

> I often wake up in the morning to a text saying "breakfast?" from my girlfriend. I already have a place to be before I'm even conscious. . . . By noon, I had read an entire 120 page book in a little over two hours. *What the hell happened?* I was reading and reflecting rather than just reading to finish the book. (Sears, 2010)

Perhaps the most profound realization throughout these papers submitted in the past three years is the sadness in which students realize they are twittering their life away, their passions evaporated by the screen for endless hours a day. The average daily use for "disposable time" (not work or school related) ranged from approximately 4.5 to 6.0 hours; but even students admitted this was an understatement.

This course utilizes several contemplative practices including sitting, walking, eating, meditation, reflection logs and commentaries, and solitary "adventures." For newcomers, meditation can be daunting. Even long-term practitioners often apologize for their lack of discipline in "sitting on their cushion." We often bracket the contemplative from everyday experience, setting the bar rather high for its achievement. While I encourage daily practice and use various tapes, readings, and *YouTube* presentations, and so on to cultivate sitting, I also encourage students to grasp what I call "stolen moments"—the episodic, brief, even fleeting moments of being present. For example, we listen to Thich Nhat Hanh's meditation in everyday life (http://www.youtube.com/watch?v=7mKJGOiOQBE&NR=1), especially where he speaks about stopping at red lights: "We should look at them [red lights] as a friend, not as an enemy . . . reminding us to breath." I ask students to think about ways to incorporate stolen moments in their day. This often leads to an insightful discussion on how we can live more fully in the present, instead of John

Lennon's admonishment that "Life is what happens to you while you're busy making other plans." For example, we've discussed stopping midway to class, taking a few "mindful steps" and then moving on, or focusing on the breath while waiting in line, or programming your computer to "ring" as a reminder to take a deep breath or yoga stretch. Even for a few breaths—they can pull back to touch the stillness. Maybe the stolen moments will turn into minutes, hours, and even days of contemplative practice. Regardless, they have reclaimed a moment of being present.

Case Study: Faculty Workshop on Distraction

During my sabbatical, I read Maggie Jackson's (2008) book, *Distracted*, and recalled thinking that every educator and parent needed to read this book. For many of my colleagues, distraction was at an all-time high. I sent out a preliminary test-the-waters invitation to see if there would be any interest in such a workshop. Within the next two hours more than 36 faculty members chimed in. Some wanted the workshop for themselves or their children. One faculty member confessed that she was ready to resign, because students' techno-intrusions were so rude. A very diverse group of faculty attended the workshop, spanning most disciplines on campus, including the law school and coaches from athletics (see Adelman, 2010).

Clearly, distraction due to technology is shifting the dynamics of the class interactions and relationships among students. Gone are the rituals of "class breaks" where students congregated to complain about a class, to discuss an upcoming exam, or to simply socialize. Many faculty members complained about short attention spans, decreased writing skills, lack of netiquette, frantic schedules, the absence of passions or discipline to cultivate a "craft," or other similar issues. This workshop included experiential, reflective, contemplative, and cognitive learning.

In discussions among students, two "factors" were suggested that influence the attentive classroom climate: distraction reduction and attention enhancement. Students argued that it wasn't enough to help reduce the distractors (such as extraneous screen activity), but that faculty needed also to work on enhancing attention. They saw these as two distinctly different issues. Students and faculty were asked how they can foster "distraction reduction" and "attention enhancement." (See answers on the website "distractionworkshop.com.")

We underestimate faculty members' desire to talk seriously about the issues of distraction. Emails from colleagues after the workshop suggested an urgency regarding the state of distraction among students and in our professional lives. One participant wrote, "I used to complain about distractions but never spent time to analyze this problem. This workshop made me sit down and find ways to control distractions in personal life and the classroom."

Conclusion

At the heart of teaching contemplative practice is a reclaiming of our lives: to live with intention and presence. All too often we hear students and colleagues speak about stress and lifestyles as though they are without choice or agency, helpless in the onslaught of demands, disempowered by technology in order to remain connected and staying current. Langer (1990) speaks of how routines, habits, and mindlessness prevail, resulting in almost automatic, robotic behavior. When I ask students if they have ever driven from point A to B and wondered how they got there, or eaten a meal and can't remember what they ate upon finishing it—they know this is more common than they would like. Granted, routines, habits, and even mindlessness have their place; but like distraction, it would be nice for mindlessness to be paradoxically intentional.

Another, more radical interpretation to teaching contemplative practice and its kindred spirits would be as an act of resistance amidst the hegemony of the screens. This is not hyperbole. If education isn't about "attention" then what are we doing? We are our attention. How can we teach or learn without attention, much less develop a craft, talent, or expertise? It is reassuring that teaching contemplative practices is spanning diverse disciplines, as part of the process for attending, observing, and reflecting. To become discerning about how we attend and focus, to cultivate being present, is not simply a "skill"—it speaks to our essence and life force. Furthermore, teaching such kindred spirits as solitude and simplicity counters the hegemony of coupledom, engagement, and consumption. It poses the question, "If we are not our screens, relationships, and consumption—then what are we?"

The subtitle of Storr's book, *Solitude*: *A Return to the Self*, is a call as poignant today as it was in 1988. As I read my students' papers that recount the days on which they reduced their mediated consumption of "the screens," I found myself saddened by their reflections. There was such wistfulness for what they felt they had lost earlier in their lives: their love of curling up with a good book, the feeling of ecstasy in one's study as a dancer, their longing to return to painting. In one class exercise, I asked students to write their obituaries, a contemplative exercise where they are asked to reflect at the end of a long life on how they will be remembered. Their obituaries reveal lives of unavoidable regrets: "I wish I had spent more time with my children" or "I regret not being there for my parents" or ". . . alas, I never pursued my passion for the piano." In a guest editorial entitled, "Tales of an Obit Maker," I wrote: "I think of an obit as a reflection pool; sometimes stagnant, other times wavering. The process usually reminds me to either get going or slow down. For me, obituaries are like a metaphor for being mindful—in the words of the late Susan Sontag, "Be serious, be passionate, wake-up" (Adelman, 2008, p. B5).

In teaching kindred spirits along with contemplative practices, we open up discussion of our curriculum, pedagogy, and research to the very issues that can deter the journey to being attentive and in-the-now. There is no question that technology will play an increasingly consuming role in our everyday lives. As such, we need to engage in a cultural critique of massive distraction, the commodification of our personal attention, and restore the virtues of solitude and simplicity. In so doing, we can reclaim the existential meaning of being present and our presence in the world and perhaps, along the way, we can rewrite our obituaries.

Acknowledgments

Seattle University, CELT Office for summer workshop on academic writing, Center for Social Justice Seminar on Contemplative Practices, and "readers" for this chapter—Hajer Al Faham, Francis Dinger, Ruan Pethiyagoda, and Kelton Sears.

References

Adelman, M. (2008, September 1). Tales of an obit maker. *Seattle Post-Intelligencer*, B5.

Adelman, M. (2009). Restorative solitude. Retrieved from <http://solitudecourse.com/>.

Adelman, M. (2010). The elephant in the living room: Distraction and its impact on students' intellectual and personal life. Retrieved from <http://distractionworkshop.com/>.

Acheson, K. (2008). Silence in dispute. In C. S. Beck (Ed.), *Communication Yearbook, 31* (pp. 2–61), New York: Lawrence Erlbaum Associates.

Barbour, J. D. (2004). *The value of solitude: The ethics and spirituality of aloneness in autobiography*. Charlottesville, VA: University of Virginia Press.

Braman, S. (2007). When nightingales break the law: Silence and the construction of reality. *Ethics and Information Technology, 9*, 281–295.

Brown, K., and Kasser, T. (2005). Are psychological and ecological well-being compatible? The role of values, mindfulness, and lifestyle. *Social Indicators Research, 74*, 349–368.

Carlin, G. (1981). Stuff. Retrieved from <http://www.writers-free-reference.com/funny/story085.htm>.

Cobb, E. (1977). *The ecology of imagination in childhood.* New York: Columbia University Press.

Colette (1966). *Earthly paradise: An autobiography.* (H. Briffault et al., Trans.) New York: Farrar, Straus and Giroux.

Csikszentmihalyi, M. (1990). *Flow: The psychology of optimal experience.* New York: Harper & Row.

Davenport, T. H., & Beck, J. C. (2001). *Attention economy: Understanding the new currency of business.* Boston, MA: Harvard Business School Press.

Deresiewicz, W. (2009, January). The end of solitude. *Chronicle for Higher Education, 55*(21), B6.

Elgin, D. (1981, 1993 Revised ed.). *Voluntary simplicity: Toward a way of life that is outwardly simple, inwardly rich.* New York: Quill/HarperCollins.

Gallagher, W. (2009). *RAPT: Attention and the focused life.* New York: Penguin Books.

Gergen, K. (1991). *The Saturated self: Dilemmas of identity in contemporary life.* New York: Basic Books.

Jackson, M. (2008). *Distracted: The erosion of identity in contemporary life.* New York: Prometheus Books.

Krishnamurti, J. (1967). *Commentaries on living (second series).* Wheaton, IL: The Theosophical Publishing House. (Original work published in 1958).

Koch, P. (1994). *Solitude: A philosophical encounter.* Chicago, IL: Open Court Publishing.

Langer, E. (1990). *Mindfullness.* New York: Perseus Books.

Long, C. R., & Averill, J. R. (2003). Solitude: An exploration of benefits of being alone. *Journal for the Theory of Social Behavior, 22*(1), 21–44.

Louv, R. (2005). *Last child in the woods: Saving our children from nature-deficit disorder.* Chapel Hill, NC: Algonquin Books.

Maeroff, G. I. (Sept. 28, 1982). Education. *New York Times* (Science section). Retrieved from <http://www.nytimes.com/1982/09/28/science/education.html?scp=1&sq/>.

Merton, T. (1958). *Thoughts in solitude.* New York: Farrar, Straus and Giroux.

Murphy, R. F. (1971). *The dialectics of social life: Alarms and excursions in anthropological theory.* New York: Basic Books.

Nietzsche, F. (1974). *The Gay Science*, New York: Vintage Books.

Peplau, L. A., & Perlman, D. (Eds.). (1982). *Loneliness: A sourcebook of current theory, research, and therapy.* New York: Wiley-Interscience.

Petroff, L. (1936). *Solitaries and solitarization: a study of the concepts, forms, degrees, causes and effects of isolation.* Los Angeles: University of Southern California Press.

Prochnik, G. (2010a). *In pursuit of silence: Listening for meaning in a world of noise.* New York: Doubleday.

Rawlins, W. K. (1992). *Friendship matters: Communication, dialectics, and the life course.* New York: Aldine de Gruyter.

Russell, B. (1930). *The conquest of happiness.* New York: Horace Liveright, Inc.

Sennett, R. (1977). *The fall of public man.* New York: W. W. Norton & Co.

Sears, K. (2010). Student paper, for Restorative Solitude. Dept. of Communication, Seattle University.

Storr, A. (1988). *Solitude: A return to the self.* New York: Ballantine Books.

Trunnell, E. P., White, F., Cederquist, J., Braza, J. (1996). Optimizing an outdoor experience for experiential learning by decreasing boredom through mindfulness training. *Journal of Experiential Education. 19*(1), 43–49.

Turkle, S. (2011). *Alone together: Why we expect more from technology and less from each other.* New York: Basic Books.

4

Contemplation

The Soul's Way of Knowing

John (Jack) P. Miller

Harry Lewis (2006), former Dean of Harvard College, has written, "Harvard teaches students but does not make them wise" (p. 255). This is a sad commentary on the university which two of the wisest Americans, Emerson and Thoreau, attended almost two hundred years ago. He also writes in his book entitled, *Excellence without a Soul: Does Liberal Education Have a Future?* that the image of the student today is a "brain on a stick" (p. 100). This image is not only held by the universities but throughout schooling that the purpose of education is to teach "marketable skills" so students can compete in the global economy. Education has become training rather than an attempt to cultivate wisdom. With the emphasis on mechanistic approaches to teaching and evaluation there is danger that our schools will become soulless. We need to provide a rich vision of the person including body, mind and soul. In this paper I focus on the soul and how it can be nourished through contemplative learning.

Soul

The idea of soul is an ancient one. Hughes (2010) in her highly praised book on Socrates argues that the main mission for that philosopher was to "explore the relationship between man and his soul" (p. 179). In the nineteenth century, soul was central to the thinking of the Transcendentalists (Miller, 2011). Emerson (1982) wrote in his journal, "Education is drawing out the soul" (p. 80). Today, Thomas Moore (1992) and others (Hillman, 1997; Sardello, 1995) have brought soul back into contemporary discourse. Moore's book, *Care of the*

Soul, published in the early 1990s, was instrumental to this process. He writes that the soul is "not a thing, but a quality or dimension of experiencing life and ourselves. It has to do with depth, value, relatedness, heart and personal substance" (p. 6). He also writes that the "soul is not the ego. It is the infinite depth of person and society comprising all the many mysterious aspects that go together to make up our identity" (p. 400). For Moore, the soul's path is not to overcome life's anxieties but to simply experience them as part of life. Through this experience one gradually gains wisdom.

Soul is usually not associated with Buddhism, but John Tarrant (1998), a well-known Zen teacher, writes of soul and spirit. Here are some of his thoughts on soul:

> Soul is that part of us which touches and is touched by the world. Through soul we connect with each other and are made less lonely—not metaphysically, but in a tangible, human way. . . . Soul connects and loses itself in the connection. It falls and falls; it falls into beauty. . . .
>
> Soul's true center is the journey of consciousness—otherwise it can identify no grand principles. Soul doesn't serve other purposes—the taste of life is its own fulfillment. . . .
>
> Soul loves to include and to learn; it is always trying to embrace things, to inhabit the brokenness of the world. . . . Soul does not abolish the difficulty of our lives, but brings a music to our pains—its gift is to make us less perfect and more whole. (pp. 16–8)

Like Moore, Tarrant views soul in terms of our life experience.

At the Ontario Institute for Studies in Education, I teach a course entitled "Spirituality in Education." I use idea of soul as the main thread. Like Moore and Tarrant I emphasize how we experience soul in our lives, which I have written about in my book, *Education and the Soul*. The main ideas found in that book, which I focus on in the course, include:

- *Soul as Energy*. One way that we experience soul is through feeling energy move through the body. Music has often been identified as helping this process as some forms have been called "soul music." When Abe Maslow talked about peak experience I believe that these experiences could also be referred to as soul experiences where we feel this energy and sometimes a connection to something beyond ourselves.
- *Work and Soul*. The soul seeks work that is deeply fulfilling. We hear stories of people changing careers at midlife and we could look

at this behavior as the soul calling these individuals to work that is more meaningful. In one of my initial teacher education courses there was a woman who had been a chiropractor for almost twenty years but was now training to be a teacher at the intermediate level. Seeing work through soul provides a different perspective on what is normally termed career education.

- *Love and Soul.* As Tarrant points out, soul seeks connections and relationships. In Japanese there is the term "en," which refers to significant relationships that we encounter in our lives. These relationships can be romantic, or platonic, but they are characterized by the sense that we are strongly drawn to another person in a way that is not readily explainable. Through soul we acknowledge the need to work with this person. Soul can also be experienced through more universal forms of love such as compassion. When Nelson Mandela was in prison, one of the ways that he was able to survive was to feel compassion for the guards. He would occasionally see glimpses of humanity in the guards and this was enough to keep him going.
- *Dark Night of the Soul.* It is inevitable that we experience loss in our lives through separation and the death of loved ones. Grief and loss can bring on what is called the dark night of the soul, where we go down. If we can be fully present to the pain and loss, the soul can deepen. Too often, however, in North American culture we deny the pain and turn away. This turning can include alcohol, drugs, television, and surfing the web.

My emphasis in the course is on the experience of soul rather than theological discussions about its existence. It is through our experiences that are best described as soulful that I believe we come to acknowledge the place of soul in our lives. I ask students to share soulful experiences in the class and they have no problem identifying such experiences in their lives. Examples include experiences in nature, loss of a loved one, or a special relationship. Sharing soulful stories allows soul to come forth in the classroom.

Currently, there is increasing emphasis on research on the brain and its relation to education. My concern with this research is physiological reductionism. Of course, there is place for this research as we learn more about ourselves, but certainly we are more than our brains. I believe that the research on near-death experiences (NDE) provides a counter to this research since many of the experiences cannot be explained through the brain. There are several documented cases of people viewing themselves from outside their bodies during the NDE. For example, people undergoing an operation see themselves on the operating table and give accurate reports of events while under an anesthetic. The best scientific summary of this evidence is presented by a radiation oncologist, Jeffrey Long, in his book *Evidence of the Afterlife*. Eckhart Tolle (2005) makes the claim that "the brain does not create consciousness, but consciousness created the brain" (p. 293). Of course, this a radical claim but one that I agree with, although I would substitute soul for consciousness. We need a more holistic view of the human being than one that focuses primarily on the brain.

Contemplation and the Soul

The soul's way of knowing is not through analysis but contemplation. As Tarrant notes, the "soul loves to include and learn" and "is always trying to embrace things." Contemplation is a form of embracing, beholding, and becoming what it embraces. Emerson (1990) wrote "A painter told me that nobody could draw a tree without in some sort becoming a tree" (p. 134).

One of the best descriptions of contemplative knowing comes from Jacques Lusseryan. Lusseryan became blind as young boy growing up in France before the World War II. After France was occupied, he was recruited into the French resistance and because his hearing was so acute he interviewed potential recruits for the resistance. However, he was caught by the Nazis and sent to Buchenwald. He survived the horrors of the concentration camp and wrote *And There was Light*. Here is his experience of contemplative knowing.

> Being blind I thought I should have to go out to meet things, but I found that they came to meet me instead. I have never had to go more than halfway, and the universe became the accomplice of all my wishes. . . .
>
> If my fingers pressed the roundness of an apple, each one with a different weight, very soon I could not tell whether it was the apple or my fingers which were heavy. I didn't even know whether I was touching it or it was touching me. As I became part of the apple, the apple became part of me. And that was how I came to understand the existence of things.
>
> . . . To put it differently, this means an end of living in front of things and the beginning of living with. Never mind if the word sounds shocking for this is love. (1987, pp. 27–28)

Contemplation then ultimately is a form of love. As Tarrant notes, soul loses itself in connection, which is another word for love. The boundary between the person and object melts away. Thoreau described contemplation as a way of seeing:

> I must walk more with free senses. It is as bad to *study* stars and clouds as flowers and stones. I must let my senses wander as my thoughts, my eyes see without looking. . . . Be not preoccupied with looking. Go not to the object; let it come to you. When I have found myself ever looking down and confining my gaze to the flowers, I have thought it might be well to get into the habit of observing the clouds as a corrective; but no! that study would be just as bad. What I need is not to look at all, but a true sauntering of the eye. (p. 99)

So contemplation is not looking but letting the object come to you and become part of you. Contemplation as a way of knowing has been absent from our education. Instead, there is an emphasis on the subject (the student) studying the object of learning and keeping that object separate. The worst kind of this learning is when the student memorizes information for a test, then feeds it back, and within a few weeks has forgotten all of this information. Forms of the scientific method also see the knower and the known as separate.

Meditation as Contemplative Knowing

If we are to teach the whole person in higher education, contemplative knowing is one way to broaden our approach to a more holistic vision of learning. One form of contemplation is meditation. Meditation involves being present and attentive as various "anchors" are used to focus the attention such as the breath, a phrase (e.g., mantra), or an image. These anchors allow the mind to focus and be present to the passing flow of thoughts and emotions. By being present to what is happening we also become part of what we are attentive to; meditation provides space for the soul to come forth.

My rationale for including meditation focuses on several points, but the most important and the one of consequence to this essay is the concept of teacher presence. Teaching, in my view, involves three basic factors. First are the theories or assumptions underlying a teaching method. The underlying assumptions and theories have been referred to as orientations (Eisner & Vallance, 1974; Miller, 1983). Second are the strategies and practices that teachers employ in the classroom. Also included here are the evaluation methods used to assess student development. The final factor is the presence of the teacher. It is this last factor which is so critical. If we recall the teachers who have had an impact on us, it is not usually the material that they taught, which we remember, but that elusive quality of presence, which somehow touched us.

Emerson (1966) in talking to teachers emphasized the importance of presence in teaching: "By your own act you teach the beholder how to do the practicable. According to the depth from which you draw your life, such is the depth not only of your strenuous effort, but of your manners and presence. The beautiful nature of the world has here blended your happiness with your power" (p. 227). Emerson refers to "depth" in the same way Moore talks about soul. We could argue that our presence arises from soul. Presence in teaching means that there is more of a chance to work from the soul rather than the ego. If we teach from the soul, teaching can become a more fulfilling and enriching experience. The most powerful teaching is soul-to-soul where we connect with students at the deepest level.

I also introduce students to mindfulness where we are completely attentive to activities in daily life. So, if I am cutting the vegetables before dinner, I am just doing that and am not lost in my thoughts as I do the cutting. Thich Nhat Hanh (1976, 1991) and Jon Kabat-Zinn (2005) have suggested different ways that mindfulness can be a daily practice that develops our presence. I particularly like Susan Murphy's (2006) description of mindfulness. "A most simple definition of mindful behavior is paying attention. This gives beauty to all things; they feel attended to" (p. 19). If we can attend to our students as Murphy suggests, we actually give them something beautiful. Murphy also describes how mindfulness is a form of contemplative knowing:

> The effort of mindfulness is to become whole-hearted. When you are whole-hearted, any action is absorbing and essentially effortless, because no one is in the way, "knowing" something about what they are doing. How strange that mindfulness is a practice of knowing less and absorbing more. (p. 20)

By "absorbing" we become what we are: mindful of, rather than being the distant "knower."

Contemplative Practices in Teacher Education

In two of my graduate courses and in one initial teacher education course I require students to meditate daily for six weeks. In another course it is an option. In the graduate courses where meditation is required, I introduce the practice in the third week of classes. I first offer a definition of meditation—

the development of *compassionate attention*—and then I offer the rationale for doing meditation, which was described above.

I then introduce the students to seven different types of meditation. We spend approximately two minutes doing each one. I suggest that they choose one to work on for the six weeks. In brief these include:

- *Observing the breath.* The student observes the breath, focusing on either the nostrils or the rising and falling of the belly.
- *Counting the breath.* The student counts the breath from 1 to 4 when they exhale. In both of these breathing exercises, I note that student should not try to control the process but breathe naturally.
- *Mantra.* A sound or phrase is repeated silently.
- *Visualization.* The student visualizes a series of images, usually from an experience in nature.
- *Walking.* This practice focuses the awareness on the foot touching and then leaving the ground.
- *Contemplation.* The student selects a short passage of poetry or inspirational text and repeats it silently.
- *Loving kindness.* Thoughts of well-being are sent first to ourselves and then to others.

Students are asked to start meditating for 5 to 10 minutest a day and over the course of the six weeks to gradually work up to 20 or 30 minutes. They a keep a daily journal describing how the process is going and they are asked to report on what the body is experiencing during the meditation and what was prominent during the practice (e.g., thoughts, sounds, etc.). Below is an entry from one student:

> Profoundly noticeable a number of times during this session was the wave of relaxation moving though my legs from top to bottom. I could feel the tension leaving the body, flowing out through the tips of my toes. Other thoughts came and went as I attempted to return to the breathing and the awareness of my chest moving up and down. My hands melted into my knees. I felt rejuvenated and ready for the rest of the evening.

I have described the impact of the meditation in other forums (Miller & Nozawa, 2002; Miller, in press). Here I cite two examples that show the impact on the student's soul. One example of the impact of meditation practice comes from an instructor at the college level. Mary is a counselor and special-needs consultant working in a community college. She works with students who have learning disabilities.

Mary took the course in the mid-1990s. Her meditation practice is insight, or Vipassana, which uses the breath as the initial focus. After starting the practice, Mary faced a battle with cancer. She then supplemented her Vipassana meditation with visualization where she would imagine the healthy cells battling the cancerous cells.

Mary meditates for about thirty minutes three or four times a week but also when she is feeling stress. For example, she meditated on the operating table before her surgery for cancer. She has also meditated in special places such as the Grand Canyon and the Pacific Ocean. Mary has supplemented her practice by attending a meditation retreat and also a program that included meditation offered at the hospital where she has been treated for the cancer. She also practices Qi Gong, which is a form of movement meditation.

Mary feels meditation has had a deep impact on her life. She says, "It's totally affected my personal life. It's enabled me to live in the present. I find when I go for a walk now, I am so busy looking at everything that's around me and I'm not thinking." Mary sees the impermanence of things, including her own thoughts. She finds it helpful to name thoughts as they arise so that if she has an angry thought she will label that thought "angry." This process helps her let go of negative thoughts.

In her work she finds that she is much more present to students when they come to her. She also finds that she is more compassionate and believes that both the meditation and her illness have led to the compassion. She feels that her ego does not get in the way in the workplace. For example, someone who is actually below her in the college hierarchy was telling her how to do her job. While other coworkers resented this, she said it didn't bother her at all. She now finds that she simply wants the best for everyone she meets and works with:

I never think someone has more than I have or someone is better off, even people who are well. I don't begrudge them their health anymore, I'm happy for them. And so the meditation may have helped here, because you become one with the larger whole that happens. . . . Meditation has made me better able to show love to other people. You know I was quite reserved before. Again the illness and meditation have probably contributed here.

Mary also recites a poem that she finds helpful in her daily life.

I have arrived, I am home,
In the here, in the now
I am solid, I am free.

Contemplative learning has the potential to be truly transformative. One woman who worked as a counselor for survivors of sexual abuse and partner assault wrote of the impact of meditation in an almost poetic manner:

Through meditation I feel that I am being gently invited to observe the nature of my own humanity. Personally I had been strongly moved and transformed through the beautiful nature of this spiritual practice. I had heard my voice and soul with amusement. I had slowly let my inner judge go away and be more in touch with the unspoken, the unseen, and the sacred part of myself. I had achieved a larger vision of my self and my reality, a vision that tenderly dilutes my fears, preconceptions, judgments and need for control. Because of meditation I had been able to transform my fear, anger, and resistance into joy, forgiveness, acceptance and love.

I can bring to meditation anything that is for the purpose of seeing it or feeling it. The reflection and contemplation offered by this practice provides a very safe and comfortable environment where my creativity, intuition, and imagination can be enlarged. I can feel, see, and reflect on my reality while I confess my own fears and personal dilemmas to the being that exists within myself. I become my own witness, my own mentor and my own source of liberation. I can unveil the many layers that cover my real nature so I can then be able to recognize my own needs and inclinations.

Meditating has also been a road of discovering for me. I first discovered the honoring power that the soul possesses for every human being. Through meditation I discovered the unconditional acceptance that is available to the heart of every human being. It is through the practice of meditation that I had better understood the meaning and importance of accepting and honoring myself and others.

This student has made the connection between her meditation practice and the soul. She has moved to a place of love and acceptance that is similar to Lusseryan. One of Thich Nhat Hanh's early books is entitled the *Miracle of Mindfulness*. In the past twenty years I have introduced meditation to over 2,000 students, most of whom are teachers, and I have witnessed many small miracles like the two cases just cited. In a class this last winter one student, who had been in my class three years ago, commented that before that class she and her husband could not conceive. It was while taking that class with the meditation practice that she was able to become pregnant and she attributed the conception to the meditation. Meditation is not a cure-all, but I believe that contemplative learning can have significant role to play in education if we are to move to a richer and more complete view of the human being capable of bringing forth an embodied wisdom. If our planet is to survive and flourish, it will need this wisdom.

Conclusion

It is my belief that contemplative practices both ground the student and at the same time provide a basic energy to my courses. Focusing on the flow of the breath is the method most often selected by my students in choosing a meditative practice. Breathing is a basic life function, and our awareness of breathing brings us into the here-and-now. It is a natural and organic process that can ground our experience. Like life itself, each breath can bring us in to the present moment. Besides grounding the students, there is also the rhythm of breathing. I have argued that in teaching we also need rhythm, otherwise the classroom becomes too static (Miller, 2010). Waldorf education has used the metaphor of breathing to demonstrate how there should be movement in the classroom. The breath, then, can be seen as symbolic of the flow of energy in the classroom. Finally, there is also mystery around the breath. The word spiritual finds its roots in the Latin, *spiritus*, which means breath. There is the space between the out-breath and the in-breath, a place of "in-between." Ferrer (2002), in his book on transpersonal theory, refers to the work of Buber and the "Between." In Buber's (1970) words: "Spirit is not in the I but between I and You. It not like the blood that circulates in you but like the air you breathe" (p. 89). Ferrer argues that the Between is the "locus of genuine spiritual realization" (p. 119). Awareness of both the flow and spaces in breathing can provide a place for soul to come forth.

Much discourse in higher education is dominated by critical theory, and Nel Noddings (2003) has identified a problem with this focus:

> A great worry for critical theorists—one that should receive far more attention that it does at present—is that efforts of critical pedagogues induce anger alienation, and hopelessness instead of wisdom and practical action. "Discussion" can deteriorate into venting and blaming thus causing increased separation among groups. (p. 104)

There is a place for critical theory in higher education but contemplative education also needs to be in the curriculum. Contemplative practices nurture awareness and holistic experience. Contemplative practices provide students with experiences that are life affirming and potentially liberating. Again, the student's comments cited above are worth repeating here. "I become my own witness, my own mentor and my own source of liberation." The experience of soul also arose through the practice. "Meditating has also been a road of discovering for me. I first discovered the honoring power that the soul possesses for every human being."

As I write this, I have just completed two sections of my course on holistic education where 48 students were engaged in meditation practice throughout the course. Reading the students' reflections on their practice, I was often moved by their comments. One student wrote, "To my surprise, feeling grew into *being* from the inside, which precipitated a sense of connectivity with the world. It was as though . . . I was lit up from the inside out." Ultimately, I believe contemplative practice is about bringing out the light within each of us. My experience in working with contemplative practices continues to inspire and deeply nourish my own soul.

References

Buber, M. (1970). *I and Thou* (W. Kaufman, Trans.). New York: Scribner.

Eisner, E., & Vallance, E. (Eds.). (1974). *Conflicting conceptions of curriculum*. Berkeley, CA: McCutchan.

Emerson, R. W. (1966). *Emerson on education: Selections* (H. M. Jones, Ed.). New York: Teachers College Press.

Emerson, R. W. (1982). *Emerson in his journals* (J. Porte, Ed.). Cambridge, MA: Harvard University Press.

Emerson, R. W. (1990). *Selected essays, lectures, and poems* (R. D. Richardson, Ed.) New York: Bantam.

Emerson, R. W. (2003). *Selected writings of Ralph Waldo Emerson*. New York: Signet.

Ferrer, J. N. (2002). *Revisioning transpersonal theory: A participatory vision of human spirituality*. Albany, NY: SUNY Press.

Hanh, T. N. (1976). *The miracle of mindfulness*. Boston: Beacon.

Hanh, T. N. (1991). *Peace is every step: The path of mindfulness in everyday life*. New York: Bantam.

Hillman, J. (1997). *The soul's code: In search of character and calling*. New York: General Central Publishing.

Hughes, B. (2010). *The hemlock cup: Socrates, Athens and the search for the good life*. London: Jonathan Cape.

Kabat-Zinn, J. (2005). *Coming to our senses: Healing ourselves and the world through mindfulness*. New York: Hyperion.

Lewis, H. (2006). *Excellence without a soul? Does liberal education have a future?* New York: Public Affairs.

Long, J., with Perry, P. (2010). *Evidence of the afterlife: The science of near-death experiences*. New York: HarperCollins.

Miller, J. (1983). *The educational spectrum: Orientations to curriculum*. New York: Longman.

Miller, J. (2000). *Education and the soul: Toward a spiritual curriculum.* Albany, NY: SUNY Press.

Miller, J. (2006). *Educating for wisdom and compassion: Creating conditions for timeless learning.* Thousand Oaks, CA: Corwin.

Miller, J. (2007). *The holistic curriculum.* Toronto, ON: University of Toronto Press.

Miller, J. (2010). *Whole child education.* Toronto, ON: University of Toronto Press.

Miller, J. (2011). *Transcendental learning: The educational legacy of Alcott, Emerson, Fuller, Peabody and Thoreau.* Charlotte, NC: Information Age Publishing.

Miller, J. (in press). "Contemplative practices in teacher education: What I have learned." In J. Groen, J. R. Graham, & D. Coholic (Eds.), *Spirituality in education & social work: An interdisciplinary dialogue.* Waterloo, ON: Sir Wilfred Laurier Press.

Miller, J., & Nozawa, A. (2002). Meditating teachers: A qualitative study. *Journal of In-service Education, 28*(1),179–192.

Moore, T. (1992). *Care of the soul: A guide for cultivating depth and sacredness in everyday life.* New York: Walker and Company.

Murphy, S. (2006). *Upside-down Zen: Finding the marvelous in the ordinary.* Somerville, MA: Wisdom Publications.

Noddings, N. (2003). *Happiness and education.* New York: Cambridge University Press.

Sardello, R. (1995). *Love and the soul: Creating a future for earth.* New York: HarperCollins.

Tarrant, J. (1998). *The light inside the dark: Zen, soul and the spiritual side of life.* New York: HarperCollins.

Tolle, E. (2005). *A new earth: Awakening to your life's purpose.* New York: Dutton.

5

Fitting in Breath Hunting

Thai and U.S. Perspectives on Contemplative Pedagogy

David Lee Keiser and Saratid Sakulkoo

Introduction

> In captivity, Aung San Suu Kyi had practiced Vipassana meditation, an ancient technique attributed to the Gautama Buddha. At first, she said, "I found it very difficult to do, because my mind was wandering, instead of being fixed on one particular place—your breathing, the rising and falling of your abdomen. I got frustrated, thinking, 'My goodness, can't I do even this little mind exercise?' But, with persistence, you get there."
>
> —Hammer, 2011, p. 24

Many teachers and parents have felt that sense of "My goodness, can't you even do this little mind exercise?" Clearly, the wandering minds of students and teachers—called monkey mind, gossipy neurons, and so on—are parts of most higher education classrooms, and challenges of teaching include frustration and unpredictable or inconsistent responses from students. In the twenty-first century, age-old challenges of holding students' attention combine also with technological innovations that offer constant stimuli. How can we help students aim and sustain their attention? How can we teach compassionately in the age of continuous partial attention?

In Thailand and the United States, two professors struggle with the challenges of contemplative teaching in public universities. One professor uses a singing bowl to illustrate a strategy for classroom management; another focuses students' attention by "hunting their breaths." On two continents a remarkable consonance illustrates not only commonalties of their university students, but also the universality of contemplative practices in higher education. Within the broad richness of contemplative teaching, representative of many world faiths and practices, the authors approach this field through a Buddhist lens. In this chapter, two professors from the Departments of Curriculum and Teaching and Human Resource Development, respectively, describe the unfolding of contemplative teaching and learning in higher education, and how the choice of terminology can help or hinder students' reactions to contemplative pedagogy.

Saratid ("Tong") is a former monk, who has for five years tried to think about how to provide meditation techniques for his students, yet wonders if it is still useful. He teaches both graduate and undergraduate classes at Burapha University in Thailand, including *Modern Concepts of Human Resources Development* (HRD), *Leadership and Ethics*, and *Research Methodology*. He believes that meditation will help all of his students be more present and focused in their studies and grounded and happy in their daily lives. As a professor, however, he feels he must couch it in different language, for example:

> I found that the term "Meditation" does not fit with the young generation. The challenging word of "Breath Hunting" hit their heart. To become a "Breath Hunter" one may need to learn how to hunt the breath. . . . I believe that class is everywhere. Everywhere can be a class. The class is in your heart not in the room. I always emphasize: do not forget your breath in and breath out.

David, a former classroom teacher, is a teacher educator at Montclair State University in the United States. He has taught a graduate course on "Mindful Teaching," and is currently a facilitator with the Compassion, Awareness and Resilience (CARE) program at the Garrison Institute. For years he has girded his courses with contemplative methods gleaned from the *Center for Contemplative Mind in Society*, meditation retreats, sabbatical research, and scientific venues. Reflecting on early trial-and-error attempts to infuse contemplative practice with university students, he remembers,

> Starting an undergraduate, prerequisite Education class, I made the mistake of giving instructions by inviting, "After I *hit the bowl*, allow the resonance of the sound to fill the room." Two dozen adolescents gazed back, both curious and humored. Belatedly, I realized my audience. "I mean, after I strike the *Singing* Bowl with the wooden stick, allow. . . ."

His undergraduate students, most of whom were new to contemplative practice, interpreted the first statement above, "hit the bowl," as a possible drug use reference; a slight change in nomenclature, however, clarified the phrase as a direction for sitting practice. Like Tong, he sees his role as educator as expansive—teacher educators need to teach the world, as well as the word. These case studies will describe two examples of contemplative pedagogies and curriculum across disparate settings. We will briefly describe some class activities from our courses, including specific contemplative practices—such as breath hunting—as well as implicit contemplative approaches to teaching. We will discuss reactions and responses of students and colleagues, and end by reflecting upon ourselves as contemplative teacher-scholars.

A Short History of the Path: Contemplative Education in Thailand

> The acquisition of intellect results in contentment.
>
> —Burapha University Motto

While the cultural contexts of Thailand and the United States are remarkably different, educators around the world face similar challenges with similar visions. In the past, education in Thailand was offered in large part by Buddhist monasteries. In general, Thai education has reflected Thai culture, including meditation and contemplation. However, the term "contemplative education" is a relatively new term in Thailand's education circles. While the term "Contemplative Education" may have originated in the United States, in Thailand, the approach has existed for over 20 years under the name "Alternative Education." The founding of the Contemplative Education Center in Mahidol University in Bangkok is an acknowledgment of public advancement of contemplative pedagogy and its integration into mainstream education (Pongbhakatheian, 2008). While it may seem surprising that contemplative practice was for many years marginalized in Thai higher education, there has been a recent uptick in interest for bringing contemplative pedagogies (back) into Academe.

At present, there are several linked contemplative organizations in Thailand, such as the Contemplative Education Network, Contemplative Research Dialogue (CoRDial), and the Contemplative Forum (Thongthavee et al., 2008). Most provide outside activities such as meditation in a Buddhist temple or meditation center volunteer work. As contemplative education expands, however, implementation needs to take into account issues of continuity, regularity, and having communities of practice as well as shared learning spaces. At the policy level, support is needed in providing facilities, personnel development, encouragement of communities of practice, development of assessment methods for this approach, and monitoring of tasks. Some argue that developing contemplative education should be undertaken at three levels: conceptual, practice, and structural (Pongbhakatheian, 2008). That is, universities not only need to frame contemplative pedagogy in their mission statements and materials, but also provide both practice settings and curricular validation for them to take hold. While some faculty use contemplative methodologies in teaching, many more university instructors would likely include contemplative practices with administrative or structural support.

This collection develops the field of contemplative education and describes and documents its legacy thus far. As this collection makes clear, the field is burgeoning, rich with momentum and growth. Still, the rich array of practice and programs outlined in this book represents outliers rather than general representatives of higher education. In teacher education, at least, even well-established fields such as social emotional learning are often peripheral, if present at all. In Thailand as well, the field seems to be emerging.

Many definitions of contemplative pedagogy serve the field in Thailand, including those by Nilachaikovit (2008) and Srisakul-Chairak (2008). According to Nilachaikovit (2008),

> Contemplative education is a specific form of transformative learning which emphasizes inner development and fundamental transformation which enhances the true understanding of interconnections between things and true love and compassion for oneself and others, based on deep understanding, all of which lead to good conscience and awareness of one's obligation to mankind and nature, and all of which are honed through various contemplative practices such as meditation, awareness practice, contemplation with the heart, learning through body and through aesthetic activities. (pp. 4–5)

Nilachaikovit (2008) offers principles of contemplative and transformative facilitation. They are the "7Cs": (1) Contemplation, (2) Compassion, (3) Connectedness (Interconnectedness), (4) Confronting Reality, (5) Continuation, (6) Commitment, and (7) Community of Practice.

Srisakul-Chairak (2008) explains contemplative education as important for how people lead their lives, both internally and externally (physically and spiritually), not only at the individual level, but also globally. The objective of contemplative education is to maintain a focus in education, particularly at the tertiary level, on developing of the inner or spiritual dimension of human beings (Pongbhakatheian, 2008). In addition, contemplative education emphasizes values, attainment of the good, beauty, and truth. It makes education about life, rather than compartmentalized learning that is unconnected to the learner's life outside of school. Similarly, in the West, we compartmentalize curriculum in higher education; in many teacher education programs, for example, the credits and courses are pre-set and limited, with no electives.

At Burapha University, there are not any contemplative courses in the Human Resource Development Center, but rather in other departments, such as Teaching and Curriculum Development, Public Health, and Nursing. Only a few provide contemplative teaching in the classroom. Yet, Alternative Education or Contemplative Education emerged and developed in Thailand over 20 years and has steadily gained popularity from elementary education to the university level. Creating a space for contemplative pedagogy, then, includes curricular as well as physical space, and visibility on course syllabi and program descriptions.

Contemplative Education in North America: Paving a Path

> Contemplative practices fall into two major classes, those that school cognition and those that cultivate compassion. We are well aware that our observation and thinking require training, but we often neglect the cultivation of our capacity for love.
>
> —Zajonc, 2006, p. 3

While many administrators might question the inclusion of love capacity cultivation in any single subject, the development of kind people and of engaged and present citizens is part of any college or university mission. In the United States, college professors can use contemplative practices with assignments that either develop school cognition (attention) or cultivate compassion or do both: in effect, a short silent sit, followed by a free writing prompt and a paired discussion of the sitting and writing (Zajonc, 2006). Contemplative educators in the United States teach their content and embrace what Kessler (2000) terms "the teaching presence," but the contemplative pedagogy movement remains in its infancy. One of the first contemplative centers in higher education in the United States is Naropa University, in Boulder, Colorado. According to their program description, Contemplative Education is, "From our perspective . . . based upon individual transformation through the cultivation of inherent spiritual human qualities, including mindfulness, awareness, empathy, authenticity, and synchronized body, speech and mind" (Garrison Institute Mapping Report 2005, p. 33). The Contemplative Education Program at Naropa is based in part on Tibetan Buddhist teachings, and prepares teachers from pre-kindergarten to higher education to bring a "nonsectarian, contemplative approach" into their classrooms. The overarching theme of the curriculum is creating mindfulness, compassion, and awareness in the classroom as well as within the educator. But Naropa and the many thought leaders and institutions represented in this text, such as the California Institute for Integral Studies and Maharishi University, have long offered contemplative curriculum to interested students.

The Center for Contemplative Mind in Society has long worked with higher education faculty to create courses that use contemplative practices to address issues of social conflict and injustice, and the promotion of peace. From this center, the Association for Contemplative Mind in Higher Education was formed to promote the emergence of a broad culture of contemplation in the academy by connecting a network of leading institutions and academics committed to the development of the contemplative dimension of teaching, learning and knowing. Across North America, professors across the spectra of subject matter and geography—from English in the Eastern United States to Psychology in the South, from Music in the Midwest to Economics in New England—now teach courses that utilize contemplative practices. For example, the late Joanna Ziegler, Professor of Art History at Holy Cross College, asked her students to look at one abstract painting for the entire semester and answer each week, "What do you see?" Ziegler (2010) reports,

> Over the 13-week semester, the painting doesn't change, but they do. If coming to know and love a work of art through sustained reflection can be so enlightening about one's preconceptions to the point of changing one's opinions, imagine if this approach were brought to bear on one's relations with other human beings.

In a September 2006 special issue of *Teachers College Record*, scholars described contemplative experiences in classrooms across North America; in one section on "teaching as contemplative practice," Canadian educator Jackie Seidel (2006) offered that "Contemplative teaching turns our work into a form of love, memory, and intimacy, reminding us of our deep life relations through time and place, and possibly having incalculable implications for our curriculum interpretation and classroom practices" (p. 1901). While Seidel (2006) referred here to teacher education, most of the entries describe academic course work in the liberal arts, music and poetry, Asian Studies, and meditation itself, rather than teacher education pedagogy. This special journal issue, based in large part on a seminal 2005 Columbia University conference on contemplative practices, "Making Peace in Ourselves and in the World," provided the higher education community with a broad sweep of contemplative possibilities and with templates and sample syllabi for faculty interested in adding contemplative components to their courses.

Now, organizations such as the *Association for Contemplative Mind in Higher Education*, the *Garrison Institute*, and the *Mindfulness in Education Network* provide teacher educators spaces to develop practices, pedagogies, presentations, and publications, all in service of developing the field of contemplative education. In order to help the field take hold, however, professors need to be able to incorporate its methods into traditional curricula. Many practices lend themselves across disciplines; for example, the cultivation of silence can be useful not only to quiet the mind, but also to allow for increased creativity and engagement. Within teacher education, for example, the cultivation of silence can manifest as increased wait time between question and response, or active listening exercises where one partner talks for several minutes and the other listens. The point in using silence as pedagogy, however, transcends individual assignments.

The Path to Teaching: Contemplative Curriculum and Field Standards

> As thin as this piece of paper is, it contains everything in the universe in it.
>
> —Hanh, 1991, p. 96

Hanh's (1991) approach to non-duality—that there is no separate reader and paper, but an interlinked chain of connections—provides a helpful paradigm for thinking about mindful higher education. Contemplative pedagogy requires that instructors dissolve or lessen the distance between student and professor, and allow for rich human interactions, not only steeped in academic formalities and titles. Within the academic field of teacher education, benefits of mindfulness, or mindful practices in education, can massage the relationship between compassionate, mindful teachers and the formation of students with better academic and social abilities, self-awareness, and emotional regulation. Yet the necessary teacher dispositions for empathy and social and emotional intelligence are often ignored in teacher education since they cannot yet be measured scientifically through empirical data. Hanh's (1991) quote may seem more relevant for spiritual or existential work than for teacher preparation, but that is exactly the point: teacher education is about interbeing. Teacher education includes developing relationships with other human beings: students, parents, colleagues, administrators, school boards, policy makers, cross-disciplinary allies, and the general public.

Many have argued that one of the primary goals of teaching and teacher education is to actively prepare students for success in society (Michelli & Keiser, 2005). However, the implementation of that goal remains a core challenge and controversy in teacher education. For example, along with pedagogical skills and content knowledge, the teachers prepared at Montclair State University must possess and/or develop certain professional dispositions that demonstrate a strong commitment to caring.

The challenge is to integrate mindful teaching practices with profession and field standards palatable to educators and education policy leaders. For example, the Montclair State University Teacher Education Program (2011) is framed by a twelve-item vision, "The Portrait of a Teacher," for preparing beginning teachers. These items include, "Create a community in the classroom that is nurturing, caring, safe, and conducive to learning." For many beginning teachers, this vision is easier read than implemented. By expanding pedagogies to include greater focus on attention and attentiveness, teacher educators can more easily foster the ability to listen and heed the classroom community. Part of teaching others how to create a harmonious and productive classroom includes the development of safety and trust. To those ends contemplative practices in Teacher Education create apertures through which deeper learning can occur, and good teaching can be learned. New teachers need to be aware of the hidden curriculum—that what is learned by students encompasses a great deal more than the subject content taught to them. This includes ways of being in school, social and pedagogical dispositions of students and teachers, and increasingly, developing social and emotional intelligence.

We wrote the following two sections in the first person, each of us briefly describing our path—how we became interested in melding our personal practices and worldviews with our chosen fields and professions. This will be followed by a concluding section.

David's Story: Seeding the Path in High School and University

I was introduced to contemplative practice in a visit to the Berkeley Community Theatre (California) by Thich Nhat Hanh while I was a graduate student there in the 1990s. Through retreats and study with teachers in Vipassana and Tibetan traditions, I have developed a practice largely steeped in basic Vipassana techniques—daily breath awareness and caring/loving-kindness practice—and have slowly begun to meld my contemplative and academic practices; said another way, I talk about being and thinking and caring in my classes, sometimes with contemplative practices. As a professor, I, as well, give scholarly presentations in local and distant communities and I developed a graduate elective course, "Mindful Teaching." I have researched the scholarship behind the practice of creating such a caring community, as mentioned in the "Portrait of a Teacher," mentioned earlier. This has since been reinforced by my work with national centers such as the Center for Contemplative Mind and the Garrison Institute. These centers, and others like them, provide secular opportunities for educators to attend to and improve their capacity for caring in the classroom. Locally, I put these ideas into practice at a local high school.

For several years, I facilitated a teacher's reading group at Montclair High School, focusing on mindfulness in the classroom. While it was a small and self-selected group, a comment from one of the participants underscores the potential for developing compassionate educators: "I think that the psychological and intellectual pause brings refreshment to our lives. The readings and the discussions have provided a force that allows me to observe myself, correct my errors, and make my teaching easier."

Another New Jersey teacher described her process of contemplative teaching in her recent Master's thesis: "I have deliberately kept my teaching of contemplative practices away from any formal spiritual or clinical tradition and in some ways I think this has made the work in the classroom less controversial in the context of my particular public school and also more amenable to my students." In fact, many professors who use contemplative practices in teaching also strive to use less controversial language and more secular references. For example, I rarely use the terms spirituality or meditation in my college teaching, but rather I encourage the development of the teaching presence and the teacher's inner life, irrespective of tradition.

It may be that the high-stakes test environment precludes public universities from overtly addressing holistic issues in teacher education. It may be that contemplative teaching, or mindfulness itself, are concepts still too esoteric for standardization and evaluation. But through the pedagogical apertures of classroom management strategies, social and emotional learning, and teacher burnout, the need for focus and attention is paramount.

Preliminary findings from the aforementioned reading group show that teachers and administrators appreciated the time to sit in contemplation, and to talk about readings on mindfulness, whenever they were able. Data from the teacher study group include teacher summative reflections, which bespeak how the simple offering of time—a weekly lunch meeting—can serve as a "place to pay close attention," or "a safe haven." One of our members summed up a recent semester:

> In the rush of modern life, the intention to take time to sit, to talk, or simply to be together may seem anathema but now, with the swirl of technological dependence engulfing much of our external

> world, the need to attend to interiority, to what's happening inside ourselves, is greater than ever before.

While making time to meet weekly was difficult, the sharing of resources and ideas appeared to impact the teachers' teaching. For example,

> I began starting each class with a "thought of the day" to focus on something other than geometry and to pass on some of the positiveness that I have gained from our study of mindfulness in education. I have not been as successful as I would like with passing on "mindfulness" to my students but hopefully I am planting seeds that will grow in the future.

The time to sit affected teachers' attitudes toward changes in the workplace they had no control over, including a new principal and a tough economy. Although one group member chose to retire early to preserve her pension, she offered this endorsement:

> During this unique time of change in our high school, along with the state budget cuts which will ultimately result in over 85 staff cuts in our district, this group has become a safe haven for staff to "take a deep breath," release their stress, and focus the mind.

Another teacher, one who uses contemplative practices such as focused writing and deep listening regularly in his Language Arts class, echoed the existential need for the space to be, rather than just do.

> Our work seems to be more important than ever. With all of the changes taking place around the school and across the state with educators, this group has been a sort of rock, a constant, where I can ground myself and bring me back to a place where I can be my best.

In summary, such responses are indicative of my students, and indicate the need for, interest in, and impact of contemplative teaching, but the marker of pedagogical and curricular transformation—the "required" course—does not yet appear in our teacher education offerings at Montclair State University. Still, as a professor charged with preparing teachers, I justify my use of contemplative practices based on the need for novice educators to cultivate their teaching presence in order to more effectively convey information and create and maintain constructive and safe classroom communities.

Tong's Story: Clearing a Path toward Contemplative Pedagogy

Through my experiences of working in the United States for 14 years, 1991 to 2004, as protocol officer at the Royal Thai Embassy in Washington, DC, as an HR specialist and Assistant Administrator in healthcare industries in Kansas and Iowa, and through my experiences as a forest Buddhist monk in 2005 and as a lecturer at Burapha University, Thailand since 2006, I have developed my personal teaching philosophy and have witnessed the practical implications of that philosophy in every classroom. My teaching philosophy focuses on the basic, good human qualities. These are kindness, compassion, a sense of involvement, honestly, discipline, human intelligence properly guided by good motivation, and the desire that no one be left behind in my class. I teach *Modern Concept of Human Development, Organization Development* (OD), *Organization Behavior* (OB), *Leadership and Business Ethics, Business for Nursing,* and *Qualitative Research Methodology.* I utilize various teaching techniques, including lectures, discussion, guest speakers, reflexive journaling, collaborative and individual projects, presentations, and examinations. I invite members of every class to have a sense of involvement, to clear their minds before studying, and to practice techniques such as "breath hunting," "knowledge sharing while drinking a cup of tea," and so on. I learned these techniques from other teachers, workshops, books, and/or journal articles. When I began to use these techniques in class, I noticed my students developing good human qualities such as active listening, sharing, empathy, and patience. As I taught, I took the time to write in a reflexive journal or weekly report to my students about what we had learned from each other. I also wrote on my lesson plans as a way to record my thoughts and observations, which might have aided my reflections. I believed all class activities enhanced the learning experience of my students as well as my enjoyment and engagement in teaching.

"Breath Hunting" or the so-called "Breathing Practice" is one of my contemplative teachings in my classes. Students can try to observe their own breathing. It takes about 5 to 10 minutes. The word "breath hunting" refers to the same meaning as meditation. I just play with the word to fit my students' age. The word meditation bores them, and they don't find it challenging or exciting enough. They are the Y Generation. Their response to my teaching is often not quite as good as I would expect, in part due to their attitudes, but also due to the presence of many mobile phones, Blackberries, and other electronic distractions. So, using breath hunting helps them focus, calm down, avoid distraction, and to clear their minds for better learning. This is a part of the preparation before I teach in the particular subject. I have found that such preparation not only helps my students focus on academic subjects, but also develop desirable human qualities of patience, perseverance, and kindness.

In most of my classes, I ask students to write reflexive journals, how they feel about the world, what they have learned from the class, and anything that they want to express. I do so, as well. I was equally willing to share who I was as a facilitator and as a person as I learned who they were as students and people. I told all my students on the first day that collectively we had more experience and were more intelligent than any of us as individuals. I wanted to instill in them the understanding of the potential we held as a group, as a community. In order for that to happen, I had to demonstrate that I wanted to get to know each of them; that I valued who they were and what they could bring to our learning environment. I think times change and people change. How do I feel when students say they're customers? I feel confused; now we have no students, only customers. Am I still their teacher? Today, education seems to be run more like a business, and in doing so it seems we have lost some of our unity and dignity; at least we show respect to each other in different ways now. In order to help me better understand and teach them, I ask my students a series of questions:

- Why are you here at Burapha University?
- Why are you being educated?
- Why do you want to be educated?
- What is the point of being educated?
- What is the point of your passing an examination and getting a degree?

It is my belief that education is not only learning from the class and textbooks, but that the class is everywhere, and everywhere is a class. And class also is in your heart! Education is not just about passing examinations, taking a degree and a job, then getting married and settling down.

Based on consumerism and industrialization, so far our students' worldviews have been changed as well as those of their teachers. Indeed, there is much evidence for material development, such as the progress in science and technology and many innovations that are followed by the advancement of communities. However, there are signs of unsustainability. Technological innovations and accomplishments have not contributed much in reducing human tension, anxieties, and hate. Science and technology have not helped us bring peace and harmony to ourselves or to our world (Wasi, 2002). Contemplative pedagogy, on the other hand, has the potential to help students gain insight into their place in this rapidly changing world. For it to flourish, however, higher education may need a broader worldview, one which includes the outer and inner realities of human existence and one which values the inner experiences of students as well as their academic outputs.

Conclusion

> At all times, it is impermanence that rules. This is something that you should meditate on. The true and correct words of the sages will not lack mention of impermanence. If there is no mention of impermanence, it is not the speech of the wise.
>
> —Ajahn Chah, 2005, p. 34

We Can't Teach the Same Students Twice: The Path in Practice

The only constant in life and in school is change: teachers need to be able to cope with, incorporate, and expect changes in order to best serve students. In the United States, with our current high-stakes testing environment, schooling and curricular structures necessitate the development of compassion for self and others, as well. While always challenging, high-stakes testing and perennial school stress make nurturing pedagogy both a challenge and an imperative. Renewing compassion and attending to social and emotional dispositions can reawaken the teachable moment and the joy inherent in learning for both teachers and students. But ultimately, what happens in college classrooms between instructor and student remains sacred and worthy of attention, even if there is a conceptual disconnect among the professoriate about the very purposes of education. That is, the magic of being together and modeling how human beings can care for one another outlives every semester. When we receive emails from former students, they more often mention the affective result of the course than the content delivery. Said another way, students' reaching out and thanking us for being with them and for being real with them bespeaks teaching that outlasts a given course syllabus and transcends a particular subject.

Each year, the *Mind and Life Institute* sponsors dialogues between scientific leaders in the West and Eastern contemplatives, including the Dalai Lama. The 2009 dialogues in Washington, DC, focused on education and human development, and included well-known educators, meditation teachers, and psychologists. Late in the two-day conference, a paraphrased exchange between two eminent educators neatly encapsulates the conundrum of proving the statistical significance of contemplative, compassionate teaching:

Linda Darling-Hammond: Your Holiness, I agree that we need compassion and kindness in our schools. How can we do research to prove to policymakers that compassion is a good thing to instill?

Dalai Lama (*through a translator*): His Holiness responds that he doesn't understand why we would research something we knew the answer to already.

(Mind and Life Institute, 2009 DVD)

While most university administrators may not know the answer to this question, certainly there is no argument that compassion hurts education. But tenure and promotion committees often focus on product, not process. A sign hanging in Albert Einstein's office read, "Not everything that counts can be counted, and not everything that can be counted counts." There may never be an ironclad way to prove that compassion is good for test scores, say, or that mindful teachers get better test results, but these are insufficient reasons to abandon the path. For teacher-educators to prepare effective teachers for the public good, they need to insure attention to social, emotional, and affective domains, as well as to measurement and test preparation. Currently, most academic testing in the United States only assesses verbal and quantitative abilities. Some question this testing surge and concomitant narrowing of curriculum, as it leads many to "teach to the test." In the words of Daniel Goleman (2006), author of *Social Intelligence*, ". . . schools themselves are a very recent artifact of civilization. The more powerful force in the brain's architecture is arguably the need to navigate the social world, not the need to get As" (p. 334).

Mindful teaching includes aligning professional and field standards with the broader goals of compassion and mindfulness, creating not pedagogical goals themselves, but rather, furthering the wider ethical purpose of schooling: to develop human potential for success in life and work. Contemplative Pedagogy, or Mindful Teaching, does not function outside of academic standards; in fact, it can augment and reshape them. The middle way is to acknowledge and strive to meet or exceed standards while at the same time not losing sight of the whole student. Our goals for remaining on the path include the need to work for kindness in the world; to renew synergies and growth from academic sharing and collaboration; and the possibilities of student cross-pollination across our two campuses.

When Tong and David first met and brainstormed ways to collaborate, we listed some of our challenges in the college classroom: plagiarism, attendance/lateness, attention, and texting in class. In universities across the globe from one another, students seem similarly distracted. Contemplative teaching in higher education has the potential to use the above challenges as opportunities to deepen our pedagogical practices and make us even more responsive to students. In a perfect world, we could bring each other's students to visit; financial strain makes that impossible for most Thais, and, of late, impossible for many American students as well. Accepting that the world is not perfect, however, and that we are all limited in some ways can also be liberating. We hope that this chapter—a small contribution to a burgeoning field—provides some cross-cultural context, and that professors interested in contemplative teaching will do so, irrespective of the setting. We hope that our work together can be an inspirational template for other academics who may think they work in isolation, that their inner teaching life is superfluous, and that they cannot reach their students. Lastly, we hope that cultural differences between professors—locations, mores, spiritual traditions, etc.—are seen as desirable ingredients in academic collaborations, rather than hazard signals. Like good sages and meditation teachers, we seek to be the proverbial fingers pointing at the moon, rather than the moon itself.

References

Chah, A. (2005). *Everything arises, everything falls away: Teachings on impermanence and the end of suffering.* Boston: Shambhala.

Goleman, D. (2006). *Social intelligence: The new science of human relationships.* New York: Bantam Dell.

Hammer, J. (2011, January 24). A free woman. *The New Yorker, 86*(45), 24–30.

Hanh, T. (1991). *Peace is every step: The path of mindfulness in everyday life.* New York: Bantam Books.

Kessler, R. (2000). The teaching presence. *Virginia Journal of Education, 94*(2), retrieved from <http://passageworks.org>.

Michelli, N., & D. Keiser. (2005). *Teacher education for democracy and social justice.* New York: Routledge, 2005.

Montclair State University. (2011). *Portrait of a teacher.* Retrieved 11 February 2011 from <http://cehs.montclair.edu/cehs/academic/cop/about.shtml#portrait>.

Nilachaikovit, T. (2008). Transformative learning and contemplative education. *The Proceeding of the 2008 Contemplative Conference of the Education for Human Development, Bangkok, Thailand* held by the Institute of Contemplative Education, Mahidol University.

Pongbhakatheian, J. (2008). Contemplative education in Thailand. *The Proceeding of the 2008 Contemplative Conference of the Education for Human Development, Bangkok, Thailand,* held by the Institute of Contemplative Education, Mahidol University.

Seidel, J. (2006). Some thoughts on teaching as contemplative practice. *Teachers College Record, 108*(9), 1901–1914.

Srisakul-Chairak (2008). Contemplative education concept and factors of contemplative hermitage. *The Proceeding of the 2008 Contemplative Conference of the Education for Human Development, Bangkok, Thailand* held by the Institute of Contemplative Education, Mahidol University.

Thongthavee, C. et al. (2008). *A report on the survey and synthesis of the basic contemplative education in Thailand.* Bangkok, TH: Institute of Contemplative Education, Mahidol University.

Wasi, P. (2002). *New human development for sustainable future.* Bangkok, TH: Moh-Chao-Ban Publishing.

Zajonc, A. (2006). Contemplative and transformative pedagogy. *Kosmos Journal, 6*(1).

Ziegler, J. (2010). Personal communication.

6

A Pedagogy for the New Field of Contemplative Studies

Harold D. Roth

Introduction: The New Field of Contemplative Studies

At Brown and a few other universities such as Amherst, Emory, Rice, Evergreen State, University of Redlands, CUNY, and Michigan, small dedicated bands of practitioner-scholars and scientists have been slowly developing the new academic field of Contemplative Studies. Financed by the Center for Contemplative Mind in Society, the Mind and Life Institute, the Frederick Lenz Foundation for American Buddhism, the Fetzer Institute, the Hershey Family Foundation, and others, these people have been forging this new and important field through their innovative research and through designing courses that incorporate the study of contemplative practices.

At Brown we have developed a flexible and integrated program of study that includes courses that have specific contemplative components and others that, while they do not, provide subjects of study necessary to round out the concentrations (or majors) that students have designed. To this point we have graduated nine students with several more in the pipeline who have utilized Brown's Independent Concentration option to design their own majors in a variety of Humanities, Arts, and Science topics that contain contemplative dimensions. Two of them are currently graduate students in Psychology and Neuroscience; two are in Medical School; one is in a graduate program in Contemplative and Peace Studies; two are teaching in public school; and two are living in a contemplative center in the United States and in Nepal.

Their selection of courses has included a variety of courses in Asian contemplative traditions that have "Meditation Labs" in them: courses that contain three hours a week of contemplative practice integrated into them. I will explain how these work below. Some have also been able to work as researchers in Dr. Willoughby Britton's Research Lab at Brown that, among other projects, is studying experiential transformations brought about by the Meditation Labs themselves. The one course required for a Contemplative Studies Concentration is "Introduction to Contemplative Studies," a "university course" that is extra-departmental: outside the perspective (and support) of any one department because of its multidisciplinary nature. From program literature:

As we conceive of it, the new academic field of Contemplative Studies includes:

1. Studying the underlying philosophy, psychology, and phenomenology of human contemplative experience.
2. Focusing on the many ways human beings have found, across cultures and across time, to concentrate, broaden and deepen conscious awareness as the gateway to cultivating their full potential and to leading more meaningful, ethically responsible, and personally fulfilling lives.
3. It attempts to:
   a. identify the varieties of contemplative experiences of which human beings are capable;
   b. find meaningful scientific understandings for them;
   c. cultivate first-person knowledge of them;
   d. critically assess their nature and significance.

As we define it "contemplation" includes the focusing of the attention in a sustained fashion leading to deepened states of concentration, tranquility, insight, and "contextualizing" orientations. These are the basis of a clear and spontaneous cognition that is able to attend effortlessly to whatever presents itself, and of compassion, love, loving kindness, and various "other-regarding" ethical orientations. Such results have become the basis of serious scientific research, in areas such as effortless attention, flowing cognition, mindfulness, and compassion.

In addition to being grounded in the philosophy, psychology, and neuroscience of contemplative experience as a *third-person* study, Contemplative Studies emphasizes "*critical first-person*" approaches. In these approaches, students are encouraged to engage directly with contemplative techniques without prior commitment to their efficacy. They then step back and appraise their experiences in order to gain a deeper appreciation of their meaning and significance.

As we have framed it, there are three principal areas of a Contemplative Studies concentration and we are developing a fourth:

Science: The study of human consciousness and of the nature and significance of the varieties of contemplative experience found predominately in neuroscience, cognitive science, and psychology. The applications of contemplative practices in heath and healing on both individual and community levels.

Humanities: The study of the role of contemplation in philosophy, the religious traditions of the world, in world literatures, and a variety of other related disciplines.

The Arts: The study of the role of contemplation in both the creation and the appreciation of the visual and fine arts, creative writing, and in the various performing arts of dance, drama, and music.

Education: The study and application of contemplative pedagogies in colleges and universities and in elementary and secondary education.

As mentioned above, there is one essential and required course for all students who concentrate in this developing academic discipline: "An Introduction to Contemplative Studies." In this chapter, I would like to focus on explaining the pedagogy behind the design of this one required course and then discuss some of the results we have observed in the ten iterations that have been taught since 2005 during the summer and the regular academic year.

A Pedagogy for Contemplative Studies: Course Rationale and Design Goals

One of the principal goals of this course is to clarify the parameters of the new academic field of Contemplative Studies. In particular, it is to present the field's intellectual and experiential foundations by introducing students to the study of contemplative practices from both the typical academic "third-person" approaches and the more innovative "critical first-person" ones. The former include philosophical, psychological, and scientific studies of contemplative experiences, and the latter include giving students first-hand experience with some of the actual techniques that are found in the wisdom traditions of all cultures, with those found in Asia being the one with which I am personally most familiar. This is done, however, in a spirit of open inquiry, with absolutely no required beliefs or dogmas or assumptions about the efficacy of these techniques. It is hoped that this gives them some experiential comfort with a range of concentrative and receptive meditative techniques to benefit them in various situations they may encounter in their lives and to encourage them to explore these techniques further in Contemplative Retreat centers. The ultimate goal of this course and of the field in general, is to sensitize students to the potential they have as human beings to explore their own contemplative experiences as the gateway to leading more fulfilling and meaningful lives. It is hoped that, if this field eventually becomes established, we will be able to develop a new generation of practitioner-scholars and scientists who have developed clarity into their own psychological patterns, processes, and potentials as a way to create paradigm shifts that will advance human knowledge.

The Empirical Directive

Because actually performing contemplative techniques in a secular classroom setting is novel and controversial, it is important to make absolutely clear to students and colleagues that the course has no interest in proselytizing in favor of any of the religions from which the contemplative practices are taken. Students should clearly understand that there is no need to believe anything; this is the key element in the "critical first-person approach" that is the hallmark of Contemplative Studies. "Critical" means just that: students engage in empirical observation of their own consciousness, comparing their experiences to the claims made by contemplative practitioners and scientists without any prior commitment to the efficacy of the practices or the truths proffered in their various cognitive frameworks.

Probably the greatest concern and opposition to Contemplative Studies courses that contain contemplative practice labs is the fact that colleagues can perceive them as proselytizing for a particular religion. To protect against this perception, it is crucial that the course design a clear and unequivocal affirmation of the critical spirit and empirical nature of the course. For example:

> This course is an example of what we call "critical first-person learning." I say "critical" because in many forms of first-person learning in the contexts of religion, one must suspend critical judgment and believe in the various truths of the tradition. There is an important place for this form of "committed" first-person learning in our private lives, but we should be careful to not require that

> kind of commitment in a secular university. By contrast, in the "critical first-person learning" about Daoist or Buddhist meditation we do in this course, the need to believe is removed. We will read and analyze a variety of texts on Buddhist meditation ("third-person learning"); we will observe how our minds and bodies work while trying out a variety of simple meditation techniques derived from these texts ("first-person learning"); and we will critically discuss these texts in light of our experiences in the meditation laboratory. You will also be asked to keep a note-card journal on which you will record brief comments or observations at the end of every lab session.
>
> Without a doubt, this kind of novel pedagogy is not for everyone. If, for any reason, there is a student who is unable to participate in the Meditation Laboratory, I will be happy to make arrangements for doing alternate work of equivalent value.

This clear statement of pedagogical orientation has gone over well with both students and colleagues.

Course Rationale

This course is structured so that students will encounter two categories of readings each week and will work on a series of relevant meditative practices:

1. Primary readings that present contemplative practices and insights from Classical Daoism and both South and East Asian Buddhism. Other contemplative traditions could readily be included here: I have only chosen those with which I am most familiar.
2. Secondary readings that introduce them to a series of important issues in the major theoretical approaches to Contemplative Studies, both philosophical and scientific.
3. Meditation Labs meet three sessions a week for an hour each time. In these labs students obtain direct critical first-person experience of techniques that are found in the primary text we are reading.

I will begin by first discussing the more theoretical secondary works and the most important intellectual foundations of the new field that they contain.

Secondary Works on Contemplative Studies

Developing the ability to be able to clearly observe and utilize one's own subjectivity in an unbiased fashion is a cornerstone of the contemplative approach. The single most important theoretical source that argues for this is *The Taboo of Subjectivity* by Alan Wallace (2000). In it he describes the history of how, over the course of the past three centuries, the subjective perspective has been incrementally written out of both science and the modern Western academy. He then makes a persuasive argument for how it can be reincorporated, through using Buddhist techniques of mindfulness (present, focused attention) that make effective introspection possible. He argues that the Buddhist tradition has developed distinctive methods for the impartial and dispassionate observation of all elements of one's experience, both external and internal. These methods lead to the development of attentional stability and vividness of focus, both of which are keys to the clear and impartial examination of one's subjective experience in genuine introspection.

Understanding human cognition as occurring through both mind and body and embracing both external and internal realms of experience is another of the cornerstones of contemplative studies. *The Embodied Mind* by Francisco Varela, Evan Thompson, and Eleanor Rosch (1991) surveys and critiques the field of cognitive science, which, they argue, has tended to ignore the embodied nature of human cognition and also ignored the extent to which our realms of experience are *enacted* by a spontaneous coordination of both our inner subjectivities and the external world of persons and things in which we are embedded. The authors argue that the Buddhist practice of "mindfulness awareness" enables a focused attention to one's subjective experience so that its embodied nature can be appreciated. This work thus presents a clear discussion of embodied cognition, essential to the combination of third- and first-person perspectives that are hallmarks of Contemplative Studies.

Another important dimension of Contemplative Studies lies in the creation, study, and analysis of what psychologist Mihalyi Csikszentmihalyi (1990) has called states of the optimal experience. These "flow" states are characterized by complete absorption in the activity being performed, altered perception of time, effortless attention, a sense of little or no mental effort being exerted, and loss of self-consciousness, among many salient qualities. Flow, or what might be called "flowing cognition," adds an important dimension to contemplative experience that includes a much greater range of human activities, particularly those that involve the creative arts: the creation and appreciation of music, painting, sculpture, and sports. This research is also central to the Positive Psychology movement, which emphasizes how to cultivate more positive mental and emotional states and traits.

There are a great variety of scientific studies in the fields of neuroscience, cognitive science, and psychology that investigate the states of attentional stability, mental clarity, calmness and tranquility, and flowing cognition that are the foundations of developing insight into the nature of our conscious experience. James Austin has written three substantive works that detail his and others' theories on the transformations of consciousness created by Zen Buddhist meditation practice: Austin (2009), *Selfless Insight*; Austin (2006), *Zen-Brain Reflections*; and Austin (1998), *Zen and the Brain.*

There are a variety of new research articles on Flow in Brian Bruya's (2010a) collection *Effortless Attention* (including a nice summary article by Austin (2010) of his ideas on "selfless insight"), and, of course, Mihalyi Csikszentmihalyi has continued his research on this topic. Excellent overviews of scientific research on meditation "states" (transient mental phenomena) and "traits" (transformations in character) are detailed in articles by Rael Cahn and John Polich (2006), and Antoine Lutz, John Dunne, and Richard Davidson (2007). Amishi Jha (2007, 2010) has studied the effects of introductory mindfulness practice on cognitive performance.

Finally, the most widely used adaptation of Buddhist mindfulness practices into a Western context is the "Mindfulness Based Stress Reduction" developed by Jon Kabat-Zinn in such works as *Full Catastrophe Living* (1990) and in an extensive body of scientific research on the applications of such practices in a wide variety of clinical contexts. Mindfulness scales have been developed by Ruth Baer (2003) and others. This scientific literature on applied meditation is another important dimension of Contemplative Studies.

Primary Works: Classics Contemplative Texts

CLASSICAL DAOISM

While it would be possible to choose from major works in many wisdom traditions that contain details of contemplative practice, experience, and insights, I have chosen ones in the principal traditions that I have researched in my own work as a scholar of classical Chinese religions and their Indic counterparts. There are three foundational works of the classical Daoist tradition that I have used in this course:

1. "Inward Training" (*Neiye*) (see Roth (1999), a short text included among 76 works in the large collection of materials from the state of Qi called the *Guanzi.* This text was likely written down circa 320 BCE but was undoubtedly transmitted orally for some time before that date. "Inward Training" is the oldest extant text on breathing meditation in the entire Chinese, and hence, East Asian religious and philosophical tradition. It contains 26 rhymed

verses that detail breathing practices and their resulting insights into the mind and nature. I have developed a series of meditations based on the techniques in these verses that helps students to develop the ability to focus on the ebb and flow of their breathing. These include "Coiling and Uncoiling" from Verse XVII (78), in which students focus on the expanding and contracting of the breathing muscles in their abdomen; "Revolving the Vital Breath," from Verse XXIV (92), in which students attend to the path of the breath from nose to abdomen and back out; and concentration on the "One Word" in Verse XIV, a mantra-like meditation on the word "Dao," the cosmic Way that infuses everything in Daoist cosmology.

2. The *Laozi*, the best-known work of classical Daoist philosophy (Lau, 1982; Henricks, 1989; Mair, 1990), that contains both passages on contemplative practice and its insights into mind and Nature and passages that apply contemplative perspectives to political philosophy (Roth, 1997). Probably completed around 275 BCE but containing older material, the *Tao Te Ching* is a collection of 81 "chapters" made up of distinct units of verse tied together by logical connectives. Contemplative practices that I have developed from this work include "Bellows Breathing," from chapter 5, in which students imagine their abdomen to be a bellows, sucking in and pushing out the breath, and "Observing the Rise and Fall of Mental Contents" from the famous line in chapter 16, "All things rise and I see thereby their return."

3. *The Zhuangzi*, a delightful collection of narratives and short essays on the experience of the Dao in everyday life that was finally completed circa 150 BCE but which contains material from the late fourth century (Graham, 1981; Mair, 1994, 2008). Meditation techniques from this work include "The Fasting of the Mind" from chapter 4, in which students concentrates on breathing into external sounds, and "Sitting in Forgetfulness" from chapter 6, which is basically an open awareness practice. (Roth, 2000).

CLASSICAL INDIC BUDDHISM

The Buddhist canonical works preserved in the Indic language called Pali contain a series of texts that the tradition regards as being the teaching of the historical Buddha, and thus dating back to the fifth and fourth centuries BCE. Among the many texts and teachings in this canon are two *suttas* (collected lectures and dialogues attributed to the historical Buddha) about the practice of "mindfulness," which involves paying complete attention to various aspects of one's moment-to-moment experience. Since the two texts are closely related, the techniques in them used in Meditation Lab are essentially the same. These two works are:

1. The *Anapanasati Sutta* ("Mindfulness of Breathing"), a short work from the collection called the *Majjhima Nikaya* ("The Collection of the Middle-Length Discourses") that presents techniques about how to pay full, nonjudgmental attention (*sati*) to different aspects of one's experience that starts first with the inbreathing (*ana*) and the outbreathing (*pana*) (Rosenberg, 1999).

2. The *Satipatthana Sutta* ("Foundations of Mindfulness"), a longer and more detailed work on similar techniques found in two inconsequentially different versions in the Pali collections *Majjhima Nikaya* and *Digha Nikaya* (Analayo, 2004). In Meditation Labs, based on one or the other of these texts, we work with mindful attention to the breathing, sometimes focusing on the whole body, sometimes counting the breaths, sometimes focusing on the breath at different physical points in the breathing cycle, such as the tip of the nose or the upper abdominal breathing muscles. We follow these texts and later interpreters and move on from there to practices that develop awareness of body and mind sensations, such as a guided "body sweep," in which students follow the sensations in their body from their forehead down the front of their body to their toes and the back to the crown of their head. We also use the technique of noting and labeling, through which a student notes an element of experience in terms of one of a set of categories such as "thought," "feeling," "sound," "image." There are a number of different systems for this that we have used but they are all derived from these two *suttas*. We also practice a very slow, methodical walking meditation based on these two sources. The more advanced practices of these texts are beyond the purview of this course.

ZEN BUDDHISM IN EAST ASIA

When Buddhism moved into China, it encountered the native tradition of Daoism and it developed in certain ways that are interesting for the study of contemplative practices. If we could describe the classical Daoist meditation techniques as "integrative," because they holistically embrace body and mind experience with breathing, and classical Indic Buddhism techniques as "analytical," because they concentrate on attending to the many distinctive elements that constitute human experience, then East Asian Buddhist contemplative techniques are a combination of these approaches. Experience is analyzed through focusing on its momentary nature, but this nature is also integrated into an underlying whole called by a number of terms including "Buddha-nature," "Buddha-mind," and "True Person."

Traditionally, Zen Buddhist teachers do not write a great deal about their practices; they prefer to give them in personal instruction. The clearest work on Zen techniques is a recent book by Katsuki Sekida (1975), a Sôtô Zen Lay Teacher who practiced with Robert Aitken Roshi's Diamond Sangha in Honolulu. Sekida in turn was influenced by Western phenomenology, the influence of which is felt in his descriptions of Zen practice. In the course we read his most important work, *Zen Training: Methods and Philosophy*, as a primary text, and use a range of contemplative techniques to which it refers. These include "Bamboo Breathing," a technique in which students exhale in stages like the nodes of the bamboo tree; working with simple *koans*, used most commonly by the Rinzai school, which are short narratives containing problems to solve that contain insights into the way consciousness works according to Zen; and the informatively entitled "Just Sitting" practice (*shikantaza*) that is emphasized in Sôtô Zen.

Mindfulness Based Stress Reduction (MSBR)

We finish the course by studying the philosophy, exemplary narratives, and techniques of MBSR, a deracinated form of mindfulness meditation practice that its founder Jon Kabat-Zinn developed for use in clinical medical contexts and that has become the most commonly used practice for this purpose (Kabat-Zinn, 1990). Kabat-Zinn stripped all Buddhist cognitive frameworks from this practice: there is no discussion of such key early Buddhist teachings as the doctrine of "no-self," the "Eight-Fold Path," the "Four Noble Truths" and so on. By stripping away a religious context, Kabat-Zinn made these techniques more palatable to an audience with strong beliefs in the Abrahamic traditions or in science as a substitute for religion. We use a number of relevant techniques from MBSR including counting breaths and body sweeps, but since we have already encountered them in our study of classical Indic Buddhist texts and practices, students have the chance to study them free of accompanying conceptual frameworks.

Course Design

The clearest way to demonstrate how these various elements come together is to examine the actual design of the version of the course I currently teach. "An Introduction to Contemplative Studies" attempts to integrate the theory and practices discussed above, to provide a balance between primary and second works and meditation techniques and in so doing to strike a balance between third- and first-person approaches to the study of contemplative phenomena.

SAMPLE COURSE OUTLINE: INTRODUCTION TO CONTEMPLATIVE STUDIES 2011 (Abridged)

Table 1. ***Part I: Methodological Perspectives: Toward a New Science of Consciousness***

WEEKLY SEMINAR	MEDITATION LAB
2/02: "Scientific Materialism" and the Disappearance of Introspection	**Daoist Reconstructive Meditations from *Guanzi's* "Inward Training:"**
Primary Texts: Early Daoist Wisdom Poetry on Meditation: Roth, ***Original Tao***, pp. 35–118 Secondary Works: Wallace, ***Taboo of Subjectivity***, pp. 3–96	1/31: Unfocused Awareness of Breathing: "Coiling and Uncoiling" 2/02: Coiling and Uncoiling 2/04: Coiling and Uncoiling 2/11–12: Daoism Lecture and Retreat by Prof. Louis Komjathy U San Diego;

Table 2. ***Art II: Psychological Approaches***

WEEKLY SEMINAR	MEDITATION LAB
2/16. The Anatomy of Consciousness and the Nature of "Flow"	**Daoist Reconstructive Meditations**
Primary Texts: Early Daoist Wisdom Poetry: Mair, *Zhuangzi*, pp. xi–xlv; 1–28; Secondary Works: Csikszentmihalyi, *Flow: The Psychology of Optimal Experience*: pp. 1–142;	2/15: The One Word As Mantra: Dao 2/17: The One Word As Mantra: Dao 2/19: Sitting and Forgetting

Table 3. ***Part III: The Phenomenology of Contemplation***

WEEKLY SEMINAR	MEDITATION LAB
3/09. Experience and the Cognitivist Hypothesis	**Theravada Buddhist Mindfulness practice**
Primary: Theravada Buddhist Meditation: *Anapanna sati sutta*; Rosenberg, pp. 198–208; Young, "How Meditation Works" Secondary: Varela, Thompson and Rosch, *Embodied Mind*: Introduction, pp. 3–84; Bruya, *Effortless Attention,* 247–86	3/07: *Mindfulness of Breath in diaphragm*: Count in-breaths to 5 3/09: Count out-breaths to 5 3/11: Mindfulness of breath at the tip of the nose **3/13: Workshop on Compassion Led by Lama John Makransky, Boston College** **3/24: Lecture by Clifford Saron, UC Davis: "The Shamatha Project"**

Table 4. ***Part IV: The Neuroscience of Contemplation***

WEEKLY SEMINAR	MEDITATION LAB
4/06. Neurological Transformations from Contemplative Practice Primary Texts: Sekida, *Zen Training*, 29–90 Secondary works: Austin in Bruya *Effortless Activity*, 373–407	**Japanese Zen Meditation** 4/04: Sekida's "Bamboo Breathing" (exhalation in stages); eyes closed 4/06: Bamboo Breathing, eyes closed 4/08: Bamboo Breathing: eyes just open
4/13. Meditation and Neurophenomenology Primary Texts: Sekida, *Zen Training*, 91–159. Secondary works: Cahn and Polich, "Meditation States and Traits" Lutz and Thompson, "Neurophenomenology"	4/11: Rinzai Zen Style: Kôan: "Does this dog have Buddha-nature?" (Jôshu's NO); eyes just open 4/13: Jôshu's NO with explanatory talk: this no is the core activity of your mind from moment to moment 4/15: Jôshu's NO; Indoor walking meditation (10")
	4/16–17: Meditation Retreat, Led by Insight Meditation Master Shinzen Young

Table 5. ***Part V: Clinical Applications of Contemplative Practice***

WEEKLY SEMINAR	MEDITATION LAB
5/04. Studies in Mindfulness-Based Stress Reduction Primary: Kabat-Zinn, *Full Catastrophe Living*, Sections IV–V; Secondary works: Kabat-Zinn, "Mindfulness-Based Interventions in Context" Brown and Ryan, Shapiro et al.	5/02: Vipassana : Body Sweep 5/04: Same 5/06: Vipassana: Open Awareness

The Meditation Labs

Organization

The 50 minute time periods of the thrice weekly Meditation Labs are roughly divided along the following lines:

- Warming up yoga practice: 10 minutes
- Meditation period: 20 minutes, expanding gradually to 30 minutes by the end of the semester as students get more accustomed to meditation

- Question and answer period: 5–10 minutes
- Journaling. 5–10 minutes: students keep journals in which they record comments or questions on the day's technique. These journals are private between the professor and student and are useful for the professor to discover who is having difficulties and, at the end of the semester, for students to gain an overview of their progress throughout the term.
- In addition, students are required to attend one or two day-long workshops from outside contemplative teachers. These augment what they are learning in the Meditation Labs.

Rationale and Method

The Buddhist tradition, from its oldest normative sources to its modern innovations and throughout all the many forms of contemplative practices it has developed as it has moved from culture to culture, has always maintained the distinction between two complementary forms of meditation: "stopping" (*Shamatha*) and "seeing" (*vipasyana*, also known as *vipassana*). These are detailed in Shinzen Young's (2006) excellent article, "How Meditation Works." Stopping is the step-by-step calming of the mind through various techniques of training the attention. These include concentrating on one object or activity, which enables one to develop being mindful—nonjudgmental of it. Seeing is the practice of clear observation, paying careful and non-judging attention to all the different aspects of one's experience, usually broken into traditional categories such as the "5 Aggregates" (*skandhas*), "12 Sense Doors" (*ayatanas*), and the "18 Sense Fields" (*dhatus*), or different aspects of experience: body, feelings, thoughts, images, and so on. It can be thought of as applying the calm and focus developed in stopping practice to one's own experience.

Along parallel lines, contemporary scientists such as James Austin conceive of two complementary dimension of meditation practice: concentrative and receptive (Austin 2010, 375, 377). The former is "voluntary, top-down practice" that leads to a narrowing of the focus of the attention ultimately leading to "one-pointedness." The latter is more "effortless, involuntary, and inclusive," in which one "learns to relax, let go, and tap bottom-up, pre-attentive, intuitive mechanisms" These techniques remain so openly available, so diffusely attuned, that they notice any stimulus arising from anywhere in the environment. I have found parallels to these categories present in classical Daoist meditation as well (see Roth, 2003, "Bimodal Mystical Experience").

Despite sources in the Buddhist tradition that claim that concentrative meditation need not precede receptive methods, I have in my own experience seen that, if one has little or none of the mental stability promoted by concentrative practices, it is extremely difficult to effectively practice receptive methods. Developing some degree of stability allows the awareness to act as a kind of lens through which one may more dispassionately observe the normal flow of conscious experience without getting pulled into it. I have therefore constructed the Meditation Labs in this course to emphasize developing concentrative techniques before receptive ones.

Starting with classical Daoist techniques, we work on concentration on the breathing within the body first ("Coiling and Uncoiling," "Revolving the Vital Breath," "Bellows Breathing"), then move to a mantra-like word meditation ("One Word: Dao"), concentrating on sound ("Fasting of the Mind"), and eventually to a more open awareness ("Sitting in Forgetfulness," "Observing the Rise and Fall of Mental Contents").

The Indic Buddhist techniques also emphasize the concentrative: mindfulness of breath (long, short, shallow, deep, etc.), mindfulness of breath through counting, mindfulness of breath with the whole body; walking meditation; noting and labeling of all things that take attention away from breathing: thoughts, feelings, images, perceptions, identified using several possible systems; body sweeps. These are concentrative techniques. We then do some beginning receptive meditations, using the noting and labeling method not as a way to return the distracted attention to breathing but as a way of fully identifying the various aspects of our moment-to-moment experience.

When we study Zen meditation techniques we begin with the concentrative technique of "Bamboo Breathing" (Sekida), move on to the combination of concentrative and receptive techniques found in kôan practice, central to the Rinzai School of Zen (Omori, 2002), and finish with the receptive technique of "Just Sitting" (*Shikan taza*), the central contemplative practice of Sôtô Zen (Cook, 1999) that is a form of open awareness.

We complete the Meditation Labs for the course with a few of the Mindfulness Based Stress Reduction techniques: mindfulness breathing through counting of the breaths and mindfulness of the body through body sweeps. In some versions of the course we also include the meditations on loving kindness (*metta*) and on compassion (*karuna*), the first two of four "Divine Abodes" (*Brahmaviharas*) (Salzberg, 2002).

It is also important to remember that these contemplative techniques represent only half the course; we are also reading, analyzing, and discussing important primary texts from these Buddhist and Daoist traditions and the secondary work I have listed above as the foundational theoretical writings of this new academic field. These readings help students to contextualize their experiences in meditation labs just as their lab experience gives them a fuller appreciation of the contemplative writings.

Qualitative Results

I have been teaching courses with Meditation Labs for over a decade: to this point I have taught 20 of them to well over 400 students. The "Introduction to Contemplative Studies" course I have been discussing had its tenth iteration in the summer of 2011. In the past few years I have given students the choice of a final assignment in which they reflected on their experience in the course. Lack of space prohibits a thorough presentation of the qualitative results I have accumulated, so I will be able to provide a few representative examples.

GS: *Over the course of the semester I have seen an increased ability in myself to observe what I am doing as I'm doing it, to monitor my progress and effectiveness and see what should be adjusted. This is a vital skill that can be applied to almost any undertaking because it usually leads to operation on the maximum level. I can check to see if I am pushing myself too hard, or not working hard enough, and this usually means that I eventually find the most effective pace in any given activity. This ability to be mindful of how I am doing something is a direct correlation to my time spent meditating. . . .*

JR: *I have noticed a definite increase in my aptitude to concentrate since starting a regular meditative practice. I can trace, using my journals, my rising skill in remaining focused on my breath and present experience from the beginning of the semester to the end.*

TH: *Still, in my first sits, I had endless difficulty just following and watching my breath; I needed to count my breaths, to block out thoughts with the work of concentration, and I was frustrated by my unending thoughts, obnoxiously interrupting my experience. Now, the thoughts are absolutely still present. But I know that I don't need to feed them with a frustration, I don't have to let them affect me the same way.*

KW: *Just as non-attachment to the thoughts as "me" was an enormous development, so too was the concept of non-attachment in general. . . . When one ceases to attach to things as "mine," there is less feeling of extreme loss or disappointment when one loses that thing. The distance one has from the emotion or thought is almost a protective barrier that keeps it from affecting one too strongly. This has helped me stabilize the mood swings that were endemic to my depression.*

KR: *Practicing mindfulness this semester has been about realizing what I have before it is gone and being grateful. It has been about welcoming both good and bad, and eventually just welcoming whatever is. It has been about realizing the difference between thinking and meditating, and the difference between sleeping and meditating. It has been about how far I have come, how far I have to go, and where I am right now. It has been about more accepting and experiencing, less grasping. About tuning my instrument. About nurturing what I knew was already inside of me, which is what drew me here in the first place. The belief that an* *enemy is just a story I haven't heard yet. The belief that the person in the other clothes, body, room, house, city, continent is still somehow fundamentally connected to me. The belief that this connection matters.*

Quantitative Results

For the past four years, clinical psychologist Dr. Willoughby Britton of the Warren Alpert School of Medicine at Brown University has been studying the effects of courses with Meditation Labs on a group of students that now numbers close to 200. She has compared them with students in other skill-acquisition courses, such as those in the Departments of Music and of Dance, with students in Religious Studies courses, and with students in courses that I teach without Meditation Labs. While she has found understandable increases in the ability to pay attention in the skill-based "first-person" pedagogy courses when compared to traditional "third-person" pedagogy courses, she has been finding unexpected changes in the emotional lives of the students in the Meditation Lab courses, including dramatic reductions in feelings of anxiety and depression and dramatic increases in compassion for self and for others. Her research is unique, rich, and complex, and will result in a series of scientific articles, the first of which is in press at the journal *Psychosomatic Medicine:* a second is forthcoming in *Frontiers in Human Neuroscience.*[1] In the former article, the authors present the data for their study that indicates that contemplative training (in contrast to music training) was associated with improvements in body awareness as well as a reduction in clinical symptoms of depression and anxiety, and with improvement in both the ability to pay attention and the ability to be nonjudgmental of oneself. In the latter article, the authors present a study that demonstrates that students who have taken courses with Meditation Labs have a singularly improved recall of positive words when compared to the control group of musicians, thus indicating a positive change in their emotional lives.

Conclusions

The contemplative pedagogies we have been developing and testing at Brown University have garnered some interesting preliminary results among the more than 400 students who have taken such courses and the 200 who have been tested. There is a strong correlation between the qualitative and quantitative results, at least at this point in the research. In the former, students self-report increased ability to concentrate on the tasks at hand and less attachment to a fixed idea of self that is continuously judging itself. This leads to a decreased fluctuation in emotional states and an ability to tolerate negative feelings that are well borne out by the preliminary quantitative research. Students also report a greater ability to simply observe themselves. These results actually fit well with some of the reported results of the contemplative traditions we are examining, particularly increased mental stability, decreased negative emotionality, and increased compassion (c.f., e.g., Shaw, 2006, 65–68, 165; Roth, 1999, 112–113; Sekida, 1975, 34; Lutz et al., 2009).

These results confirm several of the goals of teaching such courses. First, they give students the kind of direct, experiential knowledge of what is being presented in the contemplative writings that leads to a fuller and deeper understanding of them. Second, these results indicate that there are strong positive effects associated with pursuing contemplative practices within an academic context. These include increased concentration, decreased depression and anxiety, and increased compassion. Third, the broader program of Contemplative Studies established, as it is, on the foundation of a combination of the Humanities, the Sciences, and the Creative Arts, brings all three general areas, heretofore seriously divided in the modern academy, into dialogue with one another. This is a dialogue that not only demonstrates the relevance of contemplative practices in all these areas but one that also holds the potential to generate new and fruitful data, insights, and hypotheses that can help further the development of genuine knowledge about the nature of the human person.

Note

1. Silverstein, R., Brown, A., Roth, H., & Britton, W. B. (in press). "Mindfulness training improves interoceptive awareness to sexual stimuli: Implications for healthy female sexual functioning." *Psychosomatic Medicine*; Sacchet, M., Roth, H., & Britton, W. B. (forthcoming), "Neural Effects of Mindfulness/Contemplative Training," *Frontiers in Human Neuroscience.*

Acknowledgments

I wish to thank the following people for their valuable comments on earlier versions of this chapter: Shemaleiah Smylie (Brown, '11.5), and the editors of the present volume.

References

Analayo (Trans.). (2004). *Satipattaha: The direct path to realization*. London: Windhorse.

Austin, J. (1998). *Zen and the Brain*. Cambridge: MIT Press.

Austin, J. (2006). *Zen-brain reflections*. Cambridge: MIT Press.

Austin, J. (2009). *Selfless insight*. Cambridge: MIT Press.

Austin, J. (2010). "The thalamic gateway: How the meditative training of attention evolves toward selfless transformations of consciousness." In B. J. Bruya (Ed.), *Effortless attention* (pp. 373–407). Cambridge, MA: MIT Press.

Baer, R. A. (2003). Mindfulness training as a clinical intervention: A conceptual review. *Clinical Psychology: Science and Practice, 10*(2), 125–143.

Bishop, S., Shapiro, S., Carlson, L., Segal, Z., et al. (2004). Mindfulness: A proposed operational definition. *Clinical Psychology: Science and Practice, 11*(3), 230–241.

Brown, K. W., & Ryan, R. M. (2003). The benefits of being present: Mindfulness and its role in psychological well-being. *Journal of Personality and Social Psychology, 84*(4), 822–848.

Bruya, B. J. (2010a). *Effortless attention*. Cambridge, MA: MIT Press.

Bruya, B. J. (2010b). The rehabilitation of spontaneity: A new approach in philosophy. *Philosophy East and West, 60*(2), 207–250.

Cahn, B. R., & Polich, J. (2006). Meditation states and traits: EEG, ERP, and neurophysiology studies." *Psychological Bulletin, 132*(2), 180–211.

Cook, F. D. (1999). *How to raise an ox: Zen practice as taught in Master Dogen's Shôbôgenzo*. Boston: Wisdom.

Csikszentmihalyi, M. (1990). *Flow: The psychology of optimal experience*. New York: Harper and Row.

Graham, A. C. (Trans.). (1981). *Chuang Tzu: The inner chapters*. London: Allen and Unwin.

Henricks, R. (1989). *Lao-Tzu: Te Tao Ching: A new translation based on the recently discovered Ma-Wang-Tui texts*. New York: Ballantine Books.

Jha, A., Krimpinger, J., & Baime, M. J. (2007). Mindfulness training modifies subsystems of attention. *Cognitive, Affective, and Behavioral Neuroscience 7*(2), 109–119.

Jha, A. P., Stanley, E. A., & Baime, M. J. (2010). What does mindfulness training strengthen? Working memory capacity as a functional marker of training success. In R. A. Baer (Ed.), *Assessing mindfulness & acceptance processes in clients* (pp. 207–220). New York: Context Press.

Kabat-Zinn, J. (1990). *Full catastrophe living: Using the wisdom of your body and mind to face stress, pain and illness*. New York: Delacorte.

Kabat-Zinn, J. (2003). Mindfulness-based interventions in context: Past, present, and future. *Clinical Psychology: Science and Practice, 10*(2), 144–56.

Lau, D. C. (Trans.). (1982). *Chinese classics: Tao Te Ching*. London: Penguin Classics.

Lutz, Antoine, Dunne, John, & Davidson, Richard. (2007). Meditation and the neuroscience of consciousness: An introduction. In P. Zelazo, M. Moscovitch, & E. Thompson (Eds.), *The Cambridge handbook of consciousness* (pp. 499–551). Cambridge: Cambridge University Press.

Lutz, A., & Thompson, E. (2003). Neurophenomenology: Integrating subjective experience and brain dynamics in the neuroscience of consciousness. *Journal of Consciousness Studies* (JCS), *10*, 21–52.

Lutz, A., Slagter, H. A., Rawlings, N. B., Francis, A. D., Greischar, L. L., & Davidson, R. J. (2009) Mental training enhances attentional stability: Neural and behavioral evidence. *Journal of Neuroscience, 29*(42): 13418–13427.

Mair, V. (Trans.). (1990). *Tao Te Ching: The classic book of integrity and the way.* New York: Bantam Books.

Mair, V. (Trans.). (1994, 2008). *Wandering on the way: Early Taoist tales and parables of Chuang Tzu.* Honolulu, HI: University of Hawai'i Press.

Omori, S. (2002). *An Introduction to Zen Training.* North Clarendon, VT: Tuttle.

Rosenberg, L. (1999). *Breath by breath: The liberating practice of insight meditation.* Boston: Shambala.

Roth, H. D. (1997). "Laozi in the context of early Daoist mystical praxis." In Mark Csikszentmihalyi & P. J. Ivanhoe (Eds.), *Religious and philosophical aspects of Laozi* (pp. 59–96). Albany, NY: State University of New York Press.

Roth, H. D. (1999).*Original Tao: Inward training and the foundations of Taoist mysticism.* New York: Columbia University Press.

Roth, H. D. (2004). Bimodal mystical experience in the "Qiwulun" chapter of the *Zhuangzi.* In Scott Cook (Ed.), *Hiding the world in the world: Uneven discourses on the Zhuangzi* (pp. 15–31). Albany, NY: State University of New York Press.

Salzberg, S. (2002). *Loving-kindness: The revolutionary art of happiness.* Boston: Shanbhala.

Sekida, K. (1975). *Zen training: Methods and philosophy.* New York: Weatherhill.

Shaw, S. (2006). *Buddhist meditation: An anthology of texts from the Pali canon.* Oxford: Routledge.

Varela, F., Thompson, E., & Rosch, E. (1991). *The embodied mind: Cognitive science and human experience.* Cambridge, MA: MIT Press.

Wallace, B. A. (2000). *The taboo of subjectivity: Towards a new science of consciousness.* Oxford: Oxford University Press.

Young, S. (2006). How Meditation Works. Retrieved from <http://www.shinzen.org/Articles/artHow.pdf>.

Part II

Domain Specific Perspectives

7

Learning about Obligation, Compassion, and Global Justice

The Place of Contemplative Pedagogy

David Kahane

This chapter explores how contemplative and meditative techniques support teaching and learning about a key issue in contemporary ethics and political theory: our moral obligations to distant strangers. The undergraduates I have taught in departments of philosophy and political science are gripped and troubled by this inquiry into how we in the relatively privileged global north draw boundaries around our concern for others, what motivates our relative indifference to or dissociation from the suffering of distant strangers, and how these dynamics can be challenged and changed. Here, I discuss a 300-level philosophy course on "Obligation, Compassion, and Global Justice."[1] I suggest that while learning more about global inequalities, reflecting on moral principles, and getting a more vivid sense of the life experiences and perspectives of people in different parts of the world all are important to this inquiry, they are insufficient. Students also need to be supported in contemplative practice, bringing mindful attention to their embodied experiences of dissociation from and connection with their own and others' suffering.

I taught Philosophy 368 at the University of Alberta in western Canada from 2006 through 2008 to a class of 35 to 45 students, about half of them philosophy majors and remainder from other disciplines. The course was built around a cognitive and motivational puzzle relating to global citizenship and global justice. The puzzle begins with a few facts:

1. Large numbers of our fellow humans live in abject poverty (1.2 billion, by one recent estimate), go to bed hungry each night

(an estimated 800 million people), and die daily from poverty-related causes (perhaps 50,000 a day).

2. We each could prevent a portion of this suffering at minimal cost: a sachet of oral rehydration salts that can save a child from fatal diarrhea costs about fifty cents, and twenty cents buys a day's food rations distributed by the World Food Program in Sudan.
3. Almost all of us who work or study at universities in the global north spend a significant amount on luxuries we easily could forego.

Put these facts together and a sobering set of choices and trade-offs becomes visible: in drinking lattes rather than regular coffees, for example, I am paying a premium over the course of a year that could instead be used to save many human lives. When I look this equation in the eye, I come to an inexorable conclusion: many aspects of my privilege come at an unconscionable cost and ought to be given up for the immeasurably greater good that these resources could do for the world's neediest.[2]

But this brings us to the puzzle: like most students in my Canadian classrooms, I recognize this obligation and yet change almost nothing in how I live. I manage, like most privileged global citizens, to proceed relatively untroubled in a lifestyle that is unconscionable by my own standards. As decent people we nonetheless find it hard to take strangers' welfare seriously in making choices, or even to retain an awareness of others' suffering and our capacity to ameliorate it.

As my own understanding of the dynamics of dissociation from others' suffering developed, the shape of the course changed. Before getting to this, I'd like to step back and sketch the terrain of approaches to teaching global citizenship and justice, at least from the standpoint of English-speaking political theory.

Pedagogies of Global Citizenship

In the last twenty years mainstream political philosophers in the English-speaking world have systematically begun to question the assumption that justice applies only within bounded political communities. Whereas, prior to the late 1980s, political theorists did not typically even notice that their conceptions of justice screeched to a halt at national borders, debates in political theory now take it as given that many of our deepest challenges of justice (and indeed survival) traverse national boundaries, in a context of profound global interdependence. Many political theorists now aim to persuade their readers of individual and collective obligations on the part of people in the global north to redress gross inequalities of resources and power with the global south. These theorists grapple, whether overtly or implicitly, with how to motivate people to recognize and challenge their privilege and their disconnection from the suffering and the fate of those beyond their nation's borders. I see two dominant pedagogical approaches to motivating change among the privileged.

Pedagogies of Reason

Perhaps unsurprisingly, given the shape of the western philosophical tradition, the dominant way that English-speaking philosophers have tried to convince their readers to attend to the plight of the world's least well off is through rational argumentation.

Peter Singer's (1997) influential argument—which I adopted to set up the puzzle above—provides a clear example of this resort to rational persuasion as a route to changing self-perceptions, understandings of obligation, and ultimately behavior on the part of the privileged. Singer's argument is premised on the view that morality requires impartial fairness between people and that from an impartial standpoint the gross disparities in wealth and life prospects across the globe are morally indefensible. He suggests that almost all of us are impartialist in our deepest moral convictions but that we self-servingly ignore the entailments of impartiality for our everyday behavior, treating the satisfaction of our most casual desires as more important than meeting the crucial needs of strangers. The role of the philosopher is to point out this sharp contradiction between our moral convictions and our behavior so that we can see our own hypocrisy and be moved to reduce the conflict.

And yet as I have observed in my own life and my own classrooms, being rationally persuaded of a moral obligation is rarely effective in motivating change. Nor does the resilience of our privileged modes of behavior seem adequately explained by hypocrisy or weakness of the will, concepts that describe the dictates of morality being outweighed by our non-moral or immoral preferences, goals, or desires. Rather, the knowing that we achieve through exposure to rational arguments about obligation seems disconnected from the complexity of our moral being, and is eroded or displaced not by desire or by conscious, countervailing goals but by intricate dynamics of dissociation and motivation.

Pedagogies of Sentiment

A number of prominent philosophers now argue that acting ethically toward others is less a matter of applying abstract moral principles than of learning about the particularities of others' lives and so developing a sense of connection with or compassion for them.

Richard Rorty (1993), for example, suggests that the main obstacle to our offering help to distant strangers is that they don't seem like part of a valued "we." This isn't remedied, though, through abstract, principled argumentation; rather, it is through vehicles like literature that our sense of the boundaries of our moral communities can shift. We hear sad, sentimental stories about others' suffering and see that they are mothers like us, or get their hearts broken like us, or love soccer like us.[3] And out of these particular realizations comes a feeling of connection and commitment that can change both our moral judgments and our behavior.

Martha Nussbaum (1996a,b) offers a different kind of therapy of sentiment: she suggests that when we learn about the particularity of others' lives we are able to see that they share a variety of distinctively human capacities with us and so deserve our regard. This is not merely an abstract realization but a cultivation of both reason and passion that expands our circle of concern. She describes a cosmopolitan education that involves learning how distant communities and cultures live, which in turn increases our sense of appreciation for otherness and our commitment to global citizenship.

Pedagogies of sentiment seem to offer a more promising diagnosis of our dissociation from the suffering of distant strangers than do pedagogies of reason, for they offer a more complex picture of the learner. But pedagogies of sentiment do not fully account for the cognitive and motivational puzzle that I laid out earlier: giving students plenty of particularistic information about other countries and groups and people does not in fact seem to displace habits of privilege nor does it seem to seriously diminish an ongoing dissociation from others' suffering.

I would suggest that our dissociation from others' suffering is persistent because it is powerfully motivated, not mainly by self-interest, as pedagogies of reason might suggest, nor by a failure to see them as part of a relevant "we" or a common humanity, but by inchoate fear. This, at least, is what I discover when I attend closely to my own experience, say when a charity infomercial appears on my TV with the image of a starving child: a wave of sensation and emotion rushes through me, a hint of my visceral belief that if I let this suffering in (not to mention the countless reiterations of this suffering in further starving children) it will destroy me. And another discovery occurs when I attend closely to my own experience: that this recoiling from others' suffering has a counterpart in my relationship to my own suffering. Here, too, I withdraw and dissociate from emotional intensity out of a visceral conviction that I cannot stand to experience it unmediated. And there is one further discovery: that a tremendous number of my habits, including habits of consumption, serve to soothe and deaden the anxiety that arises from a fear of directly experiencing suffering—others' and my own.

My point is not that this story of my own dissociation from suffering and habits of privilege is precisely mirrored in your experience or that of my students. It is that this "deeper" story of my motivations and resistances, of my embodied and emotional experiences, is so much at odds with the narrative I would standardly offer of my life, my moral and philosophical commitments, and the kind of person I am. Just as we spend much of our privileged lives disconnected from the suffering of strangers, so we spend them caught up in narratives and self-descriptions that do a poor job of capturing the reality of our own embodied experience. This is the most profound element of our alienation: alienation from our internal realities. And this is not an alienation that gets corrected by rational reflection or by a rich sense of the particulars of others' lives.

This alienation gets corrected, I want to suggest, by the ability to observe our own present-moment experience with compassionate detachment. This compassionate self-observation of our own bodily sensations and emotional patterns requires an ability to let the usual storylines go, in order to begin to notice what's going on in us right now. It requires contemplative practices.

Contemplative Pedagogy

Philosophy 368 began with a puzzle around the entrenchment of habits of privilege: how can we recognize an obligation, or identify someone as part of a relevant "we" or a common humanity, yet still be unmoved to change behaviors that are unjustifiable by our own moral lights? Neither more information nor more careful rational reflection seems to do much to shift our deep patterns of thought, affect, or experience. We may feel concern about others' suffering or connection to distant others as we learn more about them, but these changes tend to remain superficial and evanescent without an accompanying and direct recognition of the powerful motivations and drives that underlie our persistent tendency to dissociate. This, at least, is the analysis that led me, in Philosophy 368, to complement analytical and critical approaches with contemplative pedagogy.

Contemplative pedagogy is getting increasing attention in North American higher education: a yearly week-long workshop began at Smith College in

2005, attracting about 40 educators to each summer session,[4] Naropa University initiated its own international summer session on contemplative pedagogy in 2007,[5] a major international conference was held on the subject at Columbia University Teachers College in 2005,[6] another in San Francisco in 2007,[7] and even the staid *Chronicle of Higher Education* has reported positively on the movement (Gravois, 2005). Contemplative pedagogies include a wide range of practices, but the orienting practice and experience is that of meditation. I find Arthur Ledoux's (1998) gloss helpful:

> By meditation I mean the practice of mindfulness, training the mind to focus in a steady and non-judging way on the different phases of human experience. Mindfulness is an ancient practice cultivated strongly in Buddhist traditions but which overlaps contemplative practices in many other traditions. Mindfulness practice typically begins by paying clear, steady, non-reactive attention to the sensations of ones own breathing and then extending this wise and compassionate attention to embrace all bodily sensations and then feelings, moods, thoughts, and intentions. One way to describe the goal of mindfulness is the cultivation of bare attention: the ability to focus on any aspect of life whatsoever with this calm concentration.

The contemplative pedagogies that I introduced in Philosophy 368 aimed to cultivate this kind of mindfulness.

Contemplative Techniques in Philosophy 368

Implementing contemplative pedagogies in my course on global justice felt like a dangerous leap: I had been developing my own meditation practice for only a couple of years at that point, and although I saw important implications for studying and teaching about compassion and obligation toward the global poor, I was uncertain about how to realize these. How, for example, would I present the relationship between contemplative pedagogies and the conventional forms of inquiry associated with the discipline of philosophy? I eventually realized that I did not have to resolve these tough pedagogical questions prior to the course; rather, the course could itself constitute a collective inquiry into the significance of contemplation to the issues we were studying.[8] In this and many other respects, bringing contemplation into my pedagogies marked a seismic shift in my teaching practice: it led me to give up a measure of control and authority in my classrooms and to invite students to be conscious participants in pedagogical reflection. Let me outline three major contemplative elements of the course.

Meditation

The class met for 85 minutes twice a week for thirteen weeks; in every meeting we did about seven minutes of mindfulness meditation, calmly focusing our attention on the movement of our breath (noticing the sensation of the breath, counting breaths), and returning to our breath each time we noticed ourselves getting caught up in thoughts. I was careful in explaining the rationale for meditation practice as part of the course but offered quite spare instructions for the practice itself. I would remind students to sit up straight in their seats, feet flat on the floor, arms comfortable on their laps or tables. I would remind them that the goal wasn't to stop them from thinking but rather to notice when they got lost in thoughts: the core of the practice was then to let thoughts go and return to the breath, over and over. And I would remind them of the importance of kindness toward themselves when they noticed they were thinking: this was not a contest but a rigorously gentle exploration of their own experience. After some feedback and experimentation, we decided that this period of meditation worked best if placed right at the start of class. Students were good at arriving on time and when they didn't they waited outside for the bell that signaled the end of meditation.

I had anticipated student resistance to meditating in class, imagining that some students would judge it a waste of time, or irrelevant to the course's subject matter, or unphilosophical. Instead, students were almost uniformly enthusiastic about it.[9] Based on formative and summative feedback from students, at least four things happened. First, most students deeply appreciated the chance simply to slow down. They spent their days rushing from class to class, juggling intense demands associated with school and jobs, bombarded with images and sounds, and they cherished the opportunity simply to do nothing for seven minutes. Second, many appreciated not only the break but the practice of meditation: they were curious about their internal lives and interested in training themselves to notice their in-the-moment experience in new ways. Third, they were able to see connections between meditation and the course material and were interested in meditatively exploring their relationship to suffering and moral responsibility. This was helped along by the use of a text, read across the term and alongside more philosophical articles, that discussed themes of contemplation and our relationship to our own and others' suffering (Dass & Gorman, 1988). In general, the contemplative elements of the course invited students to bring the sometimes arcane arguments of philosophers into dialogue with their own experiences and offered them a rigorous set of techniques that supported this. Fourth, meditating at the beginning of each class brought us into the room together and allowed a calmer and more careful engagement with each other; this laid the ground for better work in groups than students were used to experiencing or than I had experienced in other classrooms.

Free-Writing

It was at the 2005 Summer Session on Contemplative Curriculum Design that I came to recognize, through a presentation by Mary Rose O'Reilley, that free-writing could be understood as a contemplative practice (O'Reilley, 1993). Free-writing, popularized by Peter Elbow (1973), means writing non-stop for a fixed period of time—the only rule is that the pen keeps moving. Because writing in this way short-circuits the impulse to edit, it allows writing without so much scripting and conscious control; you get into the flow of an idea or impulse and write things that you didn't know you had to say.

I offered a prompt or question for each free-write. Several times during the term free-writes followed meditation, allowing students to process that experience. Other times, free-writes invited reflection on a particular text or a question that we'd been struggling with in discussion up to that moment.

Sometimes, when the topic of a free-write was very raw, I would let students know in advance that they would not be asked to share the writing or to include it in their portfolio. The default, though, was for the free-write to be submitted, returned by me with only a "Thank you" as comment or evaluation, and then included in a portfolio that was evaluated holistically at the end of the term. Sometimes, students would be asked to read their free-writes to one another in small groups, and here we followed a protocol that I learned from O'Reilley. Writers would be given a couple of minutes to decide if there were elements of their writing that they wished to leave out when they read aloud. Then each student would read his or her work to their peers who would listen as mindfully as they could, simply say "Thank you" at the end, then move on to the next reading.

Free-writing not only offered a mode of contemplative inquiry but also helped to alleviate some of the anxiety and intimidation that students experience around written expression. I was astounded again and again by the wisdom and authenticity of voice that I encountered in most free-writes—a much rarer phenomenon when I read students' analytical essays. I also believe that free-writing, together with other low-stakes writing exercises used in the course, helped students to grasp that writing is a way of generating thoughts and not only of representing thoughts that have already been fully worked out.

Lectio Divina

Another technique that I took from O'Reilley was *lectio divina* or sacred reading, which has its origins in the Catholic monastic tradition. For a fixed period of time—perhaps five minutes—students would focus on an assigned paragraph of text and would try to bring the mind of meditation to their reading. Rather than following thoughts about the text they would simply dwell on it, reading again and again whatever aspects caught their eye and seeing what meanings emerged. Underlining was permitted, but not note taking. We also applied this technique to photographs—in the very first class of term, for example, students moved from meditation to four minutes of contemplation of a photograph of a man cradling a starving child.

Following this contemplative reading or seeing, students might be asked to free-write to capture what had come to them, or simply to talk in groups about the experience. Students frequently expressed surprise at the meanings that they stumbled across in this way and at the connections they were able to make. Like free-writing, *lectio divina* suspended some of students' intimidation and self-monitoring and allowed them to tap into new levels of meaning, experience, and insight. Some students also expressed appreciation for the atmosphere of awe, or at least care, that contemplative reading brought to the written word: it cultivated an ethos of intellectual engagement that can be lost in the speed and instrumentality of much university reading.

Outcomes

I taught this contemplative version of Philosophy 368 three times from 2006 through 2008. Student responses were enthusiastic, as conveyed through anonymous formative evaluations conducted several times each term and through narrative comments and numerical results on formal summative evaluations. Stepping back from details, I would observe four things about outcomes.

First, student reactions made clear to me their thirst for courses that allow them to engage with their own experiences in rigorous and reflective ways, and to think carefully about questions of meaning, morality, and spirituality in their lives.[10] There is a useful distinction to be made, though, between contemplative pedagogies (which train students in particular approaches to self-observation) and holistic education (which in some forms more easily invites students to tell their habitual stories about themselves rather than directing mindful attention to what is beneath these stories).[11] I find echoes of this distinction in students' comments on the course, where a number of them noted a difference between the kind of personal perspective they were encouraged to develop in our course and invitations in other classes to "share their feelings" or "speak from their perspective" (which some of them described as irrelevant and/or infantilizing).

Second, student feedback indicated a deepened interest in issues of global justice and in their own implication in global injustice.[12] Many students indicated that they remained puzzled about their ethical responsibilities and about the dynamics of dissociation and compassion that the course had taken up. To me this uncertainty was a fruitful one, and often was held by students with real curiosity and with gentleness toward themselves. Students tended to move away from harsh judgments of themselves and others for implication in global injustice—away from a discourse of obligation and guilt that I believe distracts from our tendency (even our ability) to connect compassionately with those in need. Students became more willing to experiment with their own tolerance for letting in others' suffering, and with what this might feel like in action. And they tended to be increasingly open to the possibility that their service to those who suffer, whether by giving up luxuries for others, or volunteering, or reorienting career and life plans, might not be a sacrifice (as Peter Singer suggests) but rather a movement toward greater meaning and fulfillment in their lives.

Third, the overtly experimental quality of the course, and the amount of uncertainty we entertained together about both method and content, seemed to cultivate a less anxious, more curious, and even delighted stance toward learning. Narrative evaluation comments repeatedly said that for a course about such depressing subject matter, it really was engaging and fun. My analysis here is that in much of their educational experience students are reminded again and again of what they lack and come to treat education as a struggle to elicit praise and avoid humiliation. A range of aspects of this course, from the emphasis on compassion toward self that is part of meditation, to the cultivation of trust among students in the classroom, to the pervasive spirit of inquiry in the course, opened up for students a sense that they might in fact learn from a place of plenty, a place where they have genuine knowledge to offer one another and where there is collective pleasure in exploring tough questions.

Fourth, the sense of operating from a place of plenty rather than lack, and such genuine curiosity and joy in learning, characterized my own experience of the course. Because I made the tentativeness and experimental quality of the course methods explicit to students and invited them to be agents in this inquiry, I was freed to be uncertain, and so to be a learner in my own classroom. And because I would do classroom exercises alongside my students I got to explore my own present-moment experience of teaching (and of inquiring into the issues of the course) through meditation and free-writing, in ways that changed my sense of teaching possibility. The community, the curiosity, and the mutual support that we built in the classroom, in part thanks to contemplative methods, included me, as well: I ended up experiencing and so modeling the freedom in learning that I sought for my students, and that I now realize I was yearning for in my own experience of the classroom.

Remaining Questions

Bringing contemplative pedagogies into my philosophy and later political science classrooms (I switched departments in 2007) threw all kinds of aspects of my teaching into question. Here are a few of the questions that I continue to carry.

First, I have struggled with the experience and adeptness I should have had with a contemplative practice before introducing it into the classroom. I struggled with this in introducing simple mindfulness meditation, and again when I brought *metta* or loving-kindness meditation into political science courses on mindful social action. My response to this uncertainty has been to go ahead—to let students be participants in exploring particular practices and how we learn them. Most crucial is that I be practicing mindfulness and presence as best I can while teaching contemplative techniques. Chögyam Trungpa, a Tibetan Buddhist teacher, advised those instructing meditation that the key requirement was to remain sane while doing so—calling attention to how often we lose our present moment bearings as we teach, whether by monitoring whether we're doing it right, or thinking ahead to the next step, or getting lost in habitual stories. My ability to work diligently to remain present as I teach basic contemplative methods is as important as my expertise in particular techniques.

A second question I carry from my experiments in contemplative pedagogy extends beyond these particular methods: how much does truly effective teaching in higher education rest on one's ability to be present and grounded? Part of the fascination and richness of this question lies in the elusive meanings of "presence" and "groundedness"—I often want these to mean relief from anxiety and easy confidence in the classroom, whereas the most authentic forms of presence I've experienced are inquisitive, and often quiveringly uncertain. I'm increasingly convinced that my ability to be authentic in my role as teacher and to hold this seat with the authority of someone who is not hiding from himself is fundamental to my ability to open spaces of deep learning with students.

Third, I struggle with questions about contemplative and analytical modes of writing. I noted above the liveliness of spontaneous student writing, and the labored and intimidated quality of much analytical writing. I want to understand more about how I can support my students in writing analytically from a place of plenty rather than lack, and so in finding more authentic voices as writers. But this turns out to be a complex negotiation—not just of writing methods, but with how we can inhabit the psychic and disciplinary worlds of the academy.

Contemplative pedagogies, I have suggested, can help students to understand the habits of thought, judgment, and reaction that keep them trapped in the cocoons of their own privilege, which is also to say their own suffering. As such, these pedagogies have a pivotal role to play in cultivating a meaningful and motivating sense of global citizenship and interconnectedness. I hope I have also made clear, though, that contemplative pedagogies deepen the process of teaching and learning much more pervasively: they bring our bare humanity into the classroom in ways that allow education to be more holistic, more fulfilling, and more deeply useful to both professors and students.

Acknowledgments

My thanks to the Center for the Contemplative Mind in Society and to Naropa University for their respective seminars in contemplative pedagogy; to the Fetzer Foundation and the Frederick P. Lenz Foundation for funding these seminars; to the University of Alberta for supporting and recognizing my experiments in contemplative pedagogy; to Susan Burgraff, Meena Gupta, Cressida Heyes, Nisha Nath, Judith Simmer-Brown, and Danielle Taschereau-Mamers for many rich discussions of the topics in this chapter; and to the editors of this volume for rich and incisive questions and comments.

Notes

An earlier version of this chapter was published in New Directions for Teaching and Learning: Special Issue on Internationalizing the Curriculum in Higher Education, 2009, 118, 49–60.

1. A course syllabus can be viewed at <http://www.arts.ualberta.ca/phil368/2007-368-Syllabus.pdf>.

[2]. There is a host of well-worn ripostes to this argument (for example, saving children from starvation only leads to more suffering down the line); these are canvassed and pretty effectively demolished in Pogge 2002 and Unger 1996.

3. "Sentiment" is used by Rorty and some other contemporary philosophers—in the non-pejorative sense employed, for example, by Adam Smith—to denote an awareness of one's own moral dispositions and orientations that can arise through observation

of and interaction with others (Adam Smith, *The Theory of Moral Sentiments*, 1759). It is, in other words, a feeling toward others spurred by particular ways of seeing and interacting with them, which in turn helps shape one's moral understanding and behavior.

4. This summer session is convened by the Center for the Contemplative Mind in Society, and funded by the Fetzer Foundation. See <http://www.contemplativemind.org/programs/academic/>.

5. See <http://www.naropa.edu/cace/seminar.cfm>.

6. See <http://www.contemplativemind.org/programs/academic/05conference.html>.

7. See <http://www.heartofeducation.org/>.

8. My own meditation practice invited this movement from an "I" that protects itself by knowing, toward recognizing and embracing not-knowing as a space for community and learning.

9. Just a few students in the class had a preexisting meditation practice. The majority meditated only in this classroom (though some spoke of experiments here and there with the technique—to relax for an exam, for example, or calm down in order to sleep). In a 2010 iteration of the course, this time in Political Science, a small group of students formed a sitting meditation group that met twice weekly throughout the term.

10. This impression is supported by research results from the Spirituality in Higher Education project, led by Alexander and Helen Astin at UCLA. The extensive, U.S.-based survey found, for example, that 76 percent of college students say they are "searching for meaning and purpose in life," while more than half say that their processors never provide opportunities to discuss the meaning and purpose of life. See <http://www.spirituality.ucla.edu>.

11. For a useful discussion of distinctions and relationships between holistic, contemplative, and integral education see Sean Esbjörn-Hargens, Jonathan Reams, and Olen Gunnlaugson (Eds.) (2010). *Integral education: New directions for higher learning.* Albany, NY: SUNY Press, and especially the editors' introduction.

12. This feedback included weekly reflective writing, anonymous mini-evaluations at 3–5 points during the term, and a substantial end-of-term long-answer survey. Expressions of deepened interest came—in many forms and registers, sometimes anonymously and sometimes not—from more than 2/3 of the class. While it would be interesting to track the persistence of this increased interest over a longer period, I have not done so systematically.

References

Dass, R., & Gorman, P. (1988). *How can I help? Stories and reflections on service.* New York: Alfred A. Knopf.

Elbow, P. *Writing without teachers.* (1973). Oxford: Oxford University Press.

Esbjörn-Hargens, S., Reams, J., & Gunnlaugson, O. (Eds.) (2010). *Integral education: new directions for higher learning.* Albany: State University of New York Press, 2010.

Gravois, J. (2005). Meditate on it: Can adding contemplation to the classroom lead students to more eureka moments? *The Chronicle of Higher Education, 52*(9), A10. Retrieved October 19, 2007, from <http://chronicle.com/free/v52/i09/09a01001.htm>.

Ledoux, A. O. (1998, August). Teaching meditation to classes in philosophy. Paper presented at Twentieth World Congress of Philosophy, Boston MA. Retrieved October 16, 2007 from <http://www.bu.edu/wcp/Papers/Teac/TeacLedo.htm>.

Nussbaum, M. (1996). Compassion: the basic social emotion. *Social Philosophy and Policy, 13*(1), 27–58.

Nussbaum, M. (1996). Patriotism and cosmopolitanism. In M. Nussbaum & J. Cohen (Eds.), *For love of country: Debating the limits of patriotism* (pp. 3–20). Boston, MA: Beacon Press.

O'Reilley, M. R. (1993). *The peaceable classroom.* Portsmouth, NH: Boynton/Cook.

Pogge, T. (2002). *World poverty and human rights: Cosmopolitan responsibilities and reforms.* Cambridge, UK: Polity Press, 2002.

Rorty, R. (1993). Human rights, rationality, and sentimentality. In S. Shute & S. Hurley (Eds.), *On human rights: The Oxford amnesty lectures 1993.* New York: Basic Books.

Singer, P. (1997). Famine, affluence, and morality. In H. LaFollette (Ed.), *Ethics in practice: An anthology.* Oxford: Blackwell.

Smith, A. (1759). *The theory of moral sentiments.* Retrieved September 12, 2011 from <http://www.econlib.org/library/Smith/smMS.html>.

Unger, P. (1996). *Living high and letting die: Our illusion of innocence.* Oxford: Oxford University Press.

8

History as Dharma

A Contemplative Practice Model for Teaching the Middle East and Africa

Elise G. Young

A thin sheet of water forms itself as ice over Sale Lake. Wind flirts with dry stalks of grass. Fire falls gently across our faces. Clouds become melting snow filling our vision. This dharmic mix lies like Indra's net over the mountain range. History melts in our shoes. I rise up through the soles of my fiery wet feet and take my place in the circle to journey with this contemplative exercise. Sarah starts with notes from Lama Tenpa's class. A question in the form of a duality is not the right question to be asking . . .

I awaken our Tibetan bell:

> The Sangha is invited to go back to our breathing so that our collective energy of mindfulness will bring us together as an organism, going as a river, with no more separation. Let the whole Sangha breathe as one body, chant as one body, listen as one body, and transcend the frontiers of a delusive self, liberating from the superiority complex, the inferiority complex, and the equality complex. (Hanh 2008)

This chapter presents an approach to teaching the Middle East and Africa that utilizes concepts from Buddhist and Yogic philosophical traditions. The model also draws from African and feminist epistemologies. Although they are separate, my pedagogical approach draws on significant overlaps between particular Buddhist, Yogic, African, and feminist "worldviews." I discuss two central and related aspects to this approach: contemplative praxis pedagogy and a contemplative practice historiographical model that I call "History as Dharma."[1] That is to say, concepts emerging from Buddhist and Yogic philosophical traditions and from African and feminist epistemologies not only inform instructional methodologies but also inform theories of history.

Pedagogy itself is informed by historiography. The historiography shapes the pedagogy. For example, rather than asking students to take "sides" and propose resolution of conflict within dualistic analytical models, contemplative pedagogy encourages teachers and students to experience themselves as historical actors on a path to liberation where liberation is freed from its dualistic confines (victor/victim), and instead, is defined as a path (praxis) to freedom from samsara (hindrances). Central to these processes is transformation of our understanding of history itself—what is called history.

"History as Dharma" is an attempt to return history to its roots in philosophical systems that consider the dyad mind/body as an insufficient and reductive way of describing human being in the world. Philosophical traditions emanating from the regions addressed in this course can open a path to freedom from suffering generated by fragmentation and attachment to dualistic typologies. I envision a model of history that illuminates the cellular, fluid, ever changing nature of history, freeing history from its confines in mechanistic historiographical models.

The specific course I use to discuss this approach is a core course, "Introduction to the Middle East, Africa, Asia." I introduce students of all disciplines to these regions through case studies. For the purposes of this article, I primarily draw examples from the Middle East and Africa. An important goal of the approach presented here is to prepare students, through transformative experience, for mindful decision making about the critical issues of our times.

Given limitations of space, I briefly discuss how this approach emerged and then summarize the theory and pedagogy, concluding with samples of poetic vignettes that bring together contemplative practice principles and feminist and African epistemologies, with content introduced in this course.[2]

Background

Writing history is a relatively recent and value-laden development (for example, the colonialist claim that Africa had no history until written by Europeans). Oral history is what history is at its roots, sung, chanted, and recited as poetry, as in the tradition of the African Griot or Arab women poets. In that context, history can be understood as a "practice" opening up the central channels of the body in order to "see" beyond conceptual mind. I saw a need for students to enter the domain of history as practice in order to move beyond dualistic frameworks of the fearful mind that "jumps" to conclusion.

One motivation for the approach presented here evolved out of the devastating impact on my nervous system of working in a war zone. Both in the classroom and in the field, I found myself increasingly shutting down. I felt unable to be present for a fresh re-reading of materials I was assigning my students. How could we engage with the litany of cruelty that humans create, endure, perpetrate, without becoming hopelessly discouraged?

Applying mindfulness to the question, the Four Noble Truths (the truth of suffering, its origins, its cessation, and the path leading out of suffering) effortlessly arose as the path. A nervous system that is fragmented and depleted, interacting with fragmentation and depletion in a war zone, whether that war zone is a physical space or mental/emotional space, begins healing itself by coming back to the breath. I realized that history itself could become, and had perhaps always been, a meditation practice. This realization arose spontaneously with the study of nonviolent movements in history and as I applied mindfulness to the study of war. Playing with the space between linear time and eternity was a journey we were already on—it needed only to be brought out of concealment and celebrated. The meaning of "Budh," Awakening, became the informing principle of the pedagogy of this course—including awakening to the guru (teacher) within.[3]

Increasingly in the context of public speaking, working with organizations, and in the classroom, I have noted how dualistic historiographies inform language and thus "views" of the critical issues of our times regarding the Middle East and Africa. Disillusionment and despair regarding resolving war might in fact be the result of "unseen" conceptual frameworks limiting our abilities to be in the moment with what is.

Historiography as Contemplative Praxis

Historiographical models are based in intellectual/spiritual traditions that shape what is called history. Thus, to begin, identification of historiographical models is approached as a mindfulness practice as students look deeply into cognitive frameworks in the context of which material is framed.

In this course, I inquire into three models or theories of history: modernization theory, feminist historiography, and History as Dharma. All three are "nested" within one another (to use Richard Freeman's term regarding Yoga practices and philosophies. See Freeman, 2010). As we reflect upon our world and on historical texts, we notice that all three models reverberate, are cellular, changing, moving, shifting.

Conventional theories of history and methods of conducting historical research are based on modernization theory—the notion, emerging in the context of colonialist ideologies justifying colonialism, that history proceeds along a linear path from something called "primitive" to something called "modern"—and thus on dualistic, oppositional models of power. When historical methodologies and narratives are dualistic and hierarchical, mimicking the suffering (klesha) in the mind, history is conceptualized in the context of winner and loser, victor and victim. In this context, the study of history can fuel identification with mind states that create suffering and close the heart. It becomes difficult to extricate from, and to see clearly into, the roots of cycles of suffering and violence leading to inner torment and concomitant planetary imbalance and crisis.

Conventional historiographical models (such as modernization theory) are informed by androcentric intellectual traditions that ignore, misrepresent, conceal, and congeal gender and race, and often class, central themes of historical endeavor. Feminist historiography contextualizes history using the categories of gender, race, and class, and at best, contextualizes those categories. Exploration of feminist historiography can begin with an awareness practice in the form of open questions—for example, what has been the impact of the concealment of women in history—as we discover ways feminist methodologies can impact our view of what we call history, and thus our "praxis" of history (as a study and an action in the world). Here students discover the merging (nesting) of what is called "personal," "sociological," "political," "collective." This consciousness raising process involves of course exploration and expansion of the term "feminism" itself, rooted as it is in historical, geographical, and intellectual traditions and contexts. While feminist historiography becomes a critique of modernization theory, and one revelation is reconceptualizing what disappears/appears within the framework of modernization theory, feminist historiography itself will at points fall into dualistic thinking. Awareness of this process itself becomes a focus of observation as we move ever more deeply into the spiraling gyre of historical inquiry.

Contemplative Pedagogy and Historiography

Feminisms, Yoga and contemplative practices, African epistemologies, and other oral history traditions, are forms of consciousness-raising. History emerges as "vibration," orally recited and passed down from generation to generation.

Thus, feminisms, Buddhisms, Yoga philosophies, and African epistemologies, can become vehicles of praxis, uniting opposite patterns within the nervous system (sun/moon), opening up the core of the body to experience its innate freedom.[4] *History becomes a cellular moving, breathing form/formlessness, paradoxical and "living" both within and outside of time.* The praxis of history and the praxis of Yoga merge. Listen to Yoga practitioner and philosopher, Richard Freeman (2010):

> Nadis (energetic channels running throughout the body) become blocked by our samskaras, our old abstractions, thoughts, feelings, and desires. The physical patterning associated with these experiences—our habit of observation, the tapes that keep playing themselves over and over again within our minds—cause imbalanced flow and obstructions within the nadis. These blockages or samskaras are patterns of separation and of fear that serve to deaden the connections between the body and mind, and which cause the mind to become dull. This is a root cause of suffering. The goal of the process of hatha yoga is simply to clean out whatever is impinging the currents of movement within the nadis so that we can get an even and complete flow of breath and energy throughout the entire body, this automatically awakening the natural intelligence that lies within. (p. 47)

In Sanskrit, "samskara" refers to an "impression" left by thoughts, actions, events. Yoga traditions describe samskaras as the "seeds" of past actions, a term also used by Zen Buddhist Thich Nhat Hanh. Samskaras are created in each moment, are inherited and collective. Hanh notes, that "Our society, country, and the whole universe are also manifestations of seeds in our collective consciousness" (Hanh, 1999, p. 39). He goes on to add: "The seeds that we receive from our ancestors, friends, and society are held in our consciousness, just as the earth holds the seeds that fall upon it (Hanh, 1999, p. 47).

"Personal" samskaras reverberate in and as "public" space: thus samskaras are historically rooted. As some feminist theorists note: the "personal" and sociopolitical reverberate as nested within one another. Further, samskaras manifest as habit energies that inform our interpretations, and "prevent us from seeing anything else. . . . Our habit energies keep us from being able to perceive the reality of the present moment" (Hanh, 1999, p. 50).

Historiographical models undergird our thinking, decision-making processes, relationships with other, but remain invisible. They become habit energies. If through our education system for example, we learn to think in types and in dualistic frameworks, and we learn to look for conclusions—or more accurately, to "solidify" as though solidification itself lives as a "dualism," apart from dissolution—this will become our "habit energy."

Yoga traditions, African epistemologies, and feminisms can become "medicines," pathways to healing, conduits for unblocking nadis and "patterns of separation and fear" that create suffering in our worlds/world. Similarly, History as Dharma is a reclaiming of history as a path of healing, as "medicine."

History as Koan

In this context History is also a koan. Thich Nhat Hanh describes a koan (Chinese *gong an*, Vietnamese *cong an*) as a meditation device or riddle, solved "not with the practice of intellect but with the practice of mindfulness, concentration and insight" (Hanh, 2010, p. 1). Hanh's profound response to the violent disbanding of the meditation center at Bat Nha Monastery in Vietnam, founded by Hanh in 2007, describes what I call History as Dharma in the language of Zen Buddhism. He notes that:

> The koan "Bat Nha" is everyone's koan; it is the koan of every individual and every community. The koan can be practiced by a Bat Nha monastic, by a monk or nun studying at a Buddhist Institute in Vietnam, a Venerable in the Buddhist Church of Vietnam, a police officer, a Head of Department, a Catholic Priest, a Protestant minister, a Politburo member, a Chairman of a city's People's Committee, a Provincial Party Secretary, a member of the Central Committee, a newspaper or magazine editor, an intellectual, an artist, a businessman, a teacher, a journalist, an abbot or abbess, an international political leader or ambassador. Bat Nha is an opportunity, because Bat Nha can help you see clearly what you couldn't—or didn't want—to see before. (Hanh, 2010, p. 9)

This is a sense of history as a practice of looking deeply, allowing its dharma to arise as the suffering (and joy) we all experience (and create). The momentary cessation of suffering through the experience of interconnection, that is, the experience of "particular"/"universal" as a vibrating dyad, is put in another way in Yoga philosophical traditions. In Yoga terms we could say that historiography is about the play of Purusa (pure consciousness) and Prakrti (creativity manifesting as form).[5] As history dissolves into historiography and in this process, another layer of history emerges for contemplation, and so forth, we "recognize that our own forms of perceptions are the gateway into the matrix that ultimately connects us to everything else" (Freeman, 2010, p. 13). *The goal of history becomes the disappearance of history and it is in this vibrational energetic play between the two (appearance/disappearance) that healing takes place.* History is itself a mindfulness practice, in which sensations, interpretations, judgments, come and go. If we read history as a koan we are free to notice and to ponder a range of mental formations as they arise, whether boredom, despair, frustration, excitement), without solidifying them, hence free to receive the dharma of impermanence, non-self, and inter-being, as the gateway to love, to receiving the world in all of its paradoxical complexity, hence as a gateway to healing.

The Contemplative Classroom

> Human experiences can exist within nature, because humans are a part of nature. Humans and the remainder of nature are connected to one another. It can be argued that humans cannot have a human experience without all of nature.
>
> —Jillian Thibault, student, Introduction to the Middle East, Africa, Asia

> My first thoughts while breathing and meditating were very critical and skeptical. I thought I had better things to do, like study, but soon I became very relaxed and realized this would be an excellent way to break up the day and help myself recharge my brain and physical energy if I ever feel run down. I am very excited for this class and am excited about this new tool I have just found for relaxing, enlightening, and energizing myself!
>
> —Amir Bagherzadeah, student, Introduction to the Middle East, Africa, Asia

> This contemplation was exactly what I needed at this point in my life. I have been extremely emotional as the semester comes to an end. . . . Sometimes I feel so drowned in my emotions that I feel like I'll never feel any other way. But as the contemplation stated, even something as simple as someone passing by and smiling can make those feelings temporarily vanish. When I'm around positive energies, I feel my spirit being lifted as well. It's hard to remember sometimes that emotions are never permanent. Now when I'm feeling any type of negative way I'll be sure to think of this contemplation.
>
> —Jasmine Franklin, student, Introduction to the Middle East, Africa, Asia

While I arrange chairs in a circle, I welcome my students, addressing them as a sangha (community of practitioners), a term that I explain at length on the syllabus and come back to often. I then begin with a standing yoga pose—tadasana or mountain pose. History, I note, lives in the body, begins with the breath. Simple yoga postures can be utilized creatively, along with meditation practices, to enlarge the students' sense of geography (in the context of discussion of colonialist aspects of geographic naming) and connection to the universe.

To encourage revisioning of history through, and as, contemplative praxis, I introduce aspects of Raja Yoga such as self-study (*kriya yoga*), wisdom, or discriminative insight (*jnana yoga)*, meditation (*dyana*), concentration (*dharana*), as "vehicles" for the following: how we approach text, engaging with unfamiliar material, students' preparation for class, and how we engage with one another in the classroom, in our communities, and around the globe.

As students become sensitized through comparative case studies, to suffering, to resistance, to liberation, they begin to "read" world historical events in new ways. Their frustration or sadness or hostility or joy is no longer experienced as separate from that of the "players" whose lives we are learning about. Nor is their daily life as separate, even as some become painfully aware of the "gaps" between their situations, and those of others, either in their classroom sangha or college in general (where we have a range of class, racial, ethnic backgrounds, nationalities, religious and spiritual practices, gender identifications) or in surrounding communities, or around the globe. Mindfulness practice in daily life, including when turning on a faucet and experiencing the flow of water under ones hands, leads to heightened sensitivity to dire consequences of historical processes of privatization of water and electricity for many, whether in the United States or South Africa. History and their lives begin to be read as templates laid one over the other with points of intersection/disjuncture illuminating what hovers or shimmers beneath both. In this sense history as dharma awakens the "knowledge" that healing one's "particular" suffering is healing the suffering of the world.

From that place of awareness, I hope to nurture a spirit of inquiry, or looking ever more deeply into history as the interlinking web of Indra's net[6] where each jewel casts light on every other and each "presents" as itself and as the whole. I hope to nurture a spirit of looking more deeply into our material and lives in the mode of mindfulness rather than judgment—for discoveries or revelations rather than "answers" or "conclusions" as a final resting place. In this process we might experience a loosening of the grip of attachment/aversion to *samsara* (the wheel of suffering), or to *santosa* (contentment). One aspect of this "loosening" is expressed again by Thich Nhat Hanh's (2010) "Bat Nah" Koan. He says:

> . . . If you are caught in a personal opinion, standpoint, or ideology, you do not have enough freedom to allow the koan's insight to break forth into your consciousness. . . . Buddhism demands freedom. Freedom of thought is the basic condition for progress. It is the true spirit of science. It is precisely in that space of freedom that the flower of wisdom can bloom. (p. 9)

Ontologically speaking, "students" and "teachers" both become our own gurus (teachers), free to live in an ongoing, unfolding phenomenological space in which observer and observed merge and where, as noted, the truths of impermanence, inter-being, non-self emerge as always "shimmering" behind and within history, freeing history to become itself in eschatology. Renowned Kabbalist and spiritual leader, Reb Zalman M. Schachter-Shalom, puts it this way:

> The problem is that ego has not been seen as permeable in the conventional view. As we have created an entire reality system based on the identity of self with "the bag of skin," we come to find out that we have leaky margins, that there is a flow going through us. Perhaps this permeability is not a fault but represents a healthy membrane that is designed to allow certain substances to pass selectively. (Schachter-Shalom, 1993, p. 19)

I explore another aspect of this "loosening" of the grip of attachment/aversion with students as we apply principles of history as dharma to text. For example, Middle East historian Leila Ahmed's (1993) *Early Islam and the Position of Women: The Problem of Interpretation* inquires into processes of interpretation and solidification of Koranic Suras over time. Ahmed's focus on process evokes history as a moving, living, breathing cellular form—and this is central to her research which examines views, periods, causes, and conditions of solidification and dissolution of views of women/gender during the early period of the rise of Islam. Her discussion of Ibn al'Arabi (1165–1240), Rabi'a al-Adawiyya and Sufism, and an early Islamic movement, the Qarmatis, all describing paths to freedom from the suffering of the "inequality complex," open our vision to ways those paths are being walked in our times. Our relationships with one another across nationalist and religious boundaries depend upon these kinds of distinctions and point to our responsibility and possible "calling" as historians moving within Indra's net.

The Journey: History as Dharma via Poetic Vignettes

Evoking history as cellular, as breathing, as "medicine," I introduce poetry, music, film, spoken word/chant, to encourage awakening of the central core of the body.

The following vignettes model what is called history in the light of dharma. On the level of content and of form, they are informed by contemplative, feminist, and African epistemologies. They teach by evoking a sense of timelessness, synchronicity, and inter-being. They play with the play of *cit* (pure consciousness), *manas* (mind as organizer), *budh* (to awaken), *ahamkara* (ego function, I-maker) and the *gunas* (underlying energetic structure of all things—*sattva* (balanced, sweet), *rajas* (active), *tamas* (fixed)) (Freeman, 2003). The vignettes are an edited version of vignettes that I wrote for a presentation on History as Dharma at Naropa University in the fall of 2010. The presentation was designed to be experiential. I invited participants with music and poetry to enter the space of contemplative practice, and to engage with and imbibe the spoken words rather than to "grasp" for knowledge with the conceptual mind. "Ringing of the Bell" below marks points at which I rang my Tibetan bell and came back to the Thich Nhat Hanh chant recited at the beginning of this essay, bringing us back to the breath.

I invite you, once again, to enter the contemplative pedagogy classroom ("Sangha" in this piece refers here to students in the classroom and to you as reader of this article) and to listen to this section as chant; to breath in the space between with the ringing of the bell; to write words, images that arise; to shape inquiries. Walk into the classroom and begin to move to the music. The song is "Me and You No Be Enemy," the first song of Lagbaja's (2001) CD, *We Before Me.*

Thank you for your participation!

Ringing of Bell

> Let the whole Sangha breathe as one body, chant as one body listen as one body and transcend the frontiers of a delusive self, liberating from the superiority complex, the inferiority complex, and the equality complex.

Lagbaja is one of the most popular musicians in Nigeria. His music alchemizes Highlife, Afro-beat, juju, Jazz, pop, funk, and hip hop. Lagbaga is known for the masks he wears—he never plays without one. The name Lagbaja is Yoruba, meaning "somebody/nobody; anybody/everybody." The mask and his name symbolize his desire to remain anonymous so that he can stand for the "common" people, the nameless and faceless.

Lagbaga's lyrics are about "waking up" to kleshas manifesting as societal ills. He calls for self study as a way of awakening to history in the moment. The container is waking up to one's true self, to "we before me" to "me and you no be enemy," as the true path of liberation.

Lagbaja is a storyteller historian whose social commentary in the form of poetry had the power to heal while it informed. This materialization and dissolution of history into vibration is the interplay I am attempting to illuminate in the classroom.

Lagbaja captures the vibrational play of modernization theory, feminist historiography, and History as Dharma in his music. His lyrics speak from the ground up with a playful and contextual "analysis" (and dissolution of) of race, class, gender, age, religion, and more. As these causes and conditions materialize, they dissolve into History as Dharma in the "We Before Me," in the power of music to awaken Nigerians/us to their/our true nature beyond nationalist and colonialist politics.

Ringing of Bell

> What then are the root causes and conditions of suffering in Nigeria as expressed in Lagbaja's lyrics? What, then, is the war behind all wars?

Ringing of Bell

> Dropping into the Body.
>
> The first time I visited Jericho . . . it was during the 1987 Intifada but it has a sense of timelessness about it when I re-member it now. I was with Salwa and others from the Union of Palestinian Medical Relief Committees. I have an image of myself driving past the prison that is now a military base—it was empty—and walking across a field and looking into a dry well. Earth, Air, Fire, Ether, Water. The history of privatization of water. Vata dosha[7] becomes dehydrated. Children have problems with their bowel movements. I lift my head and at that moment of time/timelessness I hear the call to prayer. Something so visceral as though sitting on my right shoulder (they say death) took me across the river of separation. The Guru Gita to bring in Geneshe who creates and removes obstacles.
>
> We drive on. Most Palestinians in Jericho are African. Migration patterns, intermarriage. Three families of African Jews were well known in this area. Ali Mazrui says: why separate Africa

from the Middle East? The tiny body of water called the Red Sea resulted from a rift under the ocean thousands of years ago. This is historiography. British military cartographers. The boundaries are constantly shifting changing cellular—and fixed. From mushi, communally held land under the Ottoman Empire, to signing a deed to show ownership. This is modernization theory. East vs. West? From whose perspective—where do you stand—right, left, middle, in between? An ever shifting kaleidoscope of historical symbiosis solidified? I explain to my students—take this as an inquiry, these type-castings. We analyze their associations with the terms "east," "west." For a moment we wake up.

I tell them don't worry—history is medicine. I tell them a story to rock them in this knowledge, about shared folk religion in Palestine, and how Muslims, Christians and Jews worshipped at the same shrines. Changing market conditions rendered this invisible.

I tell them about the ritual days during the spring season of Saint festivals that were specifically women's days—Thursday of the plants, when Bedouin women in Gaza went out into the fields in groups, gathering herbs and flowers with which to wash their hair, chanting "what medicine for the head, oh, plant"

I tell them about Touqi Williams murdered by the State in San Quentin when I was in Berkeley in 2006. I try to explain why the crowds outside the prison felt that the State made a terrible mistake. They want to argue capital punishment. We can do that. I don't think I clearly described what that night was like—how to express the terror, whether to join those waiting at the prison or stay in my warm bed listening to the radio, waiting for the governor to. . . .

I read them Thay's play, "The Path of Return Continues the Journey," and the idea that "They killed us because they truly did not know who we were." At this moment mindfulness becomes a matter of life and death. But you told us that there is no birth and there is no death.

The Sangha is invited to go back to our breathing so that our collective energy of mindfulness will bring us together as an organism, going as a river, with no more separation.

Ringing of Bell

Reb Tirzah, singing us to the floor for prostrations in an ancient ritual of absolution. Cantor Kandler bowing in the four directions.

It took him ten minutes to sing the first syllable of the O'Leinu. I entered the cavern of his throat and when he bent his head I lay my heart against the ground and wept with joy. I sang my history every Saturday morning in Shul. I was born in 1946. One of the first awarenesses I remember of my body is asking, "Whose soul is inhabiting me?"

Did I know what reincarnation was—did I even know the word? Could it have happened so fast? Does history exist within or outside of time? Are my students willing to live in this paradox for fourteen weeks?

Ringing of Bell

In 1971 I sold everything, left my apartment for the streets, went with my friends to the Army/Navy store to buy new clothes—it was a ritual. Three years later I'm in western Massachusetts in a room above Pierce's Art Store. We have a violin, a guitar and a flute. None of us are trained. She says—"I never heard you sing like that." It was the times. I was lucky. I hand my students a ney and an oud. They roll in the grass and drink in the medicine. I am finally happy.

Fifty years old and menopausal. The nurse at the clinic says "Nature is done with you but we are not," and hands me the bottle of pills. I throw them out. Chinese medicine says nature in her wisdom stops the flow of menses so that the blood can go to nourish the organs as they age. I take lachesis—snake venom—and the hot flashes stop. Go to a gym. Take a Yoga class. I couldn't sit cross legged on the mat—my knees ached when I got out of the car. I struggle through asana and lie in corpse pose. I ask the teacher—where can I do this? In Yoga the heat rises in the body through the crown of the head and I wake up. Santosha. I like Richard's word: "milk" the body in order to investigate its true nature and unite opposite patterns within the nervous system to open up the core of the body. I think exactly: why else study history? It's so clear.

My students and I are watching the film "Colonial Misunderstanding" by Jean Marie Teno.[8] German Missionaries support colonization of Namibians—the slaughter of the Hererro people in 1904. They rounded them up in the first concentration camps—words like forced labor, founders of Apartheid. Are we still breathing? We turn to one another so that our collective energy of mindfulness will brings us together as an organism, going as a river, with no more separation. Still, I'm not satisfied. We defend, we stumble out of the room, we turn away and go back to our separate cells. I can't find the river. They want to know the assignment. I put on my glasses, pick up the chalk and go to the board: identify modernization theory in the film, feminist historiography, History as Dharma. But I don't like the assignment—it's too mechanistic, it will take them out of the moment. Just ask them: what is the drash, the teaching?

Ringing of Bell

She was called Al Haji because she had done the Haj to the Kaba in Mecca so many times. I took out my tape recorder. The daya, Hajj Anisa Shokar. All the officials in Jordan revere her—they kiss her hand when they see her in the streets. In pre-Islamic times inside the Kaba there was a circle, a sacred space called the harim, that housed the three Goddesses, Al-lat, Al-Manat, Al-Uzza, worshipped by the indigenous peoples of the Arab world. By the time of the Ottomans the harim had become the harem of Orientalist literature, housing concubines of Sultans. But Leila Ahmad raises questions about this . . . her piece is called "Western ethnocentrism and perceptions of the harem." Hajj Anisa remembered the change over during the British Mandate from dayat, midwife healer, to nurses and doctors in white. My student screams out "Modernization theory!" I ask her to explain. She reads from her notes. History proceeds along a linear path from something called "'primitive" to something called "modern." Illustration: British health administrators take control of women and reproduction, borrowing from regulations in the U.S. that put African American Granny midwives out of business. They take control of women's knowledge making, turning oral traditions of Dayat into superstition.

Ringing of Bell

In July of 1967 five young men who were volunteer workers in "School of Youth for Social Service," helping to rebuild war torn villages were abducted and taken to the bank of the Saigon River and shot. Only one survived. Thay looks deeply into "peace," "justice," "equality." In his play, a Vietnamese Nun, Mai, who had immolated herself in service of bringing attention to the suffering of the Vietnamese people in their war torn land, picks up the young men in a small sampan and conversation ensues. Mai cites the Buddha's teachings on the interconnectedness (emptiness) of things and people. Tuan, one of the murdered youth, responds:

"I agree with you sister Mai, 'Youth for Social Service' is just a label that they pasted on the objects of their hatred and fear, an object that exists only in their perception. It has nothing to do with us as persons. They shot only at the object of their fear and hatred, but because they had pasted the label of this object on us, they ended up shooting us, and we died by mistake. They killed us because they truly did not know who we were" (Hanh, 1993, p. 30).

Put another way, History is the breath and the end of history is the stop at the top of the in breath and the bottom of the out breath—pure stillness, Peace. I beg them not to take sides. They nod their heads. Jump into the Abyss, as there is nowhere else to go, as you are already there.

Ringing of Bell

I write all night and hand them my essay the next morning. I think I"ll summarize. I want them all to get an "A." I'll let them decide. I shuffle through hundreds of documents late into the night and muddle through draft after draft. I begin here:

> . . . we can only view history through what the nature of the mind is. . . . the study of history can fuel tendencies in the mind that create suffering and close the heart. . . . if the question is "one" versus "the other," it is the wrong question to ask.

Then I remember Lebanese writer Etal Adnan. I rush to the phone to call Michel. I glance at the water color she gave me of Mt. Tam. I give them the title of her last book, "In the Heart of the Heart of Another Country" and I say ". . . write from your heart as the heart of the heart of another country." They beam at me . . . as one body going as a river. . . .

Ringing of Bell

The Sangha is invited to go back to our breathing so that our collective energy of mindfulness will bring us together as an organism, going as a river, with no more separation.

Acknowledgments

Special thanks and gratitude to Dr. Stuart Sigman and the Frederick P. Lenz Foundation Residential Fellowship for Buddhist Studies and American Culture and Values for a Fall, 2010 residency at Naropa University. Thanks to the brilliant faculty, staff, and students at Naropa University. Thanks to Westfield State University Administration for their cooperation. A very special thank you to Charles Scott. An exemplary editor, his insight, dedication, and patience are greatly appreciated.

Notes

1. Dharma: Universal teachings; the way; "suchness," the wisdom of the universe. A dictionary definition of historiography notes that it is not possible to separate a record of events from a theory of history governing human society, often looked at as "laws" of change regardless of human will. (Webster's Third New International Dictionary). History then is the event: historiography is the theory of history.

2. I present an in-depth exploration of History as Dharma in a book-length manuscript in process with the working title: "What is Called History? Contemplative Practice and Teaching the Middle East and Africa."

3. Sanskrit "gu" (darkness) and "ru" (light) refers to wisdom as interpenetration of dark/light.

4. See Freeman, R., 2010.

5. See Freeman, R., 2003.

6. A metaphor for the interconnectedness of all phenomena.

7. In Ayurveda, Vata dosha is associated with air/ether element. Governs movement/activity in the body.

8. Le Malentendu Colonial, produced and directed by Jean Marie Teno, 73 minutes, Cameroon, 2004, California Newsreel.

References

Ahmed, L. (1993). Early Islam and the position of women: The problem of interpretation. In N. R. Keddie & P. B. Baron (Eds.), *Women in Middle Eastern history: Shifting boundaries in sex and gender* (pp. 58–73). New Haven, CT: Yale University Press.

Freeman, R. (2003). *The yoga matrix: The body as a gateway to freedom.* [Compact Disc]. Louisville, CO: Sounds True, Inc.

Freeman, R. (2010). *The mirror of yoga: Awakening the intelligence of body and mind* (1st ed.). Boston: Shambhala.

Hanh, T. N. (1993). *Love in action: Writings on nonviolent social change.* Berkeley, CA: Parallax Press.

Hanh, T. N. (1999). *The heart of the Buddha's teachings: Transforming suffering into peace, joy, and liberation.* New York: Broadway Books.

Hanh, T. N. (2008). *Contemplations before chanting.* Thenac, FR: Order of Interbeing, Plum Village.

Lagbaja. (2001). *We before me.* [Compact Disc]. Philadelphia, PA: Indigedisc.

Maezumi, T. (2002). *Appreciate your life: The essence of Zen practice.* Boston: Shambhala.

Schachter-Shalomi, Z. M. (1993). *Gate to the heart: An evolving process.* Philadelphia, PA: ALEPH.

9

Paying Attention

Introspection as a Ground of Learning

Daniel Barbezat

Because people ordinarily have no need to describe their conscious experience, they do not pay attention to its subtle features.

—Cytowic, 2003, p. 160

I am interested in how students can draw upon their private, first-person experience to deepen their understanding of course material and learn more about themselves and their actions. I am especially interested in this last aspect of their learning: how does what they learn in class inform their deliberations and subsequent actions? Without an awareness of their own priors, students can behave in ways that do not support their well-being. I believe the best way to support students in this inquiry is to guide them through the process of looking within, to guide them through introspection. The sort of introspection I am talking about here is not the raw attempt at describing cognitive processes, *per se*; rather, it is the exploration of the higher-cognitive order of exploring the process of decision making.

We are all subject to errors like those outlined in Chugh and Bazerman's (2007) paper on "bounded awareness." In it, they describe the ways in which we suffer "focusing failures," where there is a "misalignment between the information needed for a good decision and the information included in awareness" (p. 2).[1] This sort of issue is something with which we are all probably familiar and is one that can cause significant mischief with our decision making. In this paper, I begin with an example from my course "Consumption and the Pursuit of Happiness," illustrating the importance of students taking explicit time to undercover the latent heuristics they employ to make decisions. However, this does not happen with ease—there is cost required to support and to pay attention. After a brief background and cautionary history, I describe the ways in which we can support and sustain our students through exercises of deep introspection.

Focusing Introspection: The Ultimatum Game

In order to show students the importance of awareness concerning their decision making, I use various exercises; some of them are rather open-ended while others are more tightly directed. One of the more elaborate, directed exercises has them focus on their results from the "ultimatum game." In this game, individuals in a group are randomly combined in pairs and one person in each pair is given a "stake," such as \$20, and asked to offer the other person some part of it. If the other person rejects the offer, then both parties receive nothing. If the other person accepts, then the money is split, as suggested. Commonly, offers of less than 20 percent of the total are rejected.[2] I was interested in how the game might illustrate to my students that their unawareness of the rules used in their decision making can have profound impacts on outcomes. I had my students (n = 45) imagine they were the person offering some part of \$10. I asked them how much they would offer under conditions where they were known and where they were anonymous. As in the literature, their offers were more generous when known. The average offer while being known was \$4.83 while the mean offer not known was \$3.91. The modal amount under both conditions was \$5.00. I then asked them what the minimum value that they would accept was. The average value for this was \$3.27 and the mode was, not surprisingly, \$5.00. One would imagine that their answers might differ significantly if the monetary stakes were much higher. Finally, I asked them to re-imagine the game, this time with \$1,000 instead of \$10. The average offer now was \$360.56, with a mode (of course!) of \$500; the average minimum value accepted was \$249.14 with a mode (you guessed it) of \$500.

Clearly, students are using a dominant heuristic of an even split of the money, no matter the sum. Interestingly, though, on average, students realize the implications of this rule require them to actually reject an offer of \$400—not an insubstantial sum for any college student—and hence the average offer is a somewhat lower percentage of the total of \$1,000 than of the \$10. What is most interesting, though, is that most students who would be willing to accept \$5.00 in the first case overwhelmingly now accept nothing under \$500! The contradiction in this seems glaring. Either the commitment to *fairness* is very high or the students are really simply applying the "the even split" heuristic without thinking about the real implication of having to reject a relatively large amount. After I reported these results to the class, I took some time to speak about the apparent inconsistency of being able to accept $5.00 and, at virtually the same time, not willing to accept any value under $500. I asked the students if they came to class and were being offered $100 would they really reject that, even if someone else was leaving the class with $400? Some students reported that they now saw the cost of applying the rule and reevaluated their previous decision. My impression was that students were able to understand the consequences of applying their underlying heuristic. However, I did not stop to allow the students to imagine the amounts considered and sit with their previous decision processes and actions in any sustained, deeply introspective way.[3]

Given that our attention seems to be limited, how do we learn what is salient with experience? By way of some path to an answer, let us realize that we cannot simply focus and process everything so we must choose on what to focus. Much of this is done under our overt awareness, carried out by what Damasio calls "core consciousness." Much of the time, this immediate and central programming is right on target—shaped by an evolutionary process that has selected for the most effective responses. However, as we all know, these immediate processes can also cause us to act in ways that do harm to ourselves and others. In order to support our own and other's well-being over the long-run, we must both become aware of our own processes and, essentially, what we value and want in life. Without both of these, we are destined to repeat the failures of our past actions and become lost in a sea of overwhelming current experience.

This is a paper about the first step in this process: supporting and sustaining introspection in the classroom in order to learn more about our behavior and provide essential self-awareness/knowledge for our students. Long ago held as the central modality of scientific psychology, introspection today is often thought of with skepticism or even contempt in Western cognitive science (although it is having a bit of a *renaissance*). Introspection has long been the mode of contemplative traditions; in Buddhism, for example, introspection is explicitly required even to establish or maintain mindfulness.[4] This paper is a guide to reestablishing methods of introspection in order to change the nature of the education we provide our students. I first outline the development of introspection in the West and the serious critiques that rose up to quell its developments. After that, I suggest ways that we can meet these challenges in order to support an education that provides our students with a deeper sense of understanding of the content of our courses and themselves.

Background

In contemplative traditions, introspection has been a major source of insight and ease, and it is beyond the realm of this essay to outline the ways in which the contemplative traditions of Buddhism, Judaism, Islam, and Christianity have fostered and developed introspection. However, in the modern, Western tradition of psychology and pedagogy, introspection once had a vibrant tradition.

At the turn of the nineteenth century, Pierre Maine de Biran recognized the benefit of what we could call introspection, and later in the nineteenth century, Brentano, Wilhelm Wundt, and William James all saw what James declared, namely that: "Introspective observation is what we have to rely on first and foremost and always" (1890, p. 185). There began a research program carried out both in Europe (in Paris under Binet, and in Germany by the "Wurtzburg School" headed by Külpe) and the United States (centered at Cornell University under Titchener). These research programs were based on the idea that first-person accounts provided rigorous, primary data on which the science of behavior and mind, *psychology*, could be developed. Common to all these approaches was the idea that the subjects had to be trained, both in the fineness of the awareness of their perception and its careful articulation by the researcher, or "mediator." These cautions were forgotten over time and the critiques of introspective research often do not undertake research with subjects with any training.

Very soon these research programs were attacked, initially by the French philosopher Auguste Comte in a classic, two-pronged assault: (1) that introspection, itself, was internally contradictory, and (2) even if we set aside this foundational issue, still introspection cannot generate reliable and consistent data. Comte believed it was ridiculous that the subject be asked to examine, at the same time, what was happening, from an objective viewpoint—it was as if the subject was asked to split himself into two parts.[5] However, even in the most modern, sophisticated fMRI studies, the only way to interpret the areas that are lighting up are through interviewing the subject in real time: in effect, asking the patient if s/he is happy when the left medial, prefrontal lobe is activated. The only way we know that "happiness" or feelings of well-being are happening is through interviewing the subject and asking him or her to report—without this, we only have an image of where blood flow is especially high. However, Comte's second, empirical objection has been more damning.

It was extended through the twentieth century and made especially powerful by studies in cognitive science showing that subjects are often unable to describe the conditions under which they made decisions. The classic description of this critique is Richard Nisbett and Timothy Wilson's (1977) "Telling More Than We Can Know: Verbal Reports on Mental Processes." This paper is still cited[6] as providing strong evidence that introspection has no place in research. They review a series of studies describing subjects who cannot describe the higher-order decision making that they are engaged in. Instead of describing internal operations, they claim that the subjects' reports are rather "based on *a priori* implicit causal theories, or judgments about the extent to which a particular stimulus is a plausible cause of a given response" (p. 231). This is very similar to what I seemed to be seeing in my students during the ultimatum game exercises. Subjects seemed unable to discern their interpretations and meta-cognitions from more direct descriptions about what they were directly experiencing.

A host of studies have been used to suggest that subjects cannot properly discern their mental operations and are even surprised to hear that they might have been influenced by the structure of the experiment or outright deny that it had any effect on them. It is not my intent to respond at length to this large and very interesting literature.[7] However, it is important to recognize the boundaries of introspective study and to focus on ways that provide the best means for discovery. While these studies provide a good sense of caution in our drawing conclusions from our students' reports, they do not mean that these reports are worthless. As Pierre Vermersch (1999) points out, "What is wrong about this line of reasoning is that it moves from the premise that there are facts which are inaccessible to consciousness to the conclusion that even what is accessible to consciousness is uninteresting or non-scientific, and this *a priori*, which is not only absurd but wholly unjustified" (p. 28). In fact, I would argue that as we witness our students being unconscious of their priors, we should not throw our hands up and say they are inherently incapable of self-knowledge, as Nisbett and Wilson seem to do. No; rather, we should address this directly and develop the means for them to begin to uncover their selves. Moreover, I believe we can do this. It requires establishing the prerequisites for deep and sustained introspection.

Classroom

In many ways, we provide the clear guidelines for what is salient in our classrooms. We construct syllabi, facilitate discussions and ask leading questions, focus on certain material in lectures and ask our students to solve problems and write papers on specific, carefully crafted prompts. We repeat material and clearly signal what we consider most important. Of course this process is flexible in many ways; it results in discussions and outcomes that we cannot (and would not want to!) fully predict. To whatever extent the classroom is a creative process, we are still essentially the ultimate architects of salience in our classes. This, in itself, is not a problem; however, we can go far beyond this: we can provide and support environments to allow our students also to integrate the material of the course through a process of introspection that both provides a new access to the material that we are providing and new avenues for self-discovery and personal growth. John Dewey (1938) recognized this and he notes that education should

> . . . assign equal rights to both factors in experience—objective and internal conditions. . . . The trouble with traditional education was not that it emphasized the external conditions that enter into the control of the experiences but that it paid so little attention to the internal factors. (p. 39)

Through introspection, the students themselves are intimately connected to their own internal salience through an increased ability to focus and a greater sense of what matters to them the manner in which we can support and guide them can increase their education far beyond the content of the courses. Had I guided the students through their ultimatum games with more time for introspection, I believe we would have seen a different outcome.[8] However, such a process does not simply happen by allowing the students to have some moments to reflect; it must be cultivated through a careful training process and supported by a teacher who has developed the skills of careful listening and an intimate knowledge of introspection.

For example, we find that Wilhelm Wundt and his students (like Titchener) had clear guidelines for both the subjects and the researchers using introspection. Titchener's description of the proper training of subjects is elaborately detailed in his four-volume, 1600-page lab manual![9] The studies required systematically training subjects to report subtly and carefully what they perceived. Vermersch (1999) states this as the first step toward refining introspection: he believes in order to practice deep introspection we "need to form 'observers,' to subject them to a long training until they had become reliable in regard to what they describe." In fact, it might be "necessary to count on the expertise of such subjects to the extent that they would be the only ones capable of gaining access to certain objects of research, for example, those of short duration or which require high levels of discrimination" (p. 35). Using this approach, one cannot simply randomly select students for a study or work closely with subjects who had no training in discerning the variety of their responses.

Titchener notes: "the average student, on entering the laboratory, is simply not competent to participate as an introspective observer . . ." (Schwitzgebel, 2004, p. 61). On the flip side, the mediator/teacher cannot simply adopt these techniques as one might use a PowerPoint display. Training and attention are also required to facilitate and guide students through any meaningful process of introspection. Our focus should be on both ourselves and our students as we prepare and introduce these techniques.

Our Students' Introspection

The first writing assignment I give to my First-Year Seminar at Amherst is to ask them to select an object and observe it for 15 minutes and then write about the object without any gross interpretation: just a direct, phenomenological account. The first iteration of the paper is filled with imputations, anthropomorphisms, and conjectures, often in the very first sentence. One student, writing about a "Gatorade" bottle actually reports turning on the television while looking at the bottle "to learn what is happening in the rest of the world!" Anticipating this sort of response from them, prior to their handing in their papers, I talked a bit about the distinction of description and interpretation and had them write on their essays where they might have slipped into judgment or lost simple description. Even with this direct prompting, none of them were able to indicate all the instances of the drift away from description. They were unable to remain with their experience of the object. Many reported how "boring" it was simply to write without any embellishment. In fact, after I had them repeat the exercise, their next version was usually filled with very short, simple sentences like, "The crayon is red." I could feel their constraint—very few examined deeply—if, for example, the color they were describing was uniform; if there were scratches and if so how long, how deep? They simply were not practiced in noting, even with clear instructions. They needed practice even with an assignment as stripped down as this one, never mind being asked to witness themselves observing and applying a rule during the ultimatum game.

Prior to examining their own experiences, such as realizing that they are applying a fixed rule ("split the money 50/50"), students need to have stabilized their concentration and attention to subtle detail. Without this clarity, the sort of immediate, subconscious application of priors that Nisbett and Wilson describe will occur, and the student will be simply surprised when confronted with the fact that she or he would have actually rejected $495 while having just said that $5 would be fine to accept. As B. Alan Wallace (1999) says, "just as unaided human vision was found to be an inadequate instrument for examining the moon, planets and stars, Buddhists regard the undisciplined mind as an unreliable instrument for examining mental objects, processes, and the nature of consciousness" (p. 176). How do we encourage this sort of stability that is the ground for any meaningful introspection?

The neurologist Richard Cytowic (2002a,b) has written about the use of first-person accounts and how they led him to new discoveries of the neuropsychology of synesthesia. His method is to recognize that "Part of the problem is that patients frequently *interpret* events instead of *reporting* them straightforwardly as one would wish ideally" (2003, p. 158). Just like our students, the patients were actually slipping into metaphor or interpretation. This requires the clinician, Cytowic continues, to listen carefully and help the patient return to description. It requires that the bias in the patients is discerned by the clinician so that the patient can begin to report without embellishment. This process both requires a "training of the subjects" (p. 159) and careful listening and responses from the clinician.

How do we train our students? We need to provide our students with ample opportunity to practice focusing attention. Essential to this sort of training are various forms of relatively simple concentration practice. Yet, these practices alone will not be enough: perhaps even more radically, I believe, as I will later discuss, we must support our students in examining what they value most deeply and begin to live in accordance with it. Concentration practice in the classroom and in homework must be supported more broadly in their lives. In order to help establish a firm base for our students to examine their inner lives, we must support them aligning with their values. This is central to the objective of our courses, not something tertiary, and is a radical but necessary reorientation of the academy.

In my classes, we do concentration meditations, and I assign the students short attentive assignments like the one I described above or "Sit for 5 minutes on each of the next four days. Focus on your breath or feet or hands, something physical and commit not to move (except for your breath) for 5 minutes." Students are amazed how difficult it is, and some students simply say that they could not begin to complete the assignment. After 1 minute, many reported that they felt so anxious that they HAD to move. Either they felt this sort of agitation, or they fell into torpor and fell asleep. Classic! This is what we speak into! Agitation and torpor! It is what we face when we ask them to slow down and stop: Stop and listen. At first, all they hear is the buzzing of their incredibly busy minds or they simply shut down and drift off. This should in no way surprise us. If we are to have them maintain a reflective and introspective stance, we must first allow students to experience their own minds and have them note the difference between their chosen attention and the thoughts and sensations that arise.

When the mind and body are wild or, conversely, are sluggish and sleepy, this is just the time to do some sort of concentration-type practice—whether it be mindfulness of the body, feelings, or even mental states. In the *Samadhi Sutta*, the Buddha is reported to have explained the development of alertness and concentration:[10]

> And what is the development of concentration that, when developed & pursued, leads to mindfulness & alertness? There is the case where feelings are known to the monk as they arise, known as they persist, known as they subside. Perceptions are known to him as they arise, known as they persist, known as they subside. Thoughts are known to him as they arise, known as they persist, known as they subside. This is the development of concentration that, when developed and pursued, leads to mindfulness and alertness.

Concentration is a skill that our students have developed in all sorts of areas but have not cultivated probably in considering themselves, especially in formal, higher education. (I cannot tell you how many students have asked whether they could use the pronoun "I" in essays!) Reminding them of their demonstrated ability to focus and concentrate can help when they are struggling with this new and often uncomfortable exercise of focusing attention on their own sensations and thoughts. Prior to opening a session of deep introspection, especially when asking the student to integrate complicated tasks or material, establishing stability first provides students with the needed grounding that concentration practices can supply. As the semester rolls on, the exercises can get increasingly challenging, so the student develops finer and finer skills.[11]

Beyond the sort of in-the-trenches practice of actual concentration practice, another way in which we can support stability of mind is through an inquiry and focus on our students' moral lives. Living an ethical life consistent with one's deepest values is the ground for a calm mind. This realization can be seen throughout time and throughout traditions. Although different in important ways, Aristotle's *Nicomachean Ethics* and in Seneca's *De Vita Beata* both name the contemplative life grounded in virtuous action as the path to tranquility and stable happiness. In St. Augustine's (1999) *Confessions*, he says, "And since I loved the peace which is in virtue, and hated the discord which is in vice, I distinguished between unity there is in virtue and the discord there is in vice." In Buddhism, *sila* (virtue) is the cornerstone on which the Noble Eightfold Path is built. Ajahn Chah (n.d.), Thai Forest Meditation master, said, "Virtue is the basis for a harmonious world in which people can live truly as humans and not as animals. Developing virtue is at the heart of our practice" (p. 169). Without living in line with our deepest values, our minds are agitated and restless. Without addressing our students' deepest convictions and supporting them in living in integrity with them, we cannot truly hope to guide them in stabilizing their attention and developing the skills required for introspection. We are merely skating on top of their impenetrable, rich experience—and so, incredibly, are they.

This is something that higher education has shied away from, but I believe we are called to it now.[12] Note: we do not have to teach specific virtues, particular moral codes. What is required, though, is to support a process by which our students, themselves, can quietly and deeply inquire as to their own deepest meaning, enabling them to discover the implications of their personal values on others both locally and globally. This is not easy, and it is no wonder that we have collectively turned away from it. Trusting ourselves not to force our own convictions on others is a bold and brave act. While we cannot help but demonstrate our own convictions all the time through our speaking and actions, we need to allow students the space to discover and nurture their own values. If we are to use these methods, it is time that we, too, make *virtue* the heart of our own practice with our students.

Teachers

> When it is said that the objective conditions are those which are within the power of the educator to regulate, it is meant, of course, that his ability to influence directly the experience of others and thereby the education they obtain places upon him the duty of determining that environment which will interact with the existing capacities and needs of those taught to create a worth-while experience.
>
> —Dewey, 1938, p. 44

In any venue in which we are to use introspection, the preparation and training of our students are essential. However, this preparation begins with us; as Dewey suggests above, our duty is also to attend to ourselves. In order to initiate these contemplative and introspective methods in our classes and guide our students through them, we need to prepare and practice. I believe we need to focus on three aspects of our own development: (1) be familiar with the practices and go through them ourselves, (2) become more aware of our own biases so that we can listen and guide openly, and (3) develop and practice an open language in order to guide our students while not dominating them. These are all the sorts of cautions that clinicians face when using introspection to gather data on the nature of cognition or in diagnoses of neurological maladies. Attention to these three areas will complement the work we do with our students and foster a more effective environment for our students (and ourselves, after all) to gain more from their introspection.

I believe it is obvious that we ourselves should practice in order that we can sustain our students' attention. Knowing the sorts of difficulties encountered and the manner in which we might suggest to respond cannot be gained in any other way. It is only through our own introspection that we can foster it in others! This is, indeed, one of the areas that we have to "suffer" through in order to be able to provide for our students. As Pierre Vermersch (1999) states in his "Introspection as Practice": "To get a better idea of introspection one certainly has to practice it (which seems to have escaped the attention of numerous commentators)" (p. 33). Neurologist Richard Cytowic comes to the same conclusion in his essay on the appropriate use of first-person accounts for neurological assessments. Our own first-person accounts allow us to both understand the sorts of things are students are telling us, but equally as important, allow us to see our own biases as we confront our students.

Working with our own priors and judgments is required before we can expect to support our students in discerning theirs. I believe that this can be done through an intention and commitment of exploration. Of course, this sort of inquiry follows rather naturally from the introspection and concentration practices that we engage in to support our work, but it might not flower if the will is not directed toward it. Perhaps a place to start here is to contemplate the ways in which our preconceptions and subterranean judgments harm ourselves and our students.

In this regard, the way in which we talk with our students during these processes is incredibly important. Richard Cytowic (2003) describes his interviews with patients experiencing rather extreme synesthesia. He recounts one interaction with a patient who associated tastes with tactile experiences. After the patient had tasted spearmint, Cytowic began with the question "What is it like?" The patient responded, "Like cool glass columns." Was the patient being poetic or was he actually having a sensory experience like the one we might have touching "cool glass columns"? Cytowic pursued this by asking the subject to describe the exact sensations he actually felt rather than the broad question, "What was it like?" In the rather elaborate description that followed, Cytowic realized that the tactile qualities seemed very clear, and, in fact, found that they were stabile over time, leading him to a very different conception of this neurological condition (p. 161). Although this example seems rather simple, this sort of careful directed but not leading language can be difficult to develop. In my First-Year Seminar here at Amherst, a student wrote in his direct description that the football he was observing was "slippery." I asked him how he knew it was slippery. At first the question puzzled him. He said, "I don't know; it *felt* slippery." Question from me: "Ah, what was your experience of "slippery?" Response from him: "My hand moved quickly across the surface and I felt no bumps." Suddenly, he had shifted his perception from the gross assertion of the world outside to what he actually had access to. This sort of interaction is subtle and delicate. Vermersch (1999) cautions, "It can be done by oneself but not without a long apprenticeship and training" (p. 22). This area of guiding language should be further explored. It is an essential component of this type of work and not fully appreciated. Perhaps we could learn quite a bit from various forms of the language used in cognitive therapies; speech that draws out and guides, in a manner of speaking, but does not lead and determine outcomes. This, of course, is of great concern when using first-person-type data.

Conclusion

I started this paper with a curiosity about how we choose to focus, about how we survey and so quickly determine what is salient. This is an essential to problem solving and making choices. I was very curious about my students' responses to the ultimatum games we played. Even though we went over the results and repeated the games, the students did not seem to internalize the lessons, as if their meta-cognition of the results simply didn't sink in. In order for the lessons to be integrated into their decision making, they needed first to become aware of what they were actually doing during the process. This awareness, though, does not simply happen. In order to establish this sort of deep inquiry in our classrooms we have to begin to train our students in stabilizing and concentrating their minds. In addition, we can solidly ground this practice by guiding our students in discerning and living in line with their deepest beliefs. This moral integrity supports a calmer and more tranquil mind, necessary for the kind of work we do. Beyond this, we must also attend to our own lives through dedicated practice, attention to our own priors and the use of subtle listening and speaking. I believe that foundationally we and our students have to become mindful of our internal processes if we are to have any hope of acting in alignment with what supports our well-being. I hope that this inquiry into the conditions that support introspection has provided the means for improving our methods and giving our students the opportunity to live more meaningful and happier lives.

Notes

1. Note that this is not describing the sorts of results found from "change blindness" exercises. The issue specifically that I am interested in here is salient information that is not attended to—not any piece of information regardless of how germane.

2. There seems to be a real "taste" for fairness (thought of as a more even split) on the part of both the receivers and those making the offers. In a study by Kahneman, Knetsch, and Thaler (1986), students were given $20 and asked to choose between two binding (the offers could not be rejected) offers $18 for themselves and $2 for their anonymous partner or $10 for each. They found that 76 percent of the students chose the second offer.

3. I can hardly wait to repeat the exercises—this time allowing for this sort of sustained introspection!

4. For a detailed summary of traditional Buddhist texts on this, see Wallace (1998, 1999).

5. It is especially interesting that Comte took this position of the impossibility of the mind doing two things at once from the phrenology position that the brain had distinct centers whose operation was distinct and separate from others in the brain.

6. In Morten Overgaard's (2006) editorial on introspection for the journal of *Consciousness and Cognition*, he refers to the paper as having been still an "undisputed argument against introspection" (p. 631).

7. Even more sophisticated critiques, e.g., Habermas's "myth of the given," and the myth representation question the notion that students' thinking can be separated from public discourse and the justification of belief. See, for example, J. Habermas (1984) *The Theory of Communicative Action: Volume One, Reason and the Rationalization Society*. On the other hand, sophisticated scientific views have been explored by researchers such as Francisco Varela and others. See, for example, F. Varela, E. Thompson, and E. Rosch (1991), *The Embodied Mind*.

8. I do plan, of course, to rerun the games; this time, though, with an extended introspective exercise, allowing them to imagine receiving the money and allowing them to explore their application of the 50/50 rule.

9. For an examination of this manual (which had detailed parts for both subjects and instructors), see Eric Schwitzgebel (2004).

10. Taken from the translation by Thanissaro Bhikkhu, from <http://www.accesstoinsight.org/tipitaka/an/an04/an04.041.than.html>.

11. Taken from the translation by Thanissaro Bhikkhu, from <http://www.accesstoinsight.org/tipitaka/an/an04/an04.041.than.html>.

12. I am, of course, not alone in this observation. See, for example, Anthony Kronman's (2007) *Education's End: Why Our Colleges and Universities Have Given Up*

on the Meaning of Life or Harry Lewis' (2006) *Excellence Without a Soul: How a Great University Forgot Education.*

References

Chah, Ajahn. (n.d.). Virtue. *No Ajahn Chah: Reflections.* Retrieved from <http://www.wat-lao.org/PDFs/Bibliothek/Ajahn%20Chah/Ajahn%20Chah%20-%20No%20Ajahn.pdf>.

Cytowic, R. (2002a). *Synethesia: A union of the senses.* Cambridge, MA: MIT Press.

Cytowic, R. (2002b). Touching tastes, seeing smells—and shaking up brain science. *Cerebrum, 4,* 7–26.

Cytowic, R. E. (2003). The clinician's paradox: Believing those you must not trust. *Journal of Consciousness Studies, 10*(9–10), 160–170.

Dewey, J. (1938). Experience and education. New York: The Macmillan Co.

Dolly Chugh, D., & Bazerman, M. (2007). Bounded awareness: What you fail to see can hurt you. *Mind & Society: Cognitive Studies in Economics and Social Sciences, 6*(1), 1–18.

Kahneman, D., Knetsch, J. L., & Thaler, R. (1986). Fairness and the assumptions of economics. *Journal of Business, 59*(4): S285–300.

Kronman, A. (2007). *Education's end: Why our colleges and universities have given up on the meaning of life.* New Haven, CT: Yale University Press.

Lewis, H. (2006). *Excellence without a soul: How a great university forgot education.* Cambridge, MA: Perseus Books.

Nisbett, R., & Wilson, T. (1977). Telling more than we can know: Verbal reports on mental processes. *Psychological Review, 84*(3), 231–259.

Overgaard, M. (2006). Introspection in Science. *Consciousness and Cognition, 15,* 629–633.

Schwitzgebel, E. (2004). Introspective training apprehensively defended: Reflections on Titchener's lab manual. *Journal of Consciousness Studies, 11*(7–8), 58–76.

St. Augustine. (1999). *Confessions,* chapter XV, section 24. Retrieved from <http://www.fordham.edu/halsall/basis/confessions-bod.html>.

Titchener, E. B. (1905). *Experimental psychology: A manual of laboratory practice.* New York: Macmillan Co.

Vermersch, P. (1999). Introspection as practice. *Journal of Consciousness Studies, 6*(2–3), 17–42.

Wallace, B. A. (1999). *The bridge of quiescence: Experiencing Tibetan Buddhist meditation.* Peru, IL: Carus Publishing.

Wallace, B. A. (1999). The Buddhist tradition of samatha: Methods for refining and examining consciousness. *Journal of Consciousness Studies, 6*(2–3), 175–187.

10

Integrating Mindfulness Theory and Practice at Lesley University

Nancy W. Waring

The idea to develop an academic course in mindfulness began to solidify in the fall of 2003. That fall, I had the good fortune be among 1,200 attendees at the Mind and Life Institute meeting at MIT—an unprecedented public discourse on meditation and the human mind, featuring the Dalai Lama, Buddhist scholars and monastic practitioners, and Western neuroscientists.

At that time, the reach, track record, and promise of mindfulness meditation were already phenomenal. Thousands of medical patients with chronic pain and other debilitating conditions had completed Jon Kabat-Zinn's Mindfulness-Based Stress Reduction Program (MBSR) at the Center for Mindfulness in Medicine, Health Care, and Society (CFM) at the University of Massachusetts (UMass) Medical Center, experiencing for themselves the truth of Kabat Zinn's counsel—that they had the inner resources to respond to their situations adaptively, in ways that support healing and well-being (Waring, 2000, p. 19). Additional thousands had learned mindfulness at like-minded programs around the country and the world, many of them directed by graduates of the CFM's professional training program in MBSR.

Twenty-five years of research on MBSR had shown remarkable results—reduced stress, anxiety and panic, and symptom reduction across many conditions. One study even startled Kabat-Zinn: psoriasis patients who received meditation instructions piped into the light booths where they were receiving ultraviolet treatment experienced a skin clearing rate four times faster than that of control group undergoing the same treatment, but without meditation instructions (Kabat-Zinn et al., 1998, p. 625).

Mindfulness had begun taking root in settings other than health care. A forward-thinking law professor, Leonard Riskin, began teaching mindfulness to students in his dispute resolution classes. As a meditator, Riskin had experienced for himself the benefits of awareness of his own body and mental processes while he was engaged in delicate and stressful negotiations between opposing parties. Mindfulness reduced both his reactivity to the clients' behaviors and his self-questioning about his mediating skills, enabling him to focus sharply on the matter at hand. MBSR was being called for in corporate settings. Trained MBSR instructors were even allowed into several prisons to teach mindfulness to incarcerated men and women. A handful of psychotherapists were beginning to integrate mindfulness into their practices. Some K-12 teachers were introducing mindfulness exercises in their classrooms. The Center for Contemplative Mind in Society, with support from the American Council for a Learned Society, began offering fellowships for college professors across disciplines to develop courses that included contemplative elements.

Prior to the Mind and Life Symposium, I had considered the idea of developing a course in which mindfulness itself was the subject. Surely the principles and practices of MBSR could be integrated into an academic course that combined regular mindfulness meditation practice with rigorous academic inquiry into key findings from 25 years of research on meditation. As a professor at Lesley University in the graduate Division of Interdisciplinary Inquiry, I was well positioned to introduce such a course. The course was in keeping with Lesley's commitment to experiential education, in conjunction with critical thinking and analysis; my division is known for being hospitable to novel pedagogies.

The Mind and Life Symposium fed my enthusiasm. I was rapt as I listened to Dr. Richard Davidson describe an experiment that showed meditation-related changes in the brains of advanced practitioners. While Buddhist monks practiced compassion meditation in his Wisconsin laboratory, Davidson and his colleagues witnessed the highest frequency ever recorded in a brain rhythm called gamma oscillation, as measured by EEG. The high gamma oscillation remained even when the monks were not formally practicing. The monks, through extensive meditation practice (10,000 hours or more), had actually changed their brains. Notably, even the novice meditators in the control group showed a slight increase in gamma activity, suggesting that even short practice may effect changes in brain activity and lead to increased compassion.

What a compelling demonstration of neuroplasticity to share with students. Surely such a finding, and subsequent discoveries from the fledgling field of contemplative neuroscience, could continuously vitalize a course on the theory and practice of mindfulness meditation. The following account sets forth the pedagogical ideas underlying this now well-established course, seeks to represent students' experiences, and provides a window into the classroom.

The paper concludes with a glance at the further evolution of Mindfulness Studies at Lesley, in the form of a new, four-course Certificate Program currently offered to both graduate students and undergraduates.

Raisin Redux

A dozen Lesley University students sit in a circle, each rolling a single raisin between their thumbs and forefingers. Opening their hands, they watch intently as the raisin slides into their palms. Invited to scrutinize the raisin, they observe that it is squishy, dented, mottled, puckered. Everyone's raisin appears to have a navel. This observation prompts speculation about the raisin's life history, its journey from seedling to us, here in Cambridge, Massachusetts. Where might be the farmer who planted a seed akin to what we hold in our hands? What of the transformation from grape to raisin? Who picked it, packed it, sent it on its way? How did it end up in the dried fruit section of a Whole Foods store in Cambridge? We smell our raisins. We hold them to our ears and listen, as if to a conch shell. Can we hear the raisin? Next, we bring our raisins to our lips, noticing salivation. We focus on the sensation of the raisin as we roll it around on our tongues, the burst of sweetness as we bite into it. We chew slowly, and swallow attentively. I ask the group to ponder what it feels like to be one raisin heavier.

In the Lesley University course on the theory and practice of mindfulness, as in the Stress Reduction Program at UMass Medical School, the systematic approach to cultivating awareness begins with a raisin. This exercise well-known MBSR exercise has staying power for good reason. When new practitioners fully immerse themselves in an activity as seemingly inconsequential as eating a raisin, they begin to recognize that they are often on autopilot for more significant experiences. They see with new eyes that being fully present for whatever is unfolding has the potential to deeply enrich their lives.

Students: A Mixed Demographic

The students, like the raisins they contemplate, are a diverse bunch, including undergraduate and graduate students. Among them have been undergraduates and graduates from the University's Expressive Therapy programs, students in the Master of Fine Arts Creative Writing program, art therapy majors, psychology undergraduates, and Masters-level students in the University's professional training program in Counseling and Psychology. Others have come from the undergraduate and graduate schools of education. Several are in the Adult Baccalaureate Program—a BA program for nontraditional-age students returning to school. Since the start of the course, students have ranged in age from 18 to 57, the youngest a freshman with no declared major; the oldest a clinical social worker enrolled in Lesley's Self-Designed Master's Degree Program focusing her work on mindfulness studies.

The varied student demographic parallels the medically heterogeneous environment of the Stress Reduction Clinic. In the MBSR Program, there is no separation by diagnosis—no special groups for patients with AIDs, breast cancer, chronic pain, and other conditions. As Kabat-Zinn (1996) points out, patients' commonalities, rather than their specific diseases, help orient the group toward the shared capacity for learning, growing, and healing, versus curing a particular condition, for which a cure is usually beyond reasonable hope. Patients in the MBSR program report benefits from participating in heterogeneous groups, as they discover that membership in a community of people who have different problems enhances their perspectives, decreases their sense of isolation with their particular issues, and opens up a sense of possibility (p. 161).

So it is in the Lesley mindfulness course. In many of the students' academic courses, their classmates are likely to be around the same age and on a similar academic track. In our mindfulness course, the undergraduate endeavoring to practice mindfulness during the school day and at her evening waitressing job learns alongside the MFA student who is drawing on her mindfulness practice in her manuscript revision work, learns alongside the undergraduate art therapy student undergoing "mindful" chemotherapy for non-Hodgkins lymphoma. They are all investigating mindfulness's applications in, and implications for, their academic lives and professional practice disciplines. In their end-of-semester course evaluations, many students comment on the benefit they gain from learning with people from other age groups and working in fields different from their own.

To my knowledge, most of the students in my class are not living with the stress of serious or life-limiting illness, although one student who survived a serious spinal cord injury uses a wheelchair; and the student mentioned above was living with non-Hodgkins lymphoma when she took the course. That said, they all share a common condition: they are students, dealing with the stresses endemic to student-hood. Along with the challenges and satisfactions of learning, they are coping with performance anxiety, identity formation, career-related stress. Some are adapting to living away from home for the first time. Many of the traditional age students have jobs. The graduate students and adult learners are often balancing school, career, and family life. Our class provides an equal opportunity for all to bring mindfulness to their experiences in their academic and/or professional lives.

A Window into the Classroom

In our "go-around" in the first class, students inevitably report that they want to learn how to reduce their stress levels; they want to feel better, sleep better, and be more in control of their lives. I am always struck by how many self-identify as anxious, or depressed; some disclose that they hope that meditation will enable them to get off anti-depressants or anti-anxiety medications. (Although I welcome this information, I make sure to point out that while aspects of the course may be therapeutic, the course is not therapy, and the class is not a setting for working through personal psychological issues.) They are heartened when I report on a 1992 study from the Stress Reduction Program showing that patients who completed the program experienced less anxiety and panic (Kabat-Zinn et al., p. 936), and that they continued to feel better at follow-up three months later (p. 943).

After the go-around which reveals a dozen bright, motivated, stressed-out students, we move into the raisin exercise. (While the class is capped at 15 to foster group intimacy, the new focus on Mindfulness Studies at Lesley discussed below may lead to enlarging the class 20 to 25 students, as in the Stress Reduction Program. I would be curious to learn if as strong a sense of Sangha would emerge with a larger group.) Next, we lie on our mats on the floor, sending our mind's eye to different regions of our bodies, from the tips of our toes up to the tops of our heads, maintaining awareness of sensations during the entire process. The Body Scan is an invitation for students to experience their bodies directly and without judgment. Paradoxically, while students in Western culture are conditioned to be preoccupied with body image, many report that they are unaware of their bodily sensations much of the time. The Body Scan is an opportunity for the students to fully inhabit their bodies and befriend them, as they experience the body's potential, in concert with the mind, to bring about relaxed attentiveness.

As in the Stress Reduction Program, homework is to do the Body Scan five times a week, with guidance from the half-hour-long CD that I have recorded for them—and, following up on the raisin exercise, to eat one meal mindfully. Plus, they are assigned Part I of Jon Kabat Zinn's *Coming to Our Senses: Healing Ourselves and the World Through Mindfulness* (2005), a robust, 100-page introduction to mindfulness. The workload is demanding, and not just in terms of time spent reading or on the cushion. Mindfulness, as Kabat-Zinn notes, "is not for the faint-hearted" (p. 42). As all serious meditators know, it takes lion-hearted courage to commit to full awareness and non-judgmental acceptance of each present moment, no matter how painful or frightening or unwanted. To make such a commitment, students need to experience for themselves the central Buddhist tenet that clinging to pleasant experiences and pushing away unpleasant ones leads to suffering, while accepting things as they are leads to reduced suffering and equanimity. I like to quote the Theravadan teacher Achaan Chah's formulation and invite students to consider its high-bar third formulation: "If you let go a little, you will have a little peace. If you let go a lot, you will have a lot of peace. If you let go completely, you will have complete peace and freedom" (p. 73).

In this era of online learning, the students have the opportunity to share their responses to the homework on our Virtual Blackboard. I have become a big fan of Blackboard. That said, I have misgivings about fully online courses. The online classroom simply can't provide the depth of connection possible in a face-to-face learning environment. But Blackboard does a wonderful job of keeping our learning community connected during the week between classes. Students love sharing their postings on Blackboard and usually far exceed the weekly requirements of one brief posting on their home practice, and one response to someone else's posting. Here follows a typical Blackboard exchange in response to the mindful eating assignment:

> I used a small sugar-serving spoon, so I could take tiny bites. Yogurt, raisins, cranberries, crunchy stuff . . . the taste explodes in my mouth. The textures are very different: between the squishy yogurt, the ribs of the raisins and cranberries and the crunchy cereal. I swirl stuff around until I'm compelled to chew, which I do ever so slowly. . . . I try tiny bites trying to take a little yogurt and maybe just one raisin, or just one cranberry, or just one crunchy thing. Then I take one bite of each all together, still onto the tiny spoon. I continue to switch things around until the last bite. I notice I'm quite satisfied, so I decide not to eat the toast with peanut butter and honey like I usually do at breakfast.

Another student's response:

> I took a very different approach, going to the campus cafeteria, sitting apart from, but near a bunch of people and allowing the experience to be whatever it was. After reading your response, I want to get a sushi picnic and bring it to a park in Arlington. It's such a serene place for me.

From class two onward, the first 45 minutes of each two-and-a-half-hour class are devoted to practice and practice discussion—of the Body Scan, sitting meditation, and mindful yoga. When sitting, students do their best to follow one breath at a time, noticing when and where their minds wander, and returning to the breath, over and over again. These practice sessions routinely precede our discussions of assigned readings. When I designed the course, I decided to fold the practice sessions into the classes, rather than having a separate "meditation lab." If meditation practice induces a mind state that is both tranquil and alert, wouldn't half an hour of practice poise students for optimal engagement in theoretical discussions and analysis of the readings? The students' intense focus throughout class convinces me that practice first, academic content second, is indeed the optimal order of events.

We read all 609 pages of Kabat-Zinn's (2005) *Coming to Our Senses*, a hearty smorgasbord of philosophy, exposition, critical thinking, political commentary, poetry, and personal narrative. True to its title, the book zeroes in on the capacity of mindfulness for individual and global healing: "Imagine a politics grounded in mindfulness," writes Kabat-Zinn. Invoking the ancient wisdom of Lao Tzu from the fifth century, he continues, "Imagine a governing mindset and democratic process that knows and honors that the universe is forever out of control and that trying to dominate events goes against the current of the Tao" (p. 529). *Coming to Our Senses* is also replete with research from the Stress Reduction Program on the efficacy of mindfulness. Also considered in some detail are more recent findings on neuroplasticity, the brain's capacity to change through experience—beneficially so—through mindfulness. *Coming to Our Senses* couples the rigor of a traditional text with an acute sense of audience. It is graciously addressed to the reader and amplified by first-person accounts from Kabat-Zinn's mindful travels, with which readers can often readily identify.

Folded in between parts of *Coming to Our Senses,* and before immersing ourselves in Dan Siegel's (2008) *Mindsight: The New Science of Personal Transformation*, we study what is going on in our brains and the rest of our bodies when we are in the throes of stress and anxiety. Invariably, students are excited to peer inside their physiological and biochemical selves. By the end of our foray into our brains, everyone knows that the amygdala, the almond-shaped structure deep within, is our fear detector. They know that the horseshoe-shaped hippocampus is critical for memory and learning, and that its power is diminished by stress. They also understand that the hypothalamic-pituitary-adrenal axis enables us to respond quickly in the face of danger, but that this system is often activated needlessly by our often misguided catastrophizing thinking. They know that the adrenal glands sit atop the kidneys and make cortisol, and that too much of this stress hormone dysregulates the body in numerous ways, including compromising our immune systems. Importantly, they are pleased to learn that their prefrontal cortexes have the ability to deactivate the cycle of stress reactivity and calm the hippocampus, in the service of learning, memory, and new associations. As Daniel Goleman (2006) succinctly explains, "Stress handicaps our abilities for learning, for holding information in working memory, for reacting flexibly, and creatively, for focusing attention at will, and for planning and organizing effectively" (p. 268).

I couple the presentation of this material with Kabat-Zinn's aforementioned study of the effectiveness MBRS in treating anxiety disorders, and a more recent anxiety study. This second study, which students find especially fascinating, makes use of functional MRI and shows that the MRI-visualized amydalas of meditators have less gray matter density after only eight weeks of practice (Holzel et al., 2009). The meditators in the study also reported experiencing significantly reduced stress. Armed with this knowledge, the students realize that they have the power to reduce their own stress reactivity. They also have a window into the remarkable advances in scientific research on mindfulness over the last 20 years.

Reflective Asides

It is indeed serendipitous that mindfulness, based on the 2,600-year-old Buddhist wisdom tradition, has become a subject of scientific study. The conversation between mindfulness and science naturally invites mindfulness practitioners into the realm of science, where many of us non-scientists have previously feared to tread. I majored in English in college and met my science requirement with a course affectionately known as "Biology for Poets." That was the end of my formal science education. I went on to get a PhD in English. When I was in my thirties and got serious about sitting down and looking into my own mind, I wanted to know more about the mind and the brain. I have mindfulness to thank not only for bringing balance and sanity to my life, but also for making me somewhat mind/brain-literate.

Mindfulness is rooted in our deepest humanity. We are—to use Kabat-Zinn's formulation—*Homo sapiens sapies*: creatures who know, and who know that we know. We have a remarkable capacity to cultivate inner knowing and self-attunement, from which attunement with others naturally flows. How marvelous that mindfulness is becoming increasingly recognized and respected as a fledgling academic discipline. How important that mindfulness is creating a much-needed bridge between the humanities and the sciences. Until recently, I could not have imagined that I would be teaching a mindfulness course in which students of literature or art therapy would be enthusiastically applying their minds to scientific papers on subjects such as amygdala activity in meditators versus non-meditators, as measured by functional MRI. And, that their subjective experience of mindfulness practice, along with their new knowledge of the science revealing the mind's capacity for changing the brain for the better, would together doubly motivate students to practice.

Back to the Classroom: The All-Day

Students' academic learning and practice readies them for the all-day of practice that soon follows. That said, many find the idea of spending a day in silent practice unimaginable and anxiety-provoking. Yet for most, the All-Day is a turning point in the course. The majority of students report being gratified, proud, and grateful at the end of a day of sitting, walking, yoga, and Metta (loving kindness meditation, which students first practice at the All-Day). Many are surprised to discover feeling refreshed by a day of silence. They emerge with a deepened sense of connection with their peers. Most have more faith in the value of practice, as a way of keeping a non-judgmental eye on their minds' activities without judging themselves—and more faith that wisdom may arise through self-knowing awareness.

Some students find themselves drawn to Metta, and take it on as a regular practice after the All-Day. They are pleased to have learned a formal practice that is aligned with their expanding experience of empathy. One student comes to mind, whose father was in the hospital dying of a brain tumor. The student had a life-long difficult relationship with her father, because he was addicted to heroin, negligent of his family at best, and often seriously self- and other-destructive. After the All-Day, this student reported that she had begun regularly sitting with her father at his hospital bedside, and sending Metta both to herself and to him. She could feel pure love and compassion for him, untinged by their complex history.

The Science of Personal Transformation

Soon after the All-Day, we turn our attention to Dan Siegel's (2008) *Mindsight: The New Science of Personal Transformation*. The telephoto focus of Siegel's book is a complement to the wide-angle lens perspective of Kabat-Zinn's *Coming to Our Senses*. Siegel offers readers an overview of the triune brain—the brain stem, or reptilian brain, the limbic system, and the cortex. Then he zeros in on the middle prefrontal cortex, the profoundly integrating region that makes connections with the entire brain. Siegel is a master of personal narrative. He gives students a window into therapy sessions with his patients in which he empowers them by teaching them about neuroplasticity—the brain's capacity for change through experience. One account describes Jonathan, a young man who is bipolar. Siegel hypothesized that mindfulness practice "would help the parts of [Jonathan's] brain that regulate mood to grow and strengthen, stabilizing his mind and enabling him to achieve emotional equilibrium and resilience" (p. 86). Jonathan took to the practice, and in time, he was able to get off his mood stabilizing medication.

It is satisfying to see students resonate with the case studies which Siegel presents, such as Jonathan's. After all, our own suffering is reflected in the individuals whom Siegel treats. If Jonathan's mind, pre-treatment, was particularly unreliable, his mood swings and low self-esteem are but exaggerations of our own. One student recently noted that Jonathan's remark near the conclusion of his treatment both sparked her identification with him and captured the essence of mindfulness: ". . . my [Jonathan's] view of life is changed now. What before I thought was my identity I now realize is just an experience. And being filled with big feelings is just some way my brain gives me experiences but they don't have to say who I am" (p. 99).

Once familiarized with Siegel's accessible presentation of the middle-prefrontal regions of the brain's linkage with disparate neural regions (the entire cortex, limbic areas, brain system and the entire nervous system of the "body proper") (p. 28), students are intrigued by his positing of nine integrating functions of the middle prefrontal cortex (p. 28):

1. Body regulation (under stress, heart pounds, breath rate increases, intestines churn)
2. Attuned communication (the ability to resonate with another's feelings)
3. Emotional balance (equilibrium: when we are too ramped up, our minds are chaotic; when our emotional tone is too low, our minds are rigid or depressed)
4. Response flexibility (enables us to check our impulses and consider options before responding)
5. Fear modulation (the prefrontal cortex has the capacity to calm down the amygdala)

6. Moral awareness (mindset and behavior toward social good)
7. Insight (the capacity to connect the past with the present and the future)
8. Intuition (access to the wisdom of the body)
9. Empathy (the capacity to create images of other people's minds)

I've had occasion to hear Siegel describe how he learned about the connection between these faculties and mindfulness practice: he was on a panel with Kabat-Zinn fleshing out his research on these nine functions of the prefrontal cortex. To his surprise, Kabat-Zinn told him that mindfulness training enhances each of these functions. It was this encounter that led Siegel to posit that "by developing the ability to focus our attention on our internal world, we are picking up a 'scalpel' we can use to re-sculpt our neural pathways, stimulating the growth of areas of the brain that are crucial to mental health" (p. xii).

Chaz's Story: "Mindfulness in Mayhem"

In *Mindsight,* Siegel recounts how on one miserable occasion, he totally "lost it"—all nine functions of the prefrontal cortex that he identifies melted down in an incident involving his young daughter and son and their sharing (or not-sharing) a crepe (pp. 23–37). In response to this memorable tale of woe, one of my students wrote a dazzling account of how he managed not to lose it, but rather to call upon his middle prefrontal cortical functions, showing extraordinary adaptability and resilience in the midst of an extremely stressful situation (Southard, 2010).

I had assigned my class to attend the plenary session of a conference on Mindfulness in Education, held at Lesley and co-sponsored by the Mindfulness in Education Network, and to write a short account of their experience of the conference. The building in which the plenary was held is a former church in need of updated handicapped access. The student, a graduate student in Lesley's Counseling and Psychology Division, uses a wheelchair. On the day of the conference, Chaz Southard was accompanied by his father, who was his source of transportation and helper. Son and father found the wheelchair accessible entry to the church locked. Chaz's father went in search of a security guard. The guard was unable to unlock the entrance. Chaz writes that he tried not to identify this occurrence as good or bad, but just to see things as they were. Finally, the guard managed to unlock the entryway to the elevator, revealing a tiny, archaic lift. A sliding iron fence presented another obstacle to entering the elevator. Chaz recognized that he was caught between metal fence and dread of the elevator, and his excitement about attending the lecture. Gripped by the fight or flight response, he nonetheless managed to compose himself sufficiently to ask the guard to try out the elevator for him. The guard responded, "Sure, let me die." Amazingly (to me), in response to the guard's remark, Chaz was able to feel empathy: he felt his internal world resonating with the guard's and was able to see that the guard's experience and his were not separate.

The guard then entered the elevator and immediately got locked inside. Chaz's father managed to extricate him. Chaz writes that in response to the guards' anxiety and his father's frustration, he actually had the presence of mind to think about what to do. The guard's face was dripping with sweat; his father was seething over the guard's behavior toward his son. Short of breath and near panic, Chaz sought refuges in his breath, doing his best to focus on each in-breath and out-breath. He reports that he was consciously trying to capitalize on two of the functions of his middle prefrontal cortex—bodily regulation and fear modulation.

Chaz realized that he and his chair could not fit in elevator. If he managed to squeeze in, he would probably be trapped. The incident would create a scene, and probably the fire department would have to be summoned to free him. The terror of many other times when he had been trapped, while confined to his wheel chair, arose. Yet he was able to create a space between his escalating thoughts, and to consider and accept the situation. He was going to miss the lecture. But there was no point in allowing his "limbic lava" to explode and cause him to yell at the guard. He felt empathic, toward the guard, his father, and himself. "I was able to smooth the waves of chaos and modulate my own reactivity," Chaz writes, adding:

> Although I would have liked to learn about mindfulness from a purely academic stand-point, I can confidently state that this incident was memorable. In the future, during trying circumstances with many obstacles that I face, I hope that I will be able to react in a reasonable and healthy way.

On this occasion, Chaz returned with his father to the main campus building and meditated. (A detailed discussion of the process of writing as part of mindfulness practice in this course is beyond the scope of this paper, but without a doubt, students' writing is a mindful practice in the service of deepening awareness and understanding.)

Student Stress: What the Studies Show

Throughout this paper, I have emphasized that all too often our stress is generated by our miscreant minds spinning dreadful scenarios on the basis of little evidence, uncertain evidence, or no evidence at all. But it would be remiss not to mention that there is a time and place for hyper-arousal in the face of real threats and dangers. And certainly, some measure of arousal is beneficial for maximizing mental and physical performance. Our amygdalas are well-deserving of our respect. Consider the extreme case in favor of the amygdala reported in a recent study published in the journal *Current Biology* (Feinstein, Adolphs, Damasio, & Tranel, 2010). The subject, SM, is congenitally missing an amgydala. Consequently, she unknowingly regularly puts herself in harm's way. On one occasion when she was walking alone in a dark park at night, she was attacked by a man with a knife. The very next night, she walked fearlessly through the same park.

Yet on our college campuses, the amygdala too often carries the day. A recent front-page *New York Times* article (Lewis, January 27, 2011, p. 1) reported that record levels of stress were found in a study of 200,000 incoming freshman, with women reporting experiencing more stress, and more often, than men. Notably negative interactions with faculty affected women more than men, and women more often felt that their professors did not take them seriously. (My students are mostly women.)

According to the Anxiety Disorders Association of America (n.d.), anxiety disorders are one of the most prevalent mental health problems on college campuses. Forty million U.S. adults suffer from an anxiety disorder, and 75 percent of them experience their first episode of anxiety by age 22 (para. 1). And, stress ranks highest among factors that adversely affect college students' academic performance, according to the National College Health Assessment: Spring 2008 Reference Group Report (p. 480). The number of participants in the study was huge—80,121 students at 106 institutions for higher education. The data on stress is consistent with the College Health Assessment findings since the annual survey was first conducted in the year 2000. Surprising no one, the authors of the study conclude, that "these data expand understanding of health needs and capacities of college students" (p. 488).

Consider the foregoing information alongside key findings of a study prepared for the Center for Contemplative Mind in Society (Shapiro, Brown, & Astin, 2008). On the basis of the extant literature on mindfulness in higher education, the principal investigator, Shauna Shapiro, reports that mindfulness meditation can foster attention and improve the speed and accuracy of information processing. Mindfulness can help sustain concentration and positively affect academic achievement, as well as reduce stress, anxiety, and depression. The practice of mindfulness enhances the regulation of emotions and helps cultivate positive psychological states. Moreover, mindfulness supports creativity, interpersonal relationships, empathy, and self-compassion (pp. 9–22). The authors note that:

> Despite its importance to learning, focused attention is rarely if ever systematically trained or cultivated in most educational settings. And yet, attentional training has been the hallmark of meditative disciplines for centuries and thus the incorporation of these practices into higher education could be of great benefit. (p. 9)

Additional studies, among them a randomized controlled trial conducted by Shapiro and others, demonstrates that Mindfulness-Based Stress Reduction training both lowers stress and supports forgiveness among college students (Oman et al., 2008). Shouldn't such information be on the desk of every university president?

Wisdom from the Students

Students in my mindfulness course sometimes report general frustration with their mindfulness practices and occasional wretched sittings—full of sleepiness, agitated thoughts and emotions, physical discomfort, and self-doubt. Some bemoan the amount of reading. Yet to a person, they report that their practice and study of mindfulness is valuable and applicable to their lives as students and members of the work force. Their final papers are eloquent testimonials, not only to reduction of stress and anxiety in their lives, but to heightened compassion and self-compassion, as well as a deeper awareness of experiences as small and discreet as a raisin and as large and ungainly as their own thought processes.

One student wrote in her paper on *Mindfulness Based Art Therapy and Cancer Care:* "Believe it or not, one of the most calm and serene places that I have is the Infusion Center at Mass General hospital. . . . I love meditating during infusion . . . it's a chance for me to just sit and dedicate myself to my mind and body" (Mann, 2009).

Another student, a novelist in the creative writing program, notes that mindfulness has helped with her creative craft. She describes two of her foremost identities as "editor" and "creator." She habitually roots for the creator and has difficulty "coercing the editor" into collaborating with the creator to revise her manuscripts. She writes that drawing from Kabat-Zinn's concept of interconnectedness, from Buddhist ideas of attachment, and from her meditation practice, she has moments in which the "quarrelling contenders inside me fall silent without preference for any one." She has been able to respect both her writer and editor selves as "honored parts of my internal landscape. I hope I can translate this potential for integration and neutrality into my writing practice" (Epron, 2009).

In a third, splendid paper, one woman draws on Dan Siegel's work on the concept of secure attachment and its connection with mindfulness in an insightful self-investigation. She writes, "Not until taking this course did I realize how little intrapersonal attunement I have cultivated in my life" (Walker, 2009). She attributes her previously unexamined self-judgment to her father's lack of attunement to her when she was a child. She did not have the experience of "feeling felt." She explains that mindfulness practice, with its focus on self-acceptance and non-judgment, has offered her "a new narrative."

> I am better able to recognize that I need not be anything more or less than I am in the present moment. Over the past semester of consistent meditation, I have been cultivating an integration of mind, body, and spirit. This has helped me create a unified narrative of my past experiences, leading to a coherence of mind. (Walker, 2009)

Noting that, as she learned from reading Dan Siegel, the state of brain activation in a therapist can alter the ways in which the patient's brain is activated, she concludes,

> For this reason, mindfulness practice is especially important to me as a therapist in training. Meditation affects my personal mind states, but, as Siegel proposes, it also potentially impacts the brain, mind, and emotions of the clients I work with through our (hopefully) attuned therapeutic relationships. (Walker, 2009)

A deep bow to these hard-working, resourceful, and open-minded students. They have shown me that it is possible and beneficial to integrate critical reasoning and analysis with other forms of intelligence, such as self-knowing awareness, emotional balance, and compassion, cultivated through mindfulness meditation. Not only is this integration possible, it optimizes the educational enterprise, because from moment to moment, mindful awareness and intellectual activity are mutually reinforcing.

Challenges and Opportunities

A single one-semester course in the theory and practice of mindfulness meditation can only cover so much material. During class, I quite frequently check my watch, intent upon completing a sometimes overly ambitious plan for the week. Optimally, we would spend more time teasing out the subtleties of our practice experiences; we would dwell in the readings longer, and scrutinize the neuroplasticity studies more closely. As it is, sometimes we eat our raisins too quickly, a drawback to my more-is-better Western pedagogical conditioning, and the ongoing availability of exciting new findings in contemplative neuroscience. One consideration would be to slow the pace by teaching the course over two semesters, while modestly supplementing the course material. For now, I will reexamine the syllabus, as I do each year, looking for ways I could adjust or trim the curriculum without truncating it. And I will continue to contemplate the irony of making haste in a contemplative studies course, a conundrum for all of us who are committed to contemplative education.

Meanwhile, several other initiatives in Mindfulness Studies at Lesley have been it been realized. Along with the course explored in this paper, we offer three additional Mindfulness Studies courses. "Mindful Communications" is designed to examine and critique the theory, practice, and potential of Insight Dialogue and its roots in the Buddhist concept of "right speech." The "Principles of Mindful Leadership and Social Engagement" course provides students with an opportunity to explore how Buddhist ideas underlying mindfulness can be extended into the realm of leadership and engagement with the contemporary world. "Origins of Contemplative Practice in Buddhist Thought" examines the roots of secular mindfulness in classic Buddhist philosophy. The four courses constitute an Advanced Graduate Certificate in Mindfulness Studies, as well as a specialization in Mindfulness Studies in Lesley's Self-Designed Master's Degree Program. As of this writing, we are looking forward to launching a 36-credit Master's Degree in Mindfulness Studies in the fall of 2014. We continue to complement our academic offerings with mindful initiatives including conferences and lectures by visiting scholars, as Lesley as becomes increasingly recognized as a university that embraces the principles and practices of mindfulness.

I am hopeful, confident even, that in light of what we know about the miracle of mindfulness for integrating the brain in the service of learning, more and more such courses and programs will be offered in colleges and graduate schools around the country. When this comes to pass, what a different experience higher education will be.

References

American College Health Association (2009). National college health assessment, Spring 2008 reference group data report. *Journal of American College Health, 57*, 477–488.

Anxiety Disorders Society of America. (2011). *College students.* Retrieved February 8, 2011, from <www.adaa.org/finding-help/helping-others/college-students/>.

Carmody, J., Karleyton C., Evans, E. A., Hoge, A., Dusek, J. A., Morgan, L, Pitman, R. K., & Lazar, S. W. (2010). Stress reduction correlates with structural changes in the amygdala. *Social Cognitive and Affective Neuroscience, 5*, 11–17.

Chan, Achaan. (1987). *A still forest pool.* Wheaton, IL: The Theosophical Publishing House.

Epron, L. (2009). Befriending the editor: How merging mindfulness and writing has helped integrate my second drafts with the creative craft. Unpublished manuscript.

Feinstein, J. S., Adolphs, R., Damasio, A., & Tranel, D. (2010). The human amygdala and the induction and experience of fear. *Current Biology, 21*(1), 34–38.

Goleman, D. (2006). *Social intelligence.* New York: Bantam.

Hölzel, B., Carmody, J., Vangel, C., Congleton, S., Yerramsetti, M., Gard, T., & Lazar, S. (2011). Mindfulness practice leads to increases in regional brain gray matter density. *Psychiatry Research: Neuroimaging, 191*, 36–43.

Kabat-Zinn, J. (1996). Mindfulness meditation: What it is, what it isn't, and its role in health care and medicine. In Y. Haruki & M. Suzuki (Eds.), *Comparative and Psychological Study on Meditation* (pp. 161–170). Netherlands: Eburon Publishers.

Kabat-Zinn, J. (2005). *Coming to our senses: Healing the world and ourselves through mindfulness.* New York: Hyperion.

Kabat-Zinn, J., Massion, A. O., Kristeller, J., Peterson, L. G., Fletcher, K. E., Pbert, L., Lenderking, W. R., & Santorelli, S. F. (1992). Effectiveness of a meditation stress reduction program in the treatment of anxiety disorders. *American Journal of Psychiatry, 149*, 936–943.

Kabat-Zinn, J., Wheeler, E., Light T., Skillings, A., Scharf, M. J., Gropeley, G., Hosmer, D., & Bernhard, J. D. (1998). Influence of a mindfulness meditation based stress reduction intervention on rates of skin clearing in patients with moderate to severe psoriasis undergoing phototherapy (UVB) and photochemotherapy (PUVA). *Psychosomatic Medicine, 60*, 625–632.

Lewin, T. (2011, January 27). Record level of stress found in college freshmen. *New York Times*, p. A1, Retrieved February 6, 2011 from <http://www.nytimes.com/2011/01/27/education/27colleges.html?_r=1>.

Mann, Rebecca. (2009). Mindfulness-based art therapy and cancer care. Unpublished manuscript.

Oman, D., Shapiro, S., Thorensen, C. E., Plante, T. T., & Finders, T. (2008). Meditation lowers stress and supports forgiveness among college students: A randomized controlled trial. *Journal of American College Health, 56*, 569–578.

Shapiro, S, Brown, K. W., & Astin, J. (2008). Toward the integration of meditation into higher education. Prepared for the Center for Contemplative Mind in Society. Retrieved February 4, 2011 from <http://www.contemplativemind.org/resources/publications.html>.

Siegel, D. (2010). *Mindsight: The new science of personal transformation.* New York: Random House.

Southard, C. (2009). Mindfulness in mayhem. Unpublished manuscript.

Walker, A. (2009). Attachment and mindfulness: Research and Reflection. Unpublished manuscript.

Waring, N. (2000). Mindfulness meditation: Studies show that awareness practices promote healing. *Hippocrates, 14*, 19–21.

11

Information and Contemplation

Exploring Contemplative Approaches to Information Technology

David M. Levy

Today's information technologies are powerful tools for connection and access. But there is growing awareness that they may also function as tools of disconnection and isolation. In the spring quarter of 2006, with the support of a fellowship from the Center for Contemplative Mind in Society, I created and taught a course called "Information and Contemplation" at the University of Washington's (UW) Information School which aimed to explore this seeming paradox. Its intent would be to use contemplative practice as a lens to observe and critique current information technologies and practices, and in particular to investigate problems such as information overload, the fragmentation of attention, and the busyness and acceleration of everyday life. In this chapter, I will describe the background for the course, its content and structure, and subsequent teaching experiments based on these. I will also offer further reflections on the course structure and content as I now prepare to teach the course in the upcoming academic year.

Background

I am a computer scientist by training: I completed a PhD in computer science at Stanford University in 1979, specializing in artificial intelligence. I worked as a researcher at the Xerox Palo Alto Research Center (PARC), the think tank where the networked personal computer was first developed, for most of the 1980s and 1990s; and I now teach in the Information School at the

University of Washington, which trains future librarians, information scientists, and information system designers and evaluators.

But I am also a contemplative: I began to study Western calligraphy in the mid-1970s as a contemplative art form, and after completing my PhD, spent two years in London studying calligraphy and bookbinding at the Roehampton Institute (Levy, 1994). For a number of years I have also had a daily sitting meditation practice, and more recently have been studying the Japanese marshal art aikido, which has a strong contemplative element. As both a technologist and a contemplative, it was natural for me to ask what relationship these two kinds of practices might bear to one another.

It was in the early to mid-1990s that my questioning began to take a more specific form. In the United States at this time, cellphones were already in use, although not to the extent we see today; telephone answering machines and call-waiting were increasingly common; the Internet was making the transition from a system overseen by the military to a full-blown societal resource, and email had become a common form of communication outside the university settings and research labs where it had first been nurtured. Along with these changes, I began to notice a speedup in the culture, a growing sense of information overload, and an increasing feeling of busyness and distraction, both in the workplace and in my own personal circles. These changes in everyday life experiences caught my attention because they seemed to stand in contrast with other qualities I was trying to cultivate in my meditation practice: qualities of stillness, relaxation, and focus.

As I was reflecting on these observations, I was invited to participate in a symposium of computer scientists and social scientists to explore the topic "Presence—Being Here, There, Nowhere, and Everywhere." In my paper, titled "I'm Not Here Right Now to Take Your Call: Technology and the Politics of Absence" (Levy, 1995), I wrote about my growing concern that the latest information technologies, which were clearly being marketed as tools to connect us to one another, were at the same time also serving to disconnect us—from ourselves, from one another, and from the world. My worry was that conditions like acceleration and overload—partly growing out of our technology-enhanced connectivity—were making it increasingly difficult for us to stay connected socially, psychologically, and spiritually. Here is how I expressed it in that 1995 think-piece:

> We now look to communication technologies as essential instruments for meeting both our intimate and work commitments, allowing us to stay connected and stay in touch—not only bridging space and time, but ordering and coordinating, if not mending, the fragments of our lives.

> Yet these technologies often seem to exacerbate the problems they claim to be solving. If the telephone lets us 'reach out and touch someone' (as the familiar phone company ad used to say), it also interrupts us in the midst of other activities—even when we may actually be reaching out to touch someone. Call-waiting compounds this, allowing one phone call to interrupt another. Pagers and cellular phones increase our 'connectivity,' but at the cost of invading alone-time in cars and conversational time in restaurants.
>
> These technologies, in other words, seem to be instruments of fragmentation and absence, even as they present themselves in apparent opposition. (Levy, 1995)

When I accepted a permanent faculty position at the UW Information School in 2001, my intention was to explore such issues. Was life indeed accelerating in (some) unhelpful ways? If so, why was this happening, what roles were the technologies playing in it, and what could be done about it? These questions formed the basis for a range of scholarly initiatives over the course of the next decade.[1] And it was in the context of these ongoing concerns and investigations that I imagined a university course to explore these issues and applied for a fellowship from the Center for Contemplative Mind in Society.

Before describing the aims and structure of the course on Information and Contemplation, it is worth saying a word about the academic context in which the course was offered. The Information School at the University of Washington is an outgrowth of its School of Library and Information Science. In the 1990s, the development of personal computers and the World Wide Web led people to question whether libraries (and library schools) were still needed. Historic schools, most notably at Columbia and the University of Chicago, were permanently closed. On other campuses, however, administrators and scholars argued that existing library schools could be expanded rather than shut down, and that a new kind of school, an "information school," could be created that would train information professionals to take on the task of managing the new information flows and resources, and dealing with the range of societal problems (including intellectual property, privacy, intellectual freedom) that were being raised by the new digital technologies and practices.

The University of Washington created such an information school (or iSchool) in 2001, which now offers four degree programs: a Masters in Library and Information Science (MLIS), which was the sole degree offered by the old library school; an undergraduate major in Informatics, which trains students in a combination of computer science and social science methods; a Masters in Information Management (MSIM), oriented toward the business world; and a PhD in information science, for students who intend to teach and do research.

A Course on Information and Contemplation

The course on Information and Contemplation was offered within the MLIS program but was open to students in the other iSchool programs. A total of twelve students enrolled. Of the twelve, nine were enrolled in the MLIS, one was completing his undergraduate Informatics major, and two were PhD candidates in the Information Science program (one enrolled, one auditor).

The aim of the course, as advertised, was to use contemplative practice as a lens to observe and critique current information practices, and in particular to investigate problems such as information overload, the fragmentation of attention, and the busyness and acceleration of everyday life. The course description read:

> Today's information technologies provide instantaneous access to vast amounts of information, opening up wondrous new possibilities in education, commerce, and entertainment. But these opportunities are not without cost: the easy availability of information can turn into information overload; the presence of multiple communication sources and devices may lead to the fragmentation of attention; and the ease of acting and communicating quickly seems to encourage a pace of interaction that is unsustainable and counterproductive. In this course, we will examine the causes and effects of such trends, and will explore possible counter-measures, including contemplative practice. For thousands of years in a wide range of cultures, people have developed techniques (meditation, yoga, contemplative reading) for stilling the mind and cultivating attention. We will study and practice a variety of these techniques, and will apply the understanding gained from them to critique the speedy, fragmented, and inattentive mind states that digital technologies seem to encourage.

(The full syllabus for the course can be found on the website of the Center for Contemplative Mind in Society at <www.contemplativemind.org/programs/academic/syllabi/levy.pdf.>)

The course had three interwoven components: (1) a reading seminar-style exploration of contemporary information practices and the challenges associated with them; (2) first-person explorations of a variety of contemplative practices; and (3) a set of exercises meant to help students connect their contemplative and information practices.

Exploration of Contemporary Information Practices and Challenges

The course was conducted as a seminar, with students and instructor seated around a large table. The primary intellectual/academic course content was approached through the discussion of readings organized around particular topics. Thus, the subject of attention was explored academically by reading chapter 11 of William James' *Principles of Psychology* (James, 1890/1950) as well as an article by a contemporary Canadian psychologist, Warren Thorngate, "On Paying Attention" (Thorngate, 1988). A class session devoted to the challenges of acceleration, overload, and busyness was organized, with readings from Thomas Eriksen's *Tyranny of the Moment* (Eriksen, 2001), Jon Kabat-Zinn's *Coming to Our Senses* (Kabat-Zinn, 2005), and Peter Whybrow's *American Mania* (Whybrow, 2005). A discussion of work and leisure made use of material from Josef Pieper's *Leisure: The Basis of Culture* (Pieper, 1998) and Benjamin Hunnicutt's *Work without End* (Hunnicutt, 1988).

Exploration of Contemplative Practices

In addition to this fairly traditional academic mode of inquiry, the course provided a number of opportunities for students to explore contemplative practices. I had decided that a sitting mindfulness practice would be the base practice for the course. In the very first class session, I introduced students to the practice of sitting with mindful awareness of the breath, and returning to the breath whenever the mind was discovered to be wandering. (For some students, of course, this was not new.) Every class thereafter began with 10 or 15 minutes of silent sitting. The sitting practice provided a basis not only for talking about (and demonstrating) how greater concentration could be developed, but also the means to explore the phenomenology of first-person experience: the arising and passing away of sensations, emotions, thoughts, images, and so on.

A number of other practices were introduced throughout the quarter. These included mindful walking, free-writing, and *lectio divina* (contemplative reading). I invited Janice Giteck, a local composer and contemplative practitioner who teaches at the Cornish College of the Arts, to lead a class on contemplative listening. And I held an extra (optional) session on a weekend where the class listened to Jon Kabat-Zinn's (1990) 45-minute recording of the Body Scan exercise and practiced along (see Chapter 5 in Kabat-Zinn).

We also regularly discussed the relationship of these practices to the larger aims of the course. The practices, I explained, were meant to demonstrate ways of being—stillness, single-minded focus, mindfulness—that stood in contrast to the manic and scattered modes of interacting that are now so commonplace, and that often seem to be fueled by the use of the new technologies. They provided a lens through which to view and critique these modes of operating. And they raised the possibility that one might operate differently—more mindfully—in one's daily activities, whether while reading, walking down the street, doing email, or surfing the Web. How one might investigate such possibilities was the subject of the final thread.

Exercises Connecting Information and Contemplative Practices

The first course thread, reading and discussion, was situated firmly in the mainstream of contemporary academic practice. The second, an exploration of a variety of contemplative practices, carried the course outside the bounds of traditional practice, aligning it with many other attempts around the country (some of them reported in this volume) to introduce such practices into the academic mainstream. The last of the threads was perhaps the course's most original contribution insofar as it attempted to connect contemplative practices with today's high-tech based information practices. Through in-class exercises and homework, students were asked to bring mindfulness to some of their own information practices, to document what they had observed, to reflect on what they had documented, and to discuss these reflections with their fellow students. I will describe one such exercise, which was particularly successful, and which I have continued to use successfully in other settings, as I will explain below.

This particular exercise was offered midway through the quarter. By this time, students had spent a good deal of time reading and discussing the intellectual content of the course (thread one), and had been exploring the sitting mindfulness practice long enough to have some feeling for what it meant to tune into the breath, sensations in the body, emotions, and thoughts (thread two). Here is a slightly edited version of the exercise that was presented to the students:

Exploration of an Information Practice

For this assignment you will do a *first-person exploration* of one of your central information practices: email. Over the course of the week, you should pay close attention to your email habits and practices:

- When do you read email? How many times a day? At what times of day? For how long?
- Notice how you feel (your breathing, your bodily state, your emotions, your attentiveness) just before you start reading email, and just after you finish. Do you feel a pull (positive or negative) before you begin reading email? Do you find it difficult to stop, and if so, why?
- Notice how you feel when you read or write different email messages, or simply when you see them in your inbox. What kind and quality of attention do different email messages ask of you, and what kind and quality do you actually give them? How do your bodily, emotional, and attentional states change over the course of each email session? Do you become more energized or enervated? More or less alert? Etc.

The assignment has two parts.

Part 1: Keep a log or journal of your email sessions, noting start and stop times, number of messages dealt with, and making comments, as appropriate, in response to the above questions.

Part 2: After five days, examine your log for regularities. (You may also choose to write notes and hypotheses in your journal as they come to you during the first five days.) What patterns do you notice around your email habits? What is working well for you and what isn't? What could you imagine changing, how, and why? Write 2 to 3 pages describing your findings, relating what you found, wherever appropriate, to the readings and class discussion.

I had never created an assignment like this before, so was curious (and apprehensive) about how it might go. I was delighted to discover, a week later, that all the students had come back to class excited about the discoveries they had made. One of the most common discoveries was that they tended to go online to check their email when they were anxious or bored; some went further to note that reading and answering email did not allay their anxiety, but rather seemed to exacerbate it. As we discussed students' findings, I noticed that some of them went beyond reporting their observations to proposing changes in their email behavior (which had not been part of the original assignment). Thus, for example, a student who noticed that she was using email (unsuccessfully) to escape from anxious feelings decided that rather than going online at such moments, she might do better to attend to her breathing. I therefore suggested an extension of the assignment: I proposed that for the following class students write up personal guidelines (no more than one page) for their own email use based on their self-observations. In that next class, students shared and discussed their personal guidelines, which led to further valuable analysis and discussion. Here are some of the personal guidelines students proposed, based on their mindful observation of their own practices:

Table 1. Student guidelines

Student observation	**Proposed guideline**
A tendency to check email when anxious or bored	When anxious or bored, take a walk or meditate rather than checking email
Reading email is often fragmenting	Plan the sequence in which I read emails to avoid abrupt changes in focus
Email, compared with paper mail, eliminates important transition times	Create transition times (e.g., by taking several mindful breaths) between groups (types) of email
Email notifications as an (unnecessary) distraction	Turn off all email alerts and previews

I have devoted considerable space to this one exercise because it exemplifies an important dimension of what I was trying to achieve in the class: using contemplative practices (and the window onto one's immediate thoughts, feelings, and sensations that these practices afford) as a means to critique and potentially adjust one's information practices. Slightly generalized, the class exercise suggests a technique for helping people to assess and tune their own information practices.

1. Mindfully observe the information practice in question, noticing qualities of attention, body, breath, mood, and so on.
2. Decide which dimensions of your experience you want to cultivate or minimize (e.g., focused attention, fatigue, anxiety, relaxation, and so on.

3. Make conscious choices and draw up guidelines.
4. Share and compare.

This has become a cornerstone of the further teaching I have done since the course was originally offered, as I will explain below.

Reactions to the Course

The course was a success, as judged by the quality of classroom interactions and student written responses, the course evaluations, and my own experience (this has been the high point of my teaching career). Here is a distillation of the anonymous student comments written for the end-of-course evaluations:

- Students found the course intellectually stimulating: "This is one of the most intellectually challenging *and* satisfying classes I've taken in grad school." "It challenged what tend to be unchallenged assumptions about what knowing is and how learning is best done." "It brought light into many areas of intellectual inquiry, and stretched my thinking. The e-mail observation was especially enlightening."

- It broadened students' appreciation and understanding of the subject matter (information): "The course content and the way Levy taught it made me consider all aspects of information in a more 3-D instead of 2-dimensional way." "This course caused/allowed me to delve into areas of culture and information that I have never considered or articulated before."

- Students found value in the first-person contemplative practices: "I really enjoyed incorporating sitting meditation into each of the classes." ". . . doing contemplative practices on our own helped develop awareness of such practices and their positive effects on our lives."

- The readings and in-class discussion were highly valued: "Discussions were way more interesting—due in large part to the readings—but everyone was more engaged as well." "David guided the class discussions in a way that made room for varied perspectives—I think we were all very comfortable expressing ourselves."

Although I didn't survey my colleagues in the Information School, I have good reason to believe that the course was looked upon favorably by the majority of them. Certainly the tone was set by my dean, who was quite supportive of my efforts.

Beyond the For-Credit Course

Upon successful completion of the course, I was curious to see if a similar program of study could work not only in the classroom but in the workplace, so I next approached Betsy Wilson, dean of the UW Libraries, to see if she would permit me to offer a version of the course to working librarians. Betsy was supportive and declared the ten-week training to be professional development, thus permitting library staff to participate during work hours. I was able to offer the training twice, each time with 10 to 15 library staff in attendance. In the library version, there were no written assignments and no grades. But the results—the sense of learning and discovery—seemed to be quite similar, although I didn't undertake a formal evaluation.

Having thus attempted the course three times in a ten-week format, I was next curious to see if some of the elements could be employed within workshops of shorter duration. Over the past several years, I have experimented with different formats, offering shorter workshops, mainly to university librarians, faculty, and administrators at several universities around the country. The first of these was a day-long workshop, which provided sufficient time to explore some simple contemplative practices (mainly sitting and walking meditation) with the participants, and to talk about how such practices could be brought into the workplace to cultivate more attentive information practices. But the single-meeting format did not permit me to offer the email exercise (or a similar practice) since there was no follow-up meeting at which participants could report and discuss their findings. In subsequent short trainings, however, at conferences and campus visits, I have established a two-session format: in the first session (1.5 to 2 hours long), the contemplative practices are introduced and the email exercise is offered as homework; in the second session (which meets the next day or two days later), the results of the exercise are discussed. I have been pleased to see that even in this more restricted format, the email exercise still yields insights for the participants. (Each time I have offered the two-session workshop, some participants have come to class eager to present their discoveries—e.g., that they tend to check email when bored or anxious, and so on.) Despite this, I suspect that the short-format workshops accomplish little more than introducing participants to a contemplative perspective on their information practices; there is clearly no time for in-depth practice and learning.

Further Reflections on the Course

Five years after first offering the course on Information and Contemplation, I am preparing to teach it again (in the spring of the upcoming academic year). Overall, I am pleased with the three-part structure I initially created, which brought together, as described above, a reading seminar, first-person investigations of contemplative practices, and exercises connecting information and contemplative practices. I intend to keep this same basic structure, which by all accounts worked extremely well. But I am considering adding some new course content in light of recent cultural and academic developments. In recent years, the cultural debate about the place of the new technologies has grown. Books like Maggie Jackson's *Distracted: The Erosion of Attention and the Coming Dark Age* (2008), Nicholas Carr's *The Shallows: What the Internet is Doing to Our Brains* (2010), and Sherry Turkle's *Alone Together: Why We Expect More from Technology and Less from Each Other* (2011) argue forcefully that technological change is implicated in a widespread loss of focus and reflective capacity, while books by Clay Shirky (2011), Jane McGonigal (2011), and Cathy Davidson (2011) among others suggest that technology will ultimately enhance these capacities. (In a *New Yorker* review of a number of these books, Adam Gopnik (2011) refers to those in the first camp as the "better nevers" and those in the second as the "never betters.") When I next teach this course, my hope is to expose students to a number of these arguments, and thus help them to formulate their own critical responses.

I also hope to incorporate some of the recent scientific work on the neuroscience of meditation (see Alfred Kaszniak's contribution in this volume), which has begun to demonstrate how meditation improves cognitive control and emotion regulation. I am considering devoting an entire class to the subject of multi-tasking, for example, using recent neuroscience research to explore how multi-tasking—the rapid switching among tasks—challenges the attentional faculty, and how contemplative approaches may suggest alternatives to the fragmentation and distraction that much of today's multi-tasking behavior encourages.

Conclusion

As Jon Kabat-Zinn (2005) has observed:

> The more we are entrained into the outer world in all these new and increasingly rapid ways that our nervous system has never before encountered, the more important it may be for us to develop a

> robust counterbalance of the inner world, one that calms and tunes the nervous system and puts it in the service of living wisely, both for ourselves and for others. This counterbalance can be cultivated by bringing greater mindfulness to the body, to the mind, and to our experiences at the interface between outer and inner, including the very moments in which we are using the technology to stay connected, or in which the impulse to do so is arising. (pp. 155–156)

With nearly five years of experience bringing information and contemplative practices into juxtaposition in a variety of settings, I am convinced that the two sets of practices can, and, indeed, should be integrated. The new information technologies offer great promise, some of which has already been demonstrated. But they can be tools of distraction as much as of attentive awareness. And without the proper balance, we risk losing some or even much of their power. Contemplative practices are clearly a means to cultivate attention, and with the attention so cultivated, we ought to be in a better position to continue to craft the technologies and their practices to maintain the balance—the contemplative balance—without which human life is less productive and less meaningful.

Note

1. During the decade of the 2000s, I organized a series of conferences and workshops which brought scholars, artists, and religious leaders together to explore the problems of acceleration overload. These included the Conference on Information, Silence and Sanctuary (Seattle, 2004), the Workshop on Mindful Work and Technology (Washington, DC, 2006), and the Conference on No Time to Think (Seattle, 2008). See "No Time to Think" (Levy, 2007) for an exploration of the role of information technologies in acceleration and overload and the consequences for academic life. See "Initial Results from a Study of the Effects of Meditation on Multitasking Performance" (Levy, Wobbrock, Kaszniak, & Ostergren, 2011) for an exploration of the use of meditation to reduce the negative effects of multi-tasking.

References

Carr, N. (2010). *The shallows: What the Internet is doing to our brains.* New York: W. W. Norton.

Davidson, C. N. (2011). *Now you see it: How the brain science of attention will transform the way we live, work, and learn.* New York: Viking.

Eriksen, T. H. (2001). *Tyranny of the moment: Fast and slow time in the information age.* London: Pluto Press.

Gleick, J. (1999). *Faster: The acceleration of just about everything.* New York: Pantheon Books.

Gopnik, A. (2011, February 14). The Information: How the Internet gets inside us. *The New Yorker.* Available at <http://www.newyorker.com/arts/critics/atlarge/2011/02/14/110214crat_atlarge_gopnik>.

Hunnicutt, B. K. (1988). *Work without end: Abandoning shorter hours for the right to work.* Philadelphia, PA: Temple University Press.

Jackson, M. (2008). *Distracted: The erosion of attention and the coming dark age.* Amherst, NY: Prometheus Books.

James, W. (1890/1950). *The principles of psychology.* New York: Dover Publications.

Kabat-Zinn, J. (1990). *Full catastrophe living.* New York: Dell Publishing.

Kabat-Zinn, J. (2005). *Coming to our senses: Healing ourselves and the world through mindfulness.* New York: Hyperion.

Levy, D. M. (1994, Summer). Reflections on documents, computers and the craft of calligraphy. *The Scribe, 61,* 3–8.

Levy, D. M. (1995). *I'm not here right now to take your call: Technology and the politics of absence.* Paper presented at the Oksnoen Symposium 1995, Oksnoen, Norway.

Levy, D. M. (2007). No time to think: Reflections on information technology and contemplative scholarship. *Ethics and Information Technology, 9*(4), 237–249.

Levy, D. M., Wobbrock, J. O., Kaszniak, A. W., & Ostergren, M. (2011). *Initial results from a study of the effects of meditation on multitasking performance.* Extended Abstracts of the ACM Conference on Human Factors in Computing Systems (CHI '11), Vancouver, British Columbia.

McGonigal, J. (2011). *Reality is broken: Why games make us better and how they can change the world.* New York: Penguin.

Pieper, J. (1998). *Leisure, the basis of culture* (G. Malsbary, Trans.). South Bend, IN: St. Augustine's Press.

Shirky, C. (2011). *Cognitive surplus: How technology makes consumers into collaborators.* New York: Penguin.

Thorngate, W. (1988). On paying attention. In W. J. Baker, L. P. Mos, H. V. Rappard, & H. J. Stam (Eds.), *Recent Trends in Theoretical Psychology* (pp. 247–263). New York: Springer-Verlag.

Turkle, S. (2011). *Alone together: Why we expect more from technology and less from each other.* New York: Basic Books.

Whybrow, P. C. (2005). *American mania: When more is not enough.* New York: W. W. Norton.

12

Contemplative Pedagogy

Perspectives from Cognitive and Affective Science

Alfred W. Kaszniak

Contemplative practices, particularly meditation, have attracted a growing number of persons in recent decades, with a proliferation of books, magazines, and websites concerned with meditation, and the spiritual traditions in which this practice has played a central role (McMahan, 2008). It is estimated that there are at least 10 million meditation practitioners within the United States alone (Deurr, 2004). Meditation and related contemplative practices have also been taught within non-sectarian contexts, in hospitals, clinics, and educational settings (Duerr, Zajonc, & Dana, 2003; Hart, 2004; Salmon, Santorelli, & Kabat-Zinn, 1998; Sarath, 2006; Shapiro, Brown, & Astin, 2008). Over recent decades, there has also been a marked increase in cognitive, affective, and neuroscientific studies of meditation practice, and in the funding of these studies by the U.S. National Institutes of Health (Shapiro & Carlson, 2009).

The present chapter focuses upon scientific studies of meditation practices that are relevant for a theoretical model of the processes by which contemplative pedagogy may enhance relevant learning and transformation goals of higher education. In particular, the chapter examines research on attention, memory, emotion response, and emotion regulation, in both long-term and short-term practitioners of meditation approaches that have been derived primarily from Buddhist tradition and those modern secular forms referred to as mindfulness meditation. The focus on these particular meditation practices reflects the increasingly large body of both qualitative and quantitative research on a broad spectrum of cognitive, affective, and neuroscientific dimensions of changes consequent to practices derived from Buddhist traditions and training in mindfulness meditation.

Within the following section, a rationale is provided for considering contemplative pedagogy as relevant to Western higher education. This rationale draws from traditional and contemporary claims concerning meditation and its role as a path to the alleviation of suffering and enhancement of human flourishing. Then, a brief description is provided of the general characteristics of different types of traditional meditation practice and those conducted within mindfulness-based training programs. After this, select examples of those behavioral and neuroscientific empirical studies with the greatest relevance to pedagogy are selectively reviewed. The chapter ends by proposing some implications of research for understanding the role of contemplative pedagogy in higher education.

Why Is Contemplative Pedagogy Relevant for Higher Education?

Various meditation practices have been described (e.g., Ricard, 2010; Zajonc, 2009) as training methods for developing stable attention as an essential foundation for observing the processes of one's own mind and cultivating positive qualities such as wisdom, compassion, and happiness. For example, in Buddhist meditative practices, it is held that trained introspective observation allows insight into, and liberation from, delusive views (especially the belief that there is an essential "self" that is permanent and unchanging) that are held to be the cause of mental suffering. Careful introspection of the flow of mental experience is held to reveal that all phenomena, including the experience of self, are composite, without irreducible essence, and impermanent. However, as meditation teacher and Buddhist scholar B. Allan Wallace (2007) points out, without the training of meditation practice, introspection succumbs to either attentional excitation and scattering or drifting into drowsiness and lack of vividness.

Wallace's observation emphasizes the roles of both attention and arousal/emotion regulation in the mental training of meditation. Contemporary scientific studies of meditation mirror this emphasis in the frequent employment of measures of attention and emotion (Davidson, 2010), as will be described later in this chapter.

Why would this training of attention and emotion regulation in meditation be relevant to higher education? First, although relatively neglected in the recent past, there is now a growing recognition of the transformative potential of higher education. As Parker Palmer and Arthur Zajonc write,

> Our institutions of higher education seldom embrace a genuinely transformative view of the pedagogies they consciously, or more

often unconsciously, adopt. Our view of the student is too often as a vessel to be filled or a person to be trained. (Palmer & Zajonc, 2010, p. 101)

Transformative education encourages students to be open to change and embody various ways of knowing, being, and making meaning, through active and experiential modes of engaging ideas and information. The goal of transformative education is not merely the learning of facts or acquisition of vocationally useful skills. It also includes developing independent perspectives through digesting divergent points of view, and even transcending an individual perspective and sustaining changing and often contradictory viewpoints (Kegan, 1994; Palmer & Zajonc, 2010). Appreciating divergent perspectives, and sustaining changing and contradictory viewpoints, would appear to require both attention and emotion regulation skills. Without the ability to flexibly and fluidly shift attention, one may become fixated or stuck on one particular view. Similarly, without the ability to regulate emotion and maintain relative equanimity, encountering views that challenge cherished beliefs or appear to pose a threat to one's sense of self may elicit negative emotional arousal that can give rise to defensiveness and a narrowed focus on the familiar.

Second, there is a growing body of research evidence showing that the ability to control attention is related to individual differences in the mental resource we have for the brief storage and processing of information that cognitive psychologists call working memory (e.g., McNab & Klingberg, 2008; Vogel, McCollough, & Machizawa, 2005). Given that attention training is a key aspect of meditation practice, it has been proposed as a potential means for enhancing working memory capacity (Jha, Stanley, & Baime, 2010). Research supporting this possibility is reviewed below. Practices capable of increasing working memory capacity could have far-reaching implications for education, given that individual differences in working memory capacity are predictive of performance on aptitude measures, such as those of fluid intelligence (Cowan, Fristoe, Elliott, Brunner, & Saults, 2006). Fluid intelligence refers to that domain of intellectual abilities required for solving novel problems, in contrast to crystallized intelligence, referring to previously learned facts and concepts.

Third, chronic psychosocial stress in college students has been shown to produce long-lasting, though reversible, impairment in attention-shifting and the prefrontal brain physiological processes that correlate with attention-shifting (Liston, McEwen, & Casey, 2009). Even the relatively brief emotional arousal that accompanies acute stress can disrupt attention control. This likely reflects the dense and reciprocal interconnection of those brain regions associated with attention control, such as the anterior cingulate cortex and the lateral prefrontal cortex, with other areas commonly linked to emotion, such as the amygdala, and to motivation, such as the nucleus accumbens (for a review of this literature, see Pessoa, 2008). Randomized controlled trials of relatively brief (one month to eight weeks) mindfulness meditation training with college students have shown decreases in self-reported stress (Jain et al., 2007; Oman, Shapiro, Thoresen, Plante, & Flinders, 2008). Such reductions in experienced stress could, in turn, facilitate attention-shifting ability. Enhanced ability to voluntarily control attention is valuable not only for academic study, but also for stabilizing awareness of the contents and processes of our mental continuum. Within contemplative practice traditions, such stability of awareness is held to be critical for insight into the causes and conditions of mental suffering.

What Is Meditation?

Meditation practices taught within different traditions vary. Some practices involve maintaining mental focus on a particular sensation or somatic process (e.g., of the breath), while others involve focus upon a visual object, visual image, sound, or auditory image. Still other practices attempt to broaden the field of attention without preferential selection of any focus, gently releasing attention whenever it is pulled to any particular mental experience. Despite such variability, all of these practices can be considered as different approaches to training in the voluntary regulation of attention.

Lutz, Slagter, Dunne, and Davidson (2008) propose a conceptual framework for understanding different forms of meditation, in their broad distinction, between "focused attention" versus "open monitoring" practices. These terms describe fundamental aspects of meditation practice and connect to modern psychological constructs. According to Lutz and colleagues, focused attention meditation involves the directing and sustaining of attention on a selected object (e.g., breath sensations), as well as detecting mind wandering (thoughts unrelated to the focus, or other distractions). When mind wandering is detected, the practice involves disengaging attention from the distraction and gently (without self-judgment regarding the distraction) shifting attention back to the object of focus. Focused attention meditation can thus be considered as a method for developing attention-shifting skills, and with repeated practice, facilitating effortless and focused concentration. Such practice would also be expected to enhance the ability to monitor one's own attention and more quickly notice when mind wandering occurs.

Open monitoring meditation is typically practiced after some stability of attention regulation is achieved via focused attention meditation. Open monitoring involves no explicit focus on objects, maintaining an alert and nonjudgmental "openness" to whatever arises in the mental continuum. It also involves awareness of the conscious field itself in which mental phenomena arise, something that contemporary psychology would term meta-awareness. This calm, nonreactive and nonjudgmental awareness includes all sensations, images, thoughts, and feelings, as well as automatic cognitive-emotional interpretations or associations that arise in the stream of consciousness. However, the practitioner does not dwell upon or get lost in these experiences or associations. Rather, they are allowed to enter and pass out of mind while remaining alert and aware of the conscious field itself. Thus, open monitoring meditation emphasizes the self-monitoring skill developed initially through focused attention meditation practice, and cultivates moment-to-moment meta-awareness.

The term mindfulness has connotations of awareness, retention, and discernment. The state of mindful awareness involves remembering to attend in a discerning way to what is in immediate experience. Contemporary mindfulness practice derives from Vipassana meditation in Theravada Buddhist tradition, and involves aspects of both focused attention and open monitoring, as described above. In this practice, focused attention rests upon breath sensations, while open monitoring detects, and brings awareness to when the mind has wandered, and repeatedly, without judgment, brings it back to the breath. As skill in this open monitoring aspect develops, the practitioner learns to observe the functioning of his or her own mind in a calm and unattached manner, gaining insight into the causes and conditions of behavior (Gunaratana, 1993). As noted by Shapiro and Carlson (2009), mindfulness meditation involves intention, attention, and attitude: Intention is the personal vision for why meditation is being practiced, which may be dynamic and evolving as practice continues. Attention in mindfulness meditation ". . . is discerning and nonreactive, sustained and concentrated, so that we can see clearly what is arising in the present moment . . ." (Shapiro & Carlson, 2009, p. 10). Attitude refers to qualities of openness, acceptance, curiosity, and affection in the attention that is brought to present experience.

Jon Kabat-Zinn (1994), the originator of mindfulness-based stress reduction (MBSR), defines mindfulness meditation as a process of paying attention on purpose, in the present moment, and nonjudgmentally. MBSR is a well-defined, eight-week, systematic training program in which the central component is mindfulness meditation. MBSR was designed to provide a secular approach to teaching people how to use their resources and abilities to respond more effectively to stress, pain, and illness (Kabat-Zinn, 1990).

Behavioral and Neuroscientific Research on Meditation

Interest in the relationships between Buddhism and science has existed for over 100 years (McMahan, 2008; Wallace, 2003, 2007). However, for most of this period, interest took the form of speculation concerning whether the introspection methods of Buddhist meditation qualified as a first-person science of the mind, and debate regarding the similarities between Buddhist metaphysics and theory in the physical sciences. Despite this long-standing interest, it is only during the past few decades that a field of "contemplative science" has taken form. This field has been characterized by a rapid growth in publication of scientific studies of meditators, in which an appreciation of the details of meditation practice have been brought together with the experimental procedures of cognitive science, affective science, and neuroscience.

Given the rapid growth and consequent size of the research literature in contemplative science, the following review will only briefly describe select studies that are relevant to pedagogy in higher education. More extensive reviews of the effects of meditation on attention and emotion regulation can be found in Lutz, Slagter, Dunne, and Davidson (2008) and in Wadlinger and Isaacowitz (2011).

As already noted, behavioral and neuroscientific research on meditation has often focused on the measurement of attention, emotion, or brain structures and physiological processes that have known relationship to these psychological constructs. Experienced practitioners have been shown, through both behavioral and physiological measures, to maintain greater attention focus during mindfulness meditation practice. For example, Cahn and Polich (2009) studied 16 Vipassana meditation practitioners who had an average of 20 years of meditation experience, comparing event-related brain electrical potentials to distracting sounds during meditation with a period in which they were instructed to let their minds wander. Meditation effects (in comparison to mind wandering) were found for brain responses to the distracter stimuli, with a reduction in amplitude of the response to distracters found to be strongest in participants reporting more hours of daily meditation practice.

There are also studies demonstrating an association between meditation practice, performance on laboratory attention tasks, and related brain physiology while participants are not engaged in formal meditation. Slagter and colleagues (2007) examined 17 participants at the beginning and end of a three-month Vipassana meditation retreat, in comparison to 23 novices who meditated 20 minutes daily for one week prior to each experimental session. The attentional blink task was administered while brain electrical activity was recorded. In the attentional blink task, participants are rapidly shown a sequential series of letters on a computer screen, with two numbers embedded within the letter series. When these two numbers have relatively few letters intervening between them, persons tend to be able to report seeing the first number but fail to report the second, as though their attention had "blinked." This attentional blink effect had previously been thought to reflect a general refractory period that was thought of as a fixed characteristic of the brain. However, Slagter and colleagues found that the intensive meditation retreat practitioners, compared to novices, showed a smaller attentional blink effect for the testing session after retreat, in contrast to that before. Further, this enhanced detection of the second number was associated with brain electrical response evidence for a reduction in the persistence of brain-resource allocation to the first number. This is consistent with attention not being so persistently captured by the first number, and therefore interfering less with processing of the second. This observation is of particular interest in regard to the rationale relating attention to working memory capacity described earlier in the present chapter. Fukuda and Vogel (2011) have recently shown that the poor attentional control associated with lower working memory capacity is due to slow disengagement from distracters. Additional physiological evidence for meditation practice resulting in more rapid disengagement from mental processing is provided by Pagnoni, Cekic and Guo (2008). Using functional magnetic resonance imaging (fMRI) of the brain while participants were shown a series of words, these investigators observed more rapid return to baseline in brain activation following each word for experienced Zen meditators versus non-meditators.

In another experiment, Jha, Krimpinger, and Baime (2007) studied 17 participants in an eight-week MBSR training program, 17 meditation-experienced participants in a month-long Vipassana meditation retreat, and 17 non-meditating control participants, administering the Attention Network Test (Fan, McCandliss, Sommer, Raz, & Posner, 2002) before and after the training and retreat. In this test, various warning and spatial cues precede sequential trials in which the participant must identify whether arrows flanking a target arrow are facing in the same or different directions as the target. By analyzing the response times for these trials, separate measures of alerting, orienting, and conflict-monitoring aspects of attention can be obtained. Participants in the Vipassana retreat group, who were already experienced meditators, performed better than those in the other groups in conflict-monitoring measured at baseline, before their retreat experience. Participants in the MBSR training program showed a greater improvement than the other groups, from pre- to post-training, in their ability to orient attention to cued regions of the display. The Vipassana retreat participation facilitated greater receptive attention skills, which improved alerting to visual cues, in comparison to the other groups.

Thus, brief and longer-term meditation training appear to have differential impacts on aspects of attention. The briefer MBSR training appeared to facilitate improved "top-down" or volitional attention control, while the longer-term and more intensive practice of the Vipassana retreat group facilitated enhanced "bottom-up" or stimulus-driven aspects of attention.

In a recently published report (MacLean et al., 2010), visual discrimination and sustained attention were assessed before and after an intensive *shamatha* meditation training retreat involving more than 5 hours per day of practice for three months. Shamatha is a breath-focused meditation practice intended to develop attentional stability and equanimity. Participants were randomly assigned either to receive training first (30 participants) or to serve as wait-list controls and receive training during a second three-month retreat (30 participants). The meditation group, compared to the wait-list group, showed improvements in visual discrimination that were linked to increases in perceptual sensitivity and improved vigilance during sustained visual attention task performance. In another analysis of data collected from this same project (Sahdra et al., 2011), the intensive meditation training, compared to the wait-list group who had not yet undergone the training, was also found to result in improved performance in a response inhibition task. This focused attention improvement predicted enhanced adaptive functioning (based on an index derived from a combination of self-report measures of emotion regulation, depression, anxiety, and psychological well-being), underscoring the relationship between attention and emotion regulation in meditation practice. Although a three-month intensive meditation retreat is not a possibility for most students, there is evidence that attention, as well as emotion, changes can occur with briefer meditation training (e.g., seven-week), as described below.

The relationship between emotional and cognitive effects of meditation is also illustrated in research reported by Ortner, Kilner, and Zelazo (2007). In one study, Ortner and colleagues had 28 experienced mindfulness meditation practitioners categorize high- or low-pitched audio tones that were presented one or four seconds after the onset of pictures with emotional content versus neutral pictures. Reaction times to the tones following the emotional pictures, compared to the neutral pictures, revealed those with greater amounts of meditation experience to show less interference from the emotional pictures. These participants also reported greater mindfulness and psychological well-being in their daily lives. In a second study reported in this paper, 82 participants were randomly assigned either to a seven-week mindfulness meditation training, a relaxation training, or no training (a wait-list control group). Using the same experimental procedure as described for the first study, the mindfulness meditation training group showed greater pre- to post-training reductions in interference from emotionally unpleasant pictures. In combination, these two studies support the conclusion that both longer-term and brief mindfulness meditation practice reduces prolonged attentional sensitivity to emotional arousal.

Other studies have also provided evidence consistent with the hypothesis that longer-term meditation practice enhances emotion regulation. For example, Nielsen and Kaszniak (2006) employed an experimental procedure in which emotional scenes were exposed for very brief durations, and both preceded and followed by scrambled visual noise, a procedure termed visual masking. Masking effectively interrupts the processing of visual information at a very early stage in the brain, and those shown masked pictures are not consciously aware of what they have been shown, even though various bodily reactions to the images can be recorded. Nielsen and Kaszniak found Zen and Vipassana meditators with greater than 10 years of practice experience, in comparison with matched non-meditating controls, report higher emotional clarity in an extensive self-report inventory. Those reporting higher emotional clarity showed lower physiological (skin-conductance response) and self-reported arousal, and greater subtle positive facial expression (by facial muscle electromyography) in response to the very briefly presented and masked emotional pictures. Thus, long-term meditation appears associated with enhanced regulation of emotion very early in the emotion response process. Additional research is needed to determine whether briefer meditation training experience, as might be more feasible for students, results in positive changes in emotion regulation. However, relevant studies utilizing briefer (e.g., seven-week) meditation training have begun to appear, as described below.

Wadlinger and Isaacowitz (2011) have argued that while the attention training of mindfulness meditation practice may have a greater impact on the regulation of negative emotion, loving-kindness meditation may be more likely to increase positive emotion by bringing attention, and generating positive feelings, to the silently repeated phrases employed in such practice (e.g., "May you be safe. May you be healthy. May you be happy. May you live with ease."). In a relevant study, Fredrickson, Cohn, Coffey, Pek, and Finkel (2008) randomly assigned 139 working adults to a seven-week loving-kindness meditation (LKM) training or a wait-list group. Using statistical procedures that allow for causal inference from a time-series of correlational data, they found that, compared to the waitlist controls, LKM practice led to greater increases over time in daily experiences of positive emotions, which in turn led to increases in a wide range of personal resources (e.g., increased mindfulness, sense of purpose in life, social support, and decreased illness symptoms). In turn, these increments in personal resources predicted increased life satisfaction and reduced depressive symptoms. Surprisingly, another study found that even a few minutes of LKM practice for college students, compared to a closely matched control group that did not engage in the practice, resulted in an increase in the experience of positive social emotions and sense of social connectedness with strangers (Hutcherson, Seppala, & Gross, 2008).

Implications for Contemplative Pedagogy

The select research described above supports the hypotheses that meditation practice is associated with enhanced ability to focus attention, disengage and shift attention from distractions, maintain attention over time (i.e., vigilance), regulate emotion early in the process of its arousal, and a reduce susceptibility to attentional disruption by emotionally arousing events. In addition, particular types of meditation practice (i.e., loving-kindness meditation) appear to increase experiences of positive emotion and sense of social connectedness. Attentional focus and flexibility appear to be central in learning, and it is likely that emotion regulation facilitates openness to new experience and challenging perspectives. The results of available laboratory research are thus encouraging to those interested in the development of contemplative pedagogy. However, there is a need for much additional research on the specific impact of contemplative practices in higher education. For example, although there exists research, as reviewed above, examining the attention and emotion changes consequent to relatively brief (e.g., seven- or eight-week) meditation training, the majority of studies focus upon comparisons of long-term meditators and non-meditators. Because such studies do not randomly assign participants to meditation training, but rather recruit those with an established meditation practice, it is unclear whether observed differences between meditators and non-meditators reflect the *consequences* of meditation practice, or rather, preexisting differences related to who decides to enter, and remains engaged with a long-term practice. Thus, additional randomized controlled trials are needed, in which participants are randomly assigned to either meditation training or a control condition (e.g., a wait-list control condition wherein there is no training for the equivalent length of time as the active meditation training condition, or active control conditions in which alternative non-meditation training is provided).

Additional research is also required to address the question of what length and intensity of meditation training and practice is required to observe the desired changes in attention, emotion, or other relevant psychological dimensions. Clearly, some changes have been documented consequent to relatively brief training. However, it remains unclear whether particular kinds of educationally desirable changes require longer training and practice than is generally feasible in educational settings. It also remains unclear whether relatively brief meditation training is capable of resulting in lasting change. Few studies include the length of follow-up assessment that would be necessary to address this question. Another unaddressed question concerns the qualifications of those who offer meditation instruction. Specifically in regard to incorporating contemplative practices into higher education curricula, is it necessary for faculty to themselves have received instruction from an experienced meditation teacher, and to have a regular meditation practice? There is no available experimental research to address this question.

Finally, more research is needed that evaluates the educationally relevant consequences of meditation practice with students. A growing number of educators have been implementing contemplative practices within their courses and curricula, as described in several chapters of the present volume. However, there is almost no research available on the academic and personal transformation consequences of such innovations that would allow for relatively unambiguous interpretation.

The present author has been among those who have been incorporating contemplative practices into higher education. In a recently taught undergraduate course on the psychology of empathy and compassion, the development of which was supported by a contemplative practice fellowship from the Center for Contemplative Mind in Society, I utilized several contemplative practices. These included reflective journal commentaries based on readings; breath-focused mindful attention at the start and at various other times during class sessions; exercises in mindful attention to other bodily experience; council circle practice during seminar discussion, involving quiet and full attention to the person who is speaking; loving-kindness meditation practice during class sessions focusing on readings about research on this practice; and dyadic nonjudgmental listening practice and exercises on self versus other-focused perspective taking during class sessions focused around readings concerning research on empathy in social interaction.

Although space does not allow for a full discussion of these practices in this course, a few observations can be noted. First, structured student evaluations of the course, in comparison to both other department courses at the same curricular level, and my own previous courses, were quite positive. In regard to the contemplative exercises, most of the students reported that they enjoyed these activities and found them useful, and many reported continuing to use these practices outside of class. In addition, a comparison of pre- to post-course responses on self-report inventories designed to measure aspects of mindfulness in daily life, compassion for oneself, and empathy for others, showed statistically significant increases from before to after course participation. Further, these increases were greatest for those students who engaged in the contemplative practices outside of the class sessions.

Some of the session-by-session feedback from students was also informative. For example, their comments regarding the contemplative journal commentaries exercise were interesting. This exercise instructed students to take ten minutes, both prior to and after completing the day's reading assignment, to engage in simple breath-focused concentrative meditation, and after the second ten-minute practice, to briefly describe their experience while doing the reading. Quite often, these journal commentaries described the experience of greater attention to, interest in, and retention of the reading material, in comparison to their usual experience in doing course reading. Commentaries also noted insights into the causes (e.g., prior emotional interchange with a friend) and conditions (e.g., noise from roommates) of their experiences of distraction. The final paper required by the course supported the conclusion that students were retaining, and integrating into their life experience, what they were reading and discussing in class.

Although encouraging the incorporation of contemplative practices in higher education, such observations do not allow for unambiguous interpretation. The students in my course were self-selected, and there was no comparison to alternative approaches to teaching the course that were not contemplatively-based. Also, because several contemplative exercises were used in the course, it is unclear whether specific exercises were more useful, in terms of educational or personal goals, than other exercises. These are among the issues that future research on contemplative pedagogy should address. Such research will be important to provide faculty with an informed basis for bringing contemplative practices into the classroom and curriculum.

References

Cahn, B. R., & Polich, J. (2009). Meditation (Vipassana) and the P3a event-related brain potential. *International Journal of Psychophysiology, 72*(1), 51–60.

Cowan, N., Fristoe, N. M., Elliott, E. M., Brunner, R. P., & Saults, J. S. (2006). Scope of attention, control of attention, and intelligence in children and adults. *Memory & Cognition, 34*(8), 1754–1768.

Davidson, R. J. (2010). Empirical explorations of mindfulness: Conceptual and methodological conundrums. *Emotion, 10*(1), 8–11.

Deurr, M. A. (2004). *Powerful silence: The role of meditation and other contemplative practices in American life and work.* Northampton, MA: Center for Contemplative Mind in Society.

Duerr, M., Zajonc, A., & Dana, D. (2003). Survey of transformative and spiritual dimensions of higher education. *Journal of Transformative Education, 1*(3), 177–211.

Fan, J., McCandliss, B., Sommer, T., Raz, A., & Posner, M. (2002). Testing the efficiency and independence of attentional networks. *Journal of Cognitive Neuroscience, 14*(3), 340–347.

Fredrickson, B. L., Cohn, M. A., Coffey, K. A., Pek, J., & Finkel, S. M. (2008). Open hearts build lives: Positive emotions, induced through loving-kindness meditation, build consequential personal resources. *Journal of Personality and Social Psychology, 95*(5), 1045–1062.

Fukuda, K., & Vogel, E. K. (2011). Individual differences in recovery time from attentional capture. *Psychological Science*. DOI: 10.1177/0956797611398493.

Gunaratana, H. (1993). *Mindfulness in plain English*. Boston: Wisdom Publications.

Hart, T. (2004). Opening the contemplative mind in the classroom. *Journal of Transformative Education, 2*(1), 28–46.

Hutcherson, C. A., Seppala, E. M., & Gross, J. J. (2008). Loving-kindness meditation increases social connectedness. *Emotion, 8*(5), 720–724.

Jain, S., Shapiro, S. L., Swanick, S., Roesch, S. C., Mills, P. J., Bell, I., & Schwartz, G. E. R. (2007). A randomized controlled trial of mindfulness meditation versus relaxation training: Effects on distress, positive states of mind, rumination, and distraction. *Annals of Behavioral Medicine, 33*(1), 11–21.

Jha, A., Krimpinger, J., & Baime, M. J. (2007). Mindfulness training modifies subsystems of attention. *Cognitive, Affective, and Behavioral Neuroscience 7*(2), 109–119.

Jha, A. P., Stanley, E. A., & Baime, M. J. (2010). What does mindfulness training strengthen? Working memory capacity as a functional marker of training success. In R. A. Baer (Ed.), *Assessing mindfulness & acceptance processes in clients* (pp. 207–220). New York: Context Press.

Kabat-Zinn, J. (1990). *Full catastrophe living: Using the wisdom of your body and mind to face stress, pain and illness.* New York: Delacorte.

Kabat-Zinn, J. (1994). *Wherever you go, there you are: Mindfulness meditation in everyday life.* New York, Hyperion.

Kegan, R. (1994). *In over our heads: The mental demands of modern life.* Cambridge, MA: Harvard University Press.

Liston, C., McEwen, B. S., & Casey, B. J. (2009). Psychosocial stress reversibly disrupts prefrontal processing and attentional control. *Proceedings of the National Academy of Sciences, U.S.A., 106*(3), 912–917.

Lutz, A., Slagter, H. A., Dunne, J. D., & Davidson, R. J. (2008). Attention regulation and monitoring in meditation. *Trends in Cognitive Sciences, 12*(4), 163–169.

MacLean, K. A., Ferrer, E., Aichele, S. R., Bridwell, D. A., Zanesco, A. P., Jacobs, T. L., King, B. G., Rosenberg, E. L., Sahdra, B. K., Shaver, P. R., Wallace, B. A., Mangun, G. R., & Saron, C. D. (2010). Intensive meditation training improves perceptual discrimination and sustained attention. *Psychological Science, 21*(6), 829–839.

McMahan, D. L. (2008). *The making of Buddhist modernism.* New York: Oxford University Press.

McNab, F., & Klingberg, T. (2008). Prefrontal cortex and basal ganglia control access to working memory. *Nature Neuroscience, 11*(1), 103–107.

Nielsen, L., & Kaszniak, A. W. (2006). Awareness of subtle emotional feelings: A comparison of long-term meditators and non-meditators. *Emotion, 6*(3), 392–405.

Oman, D., Shapiro, S. L., Thoresen, C. E., Plante, T. G., & Flinders, T. (2008). Meditation lowers stress and supports forgiveness among college students: A randomized controlled trial. *Journal of American College Health, 56*(5), 569–578.

Ortner, C. N. M., Kilner, S. J., & Zelazo, P. D. (2007). Mindfulness meditaion and reduced emotional interference on a cognitive task. *Motivation and Emotion, 31*(4), 271–283.

Pagnoni, G., Cekic, M., & Guo, Y. (2008). "Thinking about not-thinking": Neural correlates of conceptual processing during Zen meditation. *PLoS ONE, 3*(9): e3083. DOI: 10.1371/journal_pone.00-3083.

Palmer, P. J., & Zajonc, A. (2010). *The heart of higher education.* San Francisco, CA: Jossey-Bass.

Pessoa, L. (2008). On the relationship between emotion and cognition. *Nature Reviews Neuroscience, 9*(2), 148–158.

Ricard, M. (2010). *Why meditate?* Carlsbad, CA: Hay House.

Sahdra, B. K., MacLean, K. A., Ferrer, E., Shaver, P. R., Rosenberg, E. L., Jacobs, T. L., Zanesco, A. P., King, B. G., Aichele, S. R., Bridwell, D. A., Mangun, G. R., Lavy, S., Wallace, B. A., & Saron, C.D. (2011). Enhanced inhibition during meditation training predicts improvement in self-reported adaptive social-emotional functioning. *Emotion, 11*(2), 299–312.

Salmon, P. G., Santorelli, S. F., & Kabat-Zinn, J. (1998). Intervention elements promoting adherence in mindfulness-based stress reduction programs in the clinical behavioral medicine setting. In S. A. Shumaker, E. B. Schron, & J. K. Okene (Eds.), *The handbook of health behavior change* (2nd ed.) (pp. 239–268). New York: Springer.

Sarath, E. W. (2006). Meditation, creativity, and consciousness: Charting future terrain within higher education. *Teachers College Record, 108*(9), 1816–1841.

Shapiro, S. L., Brown, K. W., & Astin, J. A. (2008). Toward the integration of meditation into higher education: A review of research. Retrieved from <http://www.contemplativemind.org/resources/research.html>.

Shapiro, S. L., & Carlson, L. E. (2009). *The art and science of mindfulness: Integrating mindfulness into psychology and the helping professions.* Washington, DC: American Psychological Association.

Slagter, H. A., Lutz, A., Greischar, L. L., Francis, A. Nieuwenhuis, S., Davis, J. M., & Davidson, R. J. (2007). Mental training affects distribution of limited brain resources. *PLoS Biology, 5*(6), e138. Doi:10.1317/journal.pbio.0050138.

Vogel, E. K., McCollough, A. W., & Machizawa, M. G. (2005). Neural measures reveal individual differences in controlling access to working memory. *Nature, 438*(7067), 748–751.

Wadlinger, H. A., & Isaacowitz, D. M. (2011). Fixing our focus: Training attention to regulate emotion. *Personality and Social Psychology Review, 15*(1), 75–102.

Wallace, B. A. (Ed.). (2003). *Buddhism and science: Breaking new ground.* New York: Columbia University Press.

Wallace, B. A. (2007). *Contemplative science: Where Buddhism and neuroscience converge.* New York: Columbia University Press.

Zajonc, A (2009). *Meditation as contemplative inquiry: When knowing becomes love.* Great Barrington, MA: Lindisfarne Books.

Part III

Contemplating Change

Individual and Collective Transformation in Contemplative Education Environments

13

Transformative Pathways

Engaging the Heart in Contemplative Education

Diana Denton

Entering

In various spiritual traditions the heart is conceptualized as a site of liberation or enlightenment. Considering questions of freeing consciousness, I have attended to the tantric conception of liberation as *hrydayangamibhuta*—to become something that moves in the heart (Muller-Ortega, 1989). My understandings are inspired by the non-dual tantric tradition of Kashmir Shaivism.[1] Paul Muller-Ortega (1989) in his exploration of this tradition notes that "notions of contraction and expansion of the Heart are directly related to the spiritual conditions of ignorance or enlightenment of the individual soul" (p. 122). From this perspective the heart or *hrdaya* is described as a site of vibration or movement that awakens as consciousness expands. Here the term "hrdaya refers most directly to the concept of the Heart cakra that emerged from Upanisadic and Yogic formulations" (Muller-Ortega, 1989, p. 75). The heart chakra has been described as the seat of the soul, a place of compassion and love, an embodied awareness of the Infinite—the very core of being (Maharshi, 1972/2001, p. 80). The practices of the heart are rooted in a somatic awareness of the movement of this center as it expands and contracts (Dyczkowski, 1987; Muller-Ortega, 1989).

> Through practices of the heart we move toward awakening and expanding consciousness. A heartfelt practice requires attentiveness to the stillness and movement of experience—to the multiple tightenings, contractions, fluidities, and expansions of immediate somatic

> experience. Attentiveness is the doorway to a new curriculum of breath, silence, and listening—listening in the body, listening to feeling, listening to the ordinary experiences of life—hearing (and seeing) with the heart. (Denton, 2004, p. 137)

As educator, I have followed this notion of movement conceptually, somatically and metaphorically through contemplative practice, imagination and thought as I ask: How is the heart linked to the freeing of consciousness? In trying to conceptualize an understanding that was not embedded in a specific culture or tradition, I turned to emergent somatic images. Using heart, stone, and flame as exchangeable metaphors, I explored discourses and practices to re-vitalize inner heart knowledge and embodiment (Denton, 1998, 2004, 2005a, 2005b, 2006).

In this chapter, through metaphoric innovation and a poetic sensibility, I deepen my phenomenology/pedagogy of the heart. Engaging the heart as both inner method and attainment,[2] I ask how insights and practices of the heart might continue to expand a contemplative pedagogy and vision. How is the awakened heart embodied within self, relationship, and community? An important first step in such an inquiry is the recognition of the signs of contraction and expansion in these systems. If lenses of contraction narrow our reading of the world (Levin, 1988); how might the vision of the heart expand our perception? I take as my starting point the metaphors of the heart that have informed my understandings of the inner world of the self. As a teacher and scholar of communication, I extend these metaphors from the world of the intrapersonal to networks of relationship—the realms of the interpersonal and organizational.

Kşemarāja, a tenth-century teacher in the tradition of Kashmir Shaivism states that individual consciousness "becomes contracted in conformity with the objects of consciousness" (Kşemarāja as quoted in Singh, 1990, p. 55). I use a simple image to convey this concept (Denton, 1998, 2005a, 2005b): A large black pillow. My hands clutch together pieces of the pillow, like the self that holds impressions of experience, the pillow hardens, is compressed, as impressions are embedded and "defenses" formed. If I try to remove these hardened parts the pillow will tear; it will break. This hardening of the pillow is akin to the tightening of the ego—the crust or shell that hardens around the self—constricting the heart. As the movement of the heart diminishes, "the more does the subjectivity fall until it becomes inert like a stone" (Abhinavagupta in Muller-Ortega, 1989, p. 209).

David Michael Levin (1988) describes the modern self as "a self deeply divided, a self in which reason is split off from feeling, from sensibility, and from the innate wisdom of the body" (p. 20). Citing Guenther, he notes that "the process of 'transformation' which we call 'growing up' is actually one of 'growing narrowness and frozenness'" (p. 59). I note the movement and restrictions of the self, gestures of contraction when the self is trapped in defensive psychological postures, embedded patterns of belief and behavior, or rigid conceptual frames, which result in fragmentation and separation. As Adam Kahane (2010) cautions, "Fear rigidifies us, leaves us stuck" (p. 85). Contrast this with gestures of expansion when the heart opens as a responsiveness to the seen, a listening to present experience, to the affective dimension of the self. Hrdaya means "resting place" (Muller-Ortega, 1989, p. 79). From this perspective, the heart can be understood as the place where all external experiences are swallowed back into the self, as felt response. Here they come to "rest" in the heart; in its unifying presence. As inner practice, the heart becomes the melting pot for all experience.

I have often been troubled by dualistic frames that tend to fragment the self—models that commonly address sharply demarcated levels of consciousness. In the heart, I find the "unbroken body" (Bailly, 1987, p. 44) of the self; an "undivided self-referential consciousness" (Muller-Ortega, 1989, p. 212). It is the rigid, tight, deadened defensive heart that is numb to this touch of experience. As Ronald Heifetz and Marty Linsky (2009) note:

> Calloused finger tips lose their sensitivity. Your listening becomes less and less acute, until you fail to hear the real messages from people around you, and cannot identify the songs beneath their words. . . . In the effort to protect yourself, you risk numbing yourself to the world in which you are embedded. (pp. 226–227)

Separating from experience, this self loses its agility and freedom to respond to the present. Alexandra Michel and Stanton Wortham (2009) suggest that "abstract, decontextualized concepts" are "an important part of dualistic practices" that separate "the person from the situation" (p. 30) and emphasize the importance of "clearing away people's pre-existing identities, scripts and models so that they can notice" (p. 27) the present context. Here "liberating knowledge is attained not by going beyond appearances but by attending closely to them" (Dyczkowski, 1987, p. 54). This suggests a non-dualistic vision that honors the intimate connection, the intertwining of the self with its world in a reciprocity that is "a way of being effected by what is given" (Levin, 1987, p. 62).

Dwelling in a holistic education mindset, I am concerned about facilitating these inner and outer connections—between self and the larger human and more-than-human landscape—yet I continue to be struck by the places of isolation, separation and fragmentation in the worlds of my students, colleagues, institution, and the global arena. In my organization I see contentious relationships, often characterized by defensiveness, fear, and a loss of trust. There may have been betrayals, competition, commitments that have not been met, or simply values and egos that have clashed. Here stone also becomes an apt metaphor for the underbelly of our educational environment—the blockages, hardening, or stuck places in the system. As an educator, whose pedagogy is rooted in a heart-based contemplative practice, I often find myself as a catalyst or touchstone—a fiery site where traditional Cartesian values, beliefs, and norms clash (Denton, 2011). An awareness of this underbelly and a willingness to confront the blockages, and explore pathways of reconciliation or new avenues of approach, is integral to fostering a community of practice that will embody the heart.

In my phenomenology of the heart, I have identified three methods that represent the core of my heart pedagogy and practice: dwelling in the wound, relaxing into the heart, and filling the heart. In this chapter, I apply these three as they spiral outward from the self to embody the life-world of others through poetics, metaphor and experience. I ask the question: What conditions, actions, attitudes might awaken and anchor an expansion of consciousness within self, relationship, and organizational community?

Dwelling in the Wound

> In my vision for a new interdisciplinary transformative graduate program, I have witnessed the creation and eventual dissolution of the fragile organizational structures that have held my departmental colleagues and me in place. Surrounded by dissonant choirs of institutional tension, broken trust, conflicted agendas, and challenges to both my leadership and contemplative/aesthetic scholarship . . . I find myself moving through fractured and polarized spaces.
>
> —Denton, 2011, p. 86

In my attempts to move a new graduate program forward, I watch the shadow emerge in my organization—the places of contraction and hardening—*where nothing moves*. A leader in my institution leaves a meeting as I am presenting the proposed graduate program. He departs abruptly. His parting shot as he heads for the door "Well there better not be any of that contemplative stuff in it—that's all I can say!" And so begins a chapter of wounding/conflict in my institution—a program stalled. . . . The shadow becomes visible. What had been unseen[3] now rises to the surface—is given voice and substance. Others tell me of furtive whispers that still continue behind closed doors—dismissive of my contemplative scholarship (perhaps I should not have donated my books to the university library—where they would be so easily accessible to my colleagues and their "scholarly" scrutiny). In the midst of this contraction, what is the moving heart's response? I am aware of the wound, the rising of a sadness in my being. Yet, in the sadness, there is an opening. I allow myself to feel the wound. It is this piercing that brings me back to the heart. My attention shifts to this inner center, to my own felt response. I do not defend, contract, or shut down; I listen to the wound, and then I choose to walk away.

I remember a professor during my graduate career who reminded me that one cannot critique a paradigm by standing outside of it (from a distance). A holistic orientation values different modalities of critique, the views of different perspectives; is not arched in opposition but engaged in an observant, open, compassionate listening. It is the rigidity of a perspective that freezes, tightens and contracts the consciousness of self, relationship, and organizational commuity. In my institution the shadow grows. "I notice how the tightening body, the defensive body separates from experience. The world becomes a tight place" (Denton, 2004, p. 140).

How does this tension/conflict move the organization? How does it move me? The poetic voice beckons.

tides of stone

(i)

The pebbled story:
the brutal innocence
of stone

all rivers
run into
us

face down

(ii)

the razors
of his eyes
cut
the quickening
of her seed

his severed tongue
wrapping
        her beauty
in a song

as floods waver
to a ground
        of dust

and springs
are consumed
        by her sun

(iii)

when the moon
        is shrinking

how will her
        tides be appeased?[4]

The consciousness that is tight, defended, holding a closed position, cannot shine forth in self, relationship or in our larger organizational communities. Sometimes the wounding, the burning must occur—to awaken greater consciousness. In the space of wounding there is vulnerability, an openness that may lead us to a more self-reflexive posture. "The wound is an altering of the body, a shifting of the body's tissues. The body of consciousness (a body of meanings) has its tissues damaged. The wounds of this body's experience . . . points of entry" (Denton, 1989, p. 50).

Without this pain, the self may not look deeper. Kahane (2010) offers a gentle reminder, "In healing ourselves (and others), our wound becomes our gift" (p. 130). We must have a "willingness to admit that we are part of, rather than apart from, the woundedness of our world" (Kahane, 2010, p. 132). Yvonna Lincoln and Egon Guba (2000) assert that new paradigm research is frequently concerned with the "single experience, the individual crisis, the epiphany or moment of discovery, with that most powerful of all threats to conventional objectivity, feeling and emotion" (p. 179). Such wounds hold the potential to catalyze an increase in consciousness. Levin (1988) describes truth as an *unconcealment*, an awareness informed by "authentic encounters with primordial darkness" (p. 351) that is "open to learning from the greatness—even the terror—of the night" (p. 351). In the classroom, this may mean allowing the tensions, frictions, conflicts to emerge in formal and informal educational settings. I watch the conflicts that erupt in student teams. I recall the words of a significant teacher in my life: I don't teach people, I just put them together and they learn from each other. Others respond to what the self projects; and simultaneously they see through their own rigidities and conceptual frames. Such interactions may be an opportunity to awaken consciousness, igniting a greater self-reflexivity, mirroring reflections of self and relational cultures—the deepest fears, projections and insecurities; and the inner defenses and rigidities that confine perception. Michael Jackson (1998) has noted that "disturbances in the field of interpersonal relations will register as cultural contradictions, as well as show up as knots and binds in the field of bodily intersubjectivity" (p. 13). As facilitator, I also offer a mirror; opportunities for each student to reflect on her or his contribution to the emerging dynamic through journaling and group dialogue. Learning does not always happen easily.

Dwelling in the ache of my own institutional wound, as "I watch the yielding and resistance of old paradigms and their slow burdens . . . the poetic becomes a source of presence" (Denton, 2011, p. 87) that sustains me.

duelling suns
The days
        ran into
each other

as her belly ripened

(the dawn's chorus
        rising
in her)
        to a red sun
        now yellowed
the bruise
that grows
faint

        like a blemish
on the sky's skin

where brewing
storms
        circle

        and duelling suns
        colour the horizon

as we raise
        our eyes
to her light

Celeste Snowber (2004) writes about the word *meitri* in the Buddhist tradition, "which ultimately means to have compassion for everything that comes in our lives . . . to welcome everything, even the uninvited guests" (p. 125). She asks: "How can we lean into the uninvited guests of our lives whether that is people, experiences, illnesses, broken plans, or both the delight and limitations of our own bodies. It takes strength to lean. Endurance" (p. 125). It is in the messiness of our interactions . . . the conflicts, the tensions . . . where deepenings often happen. Surprise attacks, sudden eruptions confront and hold the potential to inspire and catalyze new directions. How do I move through these spaces as educator; how do I gesture in the face of antagonism and confrontation? I notice how the Western cultural mindset gives negative connotations to conflict (Borisoff & Victor, 1998) and how these "embedded patterns lock our perceptual frames" (Denton, 2003, pp. 45–46). Thomas Crum (1988) explores the need to honor the energy given rather than opposing it, inviting us into a re-visioning of conflict.

> Ocean waves, powerful and majestic, incessantly break along coastlines throughout the world. What did it take to create this awesome splendour? Conflict—interference patterns between land, wind, and water. Who lost in this conflict? Was it the wind? Or the water? Obviously neither lost. Conflict is not contest. Conflict just is. (p. 37)

In my research on conflict and imagery in an undergraduate course on Conflict Management, students engage in contemplative imagery practice as they remember a conflict experience. As they allow inner images to emerge they are invited to relax into the image.

> From an individual perspective, staying with the image of conflict allowed participants to increase their consciousness of perceptions and attitudes, which in turn allowed recognition and examination.

> In some cases images began to shift and perceptions of conflict altered. One woman spoke of such an altering when she described conflict as an opportunity for intimacy—a deepening of connection with the other. Conflict as embrace rather than struggle. Another participant described a sense of letting go. As bodily and emotional tensions released, he did not need to hold himself so tightly. . . . Participants in the study self-reported a greater ability to "stay with conflict experience" "to work it though." Embodied images brought new voices, responses and feelings to bear on conflict experience. (Denton, 2003, p. 49)

In the poetry I watch the play and patterns of fire, wind, water and stone:

the ways of fire

(i)

We came early
to the sea
        to the stage
of her first
        storms

siloed to the stance
of another wind
        rising

in the glass
of her eyes
        shards of light
fracture
        shattering her sun

(ii)

where are the ways
of fire?

(iii)

sometimes there are
        strong rivers
in her blood

a fury of stone
        flung in
the makings
of her body

(iv)

our gaze

(burned on her skin)

arched to a
        black sky

                ruptures

and what the fire risks
we become

Christopher Poulos (2006) writes about "thin places"—thresholds where we experience a disruption between the boundaries of self and other. He suggests, "perhaps the thin places are really places within us" (p. 168)—interior spaces where we may encounter the self and all its projections, phantasms, and contractions. How does the self move through these spaces without getting caught in its own shadow or becoming burdened by the shadows of others? In navigating the hardened, stuck places in relationship it is important to attend to the self's response—to the self's feeling. But feeling can be risky territory. If one gets lost in the emotion there is the risk of getting caught in the shadow. How can this space of feeling be engaged for self and others?

Emotions can be understood as raw energy that signals to the self what is being experienced. Attending to the response to an experience, the self is beckoned inwardly. The emotion becomes a magnet that calls consciousness home. Listening to the emotion, rather than getting stuck in it, catalyzes a return to the "fire" of the heart. "A blazing energy [is revealed within] the one who dedicates himself to removing the burden of this contraction" (Abhinavagupta, in Dyczkowski, 1987, p. 190).

Here, this fiery energy of emotion is transformed to a clear flame. Rather than being lost in the emotion, it becomes the messenger that informs and guides action. The heart that moves is a centered heart that knows how to respond; that has the ability to respond. In the moving heart, as I attend to my own inner response, I am inspired to act.

How does this tension/conflict move the organization? How does it move me?

In the beginning, as I move this new graduate program forward, I am a driving force. I initiate meeting upon meeting, influencing chairs and recalcitrant committee members—before we take the graduate program proposal to a vote. The vote fails. Senior administrators (who are largely in support of the program) ask me to start again. I notice my response. The body is tired; the heart heavy. There is a different (inner) call to action. I observe, watch and eventually absent myself as the institutional "drama" unfolds. The shadow re-surfaces. What has been said behind closed doors sees the light of day. I learn to pause, to let the wounds speak, to be with what is. As I write this, I am on a one-year sabbatical dwelling in the in-between, uncertain whether my institution will open a space for this work or if I, and the work, will be called into new spaces. I live in a place of radical trust; a knowing of my own boundaries (what I can and cannot do); and an honoring of all that is still unknown—in this passage into new life.

Gibbs (1961) points to defensive communication climates—what could be characterized as the hardening of communication, the stuck spaces in relationship, and the resulting fragmentation and separation that ensues. These mounting tensions (where nothing moves) can be described as *crunch points* (Miller, Wackman, Nunnally, & Miller, 1988/1992). Here relationships deteriorate and break. Another close colleague of mine has chosen to leave. In each moment there is always a choice: do we move/respond, or stay stuck—with our rationalizations, explanations, and projections of blame? As we learn to unlock our perceptual frames, to be responsive to the immediacy of felt experience, we can be released into a new relational freedom, moving toward relational responsibility, away from the solidified perspectives of "blame and credit" to "entirely different ways of engaging with others and thus creating our world" (McNamee & Gergen, 1999, p. xii).

Images in my research on community innovation (Denton & Robertson, 2010) lend insight to manifestations of contraction and separation in organizational contexts. I am often struck by the "nodes that seem to lie on the fringes—the borderlands of our [organizational] community. We know that there are places of connection but also places of isolation and separation." In my own institution, to understand this academic system, I "must also look at its underbelly, the shadow side" conceptualized as "toxic nodes" (Denton & Robertson, 2010, p. 106).

> A toxic node is a person, organization, or network in the system where trust has been broken. There may have been betrayals, competition, commitments that were not met, or egos that have clashed. As a result, other players in the system have isolated the

> node. It has become toxic and those in the know, with experience and community affiliations, keep their distance. The toxic node can be described as a blockage, hardening, or stuck place in the system. (Denton and Robertson, 2010, p. 106)

In these hardened, stony places of relationship/organization, we must learn to be in right relationship with the seen. In honoring the self and its *objects* of consciousness (in this instance individuals, relationships, organizations, etc.) we are called to witness what is manifesting and to honour our inner response.

As a child, I would sit by the fire on cold winter evenings. I learned quickly how to *be* with the fire. If I stood too close, the sparks would burn. I would feel pain. Yet, as I respected the fire for what it was, keeping my distance, it would offer warmth. I was not angry at the fire, that it could burn me. I did not try to change it. I accepted the fire for what it was. Learning to be in right relationship with the fire of experience requires an honoring of my felt response to it; that I listen to my response; and allow myself to be moved by it (rather than stuck in rationalizations, explanations, rigidities of belief . . . "the fire didn't mean to hurt me"; "I just need to develop thicker skin"; "if only I try harder I can change the fire" . . .).

Relaxing Into the Heart

As educator, I encourage my students to listen internally to the feeling self, to the body, to the inner response. A young man in my class is troubled by his conflict-ridden interactions with a female team member. He continues to extend himself, to reach out to her to try to resolve the tensions. She refuses his overtures to meet. He feels exhausted in his efforts. I suggest that he listen to the response of his body-self; perhaps he has done enough. It is time for her to choose—to meet him halfway, or not. It must be her choice. He has done what he can. I stress that he can "care" for her and the relationship but he cannot "take care" of her or the relationship. It is an important distinction. To "take care of" implies that the other does not have the potential to provide such self-care. Implicit in this action, is the element of control. When we are "taking care" of a situation the body/psyche becomes tired; our energy is dissipated. We speak about the need to respect one's own and others' boundaries and choices—even when these choices may differ from our own; and the importance of self-care. As much as I might wish that another may change or respond differently to me, I cannot demand that this happen. The self must learn to trust in its own being/process, its own response and the being/process/response of others. Sometimes we must just let what is—be.

In tantric texts, there are descriptions of the *malas*—psychological limitations that restrict the free movement of consciousness. Karma mala is the limiting condition of "doing good or evil" (Kşemarāja in Singh, 1990, pp. 64–65)—the tendency to judge experience.

> When I judge my experience, I contract. . . . I want to move from myself, from what has been seen. I notice this also when others judge me, when criticism launched is harsh or brutal. (Denton, 2004, p. 140)

In descriptions of anava mala, it is said to bring about the sense of extreme smallness in the self because of "considering itself imperfect" (Kşemarāja in Singh, 1990, p. 64). When I am contracted I feel small. In the meanings of mayiya mala, one finds the "apprehension of all objects as different" (Kşemarāja in Singh, 1990, p. 64). Earlier, I have noticed how the tightening self, the defended body, separates from experience; how the world becomes a tight place.

Sitting in my office, as we converse, I watched him slowly relax and let go. He seems to soften. The guilt ("I am not doing enough" . . . "I am not good enough") that has hardened his consciousness releases. He has come to me because of his feelings—because he *is* feeling. This inner (and outer) conflict has risen to the surface of his consciousness. Staying with his feeling, moving through the feelings, he comes back to the self. As he leaves my office, he understands that he does not need to repair the relationship. He has learned from the experience in his own way, and she has made the choice to end the term, tensions unresolved, and to move on.

How does this tension/conflict move the relationship? How does it move him?

My young student has been at risk of getting caught in the shadow. Our conversation has offered support and understanding, a new way of entering his experience. It relieves his judgment of self—that he has not done enough—the "grip of guilt that [has] contracted the heart" (Denton, 2004, p. 139). I am reminded that sometimes, even though the "work" may not appear complete, we *have* done enough. It is time to walk away, to move out of the shadow . . . there is wisdom in timely retreat. Rather than holding on or staying stuck in an inner pattern or outer situation that is constraining, rigid, or unresponsive, as one lets go and moves, the self's presence is sometimes felt through absence. When we hold something too tightly, "it must be this way," when we try to control it, we restrict its movement. As a child, I could not control the fire, but I came to love the warmth of its dance.

Filling the Heart

> In the midst of experiences that are never predictable and often troubling, how do we offer inspiration and light?
>
> —Denton, 2004, p. 138

Abhinavagupta, another tenth-century teacher in the tradition of Kashmir Shaivism, points to the importance of nourishing the heart with "fragrant flowers which effortlessly allow for an entrance into the Heart." These flowers are "all substances—external and internal which nourish the Heart because they bestow their own nature within the Heart" (Abhinavagupta in Muller-Ortega, 1989, p. 150). As we engage the heart within self, relationship and organizational community, it is essential that we recognize and celebrate our respective callings, our gifts: those qualities, ways of being in the world that are unique to each of us. Each individual, relationship, organization has its own signature; its own fullness. Sometimes we cast long shadows in our search for what these are. But if we engage the heart as a place of sustenance, fullness, and light, eventually the shadow is dispelled. Like a small candle that brightens the darkened corners of a room, the darkness we carry can dissipate quickly. In a contemplative practice I have developed (the "Full Heart Exercise"), I invite my students to close their eyes and remember a moment of joy, a time of fullness. As they connect with the memory, I ask them to notice what it feels like; to be aware of where they feel this in their bodies; and then with each breath I invite them to let this feeling expand throughout the body, into every cell. Many students self-report that this simple exercise has had a profound effect—that as they focus on the positive image-feeling, the stresses they may have carried into the room dissolve. Several have acknowledged that they continue this practice beyond the classroom walls. In another exercise, I invite students to reflect on what is calling to them in their lives. Sometimes an image emerges or a felt response. These "callings" facilitate a deeper sense of inner connection and meaning and often prompt new calls to action.

vision-quest

(i)

We asked
the sky
to open
and you came

your tears
        the underbelly
of thunder

stunned by the
green,
tree-torn
fall

the slender
trust of grass

(ii)

Somewhere
a storm lurks
        heavy
with your breath

a slow burst of blood

where the floods
        run wild
in your eyes

and we dance, ravaged
in the wet, fragility
of their fall

Efforts to relegate contemplative scholars to the borderlands of our institutional communities persist. Yet, as we continue to embrace a vision-quest of wholeness, we will catalyze transformation. As our circles of experience touch the interior spaces of the heart, like the body of the whirling dervish, spinning to center, we court radical disruptions that move self, relationship, and our organizational communities in an ever-spiraling dance—the movement of the heart. As Kahane (2010) notes, we must "practice moving fluidly" (p. 134). Our task, as we step forward, is to support ourselves, our students, colleagues, and institutions in this movement—to recognize and articulate the shadows, callings, responses, and hearts of who we are and who we may be. In my own time of living in the in-between, I await the early signs of new life, those small movements, or quickenings, within self and other, that stir a passion, a fullness, a deep heartfelt knowing of the next pathway that is opening.

Notes

1. Kashmir Shaivism is a non-dual Hindu stream in Kashmir. Dyczkowski's (1987) *The Doctrine of Vibration: An Analysis of the Doctrines and Practices of Kashmir Shaivism* provides an excellent analysis of this tradition. Muller-Ortega's (1989) *The Triadic Heart of Siva* offers a rich analysis of the *heart* in this tradition.

2. The symbol of the heart operates on three levels: it is at once the "principle of the Ultimate," "the methods and techniques that must be employed in order to approach the reality of the Heart and transform it into a living human reality," and "the nature of the state of realization of the Heart" (Muller-Ortega, 1989, p. 2).

3. Some years earlier, a course I designed at my university that was rooted in contemplative practice—"Communicating Across Differences: Spiritual Development in a Diverse Society"—passed through similar committees with ease.

4. <www.theglobeandmail.com/news/moon-is-slowly-shrinking-scientists/article 1678756/?cmpid=rss1>, August 19, 2010. Retrieved September 2, 2010.

References

Ashton, W., & Denton, D. (Eds.). (2006). *Spirituality, ethnography, & teaching: Stories from within.* New York: Peter Lang.

Bailly, C. R. (1987). *Shaiva devotional songs of Kashmir.* Albany, NY: State University of New York Press.

Borisoff, D., & Victor, D. A. (1998). *Conflict management: A communication skills approach* (2nd ed.). Needham Heights, MA: Allyn and Bacon.

Crum, T. (1988). *The magic of conflict.* New York: Simon and Schuster.

Denton, D. (1989). *Presence.* Unpublished MA thesis, University of Toronto, Toronto, ON.

Denton, D. (1998). *In the tenderness of stone: Liberating consciousness through the awakening of the heart.* Pittsburgh, PA: Sterling House.

Denton, D. (2003). The very idea of conflict: Working with image and metaphor in a re-visioning of conflict. *Imagination, Cognition and Personality: Consciousness in Theory, Research, Clinical Practice, 22*(1), 41–53.

Denton, D. (2004). The heart's geography: Compassion as practice. In D. Denton & W. Ashton (Eds.), *Spirituality, action & pedagogy: Teaching from the heart* (pp. 136–146). New York: Peter Lang.

Denton, D. (2005a). Toward a sacred discourse: Re-conceptualizing the heart through metaphor.*Qualitative Inquiry, 11*, 752–770.

Denton, D. (2005 b). Towards a pedagogy of compassion. In J. Miller, S. Karsten, D. Denton, D. Orr, & I. Colallilo-Katts (Eds.), *Holistic learning and spirituality in education: Breaking new ground* (pp. 181–192). Albany, NY: State University of New York Press.

Denton, D. (2011). Betrayals of gravity: The flight of the phoenix. *Qualitative Inquiry, 17*(1), 85–92.

Denton, D., & Ashton, W. (Eds.). (2004). *Spirituality, action & pedagogy: Teaching from the heart.* New York: Peter Lang.

Denton, D., & Robertson, T. (2010). A kaleidoscope of innovation: Designing community impact in the Waterloo region. *The Philanthropist, 23*(3), 283–301.

Dyczkowski, M. S. G. (1987). *The doctrine of vibration: An analysis of the doctrines and practices of Kashmir Shaivism.* Albany, NY: State University of New York Press.

Gibb, J. R. (1961). Defensive communication. *Journal of Communication, 11*, 141–148.

Heifetz, R., & Linsky, M. (2002). *Leadership on the line: Staying alive through the dangers of leading.* Boston: Harvard Business School Press.

Jackson, M. (1998). *Minima ethnographica: Intersubjectivity and the anthropological project.* Chicago: University of Chicago Press.

Kahane, A. (2010). *Power and love: A theory and practice of social change.* San Francisco: Berrett-Koehler Publishers, Inc.

Levin, D. M. (1988). *The opening of vision: Nihilism and the postmodern situation.* New York, Routledge, Chapman & Hall Inc.

Lincoln, Y. S., & Guba, E. G. (2000). Paradigmatic controversies, contradictions, and emerging confluences. In N. K. Denzin & Y. S. Lincoln (Eds.), *Handbook of qualitative research* (2nd ed.) (pp. 1025–1046). Thousand Oaks, CA: Sage.

Maharshi, Ramana. (2001). The heart is the self: From the spiritual teachings of Ramana Maharshi. *Parabola, 26*(4), 80–82.

McNamee, S., & Gergen, K. (and Associates). (1999). *Relational responsibility: Resources for sustainable dialogue.* Thousand Oaks, CA: Sage Publications.

Michel, A., & Wortham, S. (2009). *Bullish on uncertainty: How organizational cultures transform participants.* New York: Cambridge University Press.

Miller, J., Karsten, S., Denton, D., Orr, D., & Colallilo-Katts, I. (Eds.). (2006). *Holistic learning and spirituality in education: Breaking new ground*, Albany, NY: State University of New York Press.

Miller, S., Wackman, D., Nunnally, E., & Miller, P. (1988/1992*). Connecting with self and others.* Littleton, CO: Interpersonal Communication Program, Inc.

Muller-Ortega, P. (1989). *The triadic heart of Siva: Kaula tantricism of Abhinavagupta in the non-dual Shaivism of Kashmir.* Albany, NY: State University of New York Press.

Poulos, C. N. (2006). Dreaming, writing, teaching: Stories from within thin places. In W. Ashton & D. Denton (Eds.), *Spirituality, ethnography and teaching: Stories from within* (pp. 167–181). New York: Peter Lang.

Singh, J. (Trans.). (1990). *The doctrine of recognition: A translation of Pratyabhijnahrdayam.* Albany, NY: State University of New York Press.

Snowber, C. (2004). Leaning absolutes: Honouring the detours in our lives. In D. Denton & W. Ashton (Eds.), *Spirituality, action, & pedagogy: Teaching from the heart* (pp. 124–135). New York: Peter Lang.

14

Contemplating Uncomfortable Emotions

Creating Transformative Spaces for Learning in Higher Education

John Eric Baugher

Modern life is replete with opportunities for witnessing the suffering of others, and the human response to such suffering is a concern shared by educators across the humanities and social sciences. In her last monograph, *Regarding the Pain of Others*, Susan Sontag (2003) considers the possibility of compassionate response, yet suggests that compassion is an "unstable emotion" and people often turn away from painful realities not simply because "a steady diet of images of violence has made them indifferent but because they are afraid" (p. 100). She continues that images of suffering could be "used like memento mori, as objects of contemplation to deepen one's sense of reality . . . but that would seem to demand the equivalent of a sacred or meditative space in which to look at them" (p. 101). In Sontag's assessment, such space is hard to come by in modern society "whose chief model of a public space is the mega-store" (p. 119) Although Sontag's concern is on the use of photographs, her exploration of the context within which an image is viewed has direct bearing on the possibility for creating transformative spaces for learning within my home discipline of sociology.

In his now classic *Invitation to Sociology* Peter Berger (1963) expresses a hope shared by many sociologists that our courses will help students become "more compassionate in their journeys through society" (p. 2). Yet just as Sontag dispels the myth that vivid photographic depictions of human suffering would inevitably inspire particular responses in viewers, so too is the relation between sociological understanding and compassionate action not so straightforward. As a consequence of reducing sociological seeing to a disembodied cognitive activity, Berger must ultimately conclude that "sociological consciousness" lends itself just as well to "malevolent and misanthropic" (pp. 175–176) actions as it does to compassionate living. In contrast, this chapter articulates a non-dualistic, emotionally embodied, contemplative pedagogy that seeks to develop within teachers and students a *sociology of self-knowledge* that opens possibilities for more skillfully and compassionately relating to the inner and outer dimensions of our experience.

Central to my pedagogic approach is the assumption that contemplating "negative" emotions such as anxiety and fear holds tremendous value for seeing the connections between self and society and for developing the capacity for human freedom and compassionate engagement with others. In the first section of this chapter I theorize the role *liminal* emotions can play in creating transformative spaces for learning in higher education by drawing connections between feminist and other pedagogies of transformation as well as my own research on the development of caring capacities in hospice workers. I then describe a specific classroom exercise I use to help students break fearful habits of mind that limit our capacity to attune to complex interpersonal dynamics in emotionally uncomfortable situations. My approach is rooted in the teachings and practices of Mahayana Buddhism, and in this section I explain how my pedagogic practice invites students to experience the distinction between classic sociological and Buddhist understandings of self-referential thoughts and feelings. I then present data from students' reflective papers from a course, "Sociology of Death and Dying," to illustrate the value of this emotionally-embodied contemplative practice. In the final section I consider some of the implications of the research and perspective presented in this chapter regarding how to more deeply realize the ideals that inform the social sciences and the liberal arts more broadly.

Holding Space for Transformative Emotions

Sociology has typically been conceived as the practice of *thinking* structurally, systematically, and critically (Eckstein, Schoenike, & Delaney, 1995, pp. 353–363). Emotions in the sociology classroom have typically either been ignored or interpreted as barriers to learning, particularly when topics are thought to be "too close to home" or "threatening" to the self-understanding and cherished values of students (Goldsmid & Wilson, 1980, p. 143; Davis, 1992, pp. 232–238). Only recently have sociologists begun to articulate the central importance of emotions in our work as educators, a turn that coincides with the death of the long-held myth in Western social science that emotions inherently stand in the way of clear thinking (Turner & Stets, 2005, pp. 21–22). Educators from diverse perspectives in the social sciences and humanities now recognize that we come to understand the mysteries of our lives and all things social first and foremost through affective, visceral experience, rather than through disembodied, abstract analysis.[1]

Encouraging students to live a sociologically competent life *is* an invitation to loss, especially in a society that celebrates individualism, consumerism, and material excess. Zen-inspired sociologist Bernard McGrane (1994) describes sociology as "examining the illusions we live by in contrast to the realities we live in" (p. 10) and he explicitly warns his students that "anyone who is afraid to shatter their image of society and their image of self should not be enrolled in this course" (p. 63). Studying human society can make students uncomfortable, anxious, or even angry, and a pedagogy that seeks to transform students' lives must skillfully engage rather than avoid such emotions. Research indicates that overcoming student resistance to sociological analyses of racism, for example, is best accomplished through creating assignments that invite *greater emotional investment* among students (Haddad & Lieberman, 2002, pp. 328–341). Similarly, male resistance to seeing sexism can be approached quite skillfully by going even closer to home and *literally* giving students the opportunity to take on the physical posture of the other (MacNevin, 2004). Sociologists typically conceive of emotions as either "positive" (e.g., happiness) or "negative" (e.g., fear) (Turner & Stets, 2005), whereas Buddhist, feminist, and other relational pedagogies do not reify emotional experience as inherently desirable or undesirable. Instead, so-called negative emotions experienced in classrooms and other educational contexts can form essential bridges to transformational learning.[2]

Perhaps the most formidable barrier to transformative education is not the emotions of students, but *teachers' own fears* of emotions in the classroom. A powerful myth that limits the possibility of transformative learning in higher education is the assumption that teachers should be in control and always able to tie things up nicely. Good lectures end with summaries of the key points students were supposed to get from what was just said, and following this same model of education, many students (and teachers) feel that discussion is "a waste of time" unless it is given meaning by some form of "teaching" at the end. Similarly, students and other persons who evaluate teachers often expect that any assignment or classroom exercise should have a clearly *definable* purpose lest the teacher appear disorganized or the assignment be dismissed as "busy work" to be suffered through as quickly as possible. Certainly, if students come away from a classroom feeling frustrated, irritated, or confused this is taken as a sign that something has gone wrong.

What these attitudes and expectations hide is that transformative learning necessitates opening to the unknown and a willingness to abide with the uncomfortable emotions that accompany such openness. My own research on hospice volunteers shows that a willingness to remain in liminal spaces where there is ambiguity regarding who one is or what one needs to do is both essential for effectively caring for dying persons and for developing one's own emotional and spiritual capacities (Baugher, in press). In the same manner, transformative learning in higher education necessitates a willingness among students and teachers to allow the space for anxiety and other uncomfortable emotions to become wonder as we *discover* what lessons are to be found in our lived experience and who we are becoming through that experience (Konrad, 2010, p. 22; Palmer & Zajonc, 2010, p. 111). And just as effectively caring for those who are dying or bereft requires the capacity to witness another's experience without trying to take away their suffering, so too does transformative learning require educators to skillfully "withhold teaching," to refuse to "neatly wrap up the messy vicissitudes of learning" even against the desires of students (Hurst, 2010, p. 41; McCrane, 1994, p. 241). As academics we are well-attuned to the importance of language in scholarship and learning, and it would serve ourselves and our students well to see that allowing silence is a "sister gift" of speaking (Halifax, 2008, p. 10). What English professor Elizabeth Dutro (2008) calls "a pedagogy of witness" (p. 433) is not a call for teachers to become counselors or for classrooms to be turned into therapy sessions, but a recognition that to create spaces for transformative learning teachers must themselves learn to become comfortable with "holding" uncomfortable emotions—our own and those of our students—in an atmosphere of inquiry and loving kindness. As feminist educator Rachel Hurst (2010) explains, silence embraces the possibility that we may learn *from* uncomfortable emotions rather than simply learn *about* them (pp. 36, 41).

Loving Kindness and the Looking-Glass Self

An implicit assumption of the dominant sociological understanding of personhood is that humans are condemned to live in the shadow of anger and fear. According to Charles Horton Cooley's "looking glass" conception of self (cited in Turner & Stets, 2005, pp. 106–107, 154), we continually evaluate ourselves according to the judgment we believe others have of us, leaving us in a near constant state of feeling pride or shame depending upon the perceived reflection of others. This understanding of the self is of grave importance since pride and shame are secondary emotions comprised in part of anger and fear (anger and happiness in the case and pride; sadness, anger, and fear in the case of shame) (pp. 18–19). Are we truly condemned to live in a near constant state of fear and anger? How might it be possible to free ourselves from the perceived controlling gaze of others that so deeply determines how we relate to ourselves and others in our daily lives?

One practice I have used in a Sociology of Death and Dying course to explore these questions involves a three-part "eye-gazing" exercise. Part I involves students pairing up with another member of the class, sitting directly facing each other, and then gradually raising their eyes until they are both gently gazing into the eyes of the other. Students are asked to remain gazing into each other's eyes in silence until a timer goes off, and they do not know in advance how long the exercise will last (2 minutes). Students are prompted before the exercise begins to attune closely to their thoughts and feeling during the exercise, and then immediately afterward are given a few minutes to take notes on their experience.

I was first introduced to this eye-gazing exercise as a participant in a weekend meditation training sponsored by the local Shambhala Buddhist center in Southern Maine and I immediately realized that I could use the practice in my sociology courses to help students directly experience the pervasiveness and phenomenological importance of the looking-glass self. I later discovered that some Buddhist groups in America have combined eye gazing in conjunction with longer periods of meditation to allow practitioners to experience quite vividly the wildness of the mind and the tendency to solidify and project onto others all varieties of discursive thoughts. As Venice Wagner (1998) of the Bay Zen Center in Oakland, California writes:

> There's a direct correlation between what happens in "eye gazing" and the manner in which we respond to events in our everyday lives. Here's an example: At work a colleague glares at me. The thought arises, "What have I done wrong?" accompanied by a tightening in my stomach and the fear that I am inadequate in some way. Instead of allowing the fear to proliferate unconsciously, I'm able to bring awareness to the situation. I note each sensation in turn, and in the noting there is acceptance and a letting go and I am liberated from my fear. (p. 113)

Here Wagner describes both the activity of the looking-glass self *as well as* a means for freeing ourselves from its controlling gaze. What sociologists call the looking-glass self, experiencing oneself as a reflection of the perceived judgment of another, could be likened to the Buddhist understanding of *samsara*, a state of ignorance in which the mind perpetuates suffering by seeking happiness in ever-shifting external and unreliable sources. In the words of Tibetan meditation master Sogyal Rinpoche, "samsara is the mind turned outwardly, lost in its projections," whereas "nirvana," or the freedom from the prison of dualistic mind, is "the mind turned inwardly, recognizing its true nature."[3] Buddhists believe that our innermost essence is pure and radiant awareness, although much human life is spent caught up in the turbulence of thoughts and emotions resulting from the discursive, dualistic mind born of identification with a limited skin-encapsulated ego perceived to be separate from others.

There is good reason to believe that the Western notion of a separate, limited self is both scientifically ungrounded and a source of much suffering in the world.[4] Yet the goal of the eye-gazing exercise is not to appeal to the logical sensibilities of students, but to create an opportunity for them to *directly* experience objects of inquiry from perspectives that differ from their everyday mindsets so that students can "become conscious of the ways their habits of mind and the structure of their imagination shape their experience of the world" (Palmer & Zajonc, 2010, p. 109). As educational psychologist Ellen Langer (2000) writes, mindful learning involves moving beyond the tendency "to confuse the stability of our mind-sets with the stability of the underlying phenomena" we are observing (pp. 220–221). Toward that end, after the initial eye-gazing exercise (Part I), I guide students in a "metta" or loving-kindness meditation for oneself (Part II) before asking them to pair up once again to repeat the initial eye-gazing exercise (Part III).

In the next section I describe in detail the loving-kindness practice, and for now I point out that this three-part exercise parallels how the Buddha first taught metta meditation to his students. The Buddha had sent a group of monks into a forest to meditate, and according to legend, the monks became frightened by tree spirits who produced all sorts of terrifying sights, sounds, and smells in an attempt to drive the monks out of the forest. The frightened monks ran back to the Buddha and asked him to allow them to practice in a different forest, although the Buddha replied, "I am going to send you back to the same forest, but I will provide you with the only protection you will need." That protection was the loving-kindness meditation which offered a powerful antidote to the fear that had earlier overwhelmed the monks. This story illustrates that the same external situation (in this case, a forest full of unhappy tree spirits) can be experienced quite differently when the mind is at rest in its radiant goodness undistracted by fear (Salzberg, 2004). In the same manner, having students return to a situation that evokes uncomfortable emotions after meditating on loving kindness for oneself invites students to directly experience a taste of freedom from the prison of fear and projected anger that defines the looking glass experience of oneself.

Students' Experiences with the Exercise

Twenty-two students enrolled in my "Sociology of Death and Dying" course in the spring of 2010 participated in this assignment, and the analysis in this section draws on students' reflective essays of their experience. The course met on Monday evenings from 7:00 p.m. until 9:30 p.m., and on March 29, 2010 I began the class meeting with the initial eye-gazing exercise (Part I) and then lectured for about an hour and a half on the assigned readings (not directly related to the exercise). During the lecture students were not aware that the class meeting that night would end with a guided loving-kindness meditation (Part II). Likewise, during the loving-kindness meditation students were not aware that there would be another round of the eye-gazing exercise to follow (Part III).

Part I: Initial Eye-gazing Exercise

All students experienced a moderate to intense degree of awkwardness, embarrassment, or anxiety during the first eye-gazing exercise. Students described their minds as being quite busy and expressed that the discursiveness of their minds and their feelings of discomfort centered on the perception that the student with whom they were paired was judging them in some way. One student explained, for example, how she tried to distract herself with thoughts of homework and everything else she had to do that night to try to push away her concerns of "what his thoughts were and how much I wanted the assignment to end." Several students expressed how their perception of time was painfully distorted because "I couldn't help but feel vulnerable and as if my partner had been judging me for some reason. All in all it was an awkward and uncomfortable two minutes that seemed to last forever."

Many students imagined that their partner was judging their physical appearance, although some also imagined that they were the object of a deeper moral evaluation. As one student expressed, "I felt like she could read through me and for some reason that made me anxious. All manner of thoughts kept flashing through my mind till eventually I had to look away." Another student described how she felt "vaguely uncomfortable" when she first heard the instructions for the exercise, and that by the time she had paired up with someone she was feeling "quite threatened and scared." During the exercise her sense of *dis*ease took the form of homophobic fears based on what she imagined the woman she was paired with might be thinking:

> I was worried about what she would think of me. Would she think I was a weirdo? Would she think I was being inappropriate?

> I was afraid that if my partner saw I was actually looking at her intently that she would think I was attracted to her. So I kept laughing and even forced a laugh a few times when I was afraid I was appearing too at ease.

Consistent with the looking-glass conception of self, these imagined judgments of the other were often turned inward and experienced as self-judgment. Many students giggled nervously during the first round of eye gazing, and for some, self-judgment took the form of irritation at oneself for "ruining" the experience of others. Several students were so overcome with anxiety that they were unable to hold the gaze with their partner, and one student articulated how her internal chatter and fear of being judged kept her from listening to "what my partners' eyes had to say." When the timer went off signaling the end of the initial eye-gazing exercise, students broke the tension in the room by immediately talking loudly, laughing nervously, and moving about in their chairs.

Part II: Loving-Kindness Meditation

Following the initial eye-gazing exercise (Part I) and lecture, I guided students in a loving-kindness meditation for oneself drawing on several of the practices outlined in Sharon Salzberg's *Lovingkindness* (2004) and Christine Longaker's (1997) *Facing Death and Finding Hope* (pp. 69–71, 200–201). The practice began with a few minutes of silent meditation, and then with eyes closed I asked students to "Visualize in the sky before you whomever or whatever for you represents pure, unconditional love in the form of radiant light, perhaps the presence of God, a saint or some other enlightened being, or maybe a parent, grandparent or another person who has expressed deep love and compassion towards you. If no particular being or person comes to mind, then simply visualize love in the form of radiant light pouring down upon you bathing you in kindness and love. Imagine that this boundless love flows directly into your heart melting away any feelings of loneliness or unworthiness and bringing you unconditional acceptance and happiness." After allowing students to rest in this feeling of unconditional love for a few minutes I then invited them to "Bring to mind a time when you were particularly kind or generous towards another person and allow yourself to feel that happiness that may come to mind in reflecting on this memory. If no particular memory comes to mind, then simply reflect on the deepest urge toward happiness within you, still resting in a sense of unconditional love and acceptance." Resting in this environment of boundless love I invited students to repeat silently to themselves the phrases, "May I be happy. May I be well. May I be safe." After several minutes of repeating these phrases, the practice concluded by asking students to let go of any particular visualization or phrase and to rest for a minute or two in a sense of fundamental well-being and acceptance. In total, the guided meditation lasted about 15 minutes.

Only one student in the course had had prior experience with loving-kindness meditation, although based on student reflective papers it appears that all were at least willing to give the practice a try. One student expressed how she tried to follow her breath and the visualizations, but she was unable to allow herself to relax: "I have never meditated before and I don't think I ever really 'meditated' at all during the assignment. I kept thinking about how much homework I had and which was the most important to get done when I got home." When the meditation ended she was left feeling "frustrated with myself that I could not allow myself to relax." Most of her reflective paper was a rumination about how highly strung she is, and the conclusion of her paper read like an apology for not being able to participate in the guided meditation and "put myself where you wanted our minds to be going." For her, the imagined judgment of the looking-glass self was pervasive throughout all three parts of the exercise.

In contrast, the majority of students described engaging deeply in the loving-kindness practice. One student expressed, for example, that this portion of the class "was that of complete relaxation full of tranquil thoughts and simple breathing. I felt every breath I took and noticed almost each exhale. There was a wonderful feeling of calm that overtook my body and I was able to completely focus on my inner self." Several students spoke of experiencing a sense of "warmth" and greater synchronicity between mind and body during the guided meditation:

> The senses in my body began to slide away so that my mind could focus on my mind and the only stimulus was that of the verbal direction of the meditation and my mind's response to the questions. Any struggle I had before with trying to 'let go' was now much easier. I could let go of any negative feeling and I could replace it with feelings of warmth.

Similarly, another woman expressed how during the meditation "I felt as though I was on a float in some type of water. I was content in my head, and my body was much less tense than it usually is in public situations."

Part III: Eye-gazing Exercise after Loving-Kindness Meditation

Immediately following the loving-kindness meditation students were instructed to pair up once again to repeat the eye-gazing exercise. The overwhelming majority of students (18/22) described a profound shift in their perspective during the second eye-gazing exercise compared to their experience with the first round of eye-gazing at the beginning of the class. Some indicated that this shift was in part because the second time "we were aware of what to expect," although many explicitly linked the shift in perspective to the loving-kindness meditation. As one student explained:

> For the second and third parts of the assignment I was able to calm down and be centered. When we were asked [during the meditation] to think of someone we loved, I couldn't think of just one person so I focused on the light. It was interesting because I felt like the light stayed with me for long after the meditation was over. It felt like a comforting feeling or some kind of protection somehow.

As a result she was able to remain "calm and centered" when gazing into her partner's eyes during the second eye-gazing exercise. Similarly, another young woman who had "the feeling of being on edge" throughout the first eye-gazing exercise expressed that as a result of the guided meditation "the feeling of anticipation was erased and I could let my body do what it needed to do without my mind interfering. As corny as it sounds, [I felt] euphoric about my life." Another student described how her feelings of nervousness and embarrassment prior to the guided meditation had been replaced by a feeling of "calm" and more vivid wakefulness explaining that "Everything was much brighter when first opening my eyes after the meditation." During the second eye-gazing exercise she took in details of her partner's face that earlier she was unable to attune to because she was too preoccupied with fears that her partner was judging her appearance.

Other students described how repeating the phrases of loving kindness during the meditation transformed how they experienced the subsequent eye-gazing exercise. One woman described, for example, that while repeating the phrases "I felt myself letting go of negative energy" and that afterwards "I found it a lot easier to focus on my partner's eyes without wanting to stare off around the room. I felt as if I were almost connected with her and that I could relate to my partner." Another student expressed that after the loving-kindness meditation "I felt as if I could focus and connect with my partner instead of focusing on my insecurities," highlighting a central theme in many students' experience of shifting from imagining the other judging oneself to feeling an appreciation and a sense of connection with the other.

> During the second experience of looking deeply I was much more grounded. I immediately felt a difference in the way I was looking at my partner; I felt focused and calm. The loving meditation definitely dismissed my apprehension about what my partner was thinking as she looked at me. After the meditation, I never felt anxious or uncomfortable because it honestly didn't seem to bother me if I was being judged or not. Looking into my partner's eyes the second time was a deep and honest experience. I looked into her eyes (never looking away to gain composure) and I completely appreciated my partner.

Students described themselves as being more receptive during the second eye-gazing exercise such that "I was able to take time to look at my partner and stop focusing on me." Even the young woman who expressed homophobic fears during the first eye-gazing exercise now allowed herself to take in how beautiful her classmate was:

> When we returned to the looking at a classmate exercise, it was very different. This time, my mind was much quieter. I sat calmly at my desk and looked at the girl across from me. I started to really notice her face, particularly the half moons beneath her eyes. She started to seem absolutely beautiful to me. I looked at her eyes, but I saw all her face and I was struck by how beautiful she was. I had a moment of disquiet when I realized that she was probably looking at me just as intently as I was looking at her, and while I was noticing how beautiful she was, she was probably noticing how ugly I was. Luckily, the thought passed about as quickly as it came, and I kept looking peacefully at my partner until the end of the exercise.

A fascinating dynamic developed between some pairs after the loving-kindness meditation whereby some students intentionally sought to care for their partners who, in turn, perceived that they were receiving care from the other. One woman who was paired with a much younger and more introverted male wrote that during the first eye-gazing exercise she noticed "how visibly uncomfortable he was looking into my eyes" to the point where "his lips were trembling" and that she too experienced "feelings of vulnerability" and thoughts that he was judging her appearance. Yet during the second eye-gazing exercise "I was completely clear with where my heart and intention was," which was to offer "love and compassion from my heart through my eyes and into him." She described the experience as "a natural state of being" that was free from concern about "trivialities such as my looks." The young man she was paired with likewise experienced a transformation in experience. He explained that during the first eye-gazing exercise he felt "very uncomfortable and confrontational," whereas after the loving-kindness meditation he felt "more related to people around me" so that "during the second round of eye contact, I actually felt a lot less dissected." Similarly, another young man wrote that although he felt more "naked" in the second eye-gazing exercise that "I could see her trying to take care of me with her gaze, to tell me it was okay that I was vulnerable."

A common theme that emerged in students' reflections was that the loving-kindness meditation enabled them to "see" more deeply during the second eye-gazing exercise once their vision was freed from the distortion of fear. One student indicated, for example, that although she was not "100 percent comfortable" gazing into the eyes of someone she does not know, the loving-kindness meditation allowed her to see beyond "my own sense of being uncomfortable" so that "I was able to really see into her eyes." She described how her partner was more relaxed this time around as well and she was able "to tune into her calm energy."

> At one point I even noticed that our shoulders were in sync with each other's breathing. That was comforting to me for some reason. I'm not quite sure why I found comfort in the fact that we were breathing in and out at the same time. Perhaps because that represented a connection. And since I do not know her or any aspect of her personal life, just being able to connect on any level—our breathing—was something I found solace in because it is my human need to relate.

This ability to see and experience more deeply the other resulted from being in a "different mind frame" following the loving-kindness practice. As one young woman explained, rather than feeling nervous about her classmate looking into her eyes, she now perceived that "she had very kind eyes and she seemed as though she was helping me through this exercise." The experience helped her realize that "I am capable of doing this simply by freeing my mind of my own thoughts and emotions." Another student found the loving-kindness meditation "amazing" because the experience allowed her to see "how easy it was for me to focus my attention when my mind was clear."

Many students expressed gratitude for what they had learned about themselves from this exercise and some indicated their intention to try the meditation again in their everyday lives. As one student wrote, "this was an interesting experiment and I am finding myself wanting to try meditation on a more regular basis to help me cope with my crazy busy life of school and kids. Thank you." Another student pondered the deeper significance of the exercise asking, "how much more meaningful our conversations might be and greater our connections might be if we stopped and really looked into each other's eyes every time we had a conversation." She indicated, that "It's a practice that I am going to try and apply to my daily living." Another student expressed how "the hazy, unclear and frantic vision I carried around with me for the majority of the day had disappeared" following the meditation such that "I felt more calm and stable and almost immediately was able to go into the calm, permanent, inevitable and sincere smile" during the final eye-gazing exercise. This experience prompted him to question the causes of "genuine happiness," specifically the value of *communing* with others rather than *consuming* stuff.

Discussion

Mission statements of colleges and universities often speak of seeking to "transform" the lives of students so they become equipped and willing to respond competently and ethically to the tremendous suffering in the world. Yet there is concern that both students and the university are out of sync with such a vision. Perhaps the dominant view regarding students is expressed in The Presidents' Declaration on the Civic Responsibility of Higher Education, signed by over 1,000 college and university presidents, which suggests that "a profound sense of cynicism" and social and political apathy are the defining features of contemporary college students in the United States.[5] Many voices within and outside the academy are also alarmed by the increasingly narrow focus of higher education on the skills needed for ensuring "competitive advantage in the marketplace." As historian C. John Sommerville (2006) writes, universities are "giving in to the pressures to follow student interests, which center on employment, and to the pressure of legislatures for some practical return on the state's support," such that "we would now be hard-pressed to find a distinctive view of life or culture being promoted by the curriculum" (pp. 87–88; see also Lerner, 2000). To the extent that universities are increasingly fashioned in the image of the corporation and run in accordance with the corporate values of efficiency, instrumentality, and materialism, they risk becoming just another arena for creating and satisfying consumer desire.[6]

I have been teaching at state schools for over ten years, and students sometimes do express concerns about how they will pay off student loans and otherwise make ends meet in the future. Yet it is a gross misrepresentation to suggest that student interests "center on employment." Recent longitudinal surveys conducted by UCLA's Higher Education Research Institute (HERI), for example, indicate that more than two-thirds of college students consider it "essential" or "very important" that college deepen their self-understanding, and nearly half have high expectations that their college will "encourage their personal expression of spirituality" (Palmer & Zajonc, 2010, p. 117). These findings resonate with representative survey data pointing to a rise in "postmaterialist values" in younger cohorts of the population more broadly (Inglehart, 1997). Perhaps it is our own commitment to the ideology of *the* American Dream of material success that inhibits professors and administrators from seeing the deeper yearning of our students for holistic opportunities to develop personally and to help create a more human society.

Others have persuasively argued that public education in the United States is blindly wedded to a materialist and competitive agenda that threatens the common good and contradicts the values of the public it is supposed to be serving (Lerner, 2000). This chapter illustrates one form of practice that runs counter to this trend (and the creative response with which students have engaged this opportunity), although here I am not simply taking sides regarding which values should be advocated in the classroom (Palmer & Zajonc, 2010, p. 152). In my courses I do regularly critique patterns of human action that contradict what I and many other social scientists believe are central values of a good society, although I attempt to do so in ways that encourage students to try on and test out their own values and yearnings.[7] The contemplative pedagogy I sketch in this chapter, however, goes beyond such controlling dichotomies of fact and value, thought and action, mind and heart. My intent with the eye-gazing exercise is not simply to persuade students that attuning to others is better than projecting our own negative emotions onto them, but to allow students to experience for themselves contrasting ways of being in the world and to help them understand how they might create the context for living more in accord with their own values. Similarly, I am not merely advocating depth over breadth of "coverage" of course content. Instead, the approach I outline centers on creating *space* for students to live the questions that arise from a direct encounter with the subject matter, and creating such space often takes very little classroom time. A few minutes of silence can go a long way, especially with students whose life rhythms leave little room for solitude.

Many of the contemplative assignments I offer in my courses draw inspiration from what Bernard McGrane (1994) calls "experiments in desocialization," which invite students to slow down whatever they are doing (or not doing) so they are able to witness more deeply what they are actually experiencing. But what is the value of asking students to gaze into the eyes of a classmate before and after being guided in a loving-kindness meditation? Students do sometimes ask what they are "supposed" to get from particular assignments in my courses, and in these moments I direct their attention away from trying to figure out what *I* might have in mind and invite them instead to focus their attention on what goes on *in their own mind* while engaging in the assignments. Like McGrane, I tell students that whatever you *actually* get from engaging in the assignment is precisely what you were *supposed* to get from that assignment. Some students did write that engaging in the eye-gazing assignment piqued their interest in meditation or in attuning deeply to subtle forms of nonverbal communication, although what is important here is their own process of discovery, meaning-making, and integration.

Based on conversations with colleagues I have had over the years it seems that sociologists believe that our work involves exposing students to new ways of thinking in the hopes that doing so might inspire them to help make the world a better place. In the words of Randall Collins (1998), these two moments, seeing through the "sociological eye" and engaging in social activism are the core "commitments" of the discipline. I share these commitments, although I see little evidence that "exposing" students to new ideas will necessarily lead them to seek to live any differently. Students, like teachers, enter the classroom full of emotionally embodied ideas of how the world works, and these ideas we live by are rarely, if ever, "acquired" through logical argumentation alone, but instead through practicing them until they become compelling ways of seeing the world. Helping students "make sense of the world differently," a primary goal of sociology courses,[8] necessitates creating contemplative spaces for students to *enact* and thereby more deeply know and feel the power of their well-worn habits of being in the world. Kuhn (1996) has demonstrated that mounting evidence against a way of seeing is not sufficient for a "paradigm shift" in the sciences, but instead requires the development of a compelling alternative theoretical lens against which to compare the older view. Transformational learning likewise requires a form of comparison, and my intention with the eye-gazing exercise is to create a context for students to experience the "same" external phenomena from within and outside their habitual cognitive-emotive patterns of engaging themselves and the world. As Sontag (2003) suggests, fear inhibits inquiry and the possibilities for responding skillfully to the suffering of others, although when engaged through contemplative inquiry, fearful ways of seeing the world can become powerful resources for seeing with fresh eyes and responding with an open heart.

The basic task of the sociologist is to see how the innermost aspects of our lives are shaped by broader social patterns and how the seemingly minor things we do everyday help reproduce or alter those patterns. The eye-gazing exercise invites students to attune to the relations between the quality of our own hearts and minds and the realities that we see and to which we are therefore able to respond, and such a pedagogic practice has direct application for the various forms of suffering that have long been the central foci of the discipline. I suggest here just one such application by returning to the hope Berger expresses that sociological thinking will help students become more compassionate in their interactions with others and "less stolid in their prejudices" (Berger, 1963, p. 175). The eye-gazing assignment described in this chapter has nothing to do with racial prejudice per se, although the kinds of embodied learning students experience through witnessing their discursive mind projecting all manner of negative emotions on an*other* could be skillfully connected, for example, with Gunnar Myrdal's (1944) classic analysis of "the Negro problem" as a "suppressed moral conflict." Myrdal (2004) observed that in mid-twentieth-century American society, blacks took on "the proportion of a menace" precisely because ordinary whites suppressed their own anxieties, embarrassment, and guilt and projected them onto the other (pp. 245–247). Adaptations of the contemplative pedagogy outlined in this chapter could offer skillful means for helping students explore how the "unavoidable dilemma" Myrdal analyzed has current parallels in relations between white and Arab-Americans in the moralizing political culture of fear in post-9/11 America. Institutional racism cannot be reduced to intersubjective processes, although in my experience as a teacher and fellow traveler on this planet living a sociologically competent life requires spaces for contemplating uncomfortable emotions and the dark thoughts they engender.

My teaching is guided by a view of students, not as disembodied minds, but as full human beings struggling to do their best and make sense of their lives and their place in the world. One consequence of my approach to teaching becoming more explicitly contemplative over the last several years is that an increasing number of students now come to me outside the classroom to explain how a course or a particular assignment has helped them to live with greater joy, sanity, and compassion. Even a course on research methods presents occasions for linking methods of knowing to the deepest yearnings of students for meaning and wholeness. And just as students benefit from assignments that engage every dimension of their being, so too do teachers need practices that sustain us and deepen our capacity to skillfully hold the uncomfortable emotions that come with teaching and living as mortal and moral beings.

Notes

1. See, for example, Christopher Dustin & Joanna Ziegler (2005); bell hooks (1994); Charles Lemert (2008); Audrey L. MacNevin (2004); Parker Palmer and Arthur Zajonc (2010); Mohammad Tamdgidi (2007).

2. See, for example, Parker Palmer & Arthur Zajonc, 2010; Rachel Alpha Johnston Hurst, 2010; Shelley Cohen Konrad, 2010; Elizabeth Dutro, 2008.

3. See <http://www.lifepositive.com/spirit/world-religions/buddhism/sogyal.asp>.

4. See, for example, Dalai Lama, 2006; Allen D. Kanner & Mary E. Gomes, 1995; Joanna Macy, 1990.

5. The *Presidents' Declaration* can be downloaded from the campus compact website at <http://www.compact.org/resources/presidents-declaration-on-the-civic-responsibility-of-higher-education-2/5275/>.

6. One indication of this cultural shift is the explicit colonization of the university with consumer idioms. On a webpage entitled "Education Redefined," for example, Ball State University students are instructed on how to "browse" for courses online and use a "course planner" to add courses to their "course shopping cart." See <http://www.bsu.edu/apps/courseplanner/courseinfo.asp>. For a useful framework for understanding this linguistic shift and its implications, see Uwe Pörksen (1995) *Plastic Words: The Tyranny of a Modular Language.*

7. In this regard I have found Michael Schwalbe's (2008) thought experiment a useful method for encouraging students to mull over the values that inform sociological inquiry. After articulating the values that guide his work as a sociologist (e.g., the belief that a good life is only possible in a society that is "peaceful, cooperative, egalitarian, and minimally regimented), he asks students to "think of the people you love and the kind of life you wish for them. Is it a life of violence, deprivation, and suffering, or is it something more like my vision of the good life?"

8. See, for example, Schwalbe (2008), pp. 1–15.

References

Baugher, J. (in progress). *Caring for dying strangers: Understanding the emotional and spiritual journeys of hospice volunteers.* Unpublished manuscript in progress.

Berger, P. (1963). *Invitation to sociology: A humanistic perspective.* Garden City, NJ: Anchor Books.

Collins, R. (1998). The sociological eye and its blinders. *Contemporary Sociology, 27*(1), 2–7.

Dalai Lama (2006). *The universe in a single atom: the convergence of science and spirituality.* New York: Three Rivers Press.

Davis, N. (1992). Teaching about inequality: Student resistance, paralysis, and rage. *Teaching Sociology, 20,* 232–238.

Dustin, C., & Ziegler, J. (2005). *Practicing mortality: Art, philosophy, and contemplative seeing* New York: Palgrave.

Dutro, E. (2008). That's why I was crying on this book: Trauma as testimony in response to literature. *Changing English, 15*(4), 423–434.

Eckstein, R., Schoenike, R., & Delaney, K. (1995).The voice of sociology: Obstacles to teaching and learning the sociological imagination. *Teaching Sociology, 23*, 353–363.

Goldsmid, C., & Wilson, E. (1980). *Passing on sociology: The teaching of a discipline.* Washington, DC: ASA Teaching Resources Center.

Haddad, A., & Lieberman, L. (2002). From student resistance to embracing the sociological imagination: Unmasking privilege, social conventions, and racism. *Teaching Sociology, 30*, 328–341.

Halifax, J. (2008). *Being with dying: Cultivating compassion and fearlessness in the presence of death.* Boston: Shambhala.

hooks, b. (1994). *Teaching to transgress: Education as the practice of freedom.* New York: Routledge.

Hurst, R. A. J. (2010). What might we learn from heartache? Loss, loneliness, and pedagogy. *Feminist Teacher, 20*(1), 31–41.

Inglehart, R. (1997). *Modernization and postmodernization: Cultural, economic, and political change in 43 societies.* Princeton, NJ: Princeton University Press.

Kanner, A., & Gomes, M. (1995). The all consuming self. In T. Roszak, M. E. Gomes, & A. D. Kanner (Eds.), *Ecopsychology: Restoring the Earth, healing the mind.* San Francisco: Sierra Club Books.

Konrad, S. (2010). Relational learning in social work education: Transformative education for teaching a course on loss, grief and death. *Journal of Teaching in Social Work, 30*, 15–28.

Kuhn, T. (1996). *The structure of scientific revolutions* Chicago: University of Chicago Press.

Langer, E. (2000). Mindful learning. *Current Directions in Psychological Science, 9*(6), 220–223.

Lemert, C. (2008). *Social things: An introduction to the sociological life* (4th ed.). Lanham, MD: Rowman & Littlefield.

Lerner, M. (2000). *Spirit matters.* Charlottesville, PA: Hampton Roads.

Longaker, C. (1997). *Facing death and finding hope: a guide to the emotional and spiritual care of the dying.* New York: Doubleday.

MacNevin, A. (2004). Embodying sociological mindfulness: Learning about social inequality through the body. *Teaching Sociology, 32*, 314–321.

Macy, J. (1990). The greening of the self. In A. H. Badiner (Ed.), *Dharma gaia: A harvest of essays in Buddhism and ecology.* Berkeley, CA: Parallax Press.

McGrane, B. (1994). *The un-TV and the 10 mph car: Experiments in personal freedom and everyday life.* Fort Bragg, CA: The Small Press.

Mohammad, T. (2007). Abu Ghraib as a microcosm: The strange face of empire as a lived prison. *Sociological Spectrum, 27*(1), 29–55.

Myrdal, G. (1944). *An American dilemma:The Negro problem and modern democracy.* New York: Harper and Bros.
Myrdal, G. (2004). The Negro problem as a moral issue. In C. Lemert (Ed.), *Social theory: The multicultural and classic readings* (3rd ed.) (pp. 245–247). Boulder, CO: Westview Press.
Palmer, P., & Zajonc, A. (2010). *The heart of higher education: A call to renewal.* San Francisco, CA: Jossey-Bass.
Pörksen, U. (1995). *Plastic words: Tthe tyranny of a modular language.* University Park, PA: Pennsylvania State Press.
Salzberg, S. (2004). *Lovingkindness: The revolutionary art of happiness.* Boston: Shambhala.
Sommerville, J. (2006). *The decline of the secular university.* New York: Oxford University Press.
Sontag, S. (2003). *Regarding the pain of others.* New York: Picador.
Turner, J., & Stets, J. (2005). *The sociology of emotions.* New York: Cambridge University Press.
Wagner, V. (1998). Eye gazing. In D. Morreale (Ed.), *The complete guide to Buddhist America.* Boston: Shambhala.

15

Contemplative Disciplines in Higher Education

Cutting through Academic Materialism

Daniel Vokey

> The essential political problem for the intellectual . . . is not changing people's consciousness—or what's in their heads—but the political, economic, institutional regime of the production of truth.
>
> —Michel Foucault, 1977

Cutting through Spiritual Materialism is the title of a book by Chögyam Trungpa published in 1973. The book is based upon a series of talks he had given in 1970 and 1971 to provide his students both with an overview of the spiritual path (as understood within his lineage), and with a description of the traps into which the inexperienced or unwary spiritual seeker might fall. He published these talks so that Westerners exploring Buddhist and other contemplative traditions in the 1970s would be forewarned of, and so more likely to avoid, the self-centered agendas that are commonly mistaken for genuine spirituality. If Buddhists agree on one point, it is that spiritual disciplines properly serve to interrupt the functioning of *ego*, defined as the collection of habitual patterns of perceiving, feeling, thinking, and acting that reflect and reinforce a false belief that we are each a permanent, independently existing subject or "self." However, precisely because interpreting experience through an "I-exist-as-a-separate-self" framework is such a deeply ingrained habit, it is all too easy to stray from the spiritual "straight and narrow." Even with the best of intentions, it is hard not to mistake spirituality for a self-improvement or personal immortality project.

> Walking the spiritual path properly is a very subtle process; it is not something to jump into naively. There are numerous side tracks which lead to a distorted, ego-centered version of spirituality; we can deceive ourselves into thinking we are developing spiritually when instead we are strengthening our egocentricity through spiritual techniques. This fundamental distortion may be referred to as *spiritual materialism*. (Trungpa, 1973, p. 3)

In this chapter, I am concerned with what I perceive to be an analogous phenomenon, *academic materialism*, meaning the sidetracks that result when certain features of our modern universities deflect transformative educational initiatives away from their emancipatory ends. By identifying some of the dynamics that can create and perpetuate academic materialism, I hope to increase the chances that efforts to integrate contemplative disciplines within higher education will yield the benefits they are meant to produce.

The contents of this chapter are presented in four sections. The first section establishes my points of departure for this project; that is, the assumptions that I ask my readers to accept provisionally if they do not already share these beliefs. The second section introduces Alasdair MacIntyre's account of the internal and external goods of *practices,* and of the tension between them, because his analysis illuminates one important way in which conflicting motivations are endemic to organizations, including institutions of higher education. Some of the competing intentions visible in contemporary universities are described in section three in light of the broader social dynamics that influence academic priorities. Section four invokes Parker Palmer's analysis of social movements to offer ideas about how institutions of higher education could become more hospitable to contemplative disciplines oriented toward transformative ends.

I. Points of Departure

Whatever insight I might have into what it means for an activity to be contemplative, and into how different forms of contemplative practice can contribute in complementary ways to spiritual development and other educational aspirations, I owe in largest part to Shambhala Buddhism. For my purposes here, however, I need not assume that my readers and I share a common understanding of contemplative education. I need only assume agreement on the three basic claims that are my points of departure. The first claim is that *the benefits (or harms) that result from the practice of any contemplative discipline depend to a significant degree upon* the view *and* the intent *of the practitioner.*

Whether we pray, meditate, chant, paint, dialogue, feast, write, or dance, it is important that we have an appropriate understanding of *what* we are doing and *why* we are doing it. This is a teaching common to many traditions, Buddhism included:

> If one has the right mental attitude, all activities, bodily action, and speech can be religious. But if one lacks the right attitude—that is, if one does not know how to think properly—one will achieve nothing, even if one's whole life is spent in monasteries reading the scriptures. (Gyatso, 1999)

For this reason, periods of study or practice within Mahāyāna Buddhism traditionally begin with reminders of "the view" (e.g., the reality of *karma*), and of the importance of rousing *bodhicitta* (the "mind of enlightenment"), which naturally seeks the benefit of all sentient beings.[1]

The second claim is that *it is important to teach and learn contemplative disciplines because of their potential to help reduce the suffering and promote the well-being of self-and-other.* The beneficial effects of contemplative practices begin with the quality of consciousness and awareness of the practitioners, but do not stop there. Training mind and heart through meditative and other disciplines can advance larger social causes such as peace, freedom, social and ecological justice, physical health, and sustainable material prosperity. This is not a new thought, of course, and the third claim is no more original. Like many others, I propose that *making significant progress toward the well-being of self-and-other requires political and cultural transformation as well as personal development.* In other words, we must promote individual liberation through social change initiatives as well as the reverse. On this view, political and cultural transformation is necessary because of the more and less subtle ways in which individual and collective suffering is perpetuated by the structures and ideologies of contemporary social institutions. On a neo-Marxist analysis, for example, warfare, oppression, injustice, the erosion of social and natural environments, unemployment, and poverty are related symptoms of political, economic, and ideological systems that prioritize profit-making over the needs of sentient beings and the health of the planet. There are, of course, other critical perspectives upon dominant social structures and ideologies that both complement and complicate neo-Marxist attention to the social reproduction of class-based hierarchies—feminist and post-colonial discourses come to mind in this regard. Their differences notwithstanding, all traditions of *systemic* critique underline the importance of attending to the inequalities reproduced by the social *status quo* and their associated ideological distortions of consciousness.

How do these three claims connect to my concern with academic materialism? The first step toward an answer is provided by Alasdair MacIntyre's account of the differences between the internal and external goods of practices,[2] the motivational tensions that can result, and the essential role of the virtues in keeping institutions oriented toward their proper ends.

II. MacIntyre and the Internal Goods of Education as a Practice

Alasdair MacIntyre (1984) defines a *practice* as any coherent and complex form of socially established cooperative human activity through which goods internal to that form of activity are realized in the course of trying to achieve those standards of excellence that are appropriate to, and partially definitive of, that form of activity, with the result that human powers to achieve excellence, and human conceptions of the ends and goods involved, are systematically extended (p. 187).

A *practice* is much more than a set of technical or other skills because it includes a shared understanding of the purposes ("ends and goods") that the skills in question are intended to serve. Because this shared understanding develops over time, a *practice* has a history in a way that the simple exercising of a set of skills does not.

> Bricklaying is not a practice; architecture is. Planting turnips is not a practice; farming is. So are the enquiries of physics, chemistry, and biology, and so is the work of the historian and so are painting and music. In the ancient and medieval worlds *the creation and sustaining of human communities*—of households, cities, nations—*is generally taken to be a practice* in the sense in which I have defined it. Thus the range of practices is wide: arts, sciences, games, *politics in the Aristotelian sense*, the making and sustaining of family life, all fall under the concept. (MacIntyre, 1984, pp. 187–188; italics added)

This definition enables MacIntyre to contrast two kinds of goods: those *internal* to and those *external* to a *practice*. Goods are internal when (a) they can only be specified with reference to the cooperative human activities and ends particular to that *practice*; and (b) they can only be recognized through the personal experience of participating wholeheartedly in those activities. Conversely, then, those who have no personal experience of engagement with a *practice* have at best a limited appreciation of its internal goods (MacIntyre, 1984, pp. 188–189). One who has never been a dedicated member of a jazz ensemble or curling team will be unable to appreciate fully what makes some performances better than others, and why those activities are pursued for their own sake as much as for any other ends. In contrast, external goods—notably such institutional rewards as wealth, power, and prestige—are only *contingently attached* to particular practices. The benefits that are specific to particular scholarly disciplines, professions, sports, and artistic practices are all distinct from monetary compensation, which can be earned in all these different spheres of activity.

Parallel to the distinction between external and internal goods is a distinction between two forms of competition. This is because, by the very nature of external goods, competition to procure them is typically more divisive within a community of *practice* than competition to excel in pursuit of that *practice's* internal goods.

> It is characteristic of what I have called external goods that when achieved they are always some individual's property and possession . . . they are such that the more someone has of them, the less there is for other people. . . . External goods are therefore characteristically objects of competition in which there must be losers as well as winners. Internal goods are indeed the outcome of competition to excel, but it is characteristic of them that their achievement is a good for the whole community who participate in the practice. (MacIntyre, 1984, pp. 190–191)

For example, only one team will take home top prize in a curling bonspiel, but the whole community of participants, commentators, and fans will benefit if the competition inspires new levels of brilliance and grace in play.[3]

MacIntyre further distinguishes *practices* from the institutions and organizations that are required to sustain them: "Chess, physics and medicine are practices; chess clubs, laboratories, universities are institutions" (1984, p. 194). As noted, institutions have reward systems that distribute the external goods of wealth, power, and prestige on a competitive basis. Given the limited nature of external goods, it is a significant challenge to create institutional structures and cultures in which the pursuit of goods internal to *practices* is not overshadowed and compromised by competition for institutional rewards. For MacIntyre, then, *the making and sustaining of forms of social life in which practices can flourish within institutional frameworks is itself a* practice *with its own internal goods*. To the best of my knowledge, MacIntyre has not named this enabling *practice* that is required for other *practices* to flourish. Although I cannot develop the idea here, it strikes me that helping an institution or community remain focused upon its internal goods is a core feature of genuine *leadership.*

By definition, those dedicated to *practices* must be virtuous to achieve their internal goods. This is because, in MacIntyre's ethics, a virtue is "an acquired human quality the possession and exercise of which tends to enable us to achieve those goods which are internal to practices and the lack of which effectively prevents us from achieving any such goals" (1984, p. 191). Particular virtues such as "justice, courage, and honesty" are required to achieve internal goods within institutional frameworks *precisely because of the need to counterbalance the effects of divisive competition for external goods.*

MacIntyre observes that, because of the number and diversity of *practices*, realization or even pursuit of their internal goods can be mutually exclusive. Consequently, without some grounds and guidelines for setting priorities among the internal and external goods we might undertake to achieve, human life would be characterized by "*too many* conflicts and *two much* arbitrariness" (MacIntyre, 1984, p. 201). What provides such grounds and guidelines is one or another comprehensive conception of "*the* good"; that is, a conception of what it means for humans to live fulfilling lives, both as individuals and as members of various social groups. In Aristotelian terms, *ethics* names the inquiry into what constitutes the most fulfilling individual life and *politics* the roughly parallel inquiry into the proper norms and priorities for the *polis* or state. From this larger perspective, in order to count as a genuine virtue, a disposition or capacity must contribute, not only to the realization of the goods internal to a *practice*, but also to a form of social life within which the various *practices* are integrated according to one or another comprehensive view of human flourishing (MacIntyre, 1984, pp. 219, 275).

How does this account of *practices* and their internal goods relate to higher education? Elsewhere, I have argued that teaching is a *practice* of creating environments in which students flourish while learning how to pursue what is genuinely good in their lives both before and after graduation (Vokey, 2003). By extension, I consider education a *practice* analogous to *politics* with the same internal good. In other words, those working to create and maintain either educational or larger political communities are properly concerned "not with this or that particular good, but with human good as such" (MacIntyre, 1988, pp. 33–34; cf. pp. 107–108).

According to this neo-Aristotelian philosophy of education, a university's teaching, research, and community engagement activities properly promote the goods internal to the different practices represented by the particular disciplines and fields associated with that university's various departments, faculties, and schools. However, its responsibilities do not stop there. A university's diverse activities should be guided by dedication to one or another conception of the overall human good "as such." Not surprisingly, this responsibility is clearly visible within institutions of higher education representing moral and religious traditions that, like neo-Aristotelian philosophy, are committed to human fulfilment. Judging by its mission statement, the University of Notre Dame is one fine example of an educational institution dedicated to the common good (http://nd.edu/aboutnd/mission-statement/). However, the responsibility to serve some vision of the common human good is also recognized in the mission statements of secular universities such as my own institution (http://strategicplan.ubc.ca/the-plan/vision-statement/). Of course, mission statements proclaim commitments to ideals that are not always perfectly realized in practice. In the next section, I consider some features of the modern university and its social context that turn research, teaching, and community engagement activities toward priorities other than—and sometimes inimical to—the common human good.

III. Postsecondary Institutions in the Twenty-First Century

Through seminars offered by colleagues in Higher Education, I have been introduced to the growing literature on *academic capitalism*, a term coined to refer to entrepreneurial "market or market-like" initiatives by universities and their faculty to obtain funding from external sources (Slaughter & Leslie, 1997, p. 8). These initiatives have been and continue to be driven by changes in the larger economic and political context. Since the 1980s, governments have looked to universities to drive economic growth and enhance competitiveness in globalized economic markets. Accordingly, they have tended more and more to target funds to applied research with tangible economic benefits, with corresponding reductions in support for other scholarly and educational activities. As a result, "academics and institutions were placed in a competitive resource environment as they vied for grants and contracts to fund basic operations and new expenditures, which were often deemed necessary due to expanding enrolments" (Metcalf, 2010, p. 493).[4]

The need of academic institutions to adapt to reductions in non-targeted funding has been invoked to explain changes in the governance and operations of universities around the globe. These changes include the increase in the number of "cost-recovery" graduate programs intended for professionals who can afford premium tuition fees; the trend toward conceiving and assessing academic productivity and "research impact" in narrow, quantifiable terms (Smeyers and Burbules, 2011); the investment of resources to expand promotional activities such as "branding" that are more usually associated with the marketing of commercial products; aggressive real estate development, including capital accumulation through the building of market-housing on campuses; the downloading of administrative responsibilities and costs from central administration to academic units; the decline in collegial governance in favor of centralized decision making, justified as necessary to enable quick action when opportunities arise to improve competitiveness;[5] the allocation of proportionately more resources to disciplines and fields "close to the market," such as business and engineering, and proportionately less to the liberal arts and humanities; the proportional decline in full-time tenure-track academic positions and corresponding rise in "casualized" academic laborers;[6] increasing expectations of research productivity resulting in the intensification or "densification" of academic workloads; the restriction on the freedom of academics to publish work or otherwise report research that might compromise the profitability of university (and/or university-business-government) investments;[7] and increasing competition by students for graduate and postdoctoral fellowships, as well as for the shrinking number of tenure-track academic positions (Jackson-Weaver et al., 2010). There is also more and more competition among postsecondary institutions (large "research-intensive" universities in particular) for (a) higher international rankings; (b) "the best" undergraduate students, graduate students, postdoctoral fellows, and faculty ("the best" typically meaning those with the longest lists of publications and grants); and (c) the most international students (who pay higher tuition fees, and/or generate income through "branch plant" university campuses in foreign countries). Such initiatives illustrate how postsecondary institutions, as well as those who study and work within them, are under increasing pressure to become more and more entrepreneurial, with an eye always upon productivity and the bottom line.

In light of MacIntyre's observations about the potential divisiveness of competition for external goods, it is not surprising that these shifts in governance, operations, and reward structures have corresponding effects upon the academy's culture and morale. Common themes in anecdotal reports and surveys include a decline in the service ethic, a strain upon collegiality, and an erosion of job satisfaction (Metcalfe & Snee, 2011). "Consequently, for many professors the academic life is bereft of pleasure, joy, and camaraderie. As cocaine is to Thompson's *Las Vegas*, competition, fear, and isolation are to the lost academic" (Stelmach, Parsons, and Frick, 2010). It is also not surprising that, as one of higher education's more vulnerable populations, graduate students are quick to get the message about what it takes to succeed in the modern academy: ". . . remember the requirements for tenure and promotion and the biggest and most important word of all: PUBLISH. Everything you do needs to 'count' somehow. The Golden Rule and love and sane living—forget them. Remember: competition and politics" (Cole, 2001).

As well as eroding the quality of academic life, academic capitalism obstructs or limits higher education's service to the common human good in a number of ways. First, it is a defining feature of capitalist economics that "value" is ultimately conceived and assessed in purely monetary terms (Allman, 2007, pp. 11–16), which erases the distinction between the internal and external goods of academic and other forms of cooperative activity. Also, as we have seen, the increasing pressure to pursue neo-liberal economic ends will incline institutions of higher education to favor forms of inquiry oriented to enhancing productivity and efficiency. In other words, *academic capitalism* can reinforce and be reinforced by *technical rationality*, a view of the relationship between scientific theory and professional practice criticized by Schön (1983, 1986), and many others since. Technical rationality understands professional competence to be a matter of selecting the most effective means to achieve predetermined ends through the application of theoretical knowledge to practical problems: theory identifies which variables must be manipulated and in what fashion to achieve desired results. Alas, technical rationality's promise of efficiency proves illusory, because the contexts of professional practice are too ambiguous and complex to allow for theory to be applied in any straightforward way. Technical rationality is not just epistemologically naïve but amoral as well. By narrowing its focus to calculations of instrumental efficiency, it leaves unaddressed important questions about the moral appropriateness of the ends and means of practical action, educational and otherwise. When technical rationality holds sway, questions about whose interests are being served and whose are not never make it to the table (Brown & Schubert, 2000, pp. 3–6; see also Davidson-Harden, 2010, pp. 584–585).

In my introduction, I observed that neo-Marxist analyses of class-based dynamics have been complemented and complicated by other forms of systemic critique, which examine how structural and ideological features of liberal democratic societies reproduce (and, indeed, exacerbate) inequality. The same holds for critical analyses of higher education: The concerns with the effects of academic capitalism noted above are complemented and complicated by theorists writing from (for example) non-white, feminist, queer, post-colonial, and/or indigenous perspectives. These critical analyses illustrate in different ways how the practices, structures, and norms of the modern academy continue to privilege the knowledges and interests of the members of some social groups over others (Marker, 2011). Many conclude that universities and colleges must, like the economic and political institutions that form their larger context, undergo radical reform if higher education is to benefit more than an elite minority (Coles, 2010). One particularly trenchant critic is environmentalist David Orr (2004) who, echoing Elie Wiesel, observes that receiving a postsecondary degree provides no safeguard against vicious conduct, "no guarantee of decency, prudence, or wisdom" (p. 8). On his analysis, so far from serving the common good, modern institutions of "higher" learning actually perpetuate the root causes of our current social and ecological crises. They do so by reinforcing such cultural biases as (a) the drive to dominate nature, and corresponding preference for forms of knowledge that afford predication and control; (b) "the dominance of the analytical mind over that part given to creativity, humour, and wholeness"; and (c) the "radical separation of self and object" (p. 8) exemplified by Descartes.

In citing Orr and other critics of the modern academy I have not, of course, presented a balanced assessment of the current and/or potential capacity of postsecondary institutions to serve the public good, nor have I offered a systematic review of the literature on academic capitalism. The accounts I have cited of the negative effects of academic entrepreneurship do resonate deeply with my own experience in postsecondary institutions over many years.[8] At the same time, I have also seen many examples of how university research, teaching, and community engagement activities can—at least in some respects and to some degree—advance noble causes such as social and ecological justice. My position is not that contemporary institutions of higher education are hopelessly compromised, but that their priorities and corresponding reward systems mirror in more and less subtle ways those operative in the academy's larger social, economic, political, and intellectual contexts. This presents educators with a variation upon the-chicken-or-the-egg conundrum: success in advancing social transformation through educational initiatives offered within public schools, colleges, and universities would seem to require prior success in making the very changes to dominant norms that the educational programs are intended to promote. A corollary of this is that we cannot assume that introducing contemplative disciplines into higher education will necessarily promote transformative change. We must acknowledge the possibility that contemplative disciplines will be taken up in ways that serve existing priorities and leave the educational *status quo* intact. For example, mindfulness meditation could be introduced into K–12 schools to help achieve their behavioral management objectives, or into university communities to improve productivity via stress-management.

My reasons for concern include two specific social-political dynamics related to neo-liberalism that are operative inside and outside higher education, limiting or undermining the benefits of educational initiatives. The first is the *individualistic bias*, the mindset that treats problems (e.g., forms of addiction) that are caused in significant part by inequitable economic, political, and social relationships (e.g., racism) as if they were simply symptoms of individual psychological pathologies and/or weaknesses of character for which the individuals in question bear responsibility. Programs for disadvantaged youth can fall into this trap. During the 1980s, I worked at an Outward Bound school that, like many service-oriented adventure-based educational programs, took inner-city "at risk" youth on wilderness expeditions. The belief was that, by improving the self-confidence of the program participants and giving them tools to manage conflict within a group, the experience would help them avoid jail and stay in school. However, even when participants did complete the course successfully, the changes in behavior achieved within the carefully structured environment of the program were very difficult to sustain when the students returned to their lives in the city. The general point is that, while such programs can have important positive outcomes for the individuals involved, they are no substitute for addressing the social and economic structures that mean some children are handicapped by their social location(s). Similarly, while contemplative disciplines might have some genuine benefits to practitioners, efforts to introduce them into public educational institutions should not function as substitutes for equity-oriented social change.

The second dynamic is *commodification*. Here, the paradigm case in my own experience is the fate of blue jeans. Denim pants and jackets were originally produced by Levi Strauss for miners and ranchers who valued the durability of the fabric. Members of the counterculture in the 1960s and early 1970s adopted denim as a sign of nonconformity—their rejection of bourgeois culture in favor of solidarity with the working class. As blue jeans became popular with young adults, however, manufacturers produced fashionable styles for the market. With the right brand or logo, jeans became a symbol of status. In this way, what meaning they had as a sign of class consciousness was neutralized by the machinery of mass commodification (Gottdiener, 2000). Radical critiques, revolutionary research programs, and transformative educational initiatives are all vulnerable to a similar fate; that is, becoming products for the academic marketplace in which publication and research grants advance academic careers. Chödrön (2005) raises similar concerns with the commodification of spiritual teachings, which can include the repackaging and rebranding of contemplative disciplines for the spiritual supermarket. In the process, contemplative techniques can be severed from the view and intention of the wisdom traditions in which they were originally practiced.

In sum: Research on academic capitalism and similar systemic critiques identify features of modern institutions of higher education and their social contexts that present obstacles to and constraints upon educational initiatives, particularly those oriented to social and ecological justice. On a Buddhist view, it is legitimate to practice mindfulness meditation to improve one's golf game, but it is unrealistic to expect self-liberation if ego's habitual patterns are left intact. By analogy, it would be perfectly legitimate to introduce contemplative disciplines to enhance the pursuit of the goods internal to different disciplines and fields within universities. However, when the objective is to support positive personal and social transformation toward more peaceful, just, and sustainable ways of life, the integration of contemplative disciplines must be part of efforts to bring the structure and culture of higher education institutions into alignment with their espoused commitments to serve the common good. In such institutions, graduate students and faculty would not experience conflict between their commitments to (for example) social and/or ecological justice and their desire for an academic career. How might our universities be changed to "make it so"?

IV. Spirituality and Social Transformation

I agree with those who maintain that attending to spirituality both individually and collectively is a necessary component of genuinely transformative *praxis* (e.g., Fernandes, 2003; Glassman, 1998; O'Sullivan, 1999). Following Parker Palmer (1998a), I believe *spirituality* is usefully defined as paths toward and/or experiences of connection to something larger and more trustworthy than *ego.* This is consistent with the Buddhist use of *ego* to mean the collection of habitual ways of perceiving, feeling, thinking, and acting that reinforce the false assumption that self-and-other exist independently. On this view, spirituality is necessary (a) to address the existential malaise or sense of fundamental disconnection that is the root cause of the greed, aggression, and indifference that drives warfare, over-consumption, and oppression (Loy, 2003); (b) to unlearn dualistic "good guys vs. bad guys" thinking, because resolving personal and social conflict successfully requires letting go of "enemy images" (Rosenberg, 2003); (c) to find sources of inspiration beyond ego to sustain us in the face of opposition (Fernandes, 2003); and (d) to discern what is and is not conducive to the human good as such (Vokey, 2001). On this latter point: To MacIntyre's argument that the virtues are required to preserve communities, institutions, and traditions from the corrosive effects of competition for external goods, I would add that becoming genuinely virtuous is essentially a spiritual path (Vokey, 2011).

In this context, however, my emphasis is upon the complementary point that *transformative* praxis *requires joining spirituality with critical analyses of and efforts to reduce systemic oppression.*[9] For one thing, we cannot address problems that we do not recognize and acknowledge. Thus, practicing mindfulness/awareness meditation facilitates personal transformative change by enabling us to see habitual patterns clearly—to recognize where we are "stuck" (Vokey, in press). Analogously, analyses of the intersecting forms of systemic oppression shows us where passion, aggression and denial have become part of the social norms we take for granted. As an important step toward institutional and social change, then, we can train in bringing such "normalized" oppression to awareness and interrupting the ways in which we participate in and reinforce unjust and unsustainable ways of life.

In his account of the four stages of genuine social movements, Parker Palmer (1998b) provides one map of the route from self-knowledge to broader institutional and social change that in particularly relevant here in its attention to reward systems that either reinforce or challenge the *status quo*. The steps he identifies are as follows:

> *Stage 1.* Isolated individuals make an inward decision to live "divided no more" finding a center for their lives outside of institutions.
>
> *Stage 2.* These individuals begin to discover one another and form communities of congruence that offer mutual support and opportunities to develop a shared vision.
>
> *Stage 3.* These communities start going public, learning to convert their private concerns into the public issues they are and receiving vital critiques in the process.
>
> *Stage 4. A system of alternative rewards emerges to sustain the movement's vision and to put pressure for change on the standard institutional reward system.* (p. 166, italics added)

The details of how Palmer's account of social movements could translate into concrete action for change would vary according to the particular contexts of those seeking to promote personal and social transformation. That said, I do see two broad recommendations following from Palmer's work for academics like myself who believe that contemplative disciplines have great potential to promote positive change. The first is that, to the extent we have become overly attached to the rewards that perpetuate the academic *status quo*, we must each "re-center" our motivation upon the ways in which our disciplines and fields can serve the common good, in part by addressing recognized human needs.

The second is that we seek kindred spirits or "communities of congruence"—perhaps at conferences and workshops hosted by groups such as the Association for Contemplative Mind in Higher Education—to renew the original narratives of academic purpose currently eclipsed by empty discourses of "excellence" and "productivity." To this end, one priority I see is to champion conceptions and criteria of academic "success" that support (rather than undermine) those committed to personal and social emancipation through "higher" learning.[10]

Conclusion

In closing, I have presented grounds for concern that contemplative disciplines will be taken up within the academy in ways that serve materialistic priorities instead of personal and social transformation toward more peaceful, just, and sustainable ways of life. I see this outcome as more likely than not if academics fail to question whose interests are being served by contemporary institutions of higher education and whose interests are not, and/or if contemplative disciplines are severed from their spiritual roots. From a Buddhist perspective, self-liberation requires that we recognize the habitual patterns that obstruct realization of our full human potential. Seeing clearly where and how we are creating the conditions of suffering provides both the direction and motivation for genuinely beneficial change. Through this account of *academic materialism*, I hope to have shown how critical analyses can play an analogous and complementary emancipatory role, by bringing to awareness the oppressive structural and ideological features of academic and social institutions.

Notes

1. Similarly, many of Atisha's *lojong* ("mind training") slogans remind practitioners of the folly of undertaking spiritual pursuits for egoistic ends (Trungpa, 1993). It is important to note that the results of contemplative practice affect view and intention as well as the reverse. For one account of how compassionate motivation, refined conceptual understanding, and direct contemplative experience can work together with other factors to promote more and more accurate insight into the true nature of things, see Gyamtso (1988).

2. To avoid confusion I will italicize *practice* when I use it, except in the context of a direct quotation.

3. See Higgins (2010, pp. 237–273) for a rich description and elaboration of MacIntyre's account of *practices*.

4. On the link between "the knowledge economy" and "knowledge capitalism," see also Davidson-Harden (2010).

5. In connection with this point, see the CAUT/ACPPU (2011) report *General assembly created out of lack of confidence in current governance of the university* at <http://cautbulletin.ca/en_article.asp?articleid=3195>.

6. According to Benjamin (2008), "Only 35% of all university instructors hold tenure-track appointments; 25% have tenure and 10% are probationary. The remaining 65% are full-time non-tenure-track, part-time and graduate assistants who provide an almost interchangeable contingent labor force."

7. See, for example, the report on the Nancy Olivieri case at <http://www.caut.ca/uploads/OlivieriInquiryReport.pdf>.

8. My experience spans roughly 20 years as a student in various postsecondary institutions in five different degree programs, plus 14 years in a variety of contract or sessional, tenure-track, and tenured faculty positions.

9. Mipham (2010) makes a similar point: "First and foremost, Shambhala is based upon a societal vision. Even though it can be seen as a path by which an individual can travel into the great depths of enlightenment, this journey has a greater purpose than that. Shambhala vision is changing the whole social paradigm. For humanity not only to survive, but to flourish and prosper, the whole question and purpose of social existence needs to be addressed. As human beings we are exceptionally vulnerable to our environment. Environment begins to color our behaviour, as well as our thought patterns. Therefore, environment needs to be addressed, and in this case, it is the social paradigm that we are addressing. If we only make some minor internal adjustments, then we are only addressing our personal dilemma, not confronting the overall societal trend."

10. Points of departure for a reexamination of academic work include Boyer's (1994) account of the forms of scholarship needed to serve the public good, as well as more recent publications on mutually-enhancing forms of university-community engagement (Inman & Schuetze, 2011).

References

Allman, P. (2007). *On Marx: An introduction to the revolutionary intellect of Karl Marx.* Rotterdam, Netherlands: Sense Publishers.

Benjamin, E. (2008). *Some implications of tenure for the profession and society.* Washington, DC: American Association of University Professors. Retrieved April 10, 2011, from <www.aaup.org/AAUP/issues/tenure/benjamintenureimps>.

Boyer, E. L. (1994). Scholarly work: New definitions and directions. In J. N. Mangieri & C. C. Block (Eds.), *Creating powerful thinking in teachers and students: Diverse perspectives* (pp. 187–194). Fort Worth, TX: Harcourt Brace.

Brown, R. H., & Schubert, J. Daniel (2000). Academic knowledge and political power in late capitalist societies. In R. H. Brown & J. D. Schubert (Eds.), *Knowledge and power in higher education: A reader* (pp. 3–13). New York: Teachers College Press.

CAUT/ACPPU (2011/Feb). General assembly created out of lack of confidence in current governance of the university. *Bulletin 58*(2), A5. See <http://cautbulletin.ca/en_article.asp?articleid=3195>.

Chödrön, T. (2005). Marketing the dharma. In S. Kaza (Ed.), *Hooked! Buddhist writings on greed, desire, and the urge to consume* (pp. 63–75). Boston: Shambhala.

Cole, A. (2001). *All I really need to forget I learned in the academy.* Available for download from <http://home.oise.utoronto.ca/~acole/>.

Coles, R. (2010). Hunger, ethics, and the university: A radical goad in ten pieces. In E. Kiss & J. P. Euben (Eds.), *Debating moral education: Rethinking the role of the modern university* (pp. 225–246). Durham, NC: Duke University Press.

Davidson-Harden, A. (2010). Interrogating the university as an engine of capitalism: Neoliberalism and the academic '*raison d'état.*' *Policy Futures in Education, 8*(5), 575–587.

Fernandes, L. (2003). *Transforming feminist practice: Non-violence, social justice, and the possibilities of a spiritualized feminism.* San Francisco, CA: Aunt Lute Books.

Foucault, M. (1977). The political function of the intellectual. *Radical Philosophy, 17,* 12–14.

Glassman, B. (1998). *Bearing witness: A Zen master's lessons in making peace.* New York: Bell Tower.

Gottdiener, M. (2000). Approaches to consumption: Classical and contemporary perspectives. In M. Gottdiener (Ed.), *New forms of consumption: Consumers, culture, and commodification* (pp. 3–32). Lanham, MD: Roman and Littlefield.

Gyamtso, T. (1988). *Progressive stages of meditation on emptiness* (2nd ed.). Oxford, UK: Longchen Foundation.

Gyatso, T. (His Holiness the XIV Dalai Lama), & Sheng-yen (Venerable Chan Master). (1999). *Meeting of minds: A dialogue on Tibetan and Chinese Buddhism.* New York: Dharma Drum Publications.

Higgins, C. (2010). The good life of teaching: An ethics of professional practice. *Journal of Philosophy of Education, 44*(2/3), 189–478.

Inman, P., & Schuetze, Hans G. (Eds.). (2010). *The community engagement and service mission of universities.* Leicester (UK): NIACE.

Jackson-Weaver, Karen, Baker, Earnestine B., Gillespie, Michael C., Bellido, Carlos G., & Watts, Anne W. (2010). Recruiting the next generation of the professoriate. *Peer Review, 12*(3). Retrieved April 10 from <http://www.aacu.org/peerreview/pr-su10/pr-su10_Recruiting.cfm>.

Loy, D. (2003). *The great awakening: a Buddhist social theory.* Boston, MA: Wisdom Publications.

MacIntyre, A. (1984). *After virtue: A study in moral theory* (2nd ed.). Notre Dame, IN: University of Notre Dame Press.

MacIntyre, A. (1988). *Whose justice? Which rationality?* Notre Dame, IN: University of Notre Dame Press.

MacIntyre, A., & Dunne, J. (2002). Alasdair MacIntyre on education: In dialogue with Joseph Dunne. *Journal of Philosophy of Education, 36*(1), 1–19.

Marker, M. (2011). Sacred mountains and ivory towers: Indigenous pedagogies of place and invasions from modernity. In G. J. Dei (Ed.), *Indigenous philosophies and critical education: A reader* (pp. 197–211). New York: Peter Lang.

Metcalf, A. (2010). Revisiting academic capitalism in Canada: No longer the exception. *The Journal of Higher Education, 81*(4), 489–514.

Metcalfe, A., & Snee, I. (2011). *"A right can of worms!!" Asking Canadian faculty about their biggest challenges.* Centre for Policy Studies in Higher Education and Training Public Seminar, UBC, Vancouver, March 8, 2011.

Mipham, S. (2010). *The letter of the morning sun.* From <http://www.shambhala.org/community/files/PDF/LetterOfTheMorningSun.pdf>.

Orr, D. (2004). *Earth in mind: On education, environment, and the human prospect* (2nd ed.). Washington, DC: Island Press.

O'Sullivan, E. (1999). *Transformative learning: Educational vision for the 21st century.* Toronto: University of Toronto Press.

Palmer, P. J. (1998a). Evoking the spirit in public education. *Educational Leadership, 56*(4), 6–11.

Palmer, P. (1998b). *The courage to teach.* San Francisco: Jossey-Bass.

Rosenberg, M. (2003). *Life-enriching education: Nonviolent communication helps schools improve performance, reduce conflict, and enhance relationships.* Encinitas, CA: Puddledancer Press.

Schön, D. (1983). *The reflective practitioner. How professionals think in action.* London: Temple Smith.

Schön, D. (1986). From technical rationality to rationality-in-action. In R. Edwards (Ed.), *Boundaries of adult learning* (pp. 8–31). New York: Routledge.

Slaughter, S., & Leslie, L. L. (1997). *Academic capitalism: Politics, policies, and the entrepreneurial university.* Baltimore, MD: Johns Hopkins University Press.

Smeyers, P., & Burbules, N. C. (2011). How to improve your impact factor: Questioning the quantification of academic quality. *Journal of Philosophy of Education, 45*(1), 1–17).

Stelmach, B., Parsons, J., & Frick, W. C. (2010). Fear and loathing in the academy. *Academic Matters, May.* Retreived July 22, 2010 from <http://www.academicmatters.ca/site_search_results.news.gk?catalog_item_id=4059#>.

Trungpa, C. (1973). *Cutting through spiritual materialism.* Boston: Shambhala.

Trungpa, C. (1993). *Training the mind and cultivating loving-kindness.* Boston: Shambhala.

Vokey, D. (2001). *Moral discourse in a pluralistic world.* Notre Dame, IN: University of Notre Dame Press.

Vokey, D. (2003). Pursuing the idea/l of an educated public: Philosophy's contributions to radical school reform. *Journal of Philosophy of Education, 37*(2), 267–278. DOI: 10.1111/1467-9752.00325.

Vokey, D. (2011). Moral education for the 21st Century: A Buddhist view. In J. DeVitis & T. Yu (Eds.), *Character and moral education: A reader* (pp. 400–412). New York: Peter Lang.

16

Transitions

Teaching from the Spaces Between

Richard C. Brown

Transitions occur constantly at many levels of the learning process. When we read, think, or create, our minds move between ideas, perceptions, and feelings. Teachers who are mindful of these changes can develop skills and practices that enhance these progressions and synchronize the many dimensions of teaching and learning. In the graduate contemplative teacher education program at Naropa University, we draw from Tibetan and Japanese wisdom sources, as well as from Western educational practices, to develop contemplative pedagogies that deepen learning. The foundation of our approach is the personal mindfulness practice of the teacher.

> Contemplative pedagogy demands that the teacher engage fearlessly in a dynamic relationship with the learning process on both personal and professional levels. Presence is not accidental; it is cultivated through meditative practices that open and clarify the heart and mind of the teacher, facilitate communication, sharpen the intellect, and foster creativity. (Brown, 2011, p. 75)

In this chapter we will begin with a contemplative exploration of the nature of moment-to-moment transitional experience—the source of insightful, creative teaching. Mindfulness lays the groundwork for the implementation of contemplative pedagogies. The ones we will touch upon here are related to transitions in teaching and learning. Teachers and students alike, within higher education contexts, benefit from mindful approaches to transitional pedagogies, which engender meaningful learning.

Mindfulness in Transitions

When we practice being mindful, we notice each distinct experience without judgment, let it go, and freshly encounter the next moment. "Transitions are like doorways. When we open a door, we think we know what we will find on the other side, but we can never be sure" (Lief, 2001, p. 15). As teachers and instructors, we often welcome the unexpected in the classroom, which can lead to creative, fresh openings for new learning. However, sometimes the door opens and we may react in a way that unintentionally shuts down learning. According to Tibetan Buddhism, our mental processes are so interwoven with emotional factors that even though we intend to create an open intellectual environment, our emotional reactions can disrupt things. For example, we may notice our irritation at a certain student whose energy and expression seems to be derailing our lesson plan. "Our basic strategy is to avoid the pain of transition. We prefer to define our world, to pin it down so that we can live comfortably within our own definition of things" (p. 18).

Rather than using our finely honed intellectual skills to quell the disruption, in mindful teaching we notice the irritation and pause briefly before acting. Mindfulness of thoughts and emotions keeps us from being blindsided in the fast-paced transitions that are constantly happening in the classroom. Usually we are moving so quickly from one experience to the next that we don't notice our emotional tone and conceptual mindset. Mindfulness creates a gap, a transitional moment that interrupts our habitual, and possibly harmful, reactions. Rather than indulging our feelings of irritation or becoming overly accommodating, we can, with practice, make peace with the feeling. Having done so, we can integrate that energy compassionately and meet the learning situation as it is. Here one of our students reflects on the value of meditation for holistic integration:

> These are all sensations, emotions, and thoughts that I would have been having regardless, but meditation helped me to acknowledge them and to relate more fully to my experience of the present moment. This acknowledgement was a kindness to myself that allowed for an inner transition—an awareness and appreciation of the changes that were occurring inside of me and around me. There was not complete peace of mind, but I was more at ease because I felt more synchronized with my own experience. (MS)

Contemplative practices which include compassion seek to incorporate our immediate inner experiences into caring learning relationships. As teachers, we begin by being kind toward ourselves and acknowledging our inner impulses.

Having pacified our feelings and thoughts, we can offer them more effectively to our students.

One important aspect of mindfulness practice that helps to pacify our harmful impulses is *direct experience* of the moment. When we notice a feeling like irritation, we practice experiencing it compassionately and non-conceptually before we let it go. We touch that emotion for an instant without complicating it with judgments or thoughts. We learn to let things be just as they are before we respond to them. This same principle applies to any ideas that may arise within us during mindfulness practice. We notice a thought and let it go; we don't think further about it. Our thoughts about our direct experience may be important later, but they are different from what we notice during contemplative practice.

Mindfulness is not an anti-intellectual approach. It is simply a method of being mindful of our thoughts, rather than blurting them out, or mindlessly running through old intellectual scripts. Being precise about the nature of our inner experiences, we learn to distinguish thoughts from feelings, which provides greater clarity of thought and actually liberates our intellectual life. As academics we are rightly passionate about the intellectual constructs we have developed during our careers. However, we sometimes unconsciously identify with those thoughts. When we equate ourselves with our ideas, our intellectual property can becomes so intertwined with our identity that any perceived threat to them becomes a threat to ourselves that we must aggressively defend. When others question our closely held ideas, we may allow our feelings to prevent open and rational discourse leading to fresh thinking. Instructors who develop awareness of their self-identification with ideas can practice noticing that and relax their grasp. Holding more gently and spaciously to our ideas leads to more perspective, humor, and freedom to explore our intellectual fields.

The *Bardo*, Emptiness, and Creativity

Mindfulness practice directly relates to the Tibetan Buddhist notion of *bardo*, which means "in-between" in Tibetan. Bardo is usually understood as spiritual instructions for dying and after-death experiences. However, according to Dzogchen Ponlop, teachings on the bardo are also intended as instructions for living in the present moment. "Every moment ceases, and that is the death of that moment. Another moment arises and that is the birth of the next moment" (Ponlop, 2006, p. 16).

The bardo teachings suggest there are actually more possibilities beyond mindfulness of successive moments. "The essence of *bardo* is discovered in the experience of nowness, in the gap between the cessation of one moment and the arising of the next" (Ponlop, 2006, p. 13). Tibetan meditators have found, through centuries of meditation practice, that there are spaces between instances of attention. It is said that these gaps are infinitesimally small and very difficult to notice. As comparatively casual mindfulness practitioners, contemplative instructors cannot be expected to notice these gaps the way that some meditation masters have done. Nonetheless, it is possible through mindful discipline to slow down, allow some space, and interrupt our flow of habitual reactions. Dzogchen Ponlop discusses the profound nature of these gaps or transitions in our momentary experience:

> If we truly penetrate [the birth and death of the moment], there is a sense of nonconceptuality—of clear awareness without thought . . . there is a sense of openness, of being nowhere. . . . In this experience of the present, of nowness, there is already a sense of non-solidity, of dissolution . . . that occurs constantly in our present life but is almost never noticed. . . . (p. 16)

This profound description of the gaps between moments reflects, among other things, the fundamental Buddhist notion of emptiness. When examined in a meditative way, our ever-changing experience is ineffable and our attempts to define it are usually insufficient. But before we dismiss this perspective as lofty philosophizing unrelated to classroom experience, we should explore echoes of this traditional wisdom of emptiness that is alive and relevant in our teaching experience.

When we notice ourselves in a transition, such as at the end of a semester, we often experience both openness and groundlessness. We may feel liberated, because our regular routine has fallen away and many possibilities lie before us. On the other hand, we may feel "at loose ends," listless, or unsure of ourselves. Sometimes we experience more of one extreme than the other, but both are related to the "dissolution" that Dzogchen Ponlop mentioned. When frameworks fall away during a transition, we experience emptiness—our ideas, momentum, and reference points no longer apply to our immediate experience. Chögyam Trungpa, Naropa's founder, called it "no-man's land," which hints at the fear this experience elicits in our conventional minds (Trungpa, 1992, p. 108).

Contemplative practice elicits our willingness to acknowledge that in that moment we are no longer conceptually in control. Contemplative practice is learning to walk confidently on uncertain ground as we move from moment to moment—to be brave enough to actually feel the profound unsettledness of transitional moments. Paradoxically, when we no longer rely upon solid ground to stand upon, we are more in touch with the simple reality of the present moment. In this empty moment, not all our previous experience and knowledge need to permanently vanish—rather they become a background, a resource. The foreground, the insubstantial present moment, is what is happening *now*. We practice perceiving the instructional opportunities that arise from that empty space without clinging to our reference points to similar classroom situations.

If we explore further the nature of the spaces between, we may see that it is a source of creativity and meaning in our teaching lives. It is in these empty gaps the creativity of transformation resides. Because the source of creativity, empty space, is formless, employing formal methods and pedagogy can be tricky. However, through contemplative practices, instructors can cultivate an attitude of openness in teaching, as one our program students describes.

> When I am mindful enough to create some gaps, empty space, in my teaching routine, I notice that my whole outlook begins to shift and I naturally move away from those old patterns that can so easily overtake me. I notice this most often when, in dealing with student behavior, one of my emotional train rides departs the station. Awareness helps me to identify the emerging pattern, mindfulness helps me throw the switch and derail that run-away train. These gaps can come in any form and at any time; they need not be anything extraordinary: a gap between my own words, between and within an exchange with a student, between direct instruction and discussion, between classes. . . . I notice that if I am mindful, the gaps continually present themselves. (DG)

"Bardos are periods of tremendous power and potential, in which the old has died and the new has not yet been born" (Coburn, 2008). By paying attention to the academic present moment and then releasing our attachment to that event, we are freer to give more energy to academic discovery. "Letting go" of the contents of experience might be better described as loosening one's grip—allowing a gap for openness and creative encounter. For teachers it is the magic in the "teachable moment," when we suddenly recognize a fresh opening, a meeting of minds, and a new way of communicating. "When one experience has died and the next not yet arisen, we are not caught, but free. . . . During these moments of heightened vulnerability, it is possible to see things freshly" (Lief, 2001, p. 16). When we are fearlessly willing to meet the open, transitional moment, then the residue of the past moment falls away.

> In that very moment, we can directly experience the non-solidity of phenomena, the reality of emptiness, or *shunyata*. At the same time, there is so much energy present—so much so that it forms into another moment. The energy brings a sense of clarity that is so sharp, it is like a clear mirror in which mind can at last recognize itself. (Ponlop, 2006, p. 17)

One of the paradoxes of contemplative practice is that as our mindfulness develops further, we not only have a clearer experience of the details of each moment, but we also notice empty space as well. The spacious, almost dream-like, nature of emptiness requires a broader context for our mindfulness practice. To engage with the profound dynamics of successive moments and the spaces in-between, we must begin to soften the dominant reference point of a self that is separate from that experience. Practicing awareness of our direct experience tunes us in to the unformed energy of that particular transitional moment. When we can maintain our awareness during transitions, then we can stay present and participate in the energetic formation of the next moment. We can "manage" transitions in the classroom, as we will explore below.

Of course, few of us can maintain constant awareness and openness. "At first, everything is vivid and new, almost overwhelmingly so. But eventually, as we adjust, that freshness dissolves, and we no longer see so clearly" (Lief, p. 17). In meditative practices we train to recognize when the "freshness dissolves," when we are closed to the present moment, and when we solidify our experience. The practice is to non-judgmentally touch the discomfort, let go of the solidity, and meet the next moment freshly. It is not about *maintaining* awareness, it is about *returning* to awareness when our attention drifts away.

It is useful to have some understanding about the nature of these empty transitional moments, so that when they arise in our teaching we can benefit from them. Even if we do not have a strong mindfulness practice, we can engage in simple teaching methods that utilize this wisdom, as we will now explore.

Wait Time

Wait Time is an established Western teaching method that clearly employs principles directly applicable to contemplative transitional practices. By examining Wait Time we can easily see how the personal mindfulness practice of the teacher can enhance this pedagogy. Important studies on Wait Time have been done since the early 1970s: Rowe (1986), Stahl (1990), and others found that when teachers wait three seconds after asking a question and before they call on students during class discussions, "many positive things happened to students' and teachers' behaviors and attitudes" (Stahl, 1990, p. 1). It was found that when using Wait Time, the number of students willing to reply increased substantially. Students also demonstrated that they knew more about the content than they did when they were called on in a fast-paced situation. The research also discovered that the while using Wait Time, teachers' interactions with students during discussions became more varied, flexible, and of higher quality. Pausing during discussions also produced "questions that required more complex information processing and higher-level thinking on the part of students" (Stahl, 1990). Furthermore, students' academic achievement test scores improved.

We have employed this excellent practice in our teacher education program at Naropa University using a contemplative twist. When *contemplative* teachers use Wait Time, they are encouraged to use the three-second pause to attend to their inner experiences, rather than just biding their time. Contemplating teachers are taught to notice, non-judgmentally, their own thoughts, emotions, or sense experiences. On a gentle out-breath, they relax their attachments to those inner experiences. This practice helps to synchronize teachers with their inner experiences and to relinquish any unconscious attachments. Having done so, teachers are able to respond more directly to what the students offer when called upon. Having stabilized their own awareness, teachers can better empathize and tune-in to the students. Experienced contemplative teachers are frequently more open to students' responses, as this teacher reports.

> I chose to back off, just quit talking so much about what I think I know on the topic and to invite "intelligent space" to participate. Students' voices were timid as they entered the space. Then I noticed more voices appearing around the topic. There was more space in the discussion, more room for the other people in the class. I felt a little lighter, a little freer and immense gratitude for my willingness to just relax a little. (DL)

Of course, an infinite variety of experiences can occur to contemplative teachers during Wait Time. They could ponder the question they have just asked the class and notice if there are any predetermined or favored responses that they expect the students to offer. If so, they could appreciate those, let them go, and become open to whatever the students may say.

Jo Ha Kyu

In our program, we have adapted the principles of *Jo, Ha,* and *Kyu* from the Japanese tradition as a contemplative basis for transitional pedagogies related to beginning, middle, and end (Worley, 2001). The Jo Ha Kyu teachings can be related to the bardo teachings. "*Bardo* is an experience of a certain duration of time, marked by a clear beginning, a sense of continuity, and a distinct end" (Ponlop, 2006, p. 13) When we pay attention to how activities begin, what they are like in the middle, and how they end, we can synchronize our teaching with the rhythms of arising, duration, and cessation that are related to mindful teaching.

Jo is said to be "an orderly beginning" (Worley, 2001, p. 130). From the perspective of the mindfulness practice of the teacher, Jo involves noticing our state of being in the beginning, before we engage in an educational encounter. Noticing who we are in the moment is, in a sense, reflecting on our inner natural order. Rather than launching straight into the class, we encourage instructors to take an instant before the start of class to tune in to their physical, emotional, and conceptual presence. "Preparing for these experiences begins with simply being who we are and where we are in this very moment" (Ponlop, 2006, p. 19). One of Naropa's founding faculty members writes about her practice before class:

> . . . I am always a little fearful before I begin to teach. That fear has the power to separate me from being fully present with my students, by lodging me securely in my thoughts (and apart from my body). So when I take the moment to include my fearful aspect, I am fully there with everyone. (Worley, 2002)

Ha, the middle, is described from the Japanese tradition as "an intensification" (Worley, 2001, p. 130). Ha is engagement in the moment—experiencing our presence fully in relation to the learning activity. Once the rhythm of the class has been established by a proper beginning, the middle takes on a different tone—a dynamic life of its own.

The momentum of the Ha in teaching presents challenges for the mindful teacher. Transitions happen so rapidly in the middle of classes, that we can easily lose awareness and lapse into habitual ways of teaching and responding. Just as in meditation, where our attention on the breath can often be absent for long periods of time, we practice returning to the present moment whenever we wake up to our mindlessness. Coming back to the present in the midst of heightened classroom intensity is the mark of a strong mindfulness teaching practice. Fortunately, pedagogies like Wait Time and others we will explore are useful methods for strengthening mindfulness in the middle of classes.

Kyu is the "culmination," the "exit" from the activity (Worley, 2001, p. 131). As we end a learning activity, we carry the residue of that experience "toward an undiscovered realm. Completing one Kyu provides open ground, a gap from which the next Jo arises" (p. 132). In order to open more fully to the next activity, it is helpful to reflect upon or notice what has just occurred. Similar to using a pause at the beginning of class, at the end we don't just mindlessly rush on to the next activity without noticing where we have been. In Russia, there was a saying, "Do a job, rest, move on to the next."

> I spent the transitional moments walking, grounding myself with who I am in the present moment, and making an effort to let go of judgments from the day. I felt much more clarity and peace in my body, versus the chaos I've felt on previous walks. (AE)

Kyu is the "arrow [flying] through the air to its destination" (Worley, 2001, p. 131). In the West we tend to emphasize hitting the target—achieving the learning outcome. It is quite different to think of the ending as the arrow flying through the air *toward* the target, rather than hitting it. In the Eastern view there are many possible results from the activity in the Ha. When we experience endings in this way, we notice what has passed and let it go. In that moment we might feel the groundlessness of not knowing what will come next. At the same time we could feel the power of that open, creative moment, without filling it, and without clinging to recent experience.

Transitional Pedagogies—Beginnings

Contemplative pedagogies can help faculty deepen learning during transitions in the classroom. When the instructor is experiencing moment-to-moment transitions on the inner level, then managing such transitions in the classroom is much easier. The selected transitional pedagogies in this section are divided into Beginnings, Middles, and Endings.

Routines and rituals at the start of classes allow for orderly beginnings. When we are able to share with our students the reasons we use transitional pedagogies, we include them in the creation of contemplative learning community, even if we don't call it that. Sometimes these methods can provoke adverse responses among students for whom they are new and seemingly irrelevant. It is important for us to be ordinary, clear, and confident in our use of transitional practices. It is better if we don't make them too "precious" and ritualistic.

> I took time out of the class to have a discussion about beginnings, middles, and ends with the students, even though it was not in the lesson plan. . . . With this awareness, students became allies in my attempt to synchronize the outer reality of changes and the inner creation of transitions for all of us. In the next class, significantly fewer students were tardy, and all of them were prepared for class. (MS)

Aspirations, whether written or verbal, are a time to reflect on the semester's journey ahead. In our summer program at Naropa, we write aspirations that reflect our intentions for ourselves in the academic program. We then hang the cards among the branches of a tree outside a classroom window. Noticing them from time to time during the summer program, we are reminded of our aspirations at the beginning.

Meditation and silence are effective ways to mark the beginning of each class. A few minutes of non-sectarian silence or breath meditation allows both faculty and students to pause and settle. When this practice is used regularly, it can profoundly affect the atmosphere of the class. Parker Palmer (1993) began his classes with a period of silence, "a time when we can still ourselves enough to begin to feel our natural connectedness to each other and the world" (p. 80). Genet Simone, an instructor in our program, introduced a moment of silence at the beginning of classes she taught at the University of Colorado.

> I put a sign on the door to let latecomers know that we were having our Moment of Silence; if they were late to class, they should just have a moment of silence in the hall until I opened the door again. I was worried about how students would deal with this radical change from the typical college atmosphere, but on my evaluations students wrote things like, "I loved that moment of silence! It was the best part of the semester for me." (Simone, 2006)

Chögyam Trungpa suggested that before beginning a lecture, teachers should let go of their plans for a few moments and stare at a blank wall in the back of the room.

Bowing at the start of classes is a practice that has been used at Naropa University since it was founded in 1974. We bow from a seated position at the start of every meeting and class. This practice begins by silently acknowledging who we are in this moment and what we are bringing to the class gathering.

In bowing we also offer ourselves in service to the others in the class. At the same time the bow is a gesture of respect to everyone else and what they may bring to the gathering.

Personal sharing is another way to create a gap from the usual momentum at the start of classes. I start my classes with a brief period of meditation, a bow, and then I take a few minutes for "announcements" from students. This is a time when students share highlights from their lives outside of class. Students have invited classmates to a protest at the courthouse and announced they have an art piece in an exhibit in the gallery. Sometimes what they offer is much more personal, "My cat died and I'm really devastated today." I often engage in sharing, myself. Sharing ourselves and our worlds outside of class creates a gap for the students. It interrupts their usual way of beginning a class and also strengthens the sense of community among us all. Furthermore, it is a reminder that contemplative study involves integrating our studies with the rest of our lives. It is, of course, important to limit the class time used for personal sharing. For me, five or ten minutes at the start of class is enough. When a student indulges in lengthy sharing I interrupt to ask them to please summarize, explaining that we have limited time. Such moments are also an opportunity for me to modulate my emotional reactivity to their ramblings.

Classroom Transitions in the Middle

During the intensity that can accompany the middle part of classroom activities, pedagogies that reinforce teaching and learning from the spacious present moment can be very helpful. These practices can be solely for the instructor, but are best when the whole learning community shares them. As with all mindfulness-based practices, the teacher must commit to regular use of the techniques over time. It is tempting to relinquish them too early, since these methods are often new and challenging at first.

The mindfulness bell, a practice made popular by Vietnamese Zen teacher Thich Nhat Hanh, is a small gong or bell, which is rung at regular intervals (usually15 minutes) during class. No matter what is happening, when the bell is sounded everything stops and all listen to the sound. When caught up in the flurry of discussion or lecture, focusing on the direct experience of the sound tends to balance the conceptual with the sensory. This practice is grounding and creates some space and grace during learning activities.

> The students were very still while the tone chimed, and it gave me enough time to reflect, honor, and respect the lesson, my students, and myself. (AE)

Naropa's president, Stuart Lord, often uses the mindfulness bell practice during his administrative meetings, and even at all-school gatherings. Smart-phones now have applications which automatically sound a gong at designated intervals. This conveniently allows everyone to participate fully in class without having to watch the clock.

Silence can be used effectively, in the middle of a class, especially in an open discussion when the words start to tumble out upon each other and the problem we are trying to unravel is getting more tangled. I try to help the students learn to spot these moments and settle into a time of quiet reflection in which the knots might come untied (Palmer, 1993, p. 80).

Quaker academic discussions employ the practice of speaking from silence. In this practice individuals wait about three minutes or more in silence before speaking in discussion. My experience of this practice at Quaker higher education conferences has been profound. The deep listening and respect was palpable.

Discussion guidelines for the class can provide a variety of ways for bringing awareness into the heart of class discussion. After a long period of discussion, the class can pause for a period of simple movement, such as standing and stretching. Another method is to have students self-limit the number of times that they speak during a discussion (Brown & Davis, 2006). When the culture of the class supports self-monitoring in this way, students learn to restrain their habitual tendencies to either leap into discussions or to refrain. "The more aggressive and verbal students . . . are forced to sort and sift what they have to say, looking for that which is essential. The quieter, more retiring students find the space to speak" (Palmer, 1993, p. 80).

Natural pauses in classroom exchanges tend to gradually develop when these pedagogies are used. In our summer program, the culture has evolved so that pauses between discussion offerings are the unspoken norm. This creates a gentle, thoughtful rhythm, which can easily transform into lively exchanges, then settle again—an atmosphere of spacious full-on engagement that feels lively, yet non-aggressive.

Unexpected interruptions occur within the middle of classes from time to time. Calling everyone's attention to a bird landing on a branch outside the window, or, less pleasantly, the loud crushing sound of a trash truck, can be opportunities for a pause and sensory awareness practice. Whether interruptions are viewed as distractions, or as opportunities to rest and wake up, is largely dependent on the leadership of the instructor and the climate of the classroom. We can use these moments to focus the class's attention on the gap that has arisen and to look freshly at the subject at hand.

Regular celebrations in the middle of semesters can create a meaningful gap in the rhythm of learning. Several programs at Naropa University celebrate Practice Week in the middle of each semester. Each program celebrates differently, but usually classes are replaced by contemplative practice sessions, panel discussions, or related social gatherings. Once each semester all of Naropa comes together for Practice Day. An all-school meditation is often followed by a talk by an esteemed contemplative. The afternoon is filled with workshop options from various contemplative practice traditions.

In our Contemplative Education summer program we have a Day of Contemplation in the middle. Our summer schedule is very full, twelve-hour days, seven days a week, so we all need a gap. But we encourage students to maintain their awareness during the day of rest and not to flop into the habitual mindlessness of a "day off." The Day of Contemplation is modeled on the Jewish celebration of Shabbat. The focus of our practice is to rest and enjoy each other's company. It begins with an evening feast the night before. On the day itself, an outing to a scenic park is scheduled, but there is no particular agenda—just resting, playing on the green, gentle walks, and a picnic. Instructors schedule assignment due-dates so we can simply pause and not worry about looming assignments. At the end of the day we reflect on our experience of that practice. What was it like to let go of anything that seemed like "work?"

Endings in the Classroom

We often teach right up to the last minute of the class period—so many important things to learn and so little time. But it is valuable to use just a few minutes at the end of class to integrate what has been learned and provide a meaningful transition to the next thing. For example, at the end of class, when reminding students about the next assignment, we might allow time and invite questions, rather than announcing it just as the students are exiting the classroom.

Reflecting and journaling on what we have learned during the class can happen in a few minutes at the end. Parker Palmer took ten to fifteen minutes at the end of class for a "corporate evaluation of how the class went. . . . Sometimes they alert us to a cognitive issue—only half the group has understood a certain point. But more often they allow feelings to emerge" (Palmer, 1993, p. 86). It is often the emotional carryover from what has happened in class that is ignored in transitions. A skillful teacher, knowing that ideas and feelings are intertwined, will help students discriminate their thoughts and emotions so the lesson is clearer and more deeply imbedded. In our Naropa education classes, we allow a few minutes at the end for students to journal about questions, feelings, and insights they have experienced. We sometimes begin the following class with time to reflect on those previous writings, thus creating continuity between the classes. Having been contemplated between classes, those perspectives often mature over time.

Ritual endings can be short and simple ways of signifying the close of class. Just as each Naropa class begins with a bow, they end that way, too. Not only does bowing together make for a crisp community marking of the end of the class, but it also gives each member a moment to appreciate what has transpired. A few minutes of mindfulness meditation can serve as a meaningful gap before leaving the class.

Closing celebrations are common in classes at the end of Naropa semesters. In our education summer program we read to each other the aspirations that we wrote and hung on the branches outside the classroom at the beginning of the semester. (This can be a particularly intuitive process when the summer rains have blurred the words on the cards.) We contemplate what those aspirations mean to us now. What have we learned? How have we changed?

Conclusion

Usually we feel we have so much content and related processing to deal with in our courses that we cannot afford time for mindful transitions. However, at Naropa we have found that devoting even brief periods of time for transitional activities allows our study of the subject to be integrated at a deep and meaningful level. Mindfulness-based approaches reduce stress levels in teachers and the enjoyment of teaching increases.

> After practicing, life always seems better . . . it's like magic. I'm less agitated, I see situations more clearly, colors are more vibrant, and I like my students more and worry about me less. (MS)

In addition, our students seem to better integrate course content, and establish more meaningful relationships to the course materials, and to colleagues.

> In our faculty meeting we worked on creating a training manual. I practiced asking "real questions," not just well crafted ones. And that generated real inquiry, reflection, and exchange. There was great discussion among all of the faculty as to why we do this

> and why we do that. We had so much fun, the hour-long meeting turned into two hours (no one looked at their watch). We only got half way through my list and everyone is looking forward to continuing. (PL)

By combining the practices and insights from the Jo Ha Kyu and teachings on the bardo, contemporary pedagogy can be greatly enriched. When we apply these practices to class periods, semesters, and to the duration of the academic journey, we can meet and appreciate the unique experiences contained within the birth, duration, and cessation of each time frame. We develop sensitivity and skillfulness in relating to each other and the course materials within these rhythms. We have a better sense of when a new educational encounter is emerging; how it can be met effectively and ended appropriately.

This approach influences how we relate to transitions throughout our lives, long after we have left our educational settings. Contemplative transitional pedagogies help us expand our focus beyond our personal reference points to a larger, energetic whole, which is richer than our singular perspective. As our sense of self expands and softens, we more easily and kindly engage with more spacious fields of study and communion.

References

Brown, R. (2011).The mindful teacher as the foundation of contemplative pedagogy. In J. Simmer-Brown & F. Grace (Eds.), *Meditation and the classroom: Contemplative pedagogy for religious studies* (pp. 75–83). Albany, NY: State University of New York Press.

Brown, R., & Davis, J. (2006). *Guidelines for contemplative discussion.* Unpublished document.

Coburn, T. (2008). *Naropa University commencement address.* Unpublished manuscript. Naropa University, Boulder, CO.

Lief, J. (2001). *Making friends with death.* Boston: Shambhala.

Palmer, P. (1993). *To know as we are known.* New York: HarperCollins.

Ponlop, D. (2006). *Mind beyond death.* Ithica, NY: Snow Lion Publications.

Rowe, M. (1986). Wait time: Slowing down may be a way of speeding up! *Journal of Teacher Education, January, 37*(1), 43–50.

Simone, G. (2006). Online lecture. *EDU635e contemplative teaching.* Unpublished manuscript. Naropa University, Boulder, CO.

Stahl, R. J. (1990). *Using "think time" behaviors to promote students' information processing, learning and on-task participation. An instructional module.* Unpublished manuscript. Tempe, AZ: Arizona State University.

Trungpa, C. (1992). *Transcending madness.* Boston: Shambhala.

Worley, L. (2001). *Coming from nothing*. Boulder, CO: Turquoise Dragon Press.

Worley, L. (2002, Sept. 15). Online discussion, *EDU635e Contemplative Teaching*. Naropa University, Boulder, CO.

17

A Call for Wisdom in Higher Education

Contemplative Voices from the *Dao*-Field

Heesoon Bai, Avraham Cohen, Tom Culham, Sean Park, Shahar Rabi, Charles Scott, and Saskia Tait

Introduction

This chapter, written as a hybrid text that blends traditional academic discourse with the narrative voices of the authors, introduces our collective "experiment" in contemplative inquiry through intersubjectivity, and explores its guiding principles, complexities, and subtleties of contemplative practice, and application possibilities in learning environments of higher education. The seven authors of this chapter have come together as a group with the specific purpose of researching the far reaches of intersubjectivity, such as accessing non-dual consciousness or awareness as a collective "field experience" and its potential to facilitate the emergence of wisdom and attendant social-environmental activism in higher education. This chapter represents the beginning stage of our journey together.

A Call for Wisdom in Higher Education

To many of us brought up in a culture that privileges speed and busyness, and productivity and consumption, contemplative practices—whether just sitting alone or engaging mindfully with others—are usually "unnatural" and difficult. We rush around frantically, work around the clock, compete relentlessly, and consume and accumulate excessively. Days and even nights are filled with busy activities, our minds are full and restless, emotions are bottled up and ready to explode or implode, shoulders permanently raised from tension, jaws clenched, and so on. Educationally, we are inclined (or forced) to consume knowledge voraciously, often in attempts to pass exams, earn degrees, and land those lucrative career positions. In the language of Erich Fromm (1997), we are preoccupied with the "having" dimension of productivity and accumulation, and ignore the "being" dimension of resting in awareness. Moreover, this ability to sit with/in one's experience, holding the space for experience to show up and present itself so that we can work with it, is indeed a difficult art to learn.

We are usually too reactive, and not spacious and tranquil enough within, to be able to sit with ourselves and observe. Our attention (and energy, too) is constantly drawn out of ourselves and disperses in all directions, and not enough is left with which we can witness and examine our own experience. Heesoon, one of the chapter authors here, humorously but poignantly characterized the dominant mode of teaching as a "vampire operation": it continually sucks and drains attention out of students. No wonder students often feel—they tell us—as though the core of their being is hollowed out, empty. In class, their life energy appears quite suppressed. We are not talking about just marginalized students.

I'm struck by how suppressed the life energy of many students in my current undergraduate class seems to be. They would all be considered privileged students: they are selected for their academic achievement and commitment to social change. They are highly intelligent and well-spoken, and they look well-groomed. Yet, I keep sensing something is somewhat missing: perhaps the "primordial confidence" that the Buddhist scholar and meditation teacher Reginald Ray (January 24, 2006, public talk, Vancouver, BC) speaks of in human beings. What is going on? (HB)

Students are not given much opportunity to attend to their inner lives, to explore their unfathomable riches, to plummet the depth, and to be nourished deeply by such engagements. Yet, it is only through such engagements that energetically charged awareness deepens and expands, connecting self with cosmos, and fully reconciling us with life and universe. Hence the motto our group would like to have for our students is: *Return Attention to Self.*

The self is unable to nourish itself with awareness and energy when its attention is continuously siphoned out: attention is needed to access awareness and embedded and embodied energy. The result of the continual drain of attention while knowledge is being accumulated is that we may be knowledgeable but are not intelligent, in the sense of being wise. Jiddu Krishnamurti also talks about our capacity to be aware as intelligence and points to the relationship between that and knowledge. He writes, "Intelligence uses knowledge. Intelligence is a state in which there are no personal [conditioned] emotions involved, no personal opinion, prejudice or inclination. Intelligence is the capacity for direct understanding" (Krishnamurti, 2006, p. 20). For Krishnamurti, intelligence is not an intellectual realization or a constructed assimilation of thoughts and ideas, conventionally known as knowledge, but is a capacity to be aware, sensitive, and clear (2006, p. 21); is a capacity to love, to act, and to be present to transformation of life from moment to moment (1975, p. 288).

Similarly, David Geoffrey Smith (2008) distinguishes wisdom from knowledge, showing that the former requires, as its precondition, the "essential unity between thought and emotion," and points out that such unity requires the discipline of mindfulness or contemplation (p. 2). (The Chinese character 心, usually translated as "mind," ideographically shows this unity, and should be translated as "heart-mind.") Smith further illuminates the aims of education in various Eastern wisdom traditions:

> In Taoism it involves finding "the stillpoint"; in Buddhism, returning to your "original face." The practice of Way—and here the key word is practice, as one never quite reaches the goal completely, finally—leads to an awareness of how the smallest details of life play into the largest consequences and effects, and that it is therefore highly important to maintain vigilance over the details of one's conduct, because how we get to here, today, depends on what happened yesterday, or indeed the moment just passed. (p. 3)

The greatest educational challenge today is not downloading more, better, sophisticated knowledge and skills into students but helping them to cultivate the unity of heart and mind (and let's not forget the em*bodied* nature of this cultivation) through the work of awareness, and bring this unity fully into all contexts of their personal, communal, academic, and professional lives. The challenge is to infuse knowledge with awareness or mindfulness of which love and sensitivity are a part, and the result is, in short, wisdom. Can our schools, from kindergarten to university, be institutions of wisdom?

In many graduate seminars on education I have been a part of, I have watched myself and fellow students grapple with the question of why it is such a struggle to enact educational ideals in practice—even despite the most earnest of intentions. For example, one colleague asked how she can unselfconsciously maintain the value of pluralism, and yet become so deeply aggravated when her children do not demonstrate her conception of a strong work ethic. The gap between our ideas about the world and our actions in it is all too often uncomfortably large. When I become aware of this yawning divide in myself, I feel immobilized and my sense of integrity and agency diminishes. In these moments of self-reflexivity and clear seeing, I have a choice: to succumb to the tension that the guilt produces and employ some means to avoid it, or to rest with/in this self-recognition and the sometimes uncomfortable sensations that emerge with it. In the later case, a new space opens up wherein I can simultaneously apprehend the limited self-identity and all the habitual urges it has come to rely on, as well as a larger "Self" that is unformed and undetermined. Through my practice, I can slowly begin to see all of the fabrications and established automatisms begin to crumble. In the wake of these little inner catastrophes, I feel a profound sense of happiness, freedom and a curious new ability to surprise others and myself. More and more, I am capable of aligning my actions with my aims and ideals. (ST)

As educators, we are striving to bring this mindful, integral contemplative praxis into our engagements with students and colleagues, and within the various environmental and institutional ecologies that support our work and study. Our formal or informal engagements with students offer opportunities to work with them in further developing mindful awareness as praxis. Moreover, these contemplative activities offer opportunities for both teacher and student to uncover, develop, and create meaning and mutual understanding in a collaborative fashion.

Inner-Outer Symmetry or Non-duality

How we, in our interiority, experience our selves, other people, and environments has direct relational and actional consequence to the world. Hence, problems of the world, such as global environmental pollution, are not just "out there," requiring us to get out and "save the planet." David Orr (1994) hit the mark squarely when he stated: "The disordering of ecological systems and of the greater biogeochemical cycles of the earth reflects a prior disorder in the thought, perception, imagination, intellectual priorities, and loyalties inherent in the industrial mind" (p. 2). If one *sees* another human only as someone to manipulate to get what one wants, then exploitation will likely happen. If we *see* Nature as nothing but dead matter and a resource base that we can exploit for human consumption, then this would result in environmental degradation and destruction. How we relate to, act upon, and treat the outer world has everything to do with what goes on in human interiority in terms of beliefs, values, feelings, perceptions, and languages that express them.

The möbius band has only one surface, and thus tracing along one side of the band inevitably leads to the other side of the band. Playfully, I call my group of fellow researchers with whom I am writing this chapter the Möbius Band. The möbius configuration of the inner-outer interrelationship illustrates our group's continuous movement of going from the inner to the outer, as well as going from the outer to the inner, each movement dynamically turning into the other. The conventional way of categorically separating the inner from the outer deprives me of the possibility of transcendence—being able to experience reality as the all-encompassing "Dao-field" through the gateway of my subjectivity. I am aware of the universe through myself, and the universe is aware of itself through me; the universe is aware of me through itself. This is a Zen moment—a kensho experience—that is simultaneously a realization of my infinite responsibility to the world. (HB)

Realizing this symmetry or non-duality between the outer environment where our behavior manifests and actions materialize, and the inner environment of thoughts, perceptions, and feelings, ethically attuned contemplative practitioners listen to the cry of the suffering world and respond to this call: not only through immediate action to alleviate the suffering of the Other but also, more fundamentally, by seeing it reflected in their own interiority, and working mindfully with the inner materials toward bringing about greater authenticity, integrity, and wisdom, and reflecting them back to the world.

Inside out. *I want to take this inside, subjective experience and bring it with me to my outside world, to connect the inside with the outside. To go inside out. I reach into the stillness, to the centre and launch it out to others and the world. And while I'm at it, why not go outside in, as well. I can travel both ways. I reach out to the outside and draw it near and into me. Now it becomes connected to inner me, but it remains separate. (CS)*

Yet, the realization of the symmetry is one of the most difficult things for humans. In a famous passage in *Philosophical Investigations*, Wittgenstein (1976) tells us that philosophizing aims at showing the trapped fly a way out of the bottle. Appropriating this captivating metaphor, we could say that the fly bottle is the metaphor for the myth of the given (Habermas, 1999): the psychological illusion of taking our contingently constructed perceptions and conceptions of reality as pre-given objective reality existing independently. At any given moment, the state of consciousness we are in, and what we experience in that moment, seems absolutely "real," hence *objective* (meaning here, "existing independently"), to experiencing subjects. There is no other reality at that moment. It is this indubitable sense of "objective" reality and truth—the sense of certainty as to "That's just how it is!"—that compels most of us to act in particular conditioned ways in that moment. When that moment has passed, and we somehow come out of that particular state of consciousness, we may find it incredulous that we acted the way we did. Sometimes we say, "I was out of my mind." It turns out that is literally true. Walsh (1990) comments: "Different states [of consciousness] are associated with different tendencies and patterns of experience and function" (p. 284). In our own group work, as well as in classrooms and in fact in all places, we have been witnessing time and again this phenomenon of being trapped in a fly bottle. How do we shatter the fly bottle and free ourselves? Cultivation of awareness holds the key. Apprenticeship to wisdom begins here.

Cultivation of Awareness

As long as we are fixated on the content of consciousness, identifying it with objective reality—"the" truth—we are like the buzzing flies in the bottle. Note however that the ordinary, everyday mind with all of its notions, confusions, and wonder is not the problem *per se*. Rather, it is our limited identification with the voice of the mind—the collapse of awareness into perceptions and judgment. In a classic metaphor, it is said that instead of seeing the sky, we remain fixated on the clouds. A passage in the Rig-Veda (Doninger, 1981) captures this dilemma "I do not know just what it is that I am like. I wander about concealed and wrapped in thought" (1.164, 37, p. 75). This limited identification (and, indeed, identity) is not inevitable; it is a choice made moment-to-moment, day in and day out. By training in repeated recognition of awareness, we gain familiarity with a natural spaciousness of mind and heart in much the same way that we gained familiarity with our limited identity and identification with points of view. In this chapter we have been referring to this capacity for witnessing what our mind does, seeing what is going on moment-to-moment in the field of consciousness, as "awareness." In the contemporary discourse and literature, more technical words like "mindfulness" (in Pali, *sati*), "presence," "the contemplative," or "witness consciousness" are used to refer to our reflexive consciousness that acts as *container or field* within which it witnesses its own epistemic *content*.

As I was preparing to write this short paper, I suddenly had a small anxious thought: "Everything I think of writing is old. There is no life in it." While sharing my thought with my partner, I noticed with her help that my anxious thought was just as old as whatever it was anxious about! It had appeared in my mind many times in the past and it was old news. On the other hand, the lightness of heart and vulnerability I felt in the moment of discovering my thought to be old felt fresh and new and created space for creativity. This simple insight evoked a question that I believe could be of service to those who wish to travel a new path in education: What is the relationship between thoughts as knowledge and awareness as intelligence? (SR)

It is through simple awareness of perceptions in their ceaseless, shifting, and dazzling array that we come into contact with a boundless identity and a freedom to express ourselves beyond ordinary limitations formed by rigidly held points of view. Fenner (2003) writes:

> When the universal panorama is clearly seen to manifest without any objective or subjective supports, viewless knowledge awakens spontaneously. Simply by not reviewing any appearing structure, one establishes the true view of what is. This viewless view is what constitutes the Buddha nature and acts dynamically as the mother of wisdom, revealing whatever is simply as what it is—empty of substantial self-existence, uncharitable and uncharacterizable, calmly quiet and already blissfully awakened. (p. 28)

The capacity to observe or witness one's subjectivity and all its activities is inherent in all of us. However, without the cultivation of this capacity, our ability to actually witness, thereby transcend, subjectivity is limited: the "fly bottle effect" is too strong to break through. Our group experiment in intersubjectivity—that is, interpenetration of each other's subjectivity and experiencing the field phenomenon of mutual attunement and resonance—therefore depends heavily on each of its member's cultivation of this capacity. Not incidentally, each of us is a long-time cultivator of various contemplative practices from diverse traditions (Theravada, Mahayana, and Vajrayana schools of Buddhism, Daoism, Advaita Vendanta, and Kashmiri Saivism).

At the heart of the canonical and commentarial texts of many great wisdom traditions, East and West, is the view that gaining familiarity with "pure presence," or the ordinary awareness within which all appearances naturally arise, abide, and resolve, can profoundly enhance our capacity to act from clarity rather than common responses such as denial, projection, repression, disavowal, and disassociation (Cortright, 2007, p. 63). It is not simplifying things too much to indicate that there is a basic distinction often made between recognition of awareness (attention is liberated or unbound) and non-recognition of awareness (attention is bound). "Awareness," in this context, does not refer to an abstract, metaphysical state, but simply to familiar, everyday awareness or attention. In this sense, as Chan/Zen is famous for articulating, "enlightenment" is nothing special. It is to recognize the natural, authentic, uncontrived nature of ordinary awareness and all that appears in, as, and through it. Shabkar Lama, eighteenth-century Tibetan yogi, wrote emphatically:

> In the unthinkable, inscrutable, ordinary nature of reality there is no difference between freedom and bondage. No matter what

> arises, when you perceive your original nature the joy arises automatically—and what joy! Relax and merge into the primal space of total presence, which is free of coming and going. Cut loose and just let it be. . . . There is not so much as a mote of dust upon which to meditate, but it is crucial to sustain unwavering attention with presence of mind. (Dowman, 2003, pp. 97–98)

I recall many years ago driving into the far end of the parking lot at the University of British Columbia. I was arriving to write an exam. It was winter. The sun was very low in the sky and the light was a pale yellow. I recall thinking how nice it would be to just keep driving in the direction I was going, south, all the way to California. In the flicker of a moment I suddenly felt unified with everything. I felt the bliss and joy that Shabkar Lama describes. I am now reminded of Robert Thurman's statement, "Reality is bliss." (March 18, 2010. Public talk at the University of British Columbia, Vancouver BC, Canada.) (AC)

The idea of cultivating mindful awareness or reflexive witnessing consciousness is simple enough, even if difficult to practice. It can be summarized in one pithy statement: "Simply sit there." When we simply sit (or walk, move about), without the usual distracting and consuming stimuli from the external environments that pull and grab our attention, our attention is thus released to attend to itself, which is what creates self-reflexivity and a sense of the "container" (or field) within which we can rest and watch what arises in the field. To simply "sit there" can be understood as resting in or as awareness, the pure presence that beholds all appearances moment to moment in all states (waking, dreaming, and sleeping). By sustaining recognition of this pure presence amidst the ebb and flow of day-to-day perceptions, there is a freedom to listen, learn, and respond to all situations in life with wide-awakeness, attentive care, and creativity. We are no longer bound to enact conditioned or patterned responses because there is recognition of the spaciousness surrounding every perception. Staying present in any moment of experiencing ("sitting there") is a moment of non-reactivity, which is itself a moment of action. Since whatever one reflects on eventually becomes the basic inclination of the mind, not reacting in habitual ways (usually some form of aversion or attraction) creates new patterns, which in effect create new and more wholesome patterns of mind, body, and speech: an embodied process.

I stand in one spot as my sifu (teacher) checks my posture. I think I've relaxed my shoulders enough, but his steady hand tells me I can release even more. Hidden tension is suddenly released. I now feel my weight stack up in a straight line that balances with a subtle wavering between my two feet. I feel a sense of rebound from the earth. As I allow the weight of my body to push against the ground, the force somehow bounces back up through my entire body. There is a sense of being lighter and heavier. A feeling of vulnerability moves through my body, and reactively my chest and shoulders bulge and stiffen, the sensation of stiffness and hardness granting me a perceived sense of security. Then again, under my sifu's calm and gently guiding hand, I soften and relax the chest and shoulders, and a wave of calm bathes this sense of being wide open. (SP)

Inner Work

Simply sitting (known as *zazen* in Zen), however, is one of the most difficult things to do for most humans, not because the mechanics of sitting is difficult (although lengthy sittings can be painful), but mostly because what happens inside us when we sit (stand, move) is difficult to *be with*. During our sitting, all kinds of personally difficult emotions can arise, for example, anger and aversion, that are a part of the psychological constructions of defense mechanisms that have been created to protect our vital core and simultaneously defend against further intrusions and the attendant pain. Unless these psychological wounds and scars are adequately addressed, the mindful awareness cultivation would in fact have a difficult time taking root in the afflicted individual. In the process of sitting with our own mind, we become intimate with our experience moment by moment. We get right inside our experience, and get to sit in the midst of it, and often, we find ourselves in the midst of raging fire, deluges, and all manners of agitations from past experiences and future worries and plans. That is what makes it difficult to sit. And once we succumb to the agitations, we may find ourselves back in the fly bottle.

A friend of mine mentioned to me that whenever conflict arose, his emotions became so overpowering he was unable to respond in a way that was helpful. I suggested that in the moment as the tide of emotion was overtaking him that he internally name and acknowledge the presence of the emotions. Several months later he said this small bit of advice changed his life. He got along better with family and coworkers because he was able to respond in ways not possible before. Acknowledging or witnessing one's internal emotional landscape even in small ways seems to enable what might seem as impossible transformations. (TC)

There are approaches based in humanistic-existential psychotherapy that, when combined with contemplative practice, are effective in working with these psycho-physical constructions that serve as both armor and prison. These constructions can be identified, their intent can be unearthed, and the surrounding dynamics can be brought into awareness. As well, the associated and unconscious identity construction can be made conscious, the relationship between the conscious and unconscious dynamics and ego structures can be resolved and integrated, and flexibility and personality structures that have been frozen can be thawed. The process we outline here is complex and difficult to undertake unless there is enough support from mindful awareness (as discussed in the last section) that can safely contain these volatile constructions while their deconstruction takes place. This leads to a person feeling that she or he has a personality rather than that it has her or him, and the life force is able to emerge more freely.

As a child I was told by my mom not to run around and be noisy on a regular basis. I was told, "You will get overheated and get sick." No doubt my mom believed this and had the very good intent of looking after my well-being. The net effect over years was that I suppressed my tendencies to be expressive and particularly in front of others. I developed a personality structure that was somewhat frozen. I often felt unhappy and estranged from others and my surroundings. This frozenness insinuated itself into my physiology and, ironically, I seemed to get sick more frequently than one would normally expect. Over many years of inner work I have been able to turn the inner ice back into water by applying the heat of my attention, allowing the attention of others, and working with the fragments of myself to re-integrate them into a whole identity that is now allowed to be more expressive and warm. I am still working on this. (AC)

Of courses, serious personal wounds and scars need to be taken care of in psychotherapeutic work, and we are not implying that inner work in educational contexts can replace that. However, insofar as our general condition of humanity is the fly bottle situation, and we have the evidence of suffering due to the fly bottle condition all around us, working on liberating ourselves from our conditioned patterns of thinking and acting does become a general educational project. Teaching for advanced knowledge and skills, while necessary for competency training in higher education, is not sufficient, is inadequate, for fulfilling the mandate of education whose larger and ultimate aim should be to help human beings to become whole, wise, and compassionate.

Integration and Integrity

Often contemplative or meditative practices are seen as mental activity, even confined to the brain (Austin, 1998; Flanagan, 2002). Not only people who are unfamiliar with contemplation but also some of the practitioners themselves labor under such notions. Hence, it is important that we state plainly that the cultivation of contemplative awareness crucially requires the holistic approach of integrating body-mind-heart-spirit—in short, the whole-person approach that, when well extended, will implicate the whole cosmos. Recall the non-duality of inside and outside we explored previously; in the same vein, the whole-person and the whole-cosmos are implicated in each other (Bohm, 1980). Both the Daoist and Zen traditions are explicit about this. In fact, in these and other Asian traditions, the philosophy of body-mind-heart-spirit interconnection is a given. We may forget this, or ignore this, but like the air, it is always there, whether we acknowledge it or not. However, by recognizing and learning to work with the body-mind-heart-spirit interconnection, we can learn to live more sanely, ethically, and wisely.

Recognizing that the cultivation of contemplative consciousness involves all manners of breath work, bodywork, emotional work, and spiritual practices in addition to any text-based scholarship activities, all of us in our group have been engaging in various forms of Yoga, marshal arts, qi gong, neigong, Zen arts, and spiritual rituals and practices. All these practices are not adjunct or ancillary practices but are central and critical to the cultivation of contemplative consciousness.

For instance, Daoism is rich in cultivation of tranquility that involves breath, body, mind-heart, and spirit. The Daoist text, *Nei Ye* (Inner Cultivation), written about 2,500 years ago, treats tranquility or equanimity as the ruling principle of humans. The text states that pleasure and anger, accepting and rejection are the "devices of human beings." Therefore the sage "[a]lters with the seasons but doesn't transform; [s]hifts with things but doesn't change places with them" (Roth, 1999, p. 58). Conscious alignment of the heart-mind with *Dao* whereby one empties the mind of emotions, desires, thoughts, distractions, enables greater expression of mental attributes of virtue to emerge and deepen mental tranquility. Here, *Dao* (道, also romanicized as "tao," literally means "way") refers to the wholeness of reality full of creativity and potentiality. As well, this reality is endlessly open to human participation: this is why it is called the Way. To emphasize this vast openness and rich creativity for human participation, our group has adopted the term, *Dao*-field, that Cohen and Bai (2997) coined, to speak of the *Dao*.

According to *Nei Ye*, conscious alignment with tranquility enables the virtue of the mind or the numinous mind to emerge, which results in a deeper awareness of *Dao* whereby one's health, behavior, desires, and circumstances—all becomes aligned with *Dao*. What further results for the practitioner is conscious presence of *Dao* in one's life and one's daily cultivation. One always sees a way, finds a way, and moves forward.

A friend and I come across an old woman feeding white bread to birds in a park. My friend becomes tense and stares at her with blazing eyes. He tells me he's angry and wants to do something, but he is trapped inside his anger. In response to my friend's psychological paralysis, my breathing and my body are being activated in connection with the ground. Suddenly, I find myself walking towards her and call out in a humorous tone: "Hey, you got any bread for me? I'm hungry too"! The woman smiles and comes my way, telling me that she has no use for the bread because it upsets her stomach. "Oh no," I say, "white bread has very few nutrients and not very much energy—they would be better off with nuts and seeds." My friend relaxes and joins us in a dialogue about ecology. Shortly after the woman leaves, we see her telling others in the park about what she has just learned. (SP)

There is the same emphasis in Buddhism on the cultivation of tranquility. Why? Tranquility is the key catalytic ingredient in turning an ordinary, busy-minded dualistic consciousness into the non-dual contemplative witness consciousness. Without such consciousness that enables humans to transcend their conditioned patterns of thought and action, we may very well end up taking permanent residency in the fly bottle. Superior intellect is no guarantee that we will not be trapped in the bottle.

The absolute importance of cultivating tranquility cannot be emphasized enough, especially in these times of increasing speed and stress. "Just sit" as in Zen might appear too passive as if it means doing nothing. Speaking as a Daoist, just sitting may be better characterized as "creating the conditions for emergence of growth." We are familiar with this "creating conditions" and rely on it every day. For example, when we fall asleep, we align with the fundamental principles of sleep, such as being physically and mentally tranquil. When we do this, all on its own sleep emerges. In sitting, too, we need to create conditions that allow the emergence of awareness. The Daoists amongst us would talk about aligning ourselves with the universal life force, *qi* (氣), which engenders growth in every living being.

I have found that it isn't necessarily unwavering attention that brings on a different kind of awareness. Perhaps is my low level of cultivation but I find that rather than attention, it is a matter of setting one's intention and persistently creating the conditions that enable the awareness that is always present to surface while everyday thoughts recede somewhat into the background. I would say that if the conditions are right the awareness or perhaps I should say presence arrives like a welcomed guest. I appreciate the guest very much. (TC)

Again, like the *Dao*, the universal life force, *qi*, is not something esoteric and mysterious, and we should be careful not to turn it into an exotic thing. *Qi* is present everywhere: when children grow into adults, when our bodies heal after injury, when we recover from emotional loss, when we plant a garden. In most cases, it is a power that does its work quietly, generously, all on its own without our intervention or thanks. In just sitting it might appear that we are doing nothing, but if we practice and trust in the principal of life in each and every one of us, action emerges subtly in the form of healing and growth.

Classroom as *Dao*-field of Intersubjectivity

In our group work, as in our classroom teaching, we practice sharing our inner life, inviting and giving feedback, listening to both what is said and not said, and meeting each other in the emergent space of the Buberian I-Thou encounter. An intersubjective contemplative praxis opens us to and engages us with the *Dao*-field, the sphere of relationality and creativity that extends, in terms of human participation and practice, from the self right out to the whole cosmos. Thus intersubjectivity becomes a way of life. In the *Dao*-field, we can experience a meaningful association—or *interpenetration,* to emphasize the intersubjective aspect—of persons and things that are bound together in varying degrees of destiny.

When I introduce contemplative practices in undergraduate business classes I start by saying something like this: "For most of your career in school you have studied the world outside as if who you are and what you do has little do with how the world is. This time, you are going to have the opportunity to study how you and the world are hinged together. The self and the world, mind and body, interpenetrate. If you want to change the world, change yourself. In particular, you are going to learn about yourselves by paying attention to your emotions as experienced in your body." The students are requested to keep a journal of their inner experiences and discoveries. With some relatively simple exercises that include contemplative practices, I am always amazed at the insights and transformations witnessed by students. Some students talk about being able to change in ways considered not possible before. Others talk about profound changes in relationships at work or in their personal life. My experience is that contemplation in the classroom makes a positive contribution to the personal and professional lives of students. (TC)

Martin Buber (1947/2002) contends that a longing for and mindfully dialogical engagement with others brings the awareness of haecceity, of presence, and from this the "presentiment of a world-wide dialogue, a dialogue with the world-happening" (p. 43). We become aware of what Buber (1958/2000) referred to as the "eternal Thou":

> He who enters on the absolute relation is not concerned with nothing isolated any more, neither things nor beings, neither earth nor heaven; but everything is gathered up in the relation. For to

> step into pure relation is not to disregard everything but to see everything in the Thou, not to renounce the world but to establish it on its true basis. (p. 80)

What Buber (1965, p. 62) referred to as a "synthesizing apperception" finds pure relation embodied in all beings and the "whole stuff of life" where the "holy primary word makes itself heard in them all" (1985/2000, p. 108). Imagine what our classroom experience would be like if we practiced this kind of engagement.

I give my undergraduate class an assignment for the week: go on at least two 20-minute silent walks that have no particular destination planned out and write about it afterwards. One student wrote:

I came across a house that had a very cottage-like aura and it also had beautiful stained-glass windows. I stood there for a while just staring at them. It felt so great not to be obliged to talk to anyone or have to think about anything in particular. I walked slowly and enjoyed the peace that I felt. I was also very aware of my breathing. While walking I felt free of the need to race against time and rush. I felt my body relax and move freely. After this walk, I went home to do some creative writing in my journal. I was so surprised because I had a lot I wanted to write about! The words just flowed freely and I was able to write about a vision for my future that I didn't think I knew. (SP)

Emergence is about giving birth to new futures—to that which we did not nor could have known to exist (Varela, 1999). Flowing with an open awareness across the crucible of "me and we," moment-to-moment invitations into possibilities emerge through the *Dao*-field—reality as "a field of infinite possibilities of perception and action" (Cohen & Bai, 2007, p. 7). It is in the presenced, witnessing relationality with the Other in our immediate lifeworld (such as our classroom) where we gain self-mastery, and we learn to embody care and ethical action and to align ourselves with the *Dao*-field. In an earlier narrative, moving toward and befriending the woman in the park arose out of dwelling with awareness of the inner and outer world, a dynamic crucible that brought about an unexpected response, one that opened up the possibility to know a deep interconnectivity with other beings. How we speak, how we listen, how we regard each other, how we breathe together, how we support each other, how we teach and learn from each other: every moment of being and interaction in our classroom gifts us with the riches of the *Dao*-field.

We began this chapter with a concern about how we spend our busy lives focused on the outer world, accumulating things and information. However, in our experience right before us, available to all, is an inherent wisdom from within that, given the right conditions, can emerge and guide us on the path of life.

We hope that our personal stories and theoretical explorations inspire others to collectively cultivate a *Dao*-field to emerge within their classes and invite students to participate in life-affirming and nourishing discoveries and transformation. We believe this is immensely rewarding to both teacher and student alike.

References

Austin, J. (1998). *Zen and the brain: Toward an understanding of meditation and consciousness.* Cambridge, MA: MIT Press.

Bohm, D. (1980). *Wholeness and the implicate order.* London: Routledge & Kegan Paul.

Buber, M. (1947/2002). *Between man and man* (R. G. Smith, Trans.). London: Routledge.

Buber, M. (1958/2000). *I and Thou* (R. G. Smith, Trans.). New York: Scribner.

Buber, M. (1965). Distance and relation. In M. Friedman (Ed.). *The knowledge of man: A philosophy of the interhuman.* New York: Harper & Row.

Cohen, A., & Bai, H. (2007). Dao and Zen of teaching: Classroom as enlightenment field. *Educational Insights, 11*(3). Available from <http://www.ccfi.educ.ubc.ca/publication/insights/v11n03/articles/bai/bai.html>.

Cortright, B. (2007). *Integral psychology: Yoga, growth, and opening the heart.* Albany, NY: State University of New York Press.

Doniger, W. (1981). *The Rig Veda: An anthology of one hundred eight hymns.* London: Penguin Books.

Dowman, K. (Trans.). (2003). *The flight of the garuda: The Dzogchen tradition of Tibetan Buddhism.* (2nd ed.). Somerville, MA: Wisdom Publications.

Fenner, P (2003). Nonduality and Therapy: Awakening the Unconditioned Mind. In Prendrgast, J., Fenner, P., & Krystal, S. (Eds.), *The sacred mirror: Nondual wisdom and psychology* (pp. 23–56). St Paul, MN: Paragon House.

Flanagan, O. (2002). *The problem of the soul: Two visions of mind and how to reconcile them.* New York: Basic Books.

Fromm, E. (1997). *To have or to be.* London: Continuum.

Habermas, J. (1999. From Kant to Hegel and back again—The move towards detranscendentalization." *European Journal of Philosophy,* 7(2), 129–157.

Krishnamurti, J. (2006). Krishnamurtion education. Ojai, CA: Krishnamurti Foundation Trust.

Orr, D. (1994). *Earth in mind: On education, environment, and the human prospect.* Washington, DC: Island Press.

Roth, H. D. (1999). *Original Tao: Inward training and the foundations of Taoist mysticism.* New York: Columbia University Press.

Smith, D. G. (2008). *Widsom responses to globalization: A meditation on Ku-Shan.* Lecture presented at Simon Fraser University, Faculty of Education on April 8, 2008. Burnaby, BC, Canada. Retrieved online on September 18, 2011 from <http://attheedges.org/reading_room_files/Ku-shan%20meditation.doc>.

Stone, M. (2008). *The inner tradition of yoga: A guide to yoga philosophy for the contemporary practitioner.* Boston, MA: Shambhala Publications.

Varela, F. J. (1992). *Ethical know-how: Action, wisdom, and cognition.* Stanford, CA: Stanford University.

Walsh, R. (1992). Can Western philosophers understand Asian philosophies? In J. Ogilvy (Ed.), *Revisioning philosophy* (pp. 281–302). Albany, NY: State University of New York Press.

Wittgenstein, L. (1976). *Philosophical investigation* (G. E. M. Anscombe, Trans.). Oxford: Basil Blackwell.

Part IV

New Frontiers of Contemplative Learning and Instruction

18

Considerations for Collective Leadership

A Threefold Contemplative Curriculum for Engaging the Intersubjective Field of Learning

Olen Gunnlaugson

Traditionally, the prevailing pattern of academic learning across disciplines is to strengthen individual learner's critical, analytic, and deliberative abilities to the neglect of other essential individual and collective modalities of knowing, learning, and being. Within the past decade, a widespread and growing academic interest in contemplative studies has emerged in response to the shortcomings of the current mainstream academic model of scholarship. As a movement of thought and practice directed toward rigorous transformative approaches to adult instruction, learning and knowing, the emerging field of contemplative studies has stimulated important research and scholarship across disciplines (Roth, 2006; Zajonc, 2006). While many of these contemplative approaches have been applied from a predominantly first-person standpoint—a response in part to the prevalence of third-person learning approaches that typify traditional academia, as I have pointed out elsewhere (Gunnlaugson, 2009)—such an approach has led to an omission of second-person approaches that inspire deeper shared and co-emergent contemplative states of knowing and generally move individuals toward a more common focus and collective discernment in their learning process. Unlike either third- or first-person methods, second-person approaches offer the benefits of rich engagement not only within, but also between participants and the intersubjective field of conversation. From this learning milieu, dynamic shared contexts for collective leadership processes can emerge in contrast to a more individual-centered ethos within groups, classrooms and teams.

As an alternative to the enduring epistemological habit of privileging first-person individual approaches to learning, in this chapter[1] I explore specific aspects of three distinct second-person contemplative approaches: Scharmer's practice of presencing (2001, 2007; Scharmer, Senge, Jaworski, & Flowers, 2004), Varela's three gestures of awareness (2000; Depraz, Varela, & Vermersch, 2003) and Quaker discernment (e.g., Loring, 1999; Palmer, 1976). Additionally, I examine the traditional first-person contemplative practices underlying each of the three collective practices, and identify how each contributes to opening the collective contemplative mind in classrooms, groups, and teams. In doing this, my intention here is to continue establishing, legitimizing, and advancing the project of bringing an intersubjective approach to our instructional methods and processes.

Re-balancing the Epistemological Foundations of Contemplative Methods

Unlike critical and reflective modes of thinking that are oriented toward external content in the attempt to gain objectivity, in first-person contemplative knowing there is generally a figure/ground reversal of the habitual structuring of one's attention as one engages in thinking in order to foster deeper awareness, concentration, and insight in the present (Hart, 2004). Rather than habitually directing one's thinking processes from the momentum of conditioned thought, self-referencing, or past associations, the objective of contemplative knowing from the first-person perspective involves attending more carefully to one's thoughts in order to access a more unconditioned awareness, and in turn a more clear, wise, and compassionate source of knowing that is always already present. There is a kind of primary if not taken-for-granted interiority of the individual that informs first-person processes of contemplative knowing, yet there also is a hidden intersubjective dimension of learning and knowing that cannot be satisfactorily addressed pedagogically by first-person methods. For example, a more conventional second-person process such as discussion might be described as an exchange between situated individuals (two or more) focusing on a particular subject from intermingling first-person positions. A second-person position from the perspective of a group discussion is a collection of unique and distinct first-person positions.

However, within intersubjective theory, there is the notion of the "intersubjective field" that forms between any two or more persons where there are always at least three points of view: mine, yours, and ours together (Orange, 1995). In spite of the challenges of conveying the perspective of "ours together" in a satisfying third-person manner, there is a growing consensus on the significance of this second-person perspective as represented by such constructs as the intersubjective field. Support for this notion has surfaced within and across the fields of leadership development (Isaacs, 1993, 1996, 1999; Jaworski, 1996; Scharmer, 2007; Scharmer et al., 2004), dialogue education (Arnett, 1992; Gunnlaugson, 2006), consciousness studies (de Quincey, 2000, 2005; Hargens, 2001; Thompson, 2001), contemporary psychotherapy (Orange & Stolorow, 1998; Stolorow & Atwood, 1996) and collective intelligence (Atlee, 2003; Hamilton, 2004; Por, 1995), among others.

As an advocate for collective wisdom processes, Chris Bache's (2008) research is founded on the view that classroom learning processes informed by the intersubjective field bring about a markedly transformative quality of experience for students. Along the lines of Bache's explorations, Christian de Quincey (2005) has experimented with Bohmian dialogue in his graduate classes:

> I include sessions devoted exclusively to the second-person approach to consciousness studies. Almost without exception, I'm moved and surprised each time at how deeply people can go in shifting from our typical modes of thought to embodied, authentic self-expression, even in periods as short as a couple of hours. (2005, pp. 163)

Jonathan Reams (2007) has also applied Bohmian dialogue in his courses on leadership studies as a means for transforming students' ways of knowing and being together. Similarly, Maureen O'Hara's (2003) research indicates "there are certain moments in a group's life in which an extraordinary level of alignment and attunement occur between individual members and the group consciousness" (p. 73). Ettling and Gozawa (2000) have explored the implications of co-creating a field of mutuality with groups as a means for fostering collective wisdom and a felt sense of shared humanity. Much of this descriptive research characterizes specific aspects of the transformative dimensions of intersubjective experiences. Yet further research is needed to better understand the ways in which second-person contemplative processes are capable of advancing collective aspects of leadership development. Toward this end, the remainder of this chapter will outline second-person contemplative practices for engaging these specific regions within the intersubjective domain of group life.

In his proposal for a new field of contemplative studies, Roth (2006) advocates integrating critical third-person and first-person approaches to contemplative study, to which I have responded by advocating critical second-person study (Gunnlaugson, 2009). Building on Sarath's (2009, p. 2) point that with each contemplative approach, certain first-, second-, or third-person aspects tend to prevail, in the next section I will also explore the implications of first-person contemplative practices of presence, mindfulness and discernment in contributing to the development of a second-person contemplative process-method. While it can be argued that participants in conversation are always participating intersubjectively (whether they are aware of this or not), this article outlines a language and set of distinctions for engaging certain intersubjective fields (Scharmer, 2007, p. 237) by advancing a set of second-person contemplative practices for groups to experience the transformative aspects of collective wisdom and leadership processes.

Engaging the First-Person Practice of Presence

In spite of living in a historical period of increased distractions, interruptions, and complexity, from the perspective of the wisdom traditions, the possibility always exists for cultivating relaxed attention, awareness, and intentionality—that is, presence. The experience of presence—the practice, condition, or state of abiding in embodied present-moment centered awareness—is the quality of attention that we embody in each moment. Bugental (1987) elaborates on presence as:

> a name for the quality of being in a situation or relationship in which one intends at a deep level to participate as fully as she is able. Presence is expressed through mobilization of one's sensitivity—both inner (to the subjective) and outer (to the situation and the other person(s) in it)—and through bringing into action one's capacity for response. (pp. 26–27)

Kessler (2000, pp. 7–9) claims an instructor's presence develops from cultivating discipline, being present and having an open heart. Solloway (2000) delves further into presence as a means for exploring further "what our conditioning shuts to the background" (p. 30).

Facilitating from presence can help uncover a liminal space of underlying wholeness that enables us hear more of what our students are saying that might not be immediately obvious. Instructing from presence requires learning how to abide more fully in this quality of awareness through some form of formal silence or stillness-based contemplative practice, which can then be deployed to witness our discursive thoughts, feelings, and interior processes while we facilitate, teach, or coach our students. As an instructional process, engaging others from presence inspires a way of relating with our consciousness and our students that stands apart from our more automatic and conditioned ways of being that obscure creative engagement. Instructing from presence involves the disciplines of carefully attending to our inner and outer environments, ensuring that deeper instructional intentions, learning goals, and objectives are not forgotten amidst opportunities for spontaneous action and emergence. To further illustrate the importance of engaging presence, I will now introduce presencing as a second-person contemplative process-method for collective wisdom.

Presencing from the Intersubjective Field

Otto Scharmer's (2000; 2007; Scharmer et al., 2004) notion of presencing offers a second-person method and framework to guide presence-based conversation and inquiry. For our purposes, I will focus on two specific contexts of Scharmer's (2007) account of presencing, which involve ways of leading from presence. First, I examine presencing as a field structure and meta-process of conversation (Scharmer, 2007, pp. 238; 297), and secondly as a way of engaging presence for the purposes of apprehending new knowledge in conversation.

For the first meaning, let us now turn to Scharmer's (2007) work on conversation, where he distinguishes between four basic second-person intersubjective fields:

ENACTING EMERGING FUTURES

PRIMACY OF THE WHOLE

PRIMACY OF THE PARTS

PRESENCING

generative flow
collective creativity
stillness and grace
listening from the emerging future
other = highest future Self
rule-generating

DIALOGUE

inquiry, reflection
I can change my view
listening from within
(empathic listening)
other = you
seeing onself as part of this current whole

DOWNLOADING

talking nice
polite, cautious
don't speak your mind
listening = projecting
rule-conforming

DEBATE

talking tough, clash
I am my point of view
listening from outside
other = counterpart
rule-conforming

REENACTING PATTERNS OF THE PAST

Figure 1. The Four Fields of Conversation (Scharmer, 2007, p. 274)

In the above framework, Scharmer depicts how conversations move counter-clockwise from relatively closed and inauthentic fields of conversation in the lower left-hand quadrant (i.e., downloading) through debate, dialogue, and finally presencing. For Scharmer, the field of presencing in part builds from the earlier habits of listening and speaking that characterize the three previous fields of conversation. Awareness of how we enact these three previous fields of conversation and the characteristic structures of attention that define each field is helpful in moving into the fourth field of presencing. For example, reenacting past habits of discussion within groups—a key aspect of the field of downloading—generally does not bring forth empathic insights into the perspectives others are speaking from or foster a deepened co-creative process. To work with presencing, it can be beneficial to introduce and explore the dynamics of learning from the previous three fields of conversation. However, with other groups it may only take part of a session or a few sessions to move into presencing, depending on a number of different contextual factors unique to each class. Contextual factors include participants' previous experience with contemplative methodologies, degree of interest in engaging collective learning processes, familiarity with the presencing practice, and so forth. Each field of conversation, for Scharmer, contains within it a characteristic intersubjective pattern that is informed by particular forms of engagement in listening and speaking within the group. From instructing and facilitating Scharmer's model in different contexts, I have found that participants can roughly self-assess when they are in a particular field as well as the group's intersubjective pattern of engagement. Interestingly, the quality of listening and speaking is influenced by the field dynamics of conversation, particularly in reflective dialogue and presencing, where shared group intentions play a generative role in how the conversational process unfolds.

This brings us to the second meaning of the term presencing, which involves orienting from presence. Scharmer et al. (2004) describe presencing as becoming present "to the larger space or field around us, to an expanded sense of self, and ultimately to what is emerging through us" (p. 91). From this passage, Scharmer builds on the previous meanings of presence by identifying specific contexts for instructors and participants to explore the practice of presence (a) in the intersubjective field of learning, (b) as an expanded or distributed sense of self, and (c) in a transpersonal process for unfolding new knowledge. Presencing, as a conversational practice, arises from establishing ourselves in presence and then connecting with specific contexts or sources of our experience while we participate in conversation in order to uncover new forms of tacit-embodied and self-transcending knowledge (Scharmer, 2007, p. 255).

How do the above three contexts for presence take shape in groups? Briefly, attending to the field dynamics of a group conversation helps open up a meta-perspective, which can be useful in articulating or sensing the emergence of the "ours together" perspective mentioned earlier on. When we bring our attention to what Scharmer describes as an expanded sense of self, this might involve encouraging participants to experiment with shifting their awareness from their individual perspectives to the group's, and ultimately attempting to observe from "multiple points of view simultaneously from the surrounding field" (Scharmer 2007, p. 169). Finally, in becoming present to what is emerging through us, the group or conversational field itself becomes more of an "enabling presence" (p. 181). This allows everyone to see more of who we are, which helps open the intersubjective space for deeper issues, questions, and realizations to surface. When in the facilitative role, I have found it helpful to invite participants into shifting the place of their perception from our individual viewpoint to considering the perspective (not only cognitively, but also emotionally and kinaesthetically) of an intersubjective view or shared source of attention in the intersubjective field of conversation.

Presencing draws upon presence, but the intention and purpose are different. With presencing, we cultivate presence as a basis for apprehending, seeing, and sensing into emergent (that is, not-yet-known) possibilities and knowledge with our students. Building on presence as an embodied quality of being, Scharmer (2007) reframes presence as a precondition for experiencing a deeper source of who we are, as a form of deeper interrelated engagement with others and as a collective vehicle for unfolding new knowledge in conversation. Presencing as a field of conversation offers a different learning environment than downloading, debate, and even dialogue, helping create the conditions for contact with deeper forms of tacit embodied and self-transcending knowledge. For Scharmer (2007, p. 255), tacit embodied knowledge is based on lived experience and relates to the reality within, in contrast with self-transcending knowledge, which is tacit knowledge prior to its embodiment. Jackie Seidel (2006) offers a perspective of this process:

> Catherine Keller (1986) wrote that we can feel the future forming in ourselves now, for this my present self will be endlessly taken up and reiterated. The future will—if only to the most trivial degree—feel this present. My soul, my body, my world: ongoing, they will have to take me in. So if I learn to feel the subtle movement from past to present, I may begin to discern the transformation of vast relational patterns, personal and social, as they roll through my present. (pp. 246–247)

The practice of presencing then requires shifting from (a) learning from and reflecting on the past or pre-existing explicit knowledge, which is well known and underlies all conventional learning methodologies (Scharmer 2007, p. 7), toward (b) learning together from the emerging future by collectively sensing into and intuiting not yet embodied or known possibilities. As such, presencing offers a dramatic contrast to traditional instructional objectives that involve acquiring or replicating past or preexisting knowledge. As a form of collective learning, presencing involves a specific shift in our place of perception from current reality in the present to perceiving from the source of what is emerging in our experience (Scharmer, 2007, p. 163) as a basis for unfolding new knowledge about a specific issue, topic, or subject. Learning to be with others in the creative tensions of "ambiguity" and the "not-yet-known" (Fels, 2004) helps open up a generative conversational context. As a contemplative form of second-person knowing, presencing offers a subtle basis of knowing oneself through a fundamental shift in the locus of our awareness from a localized and separate self to a de-centered and distributed sense of self that is attentive to what is emerging through the field of conversation. Scharmer (2005) elaborates:

> People usually enter into an experience of presencing by noticing a change of social space (a decentering of the spatial experience), of social time (a slowing down of the temporal experience to stillness), and of self (a collapsing the boundaries of the ego). The outcomes of this process include a heightened level of individual energy and commitment; a heightened field quality of collective presence and energy, and profound long-term changes. (p. 13)

From the connected quality of self and knowing that emerges when group members are presencing together, shared presence tends to invite a way of listening and being that is attuned initially to one's own interior promptings, but then gradually more and more to the subtle depths of what wants to emerge from or through the group field of conversation. As we become increasingly receptive to the group field of conversation and the moment-by-moment unfolding of the presencing process with others, this tends to elicit more authentic, collaborative, and co-creative ways of learning together.

Mindfulness

Mindfulness practice, both as defined within Eastern traditions and a Western social science perspective, provides a basis for cultivating enhanced learning experiences. Gunaratana (1992) points out that mindfulness training teaches us how to examine our own perceptual process with fine-tuned awareness, so that we see our own responses with calm and serene equanimity. Advocate for mindful learning, Harvard educator Ellen Langer (1997) unpacks the cognitive implications of mindfulness in the context of learning:

> When we are mindful, we implicitly or explicitly view a situation from several perspectives, see information presented in the situation as novel, attend to the context in which we are perceiving the information, and eventually create new categories through which this information may be understood. (p. 111)

Mindfulness then cultivates a flexible and alert state of mind, allowing us to know something more vividly. Susan Walsh (2003) expands further on different aspects of this interior relation:

> Through foregrounding breathing, and returning at all times to the ever-changing sensing body, the impermanence of thought too becomes evident. What seems gripping in the moment passes with the breath. A multidimensional space opens around experience, how we encase it in language. We notice how thought works, its habits, its familiar haunts and pathways. We observe, witness. Stay with. (p. 2)

In applying mindfulness to our thinking, we begin noticing our thoughts as we speak and listen to others. With sustained practice, this develops a disposition of non-interfering and non-judgmental witnessing of our thought process. Heesoon Bai (2001) acknowledges that mindfulness frees us from the "tenacious grip of the abstract, disembodying conceptual mind (intellect)" (p. 97) by recovering our roots in "non-discursive, embodied awareness" (p. 92). By attending closely to what is happening moment-to-moment without getting caught up in thoughts that obscure this non-discursive awareness, we win some distance from the obsessive and habitual nature of thinking, as Bai points out. By becoming more mindful of our thought process in daily life, we are effectively training ourselves to see and perceive life more directly as it is rather than through a screen of thoughts and concepts (Gunaratana, 1992).

This brings us to the second application of mindfulness with our emotions. Awareness of our emotional state is central to the capacity of emotional intelligence (Goleman, 1997). Mindfulness training provides a way to cultivate emotional balance and decrease the hold of habitual patterns that obscure perception and impair our judgment, developing a distanced or decentered relationship with our experience, in turn decreasing emotional reactivity. Mindfulness then cultivates an experience of emotions as impermanent entities with which we can work and not become as entangled—teaching one to approach experiences with acceptance, open-ended curiosity, and self observation without judgment (Bishop et al., 2004). Zukav & Francis (2001), in their discussion of emotions, provide the image of standing on a bridge and noticing the river beneath, accepting where and how it flows, which cultivates an attitude of being-with our emotional state, where, if we happen to fall into the river's currents, we return our awareness to observing the emotional currents from our previous location on the bridge. Being mindfully attuned to our emotional state in such a fashion, particularly in moments of emotional distress, helps us discover first-hand how our emotions affect and infect our words and actions in group contexts of inquiry.

Mindfulness of the body requires that we attend to our breath and return to it when experiencing emotional tension. The physical act of breathing is at once material and metaphorical, helping us develop a grounded connection to our immediate experience and situation. It is a practice anchored in our physicality—bringing about a heightened and purposeful awareness of sensations. With a diffuse focus on the breath, we can move toward re-inhabiting our bodies as the mooring and support for mindfulness in our conversations.

As I examined presencing in relation to its roots in the first-person contemplative practice of presence, in the next section I will delve further into intersubjective mindfulness by building on a specific first-person practice. I will attempt to convey the importance of intersubjective mindfulness in groups. Traditionally, interior forms of mindfulness are taught (mindfulness of one's thoughts, emotions, body, and breath), yet when taken up within the intersubjective field, exterior forms of mindfulness can also be cultivated (Kabat-Zinn, 2005) as the outer counterpart to the inward cultivation of moment-to-moment non-judgmental awareness or mindfulness (p. 448). While an intention of first-person mindfulness is to foster clarity and individual presence through mindfulness of body, mind, emotion, and spirit, with the practice of intersubjective mindfulness, a core intention is to engage this presence in relating with others through contemplative processes in conversation.

Three Gestures of Becoming Aware in the Intersubjective Field

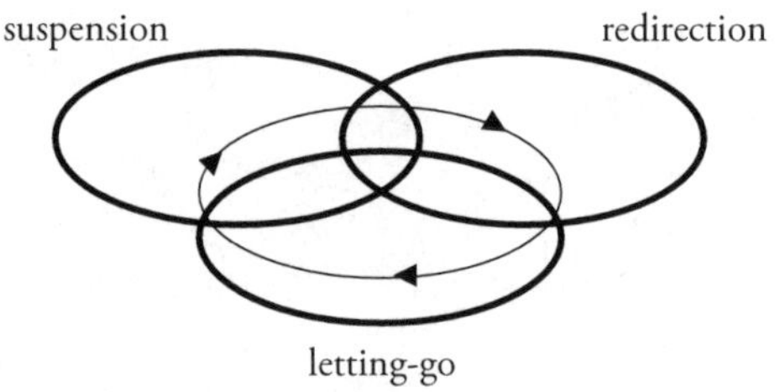

Figure 2. The Three Phases (Depraz, Varela, & Vermersch, 2000, p. 135)

I now turn to the late Francisco Varela's (2000) three-phase structuring of the act of becoming aware, which consists of suspension, redirection, and letting go. Though this cycle incorporates elements of several contemplative practices, it most closely resembles the practice of mindfulness. In the following section, I will examine each phase with an interest in its pedagogical contribution for fostering intersubjective mindfulness. A key difference between second-person forms of mindfulness and a group practicing mindfulness is that the former situation takes place with a shared collective intent. In other words, the process and content of conversation become the objects of mindfulness, whereas having a group individually practicing mindfulness may not necessarily involve either a shared second-person content or shared second-person process of mindfulness. As an example, one person could be practicing mindfulness of one's body, another mindfulness of their emotions, and still another mindfulness of thought and be faintly aware of what is unfolding in the group field of conversation.

When practiced by an individual, suspension creates an interior space for the reconsideration of thought, emotions, and underlying assumptions and patterns. When practicing suspension in the context of conversation, the act of suspension by one or more opens a shared space within the intersubjective field. Adapted as a second-person contemplative practice, suspension involves slowing down our communication so that we can more clearly comprehend the complex nature of a particular issue, subject, or everyday situation. As a contemplative practice, suspension involves holding the complexity of our assumptions, biases, histories, and habitual ways of engaging with one another in conversation so they can be mindfully attended to, felt, and reflected back to the group. In learning to hold these tensions of thinking with others (as representations of a more comprehensive and complex reality), creative space can be opened to address the deeper incoherence of the process of thinking itself (Bohm, 1996), which when left unsuspended, tends to weaken our grasp and diminish our comprehension of this deeper complexity. Suspension, then, for creative purposes, helps develop a shared willingness to be tentative, curious, and ultimately less invested in advocating or defending our existing knowledge. Suspension also prevents us from slipping into discursive, disembodied ways of knowing insofar as the practice draws on the physiological and kinaesthetic correlates of our thoughts through felt awareness of our thoughts, emotions, breath, and other faculties moment to moment.

Varela (in Depraz et al., 2003) describes the second gesture of redirection as involving learning to subtly move our attention away from the content we have "suspended" and to sense into, be with, and perceive what is trying to emerge. Redirection is also helpful in the practice of presencing, insofar as what is arising requires our attention, and to the extent that we are attending to what has arisen, we are no longer following the leading edge of emergence. As a second-person contemplative practice, redirection involves a subtle but discernable change in the location of one's habitual mode of paying attention from what has arisen or been shared to listening from the deeper collective interior context in which the content of a particular conversation arises from. Redirection also asks that in addition to attending to the level of thought and language in a conversation, we also consult with and redirect our attention toward the underlying source of our experience as we inquire into or discuss something. Initially, this can be confusing, insofar as distinguishing between the action of reflecting on past knowledge and holding a context out of which new knowledge can emerge is generally not clear to the untutored eye and ear.

An approach that I have found helpful is to invite others to periodically redirect attention to different levels of their experience as the conversation unfolds, engaging a mode of sensing that is similar to Gendlin's (1997) subtly embodied felt-sense, where we listen on different levels to the larger gestalt of what others are sharing, as well as the deeper source of our individual experience. Zajonc (2003) elaborates:

> The idea of redirection is difficult because often we have wrong expectations. To redirect, to step into a space and—as opposed to going with the conventional set of expectations, going with what we know to be the case already, going with a habit and so forth—to stop and truly redirect to what's right now, right there is enormously difficult. To realize, as something is emerging, that's what's important, this shifts everything. And if you're attentive and can suspend judgment and hold on to that redirected attention, you're nurturing a part of your own consciousness that is otherwise neglected. (p. 25)

As Zajonc points out, redirection follows from the holding gesture of suspension and involves shifting our attention back into the arising present moment—into presence. From presence, you have effectively shifted your attention from outside of yourself to the inside of yourself (the first-person contemplative turn), which then expands or opens to include the inside of us (the second-person contemplative turn).

Following redirection is Varella's disposition of letting go, which Scharmer (2007) describes as letting come. In the context of conversation, letting come involves a recursive movement of attention toward abiding in presence and being with the unknown—that is, entering into a receptive state of listening for new meaning, knowledge, and insights to emerge in one's awareness.

Applied as a second-person contemplative practice, letting come takes place in shifting one's attention from "looking for something" to "letting something come to you," to "let something be revealed" (Depraz et al., 2003). Depraz et al. elaborate:

> You actively pay attention but at the same time you wait, since what you're reflecting on is by definition tacit, pre-reflective or pre-conscious. Thus you have to balance yourself between a sustained act of attention and not having immediate fulfilment. . . ." (p. 37)

With practice, the third gesture of letting come fosters receptivity to the subtle textures and nuances of what is emerging within the inquiry in the conversational field. Letting come, when followed from the practices of suspension and redirection, helps create the conditions for collective receptivity to what is arising from the conversational field with a particular subject of inquiry.

Discernment

Discernment in academic settings tends to be influenced by the Classical tradition of Western philosophy. Olivia (2004) elaborates on discernment as a form of critical thinking and third person learning:

> An example of this from the Greek philosophical tradition is in Plato's Apology. Here, Socrates makes his famous observation that "the unexamined life is not worth living" (Ap. 38a). According to Socrates, in order to live a moral and ethical life, we should examine not only what we believe, but also why we believe what we believe. In the Socratic method of philosophy, we examine our minds and see if our thoughts, our perceptions, our behaviours, our biases, are rooted in Clear Seeing, come from some form of truth, or instead are simply rooted in habits of mind. According to Socrates, much of what we believe, that is, much of what we take to be our personal beliefs, are actually conditioned by our culture. And much of what are our personal beliefs are simply habits of mind, habits that are so often repeated that we take them to be true. Coming from the classical tradition, then, examination, questioning, becoming aware, allows us, invites us, to go beyond what we take to be givens. In academia, we call this process of examination and questioning, this practice of discernment, "critical thinking." (p. 1)

In the context of critical thinking, discernment involves separating, dividing, or distinguishing with the intellect, getting at what is hidden or obscured as a means for a more developed and critical understanding of an existing body of knowledge. It is important to address briefly the limitations of discernment. While it may help us locate certain words, new insights, or knowledge, the deeper source of our experience can become remote to us, or our finitude and conditioning can prevent us from living into such discoveries. There can also be false or misleading forms of discernment that surface or lead to confused, deluded, or defensive experiences that reinforce ego boundaries and so forth.

Contrasted with critical thinking, in the Quaker tradition practitioners cultivate discernment through shared implicit rituals and deep listening, which involves opening to dimensions of wisdom that lie beyond one's presently held ideas, assumptions, and current understanding.

Three Phases of Discernment: A Second-Person Contemplative Practice

> Another important feature of the meeting for learning is that it places trust in the group itself. In conventional education the group is only an accident; it just happens to be more convenient for a teacher to deal with individuals in a group rather than separately. But in a meeting for learning the group assumes an importance at least equal to that of any individual in it—just as a meeting for worship is more than a collection of individuals in meditation. In a meeting for learning the roles of teacher and student continually move from one person to another, and it should be impossible at any moment to anticipate who will be teacher next.
>
> —Palmer, 1976, p. 3

Discernment in the intersubjective field occurs (a) intrapersonally in the dynamic tension between multiple qualities of awareness arising in one's consciousness, as well as (b) interpersonally due to the engaged subjectivities of two (or more) persons, and (c) transpersonally through ongoing attention to deeper immanent and distributed presence. Because discernment involves a dynamic process of attention that flows through the intrasubjective, intersubjective, and transpersonal contexts, I have found it helpful to work with a discernment cycle in groups.

The first part of the cycle, intrapersonal discernment, was covered in the above section. Interpersonal discernment, the second part, takes place in the identification of qualitatively different and often unpredictable occasions that take place in groups, which have potential to shift the intersubjective field to a deeper mode of collective engagement. Transitional moments have the potential to pull the participants into a shared present together—an emergent property of the intersubjective field. Such shifts are essential for doing second-person work. And such transitions often surprise everyone, in that it is generally not predictable though it may be expected or hoped for. With groups informed by second-person contemplative principles, transitional moments can lead to a deepening of presence and presencing in the intersubjective field. When this shift happens and has been performed and mutually recognized and integrated, a new intersubjective state comes into being within the field. With practice, this new state helps provide a distinct intersubjective context or field of conversation to which the group has more stable access.

Through the encounter between participants and the group field, there is a collective coming into presence both in silence (feelings, images, body awareness) and in language (words and thoughts), opening the way for new meaning and discoveries to be discovered. Such shifts have the potential to shift the conversation in the direction of presencing or greater collective intelligence, increasing the collective process and quality of attention, with the proof of discernment being its knowledge and life-transforming fruits (increased presence, clarity, acuity of thinking and feeling, etc).

Within the intersubjective field, participants bring their unique subjective perspectives, which helps build the relational dimension of the field. Here participants potentially perceive and receive each other in ways that bring increased awareness and deeper meaning to their encounter. Discernment within the intersubjective field plays out on a continuum from ordinary experiences (involving judgment and discrimination) to the heightened presence of extraordinary learning experiences (involving intuition and presencing). When discernment evokes the latter, the field of presencing tends to deepen as the participants are changed in some way through the dialogical encounter. However, presencing can just as easily break down when the opinions of vocal members start to prevail over participants and are no longer coming from presence or being mindful of what is emerging. The process of discernment takes place on three levels—mindfulness of what is arising in our perception, of what is arising in the group field, but also of what is tacit, felt, or hidden from our conscious awareness and received through deeper intuition or the source of our experience.

In terms of the third part of the cycle—transpersonal discernment—I return now to the insights of Parker Palmer (1976), "A meeting for learning will know when to cease moving and talking, to cease pursuing truth, and to wait in silence for truth to come into its midst. Some of my most important moments of learning have been in such stillness—as insight coalesced, as knowledge settled in, or as a simple receptiveness" (p. 5). Parker's articulation of transpersonal discernment through a listening and attending to occasions of silence indicate a reverential disposition toward conversation and learning as sacred process. Questions asked well can invite subtle changes in the intersubjective field. Questions received well hold our attention to what is arising from within us as well as the field of conversation. Questions contemplated well can open up space and slow down time, inviting a deeper space of emergence and sense of participation within a common horizon of shared experience and inquiry. When learning reaches this point of the amplified quality of silence Palmer writes about, new horizons of collective contemplative learning emerge.

Closing Thoughts

Navigating the intersubjective terrain of group life is no easy feat, particularly as the conversational field of presencing as well as processes of shared discernment and intersubjective mindfulness among others tend to be foreign or indistinct to the untutored eye. Nevertheless, contemplative explorations of second-person territory via the process-methods introduced here can support new capacities for engagement with sufficient practice, and in turn broaden and deepen our canvas of the existing possibilities for contemplative learning in classrooms, groups, and teams. It is important to remind readers that the practices introduced in this chapter are useful in bringing about direct experiential discoveries of the intersubjective potential of groups, as well as new phenomenological territory for engagement. As intersubjective check points or guides for orienting our awareness in a more skilful fashion, these second-person contemplative practices offer a means for engaging this latent territory of group life, as well as a means for generating, enacting, bringing forth, and illuminating heretofore absent yet arguably crucial shared dimensions of learning and experience.

As I have pointed out, the prevailing instructional stance of approaching contemplative learning experiences from the first-person perspective alone is problematic to the extent that a rich and complementary set of second-person processes of contemplative instruction, learning, and knowledge creation are overlooked. A similar argument can be made against the traditional approach of privileging third-person forms of learning. Thus, as instructors and facilitators aspiring to work toward a more balanced and integrated approach to collective wisdom and leadership development, this article advocates second-person approaches as a vital overlooked dimension of academic contemplative practice.

Note

1. A different version of this essay will appear in an upcoming issue of the *Journal of Transformative Education.*

References

Arnett, R. (1992). *Dialogic education: Conversation about ideas and between persons.* Carbondale, IL: Southern Illinois University Press.

Atlee, T. (2003). *The Tao of democracy: Using co-intelligence to create a world that works for all.* Cranston, RI: The Writer's Collective.

Bache, C. (2008). *The living classroom: Teaching and collective consciousness.* Albany, NY: State University of New York Press.

Bai, H. (2001). Beyond the educated mind: Toward a pedagogy of mindfulness. In B. Hocking, J. Haskell, & W. Linds (Eds.), *Unfolding bodymind: Exploring possibility through education.* Brandon, VT: Foundation for Educational Renewal.

Bishop, S. R., Lau, M., Shapiro, S. L., Carlson, L., Anderson, N. D., & Carmody, J. (2004). Mindfulness: A proposed operational definition. *Clinical Psychology: Science and Practice* (11), 230–241.

Bohm, D. (1996). *On dialogue.* London: Routledge.

Bugental, J. F. T. (1987). *The art of the psychotherapist.* New York: W. W. Norton & Company.

Depraz, N., Varela, F., & Vermersch, P. (2000). The gesture of Awareness: An account of its structural dynamics. In M. Velmans (Ed.), *Investigating phenomenal consciousness* (pp. 131–139). Amsterdam: John Benjamins.

Depraz, N., Varela, F., & Vermersch, P. (2003). *On becoming Aware: A pragmatics of experiencing.* Amsterdam: John Benjamins.

de Quincey, C. (2000). Intersubjectivity: Exploring consciousness from the second person perspective. *Journal of Transpersonal Psychology, 32*(2), 135–155.

de Quincey, C. (2005). *Radical knowing: Understanding consciousness through relationship.* South Paris, ME: Park Street Press.

Ettling, D., & Gozawa, J. (2000). Morphogenic fields: A call for radical thinking and being. In K. Klenke (Ed.), *2000 Aom/IAom Proceedings Project 2005, 18*(4), 61–71.

Fels, L. (2004). Complexity, teacher education and the restless jury: Pedagogical moments of performance. *Complicity: An International Journal of Complexity and Education, 1*(1), 73–98.

Gunaratana, H. (1992). *Mindfulness in plain English.* Boston: Wisdom Publications.

Gunnlaugson, O. (2006). Exploring generative dialogue as a transformative learning practice within adult & higher education settings. *Journal of Adult and Continuing Education, 12*(1), 2–19.

Gunnlaugson, O. (2009). Establishing second-person forms of contemplative education: An inquiry into four conceptions of intersubjectivity. *Integral Review, 5*(10), 25–50.

Hamilton, C. (2004, May–June). Come together: the mystery of collective intelligence. *What is Enlightenment* (25), 56–77. Retrieved from <http://www.enlightennext.org/magazine/j25/collective.asp>.

Hargens, S. (2001). Intersubjective musings: A response to Christian de Quincey's "The Promise of Integralism." *Journal of Consciousness Studies, 8*(12), 35–78.

Isaacs, W. N. (1993). Taking flight: Dialogue, collective thinking, and organizational learning. *Organizational Dynamics, 22*(2), 24–39.

Isaacs, W. N. (1996). The process and potential of dialogue in social change. *Educational Technology, 36*(1), 20–30.

Isaacs, W. N. (1999). *Dialogue and the art of thinking together.* New York: Currency Doubleday.

Jaworski, J. (1996). *Synchronicity: The inner path of leadership.* San Francisco: Berret-Koehler Publishers.

Kessler, R. (1998). The teaching presence. *Forum* (35), 30–37.

Langer, E. (1997). *The art of mindful learning.* Reading, MA: Addison-Wesley.

Loring, P. (1999). *Listening spirituality: Corporate spiritual practice among friends.* Washington Grove, MD: Openings Press.

O'Hara, M. (2003). Cultivating consciousness: Carl R. Rogers's person-centered group process as transformative andragogy. *Journal of Transformative Education, 1*(1), 64–79.

Olivia, N. (2004). The practice of discernment in contemplative education. Retrieved July 10, 2010, from <http://www.asianetwork.org/exchange/2004-fall/anex2004-fall-olivia.pdf>.

Orange. D. (1995). *Emotional understanding: studies in psychoanalytic epistemology.* New York: Guilford Press.

Orange, D., Stolorow, R. (1998). Self-disclosure from the perspective of intersubjectivity theory. *Psychoanalytic Inquiry, 18,* 530–537.

Palmer, P. (1976). *Meeting for learning: Education in a Quaker context.* Wallingford, PA: Pendle Hill Bulletin.

Por, G. (1995). The quest for collective intelligence. In K. Gozdz (Ed.), *Community building: Renewing spirit and learning in business.* Pleasanton, CA: New Leaders Press.

Reams, J. (2007). An experiment in education for states. *AQAL: Journal of Integral Theory and Practice, 2*(2), 50–71.

Roth, H. (2006). Contemplative studies: Prospects for a new field. *Teachers College Record, 108*(9), 1787–1815.

Sarath, E. W. (2009). Jazz, creativity, and consciousness: Blueprint for integral education. In S. Esbjörn-Hargens, J. Reams, & O. Gunnlaugson (Eds.), *Integral Education: New directions for higher learning* (pp. 169–184). Albany, NY: State University of New York Press.

Scharmer, O. (2001). Self-transcending knowledge: Organizing around emerging realities. In I. Nonaka & D. J. Teece (Eds.), *Managing industrial knowledge: New perspectives of knowledge-based firms* (pp. 68–90). Thousand Oaks, CA: Sage Publications.

Scharmer, O. (2005). Excerpt from: Theory U: Leading from the emerging future presencing profound innovation and change in business, society, and the self. Retrieved March 01, 2010, from <http://www.solonline.org/repository/download/Theory_U_Intro_Sept_05.pdf?item_id=8892547>._

Scharmer, O. (2007). *Theory U: Leading from the future as it emerges.* Cambridge, MA: SoL Press.

Scharmer, O., Senge, P., Jaworski, J., & Flowers, B. (2004). *Presence: Human purpose and the field of the future.* New York: Society for Organizational Learning/Currency.

Seidel, J. (2006). Some thoughts in teaching as contemplative practice. *Teacher's College Record, 108*(9), 1901–1914.

Solloway, S. (2000). Contemplative practitioners: Presence or the project of thinking gaze differently. *Encounter: Education for Meaning and Social Justice, 13*(3), 30–42.

Stolorow, R., & Atwood, G. (1996). The intersubjective perspective. *Psychoanalytic Review, 83*, 181–194.

Thompson, E. (2001). Empathy and consciousness. *Journal of Consciousness Studies, 8*(5–7), 1–32.

Varela F. (2000). *The three gestures of becoming aware (interview with Claus Otto Scharmer)* Dialogue on Leadership. Retrieved February 11, 2010, from <http://www.presencing.com/presencing/dol/Varela-2000.shtml>.

Walsh, S. (2003). Being-with, letting go: mindfulness. *Educational Insights, 8*(2). Retrieved February 1, 2010, from <http://www.ccfi.educ.ubc.ca/publication/insights/v08n02/contextualexplorations/sumara/walsh.html>._

Zajonc, A. (2003). Investigating the space of the invisible: Arthur Zajonc in conversation with Otto Scharmer. Retrieved June 15, 2010, from <http://www.collectivewisdominitiative.org/papers/zajonc_interv.htm>.

19

Buberian Dialogue as an Intersubjective Contemplative Praxis

Charles Scott

Introduction

Recent scholarship (Bache, 2008; Bai, 2001; de Quincey, 2000; Gunnlaugson, 2009; Isaacs, 1999; Scharmer, 2007) has pointed to intersubjective dimensions as manifestations of second-person, relational approaches to contemplative practice, particularly in educational contexts. As Wilber (2006) asserts, second-person approaches have had an established place in the major, mostly devotionally religious, contemplative traditions for centuries. These approaches have centered on developing relationships between the individual and what is held as divine or the Ground of Being. However, there is a scholarly interest in these approaches, their value to us in developing interpersonal relationships, and how we might implement them in secular educational institutions (Bai, Scott, & Donald, 2009; Gunnlaugson, 2009; Seidel, 2006). As Olen Gunnlaugson (2009) points out, there is a need to develop more nuanced and context-appropriate applications of second-person approaches in contemplative practices, especially in the context of secular educational institutions, particularly when we consider their use in pedagogical practice. To this point, several scholars have noted the benefits and challenges to using dialogical second-person principles and practices in educational settings (Bai, 2001, 2009; Bingham & Sidorkin, 2004; Blenkinsop, 2005; Scott, 2011), and now scholars are exploring intersubjective dimensions of contemplative practice.

Arthur Zajonc (2006) outlines the following features of contemplative inquiry, or what he calls an "epistemology of love" (p. 1745): respect, gentleness, intimacy, participation, vulnerability, *Bildung*, and insight. These qualities of an epistemology of love move us into the relational aspects of contemplative practice. Zajonc also points to the significance of opportunities for meaning-making among university students; the research on the importance of spirituality for college students by Astin, Astin, and Lindholm (2011) also highlights the importance of spirituality and the "big questions" for students. Intersubjective engagements are ideally suited to inquiry into meaning and the "big" philosophical and spiritual questions as an approach to contemplative practice, thus addressing these needs. Following from the work of Zajonc and that of Gunnlaugson, I want to suggest that Martin Buber's philosophy of dialogue as a relational, ontological orientation that offers a comprehensive, integrated theoretical and practical framework for an intersubjective, second-person form of contemplative practice. Gunnlaugson (2009) suggests that contemplative education integrates contemplative practices which foster knowing characterized by "wholeness, unity and integration" (p. 26), and I would suggest Buber's praxis of dialogue is characterized by epistemologies of wholeness, unity, and a profound integration of body, mind, and spirit, as well as a recognition of the immanence and transcendence of the sacred. I am suggesting that Buber's *praxis* of dialogue is by nature contemplative: it develops and works through the dimensions of contemplation I outline below.

Buber's ontological model of dialogue (1947/2002, 1957, 1958/2000, 1965) emerges out an epistemic stance of relationality and is based in the presence and systematic practice of a number of dialogical capacities that are themselves contemplative in nature. In this paper, I will outline these capacities in detail as a means of pointing to their cultivation as both formal and informal second-person contemplative practices. I further consider educational curricula and pedagogical approaches through which students and educators can develop these capacities in establishing an intersubjective, contemplative *praxis*—a reflective and practiced life of dialogue which embodies contemplative practice in the everyday.

I am considering contemplation as intentional, disciplined acts and ways of being which concentrate the attention and develop insight, serving to deepen a centered, present, receptive, empathic awareness of oneself and one's connectedness to others and the various physical, sociocultural, historical, and spiritual ecologies that surround one. Contemplation is marked by such an increase in subjective, intersubjective, and objective awareness.[1] Contemplative ways of knowing, while at time intuitively distinct, also complement, build on, or work through sensory, somatic, empirical, affective, and rational ways of knowing (Thurman, 2006; Wilber, 1999).

Buber's Philosophy of Dialogue

Buber's (1958/2000) philosophy of dialogue centers on an ontological orientation to the development and creation of *I-Thou* relationships. The other—be it another person, an animal, a plant or tree, or even a stone—is seen as *Thou.* This stands in contrast to apprehending the other as *It,* where we instrumentally see the other only objectively, as something we can use or classify. Buber uses "*Thou*" to denote something unique and ineffable, whole, Other, and perceived as connected to everything. Moreover, a *Thou* is made *Thou* through relationship to an *I.* Conversely, an *I* is made fully *I* through a relation to a *Thou;* we "take our stand in relation" (p. 20).

Dialogue for Buber is essentially and fundamentally a state of being, an *ontological turning toward the other* made possible through the perception of the other as *Thou.* Such a perception of the other as *Thou* rests in the ability to turn in response and responsiveness to that other. I recognize the other addressing me as an independent being and one to whom I can respond out of fidelity. Unlike the world of the *I-It* relationship, the *I-Thou* relationship exists outside the confines of time and space. Moreover, it is ontologically unique: beingness now exists in the sphere of the between, in our meeting together. This is why for Buber, "All real living is meeting" (1958/2000, p. 26). Buber characterizes the moment of meeting as revelatory, a moment in which we change. It is not an experience, something to be catalogued, but rather represents a moment where something happens. "At times it is like a light breath, at times like a wrestling-bout, but always—it *happens*" (1958/2000, p. 104). While Buber initially saw these "immortal" meetings as fleeting and transitory, he later outlined a developmental model of dialogue (1947/2002, 1965); as one cultivates the dialogical life, the moments stretch and gradually become more permanently established.

Turning itself includes and is made possible by the practice and manifestation of an integrated series of what I term dialogical "capacities" or "virtues" (cf. Aristotle, 2000; Rice & Burbules, 1992). Buber's writings include extensive and repeated references to them, as well as comprehensive expositions of their significance and characteristics. These dialogical virtues or capacities include becoming aware; confirmation of the other; presence; empathic inclusion; openness and receptivity, what Buber termed the "holy insecurity"; the ability to comprehend paradox; and an ability to apprehend holistically and systemically—what Buber (1965) termed a "synthesizing apperception." They represent the intersubjective as a way of being. In turn, I am suggesting that these represent capacities we can develop as part of an intersubjective contemplative praxis. It is a praxis grounded in conscious and reciprocal reflection and practice, whose foundations rest in contemplative ways of being in the world: specifically, the desire to enter more deeply into meaningful relationships with others, deepening one's sense of connectedness to others and the world.

The Dialogical Virtues

I am suggesting that intentional development of the virtues present in Buber's conception of dialogue can represent an integrated form of contemplative practice that is rooted in intersubjectivity.

Buber adopts an integral (Wilber, 2006) approach to dialogue. That ontological re-orientation is made possible by and enacted by the "whole person" (Buber, 1948, p. 20): body, intellect, emotions, and spirit contribute to a wholly integrated, ontological re-orientation of being in dialogue. Thus, their faculties all contribute toward the possibility of turning. "So it is not just with his thought and his feelings, but with the sole of his foot and the tip of his finger" (1948, p. 27) that a person is capable of turning to the other. Turning thus represents a deeply integrated and interwoven constellation of virtues that make it possible.

Becoming Aware

Buber (1947/2002) writes, "The limits of the possibility of dialogue are the limits of awareness" (p. 12). Becoming aware of the other is central to the entire process of turning in the dialogical encounter: turning to the other begins with awareness. And to the degree that listening is at least partially synonymous with awareness—at least in the most liberal definition of listening—then other dialogical educators and scholars of dialogue would agree to its centrality (Bohm, 1996; Isaacs, 1999; Senge, 2004). "I consider a tree" (Buber, 1958/2000, p. 22). With this phrase in *I and Thou*, Buber begins the development of an integrated, contemplative approach to dialogue. He can have an objective relationship with the tree, noting its size, various other physical dimensions, processes, and capacities: classifying it. The tree as object, as *It*. But ". . . if I have both will and grace . . . in considering the tree I become bound up in relation to it. The tree is now no longer an *It*. I have been seized by the power of exclusiveness" (p. 23). He now perceives the tree an as ontological presence *and* that he is in relationship with that presence. One feels addressed, one can respond, and so a relationship is forged. While the word and response may come through speech, neither call nor response is limited to speech or to humanity. They can occur with an animal, plant, or even a stone; we exclude nothing from the series of things and events that can address us.

The challenge we face is becoming aware—of presence, of signs and calls, of otherness, and of relation. We are, as Buber (1947/2002) writes, "Encased in an armour whose task is to ward off signs" even though they are all around us, happening "without respite." He adds, "The waves of the æther roar on always, but for most of the time we have turned off our receivers" (p. 12). Our contemplative challenge is to throw off the armour (see the section below on the "holy insecurity"), turn on the receivers, and fine-tune their sensitivities—through practice. The awareness begins with and extends out from our sensuous, aesthetic, emotional, intellectual, and contemplative knowing of the world and our refinement and discernment of that knowing, requiring that we slow down to notice.

Confirmation

Emerging out of and intimately related to our becoming aware of the other and the other's address to us is our confirmation of the other as Other. We apprehend and confirm beingness and wholeness—haecceity or suchness (*Tathātā*). As Buber (1947/2002) writes: ". . . out of the incomprehensibility of what lies to hand this one person steps forth and becomes a presence" (p. 25). Buber's concept of confirmation calls forth respect for the other in what Buber calls its "elemental otherness" (1965, p. 69) and its "primal setting at a distance" from us (p. 60). Confirmation opens up the possibility of an *I-Thou* relationship.

> Only he who himself turns to the other human being and opens himself to him receives the world in him. Only the being whose otherness, accepted by my being, lives and faces me in the whole compression of existence, brings the radiance of eternity to me. Only when two say to one another with all that they are, "it is *Thou,*" is the indwelling of the Present Being between them. (Buber, 1958/2000, p. 30)

Buber (1947/2002) sees confirmation as a breakthrough: the shattering of solitude into a "strict and transforming meeting" (p. 239). Meeting—the development of Thou—represents our beingness in the between. As the word "strict" suggests, such a contemplative effort is disciplined and rigorous. The other and I come into the fullness of being *through* these relationships, being confirmed as ontologically whole in the *I-Thou* relationship.

The next aspect of the dialogical turn is the empathic ability to include another's experience and views in our own without any loss of our own perspective or sense of identity.

Inclusion

Eros—longing for unity and fulfillment—can propel us to a movement of "experiencing the other side": being able to apprehend what the other is experiencing. This deep, empathic apprehension of another's experience, sensation, emotion, or thought "makes the other person present" (Buber, 1947/2002, p. 114). Buber calls this "inclusion" because I have both the apprehension of my own experiences, sensations, emotions, and thoughts *and* those of the other. Inclusion is an "extension of one's own consciousness, the fulfillment of the actual situation of life, the complete presence of the reality in which one participates," where an individual, without sacrificing any personal perception or reality, "lives through the common event from the standpoint of the other" (p. 115). Empathic inclusion is an extension of both awareness and confirmation and contributes to their fulfillment.

The entire *I-Thou* relationship is predicated on the empathic ability of the individual, as a full presence, to encounter the other, no longer an *It* bounded and limited and egocentrically "experienced" but as an unbounded *Thou*, moving beyond the boundings of egocentricity to a wider and more inclusive, dialogical sense of self. Buber's concern for the ontological primacy of both *I* and *Thou* leads us naturally into the next dialogical virtue—Presence.

Presence

Jackie Seidel (2006) notes that contemplative practices bind or return us to the present, in "this interconnected moment" (p. 1904). We become connected not only in time but also in place—here, now. Coming into full presence in such interconnected moments was an essential part of the dialogical engagement for Buber. Both *I* and *Thou* come into being through dialogical engagements; there is no dialogue without the full presence of an *I*. "Becoming a self" is a relational process, but the corollary is also true: bringing a full presence to the engagement contributes to it becoming a dialogue.

Thus, I come to the encounter with my presence, and through my committed engagement, I place myself squarely in the here-and-now, in the meeting with the other. To the degree that I place myself thusly, the present remains something that is "continually present and enduring" (p. 27). Buber later emphasizes the taking of a stand in destiny in the second part of *I and Thou*, where he says of the free person that:

> . . . he knows that he must go out with his whole being. . . . He listens to what is emerging from himself, to the course of being in the world; not in order to be supported by it, but in order to bring it to reality as it desires, in its need of him, to be brought—with human spirit and deed, human life and death. (pp. 64–65)

Buber (1947/2002) also notes that the dialogical person gives an "answer from the depths, where a breath of what has been breathed in still hovers" (p. 77), and does so without prompting. Such a person is aware of the historical and community contexts which shape her or his actions; such a person "does not spare himself" in manifesting a presence in words or actions (p. 78). This is the person who thinks "existentially," who "stakes his [sic] life in his thinking, and is "standing his test" (p. 95). Even though our response may be wholly inadequate, it is what is required. Our existential offering to another is "Surely a presence by means of which we are told that nevertheless there is meaning" (p. 16).

Thus the teacher acts directly, with the whole being, and in an informed spontaneity. Persons of presence are the bearers of personal conviction who may have to show opposition to others. But they still confirm them as partners.

Our presence, too, is a response to the world; the conviction it embodies requires, then, that we be open and receptive to others and the world, to what the present and future bring, and that we be willing to live on the edge of uncertainty, empty and waiting.

The Holy Insecurity

Buber (1947/2002) emphasizes genuine dialogues where presence is felt and there is "speech from certainty to certainty," but also emphasizes that dialogue includes communication from "one open-hearted person to another open-hearted person" (p. 9). The contemplative eros of dialogue is a call to the unknown and even, in some of its utmost manifestations, to apophatic ways of knowing. We can only receive the world if we make ourselves open and receptive to it. This spirit of openness is lived in the insecurity of going forth into a world where there is the uncertainty of meeting and what new situations might bring. For Buber, the only certainty is the uncertainty of meeting, of life itself. Such openness was so significant for Buber that he deemed it a "holy" act. Those who tread this path live and wrestle with that which is changing, new, and possibly unknowable; they tread the epistemic path of what he famously calls the "narrow rocky ridge between the gulfs where there is no sureness of expressible knowledge but the certainty of meeting what remains, undisclosed" (1947/2002, p. 218).

One is called to trust. At the heart of Buber's philosophy of dialogue is existential trust: of self and others, of the present and unfolding moment, of the unknown and unknowable (Friedman, 1967). One refuses the security of either-or for the uncertain possibilities of both-and. The final response of Buber's philosophy of dialogue and the attendant holy insecurity is that: "This very world, this very contradiction, unabridged, unmitigated, unsmoothed, unsimplified, unreduced, this world shall be—not overcome—but consummated" (Buber, 1948, p. 26). The movement is one of inclusive embracing.

Tim Lilburn (1999), like Buber, calls for attention in these moments of unknowing: "Stay with it and the carefully attentive befuddlement unravels into a fidelity to the branch, a setting down of stakes, an alongside-ness, a fretful proximity to the branch that is as far as it can be known" (p. 29). And that fidelity may require us to resolve the complexities, uncertainties, and paradoxes that lie before us.

The Unity of the Contraries: The Capacity for Paradox

Friedman (2002) notes that Buber's "narrow ridge" of uncertainty is a "paradoxical unity" of what we usually see as alternatives—I and Thou, love and justice, dependence and freedom, security and insecurity, being and doing, and the individual and the collective. Buber resolutely claims that the oppositions themselves are not problematic, that we allow them to obscure the complex, inherent, and transcendent unities they contain. Buber, Avnon (1998) notes, had an affinity for the pre-Socratic Greeks who had more attunement with the flowing, contrarian, Heraclitean *Logos* than with the ordered and rational Socratic or Aristotelian one. Buber's affinity for the Heraclitean *Logos* stems from his belief that the reality of meeting precedes analytical thought.

Buber (1947/2002) encapsulated paradox when he wrote about transcending the either-ors (see, for example, pp. 236ff). Our rational culture tends toward the binaries of either-or and opposites and has difficulties seeing transcendent unities in things which appear to oppose one another. We readily see differences in language, culture, religion, nationalities, and market systems, generating endless schisms. Some of these binary positions can only be resolved in paradox where both-ands replace the either-ors, some of which do not logically fit together. For example, Buber confirms the ontological uniqueness and separateness of *I* and *Thou*, and yet acknowledges a transcendent unity. Meeting itself is fundamentally wrapped in paradox. One acts to fulfill the dialogical meeting . . . but one doesn't act; dialogue emerges out of being. One goes forth with one's whole being but one does not intervene—and at the same time, one does not merely let things happen!

Celeste Snowber (2002) suggests a practice of "paradoxology": where students and teachers work to examine the paradoxes involved in their lives, teaching, and research, adding that understanding paradox can help us understand the other. Arthur Zajonc (2006) offers the example of students in his courses grappling with what he calls the ability to sustain contradiction. He suggests that rather than trying to resolve paradoxes into either-ors, they learn to sustain the presence of paradox, concluding, "When we deny that complexity, as a society we quickly decompose into warring ethnic and religious factions vying for dominance" (p. 1754). Buber (1948) felt the ability to embrace paradox was central to dialogue: "The unity of the contraries is the mystery at the innermost core of the dialogue" (p. 17).

A Synthesizing Apperception

One of the paradoxes Buber (1958/2000) mentions in *I and Thou* is that the *Thou* is whole and exclusive and our relation with each *Thou* is unique. However, the relationship with what Buber calls the *Eternal Thou* is "unconditional exclusiveness and unconditional inclusiveness in one" (p. 80). Everything now is related and we see relationality everywhere. This is an expression of what Buber (1965) calls a "synthesizing apperception," the ability to see a transcendent wholeness in and connections between things: "the apperception of a being as a whole and as a unity" (p. 62). In a passage from *I and Thou*, Buber (1958/2002) writes, "He who enters on the absolute relation is not concerned with nothing isolated any more, neither things nor beings, neither earth nor heaven; but everything is gathered up in the relation" (p. 79).

Significantly, this synthesizing apperception is born of Eros. The passionate longing for dialogue, Buber (1947/2002) contends, brings the awareness of haecceity and from this the "presentiment of a world-wide dialogue, a dialogue with the world-happening" (p. 43). We can experience a meaningful association of persons and things that we find bound together in varying degrees of destiny.

Turning to the Other: A Contemplative Praxis of Dialogue

The sum of the dialogical turning to the other is a meaningful engagement with the other, be it a person or persons, another member of the biosphere, an inanimate object, or the world itself. An ethos of dialogue allows, encourages, and fosters new, connected understandings developed collaboratively through relational epistemologies. It embodies an integrated approach to knowledge through the body and senses, through feelings, hopes, and longings that connect to the everyday occurrences of our lives.

Buber's integrated model of dialogue provides us with a basis for a contemplative praxis of dialogue rooted in the intentionality of the here-and-now of each relationship and each moment. Dialogue as an ontological orientation of turning to the other can be developed through systemic practice. Dialogue takes work and its path can be long, twisty, dark, unknown, and full of surprises along the way. It is a commitment to a dialogically contemplative way of being in the world—relational and mindful—and its continual development. With the intention of deepening relationships, educational engagements (in and beyond the classroom) thus become opportunities to practice these dialogical virtues.

Through educational practice and even more as a way of life, we establish dialogue through the integrated efforts of body, mind, and heart. I suggest here two practices that can facilitate the development of these contemplative, dialogical virtues: artistic practices and the pedagogical practice of dialogue itself. Along with the obvious study of Buberian dialogue, these can be creatively incorporated into educational programs and can be used with any number of other contemplative approaches, such as focusing the mind, developing mindfulness, or extending compassion to the world.

Artistic Practices

Artistic practices offer opportunities to engage in "slow" pedagogy (Payne & Wattchow, 2009): opportunities to slow down and become aware, and to allow that awareness to lay the foundations for the other dialogical virtues. We can create opportunities where students have sufficient time to interact with their environment artistically. Buber (1947/2002) felt art and art making were dialogic in nature, also writing (1958/2000) that art as an appearance demands and helps unfold the fullness of one's own being and engagement with the fullness of another as *Thou*. Elsewhere, he adds:

> True art is a loving art. To him [sic] who pursues such art there appears, when he experiences an existent thing, the secret shape of that thing. . . . This he does not see only with his eyes, rather he feels its outlines with his limbs; a heart beats against his heart. Thus he learns the glory of things. (Buber, 1957, p. 29)

As artists, we are required to attend fully to the other, to come to confirm its presence creatively, and to realize and then to express, as fully as we can, the reality and perspective of the other. The encounter is both existential and sensory; the artist's encounter is a "meeting with the world and ever again a meeting with the world" (Buber, 1965, p. 151). The artistic encounter is demanding. The "risk" is that a person may withhold nothing; the whole being is required (Dunlop, 2008).

Frederick Franck (1973) asks students to look more deeply: "We know the labels, but don't know the wine" (p. 4). Students would observe a subject carefully for extended periods to develop a sense of the subject's presence and relational context, to engage in drawing rapidly, without looking at what they are drawing, attempting to capture that felt sense of the other's presence, wholeness, and connectedness, rather than representational "accuracy." Students can then share their works and understandings with each other, outlining the meaning of the subject and their sense of connectedness to it as depicted in the representation. Peter London (2003) points to the need for a holistic approach with artistry: engagement with the mind, senses, emotions, heart, and spirit; these offer "a replete and durable sense of being in the world" (p. 2). Similarly, Thomas Merton (Merton & Griffin, 1970) used photography as a means of approaching the "hidden wholeness" of a subject, arguing for the need for a slow, sustained, and attentive engagement with the subject. Thus, students can be instructed not only in the basic arts of composition and exposure when engaging in visual arts, but can also be instructed to try to sense and depict the essences, meanings, and ecological contexts of their subjects.

I will have students working with photography, for example, spend considerable time focusing on a subject in their attempts to enter into a dialogical relation that reveals what they feel are its essential characteristics; this requires them to be still or appropriately position their bodies, their minds, and to focus their attention. Students will compare images, offering feedback about the subject, its portrayal, meaning, and the nature of our engagements with the subject. As well, students will engage in reflective writing about the subject, furthering their research. These activities in turn lead to further opportunities to re-photograph the subject to engage more fully with it, to reveal the *Thou*. These principles and practices apply to all artistic forms of engagement that can enhance the awareness of the other and provide an empathic confirmation of its presence. The artistic practice itself becomes an almost ritualized, respectful engagement between students, teacher, and the artistic subject (Loori, 2004).

An Intersubjective Pedagogy

A pedagogical approach based on dialogue obviously makes sense, including many opportunities to engage in dialogue in classes, with an understanding that it includes but also transcends mere conversation. Dialogue takes more time, particularly if we are to listen, offer reflective moments between comments instead of rushing in with a response, and if we are to probe more deeply into each other's comments and meanings. Our educational engagements become opportunities to deepen our embodiment of the dialogical virtues, offering a perfect opportunity for the development, practice, and manifestation of dialogue as a contemplative praxis.

In the classroom, dialogues can be careful yet authentic, methodical yet yielding to the unknown, and can be practiced in ways that give space and time to intersubjective encounter, to the possible unfolding of *I-Thou* relationships and *Logos*, and to the revelation of what might be held as sacred to the participants. The dialogues can occur in conversation, in artistic practices, or shared practice of formal contemplation. All of these deepen the intersubjective meeting, and in and through that intersubjective meeting learning occurs. Our classroom engagements become intentional efforts to embody the virtues of dialogue as a means of contemplative practice.

In these mindful engagements, what can emerge is a more collective sense of "we" or what Buber (1947/2002) referred to as the "sphere of between" (p. 241). It is a collective sense of "we" without the loss of *I* or *Thou* in which there is the "logos that is common to them all" (1965, p. 103). Logos, this sense of meaning, attains its fullness only in the intersubjective sphere of between. The educational project now becomes this development of Logos and the mutual exploration of its significance to us, regardless of the specific subject matter; such explorations are *dialogos*: the flow of meaning between. The aims of our education efforts, for example, and how these aims connect meaningfully with the rest of our lives, become relevant explorations. As well, conversations can shift to the participants' meta-analyses of the nature of the engagements: a shared or developing meta-awareness of nature of the intersubjective engagement. Such analyses not only allow for deepening awareness of intersubjectivity but also can lead to a dramatic dénouement of the dialogical virtues—the flowering of an intersubjective contemplative practice.

Conclusion

We live in a world of increasing complexity, change, and connectedness. The need to develop our relationships with others and the more-than-human world is evident. As part of our efforts as educators to deepen these relationships in effective and meaningful ways, we can contribute by helping students develop dialogical ways of perceiving and interacting with others. We want to bring mindfulness into our engagements with our students (Seidel, 2006), and our engagements with others and the world.

Buber's philosophy of dialogue offers us a comprehensive, rigorous, and reflexive praxis of dialogue that serves as an intersubjective, mindful form of contemplative practice. Further, in acknowledging both the roles of body, intellect, emotions, heart, and spirit in dialogue and also an awareness of the ecological situatedness of the dialogical praxis in the contexts of self, others, and the world (Wilber, 2006), Buber's model of dialogue offers a contemplative praxis that is integrally grounded. It serves individuals in creating meaning and meaningful, sustainable relationships, serves groups and organizations in fostering understanding and effective relationships, and can serve in developing a more global commons.

The intrinsic value of dialogue as a contemplative practice lies in its ability to create, uncover, explore, and develop meaning; to manifest an *I-Thou* relationship which reveals and affirms self and other; and to serve as a way of being in and with the world. This creation of meaning in and through relationships reveals what is sacred in ourselves, others, the world, and our relationships—a vital need for any society. At the conclusion of *A Secular World*, Charles Taylor (2007) decries the "triumphant grasp of the world, intellectually and practically" (p. 773) the instrumentalism and ontological separateness of our secular world has wrought. He calls for the revelation of the sacred. Buber (Buber & Friedman, 1964) writes:

> The crisis that has come over the human world has its origin in the dehallowing of existence. . . . True education is never in vain, even if the hour makes it appear so. Whether it manifest itself before or in or after the threatening catastrophe—the fate of man will depend on whether the rehallowing of existence takes place. (p. 62)

Dialogue can represent the challenge of both the educator and education. Dialogue as a form of contemplative education serves to bring the sacred into our educational encounters. In the end, all that is left to form, Buber (1947/2002) suggests, is the image of what is sacred; that image is formed within and between us as meaningful relation. It dwells here, immanently, in the dialogical relation. It dwells here, transcendentally, in the sphere of between. Dialogue becomes the revelation of the sacred in the sphere of the between, in the meeting of *I* and *Thou*.

Note

1. This concept of contemplation draws from the work of Hart, 2004; Roesner & Peck, 2009; Sarath, 2006; and Seidel, 2006.

References

Aristotle. (2000). *Nicomachean ethics* (R. Crisp, Trans.). New York: Cambridge University Press.

Astin, A., Astin, H., & Lindholm, J. (2001). Cultivating the spirit: How college can enhance students' inner lives. San Francisco: Jossey-Bass.

Avnon, D. (1998). *Martin Buber: The hidden dialogue*, Lanham, MD: Rowman & Littlefield.

Bai, H. (2001). Cultivating democratic citizenship: Towards intersubjectivity. In W. Hare & J. Portelli (Eds.), *Philosophy of education: Introductory readings* (3rd ed.) (pp. 5–10). Calgary, AB: Detselig Enterprises Ltd.

Bai, H. (2009). Re-animating the universe: Environmental education and philosophical animism. In M. McKenzie, H. Bai, P. Hart, & B. Jickling (Eds.), *Fields of green: Restorying culture, environment, education* (pp. 135–151). Creskill, NJ: Hampton Press.

Bai, H., Scott, C., & Donald, B. (2009). Contemplative pedagogy and revitalization of teacher education. *Alberta Journal of Educational Research, 55*(3), 319–334.

Bingham, C., & Sidorkin, A. (Eds.). (2004). *No education without relation.* New York: Peter Lang.

Blenkinsop, S. (2005). Martin Buber: Educating for relationship. *Ethics, Place, and Environment, 8*(3). 285–307.

Bohm, D. (1996). *On dialogue.* London: Routledge.

Buber, M. (1947/2002). *Between man and man* (R. G. Smith, Trans.). London: Routledge.

Buber, M. (1948). *Israel and the world: Essays in a time of crisis.* New York: Schocken Books.

Buber, M. (1948/2002). *The way of man: According to the teachings of Hasidism.* London: Routledge.

Buber, M. (1957). *Pointing the way: Collected essays.* New York: Harper & Row.

Buber, M. (1958/2000). *I and Thou.* (R. G. Smith, Trans.). New York: Scribner.

Buber, M. (1965). The k*nowledge of man: A philosophy of the interhuman* (M. Friedman, Ed., R. G. Smith & M. Friedman, Trans.). New York: Harper & Row.

Buber, M., & Friedman, M. (1964). Interrogation of Martin Buber. In S. Rome & B. Rome (Eds.), *Philosophical interrogations: Interrogations of Martin Buber, John Wild, Jean Wahl, Brand Banshard, Paul Weiss, Charles Hartshorne, Paul Tillich* (pp. 13–118). New York: Holt, Rinehart and Winston.

Burbules, N. (1993). *Dialogue in teaching: Theory and practice.* New York: Teachers College Press.

de Quincey, C. (2000). Intersubjectivity: Exploring consciousness from the second person perspective. *Journal of Transpersonal Psychology, 32*(2), 135–155.

Dunlop, R. (2008). Open texts and ecological imagination. *Canadian Journal of Environmental Education, 13*, 5–10.

Franck, F. (1973). *The Zen of seeing: Seeing and drawing as meditation.* New York: Vintage Books.

Friedman, M. (1967). *To deny our nothingness: Contemporary images of man.* New York: Dell Publishing.

Friedman, M. (2002). *Martin Buber: The life of dialogue* (4th ed). London: Routledge.

Gunnlaugson, O. (2009). Establishing second-person forms of contemplative education: An inquiry into four conceptions of intersubjectivity. *Integral Review, 5*(1), 25–50.

Hart, T. (2004). Opening the contemplative mind in the classroom. *Journal of Transformative Education, 2*(1), 28–46.

Isaacs, W. (1999). *Dialogue and the art of thinking together.* New York: Currency Books.

Lilburn, T. (1999). *Living in the world as if it were home.* Dunvegan, ON: Cormorant Books.

London, P. (2003). *Drawing closer to nature: Making art in dialogue with the natural world.* Boston: Shambhala.

Loori, J. (2004). The *Zen of creativity: Cultivating your artistic life.* New York: Ballantine Books.

Merton, T., & Griffin, H. (1970). *A hidden wholeness: The visual world of Thomas Merton.* Boston: Houghton Mifflin Co.

Payne, P., & Wattchow, B. (2009). Phenomenological deconstruction, slow pedagogy, and the corporeal turn in wild environmental/outdoor education. *Canadian Journal of Environmental Education, 14,* 15–32.

Rice, S., & Burbules, N. (1992). Communicative virtues and educational relations. *Philosophy of Education Yearbook, 1992.* Retrieved from <http://www.ed.uiuc.edu/EPS/PES-Yearbook/92_docs/rice_burbules.HTM>.

Roesner, R., & Peck, S. (2009). An education in awareness: Self, motivation, and self-regulated learning in contemplative perspective. E*ducational Psychologist, 44*(2), 119–136.

Sarath, E. W. (2006). *Meditation, creativity, and consciousness: Charting future terrain within higher education, 108*(9), 1816–1841.

Scott, C. (2011). *Becoming dialogue; Martin Buber's concept of turning to the other as educational praxis.* Unpublished doctoral dissertation, Simon Fraser University, Burnaby, British Columbia.

Seidel, J. (2006). Some thoughts on teaching as contemplative practice. *Teachers College Record, 108*(9), 1901–1914.

Senge, P. (2004). Preface to Routledge classics edition of "On Dialogue." In D. Bohm, *On dialogue* (pp. vii–xiv). London: Routledge.

Snowber, C. (2002). Bodydance: Enfleshing soulful inquiry through improvisation. In C. Bagley & M. Cancienne (Eds.), *Dancing the data* (pp. 20–33). New York: Peter Lang.

Taylor, C. (2007). *A secular age.* Cambridge, MA: Belknap Press of Harvard University.

Thurman, R. (2006). Meditation and education: India, Tibet, and modern America. *Teachers College Record, 108*(9), 1765–1774.

Wilber, K. (1999). Eye to eye: The quest for the new paradigm. In *The collected works of Ken Wilber* (pp. 137–432). Boston: Shambhala.

Wilber, K. (2006). *Integral spirituality: A startling new role for religion in the modern and postmodern world.* Boston: Shambhala.

Zajonc, A. (2006). Love and knowledge: Recovering the heart of learning through contemplation. *Teachers College Record, 108*(9), 1742–1759.

20

Contemplative Pedagogy and Compassionate Presence

Joanne Gozawa

In this chapter I inquire into the significance of a non-instrumental consciousness to compassionate presence and to contemplative meditative-type practice and pedagogy in the context of learning. By non-instrumental I mean that the locus of agency is not in the individual ego and that consciousness is not entirely a willed affair. The inquiry then, is to discover how we educators are to *be*, if not only the agent who actively directs a contemplative attitude for teaching and learning.

My exploration is significantly influenced by contemporary Jodo Shinshu (Shin) Buddhist thought (Ueda & Hirota, 1989) with its understanding of the mutual relationship between human existence (samsara) and infinite wisdom and compassion (nirvana). Unlike many other Buddhist traditions, Shin, a sect prevalent in Japan, does not subscribe to direct practices that seek to eliminate the ego and its desires, and thus Shin does not believe that individual emptiness is possible. Rather, the tradition embraces the imperfection of human existence, recognizing that human will, whether in the service of human good or human evil, causes harm in that it perpetuates the life of cause and effect (karma). Shin's realization is that human consciousness, if awake to its limitations, experiences its embeddedness in a limitless consciousness and simultaneously brings it forth. This mutual, co-creating relationship of finite and infinite, with its absence of judgment and its mental presence to things as they are (in Japanese, *sonomama*), makes available to human ways of knowing, an unconditional and inclusive patterning that can evoke a compassionate turn of heart. It is this heart opening, I suggest, that enhances capacity for profound depth in teaching and learning.

The methodological approach this chapter takes to more wholly draw the reader into its content is to present the learning environment as a subject who is animated by transpersonal and archetypal collective energies (Jung, 1990). I imaginatively suggest that she[1] (the environment) and learners are unwittingly in a co-creative relationship that can restrict or enhance depth of learning. I also offer a few stories to ground abstractions in experience so as to engage readers further.

Environment's Personality—A Story

My family attorney Layna (not her real name), obviously educated and clear thinking, told me that she consulted with her sixth-grade educated mother from the old country when it was time to choose between two equally prestigious private schools for her daughter. Grandma visited each school and felt instantly that the first was cold and like a "jail." Arriving in the parking lot of the second school, she already knew that this one was "right."

Environment and Her Ways of Knowing

As American-born educators, we are likely less conscious than Grandma of the feelings that live in learning milieus (whether physical or virtual), tending instead to focus exclusively on the subject matter and the students' abilities to know it. In a matter of speaking, we are apt to think more about inhabitants than habitats (Nisbett, 2003) and just as likely, were it called to our attention, to relate to the learning environment as an object rather than as subject. A learning environment as an object is a thing we act upon, manipulating its physical attributes through our will. As subject, however, environment becomes someone to engage and who is engaged with us. She and we are informed by our mutual *being*.

Thus, an I-Thou relationship (Buber, 1970) with environment is envisioned here. Consideration for such a mutual relational epistemology with the transpersonal and insubstantial is rare in Western thought (de Quincey, 2005), and thus an intersubjective awareness between learners (including instructors) and the learning environment may be difficult to imagine. Resistance may come from the habitual mindset of privileging I-It knowing and the belief that considering I-Thou knowing disrespects the former. However, considering a being-to-being relationship with environment is not to suggest that object-oriented consciousness is not powerful, nor that it and subject-oriented consciousness aren't integrated in experience. Rather, this chapter explores the relationship to the learning environment with an I-Thou awareness to open the way for future discussions on the nuances of relational knowing and on the quality of its integration with I-It knowing. Ultimately the intention is to spur further conversations about the significance of non-instrumental ways of knowing to contemplative pedagogies.

To continue then, I imagine the *environment as learner*, as subject, mutually engaged with learning persons. Far from inert, the environment in this understanding is alive with transpersonal and collective energies that have the potential to support or thwart learning. Further, I propose that a contemplative pedagogy, practiced with a non-instrumental, *listening for, being of* attitude, can awaken a compassionate presence in the learning environment. In turn, a compassionate environment fosters potential for deepened learning amongst her inhabitants. The premise is that learners, regardless of the subject matter at hand, penetrate more profound levels of understanding when environment is compassionate. Be aware, however, that I am proposing that it is only when environment awakens (that is, learns) compassion that compassion finds its simultaneous expression in educators and learners. With this proposition, the boundary between inner (subjective) and outer (objective) realities needs to be reconsidered, as well as the meaning of compassion itself.

Jungian psychology, consciousness studies, and Shin Buddhist thought can help ground this culturally counterintuitive idea of *environment as learner*. All of these discourses must use metaphorical language to discuss the invisible and the allusive. It is from these varying metaphorical descriptions that I intend to tap an imaginal hermeneutic, after Heron's (1992) "up-hierarchy"[2] of human mind. This model posits that conceptualizations that enlist affective and imaginal modes of mind attune knowers to *being* even as they attempt to language their perceptions. The model describes whole-person learning, and it is with this holistic understanding that I create scaffolding for discussing how contemplative pedagogy and compassionate presence transform what's possible in sites of learning. The following engagement with the aforementioned discourses are then not meant to be definitive or comprehensive; rather, they intend to invite readers into the flow of intuitive knowing that sees through to what is difficult to grasp.

Jungian Psychology and the Transpersonal

Jungian psychology offers the concepts of the collective unconscious and oppositional archetypes (Jung, 1990) to help illuminate a dimension of reality that is transpersonal: that is, beyond individual persons. These Jungian concepts offer a glimpse of the invisible elements that animate the field of encounter or what I am calling *environment*, but as a subject that is alive and dynamic.

In Jungian terms, one might say that environment's polarized archetypes vie for expression, and if they are not mutually integrated, they relate crudely to one another. One becomes superior at the expense of the other. The superior archetype develops in the extreme, and the underdeveloped inferior complement creates its own havoc. Environment, haunted by the hubris of the exalted superior and the agitation of the repressed inferior, can only offer patterns of relating that are fragmented and contentious. In turn, environment's inhabitants perpetuate these patterns of knowing as normative. Jungian, feminist literature (for example, Goodchild, 2001) exposes the imbalance between the most fundamental archetypes: the anima and animus, feminine and masculine. In a patriarchal society, the culturally formed psychic structures offer unbalanced anima-animus patterning to meet the world. Inhabitants, while finding this patterned way of relating effective at one point in their people's history, find it no longer adequate for increasingly complicated social and political realities.

The cultural complex (Gozawa, 2009; Singer & Kimbles, 2004), a contemporary Jungian idea, associates this understanding of patterned ways of relating and knowing to the cultural level. A complex unleashes pent-up negative energy when a novel situation, requiring a more whole response than the culturally habituated one, brings the imbalance of opposites to awareness. Environment's archetypal inferior, vindicated but still held captive, and the archetypal superior, redoubling efforts to remain triumphant, flood the environment with its complex-polluting energy, marinating inhabitants in negativity and defensiveness. Thus, when a habituated cultural pattern of relating fails to adequately meet the other (whether other persons or conditions), a cultural complex unleashes propensities to project, to vilify, or to wither and withdraw. In the overwhelming feeling, the ability of participants to adapt creatively, to learn, is thwarted.

Cultural Complexes Aroused—A Story

I offer the following from my teaching practice to ground the cultural complex and its dynamic in experience. In this story the catalyst is the cultural complex and the protagonist is the listening-for, being-of attitude.

In an online graduate class on culture and myth offered by a transformative studies program, an asynchronous conversation took place amongst learners regarding an item in the news about a Louisiana justice's refusal to issue a marriage license to an interracial couple. An African-American student from the South posted a link to the article and asked, "How's this for a major setback in societal transformation?" A white woman student from California posted, "Ridiculous," while another white student, a man from Australia, commented, "I don't know U.S. history as well as you do, but I seem to recall the idea of a black and white couple even dating would have raised the (violent) ire of a good many white folk, and perhaps black folk too." He continued, ". . . does ridiculing the action help to change it?" He went on in his reasoned way: ". . . could this couple have gone to another State rather than publicly attack, or litigate against, this individual by branding him and his decision as 'racist'?"

In this scenario the cultural complexes were all on alert and could have easily been further triggered, compromising a normally trustful environment and taking away any learning potential. The emotionally divested rational-masculine who is the superior archetype in most academic settings, could have retained its superiority, inflating its sense of entitlement. But by the same token, the often-repressed feminine archetype could have just as well taken on a pseudo-masculine air and feigned an exclusively rational response or could have expressed itself as the disempowered, feminine-victim archetype. How could the polarizing dynamic amongst these complexes turn to whole making? A learning environment that could hold all complexes in its compassionate presence could dispel the gathering dark feelings. I as the instructor, to appeal to such a whole-holding presence, needed to be of *sonomama*, non-judgmental consciousness. Only then would I be able to listen deeply and hear all involved as they each experienced themselves—as good people. As it turned out, I was able to post something that helped all to stay heartfully, yet critically, engaged. What allowed me to be of such a presence? I suggest it was a *listening-for* and *being-of* attitude, the focus of this chapter. I continue that exploration through Jungian concepts in the next section.

More about Jungian Psychology and the Transpersonal

The collective unconscious and the cultural complex are transpersonal concepts that help us consider environment as a collective, animated, archetypal presence that, although distinct from individual inhabitants, has a constitutive effect on them. This presence compels a patterned way of knowing and of relating dualized pairs. Thus, were the archetypal pairings to become more complementary and nuanced, one could say that environment "learned" a new, enhanced pattern of relating, and a more compassionate one as in the story above. Psychology generally, however, is focused on individual therapy and not on environmental therapy, except to notice, for example, that in the relationship between therapist and analysand (Hobson, 1985; Ulanov1996), or between mother and infant (Benjamin, 1988), or in group dynamics (Smith & Berg, 1987) there is a third participant—the many relationships that contribute to and comprise the unfolding dynamics between participants, emerging out of the ever-present and unfolding collective and archetypal patterns. One might then imagine this third element that surrounds the participants as *environment*. Conventional thinking might posit that the feel of the environment is solely attributable to the residual effect of the quality of how individuals relate. Yet it is clear, from the Jungian perspective, there is something that is independent of participants and a priori to their form of relating.

What I am calling *environment* then, in Jungian terms, is related to a particular complex of psychic energies that pattern the relationships of archetypal pairs and gives environment its personality. Grandma, introduced earlier, could easily distinguish the personalities of schools, their warmth or constrictiveness. Were Grandma to have witnessed the online class in the previous story she would surely have felt the shift in what the environment compelled. At first, contention threatened to set the pattern of engagement in that form, but then, compassion became the order of the day. In Jungian terms, it is the transpersonal, collective, and cultural unconscious that stirs environment's latent affect and concomitantly all that inhabit her.

Is what I term *environment* simply attributing an unnecessary heuristic of place and presence to the Jungian notion of the collective unconscious in order that we may more easily attune to her dynamic? This is a question worth considering—what is gained, if anything, by attributing both subjectivity and environmental, ecosystem-like imagery to the idea of the collective unconscious? What do we conceive more readily were we to imagine the collective unconscious as an animated environment with collectively formed personality?

To cast environment as person-like in the drama of learning allows me to imagine instructor and learner also as persons. We, persons and environment, are mutually engaged with each other. Further, environment's more beneficial, collective patterns of relating may lie unrealized. If these patterns are not awakened in environment through participants' listening-for attitude, her inhabitants collectively are also deprived of them. This conjuring of environment as subject allows a potential, if only temporary, suspension of prevailing Western cultural attachment to objectification. It allows me to see beyond the limitations of my existing repertoire of words and concepts by evoking imagery. (See de Rivers & Sarbin, 1998; Heron, 1992; Jones, Clarkson, Congram & Stratton, 2008; and Murray, 1986 for a range of discussions on imagination.)

In this imagining of learning environment as alive, I come to feel that she calls to me as I call to her; we listen for each other; we become mutual subjects. Further, she as habitat and I as belonging there, conjure a symbiotic, caring, and constitutive relationship precipitating perhaps a residual feeling of trust and of heart opening. In this imaginative moment, my relationship is not to *do to* environment; rather it is to *be with* environment. This pattern of relating, of recovering *being*, also affects my relationship with learners. I can imagine being with them rather than just doing to them; I can be more open to meeting their persons in the psychological, personhood sense (Heron, 1992). We, learners and instructor, as with environment and instructor, become mutual subjects, manifesting an enhanced pattern of relating that blurs the line between subject and object. To be a mutual subject with environment opens the way for instructors to be mutual subjects with learners. Additionally, this mutuality allows a more integral (inner-outer; spirit-matter) dimension to learning. The fostering of the relational way of being when better integrated with the urge to direct action in the world, transforms what is possible.

In this imagining of a subjective environment, what else is realized? First, that the collective unconscious conjured as environment speaks more concretely to the underlying ambiguity—that environment is at once separate from us and constitutive of us, whether as nurturer or nemesis—and that inner and outer are dynamically related. Our participatory relationship with environment as subject substantiates our existence, our being, and hones our self-awareness. We are not simply *in* an environment but *of* her and with her. As educators, we are allowed to consider more deliberately the feel of her presence and our unwitting participation in maintaining the limits or enhancing the possibilities of that presence to learning. We can further our gaze, from simply the subject matter at hand and learners as objects, to how we are with learners as mutual beings. And, finally, we might feel at a visceral level, beyond our directed reasoning, that environment's compassion is awakened when we attune to her as subject, as *being*. In that primal moment, awareness shifts and who is knower—ego-self or other—is ambiguous. To remember to listen for, to embrace not knowing, awakens the environment to compassion. I will return to this theme of compassionate presence, its relationship to contemplative pedagogy and integral learning, in subsequent sections. However, first I take up considerations of unity and dualism in the next section.

Consciousness Studies, the Yearning for Wholeness

We are so accustomed to distinguishing figure from ground and self from surround that thinking otherwise takes effort. The separation from unity consciousness that leads to duality and consciousness is discussed as the evolution of human consciousness (Low, 2002). To understand that consciousness is duality arising from unity is to know that humankind suffers an intrinsic ambiguity that is inescapable. The prevailing tension provides the dynamic for creativity and the perpetual unfolding of human consciousness. This paradox of the human condition, of its virtue and volatility, is significant to this chapter as it considers humanity's "sacred wound" and illuminates the need for an awakened compassion. However, prior to exploring that idea, there is consciousness itself, as the emptiness that is full. I turn to this paradox first.

When trying to define consciousness, one instantly sees the conundrum. Its presence is taken for granted and yet when one turns to substantiate it, it disappears. I appreciate Combs' (2002) commentary on consciousness for the image that it compels. He writes, "Like a polarizing magnetic field that draws iron filings into formations of multiple ellipses, consciousness aligns the processes of the mind into patterns with direction and purpose" (p. 7). Suggested herein is the idea of a form-inducing presence that itself is not form but patterning that arises from the relationship of polarities. I propose that environment awakening to compassion can induce patterns of mind with direction and purpose significantly changed from patterns enacted when compassion lies dormant and unimaginable. This may seem less-than-provocative if one substitutes the term *consciousness* for *environment*. However, *environment*, I suggest, provides a more accessible image than does consciousness. *Environment* more readily suggests that persons do not will themselves to be compassionate nor can compassion be thought of as a commodity that is granted or withheld. The eco-system like dynamic conjured by *environment* is a participatory one (Ferrer, 2008) in that the template for relationship is emergent and dynamic and perpetually created by the habitat-inhabitant relationship as a whole. Thus, environment must realize compassion, must be compassion, before its inhabitants can be compassionate. One might say that compassion must awaken in the greater consciousness, must become a patterning before it is realized in the collective and individual consciousness. This isomorphic relationship (what this chapter has conjured as habitat and inhabitants), according to consciousness studies, envisions whole and part as mirrors of each other. In another words, one is not separate or beyond the surround. The one is the whole and the whole the one—environment as a collective system of relational patternings are mirrored in her inhabitants.

Thus, concepts from Jungian psychology and consciousness studies support the idea that there is a dimension of reality that is transpersonal and anticipates forms of relating that gives some tangibility to environment as subject and as learner. However, as with *collective unconscious*, is there call to imagine *consciousness* as animated environment? Are we too modern and beyond such imagining? Those questions are considered in later sections of this chapter.

For now, I turn to discuss the implications of the "sacred wound" (Low, 2002; Romanyshyn, 2007), the duality of consciousness.

Concepts from consciousness studies bring the human condition into inquiry for closer consideration. The human condition has been described as the tension between humankind's yearning for eternity and the finiteness of its mortal body (Gozawa, 2000). Similarly, Low (2002) writes, "A deep intuition of unity is violated, split in two incompatible halves—a mind half and a body half—each with its own demands" (p. 17). The dynamic of this intrinsic conflict has fueled consciousness and human life and has been characterized by religions as the struggle between the divine and the demonic, of good and evil inherent in humankind. The outer manifestations of violence are attributed by some in consciousness studies to this un-resolvable innate tension, while the creative marriage of psychic contending poles are said to hold evolutionary promise (Low, 2002).

If the inherent tension in human being is unavoidable and un-resolvable in a direct way, can an indirect approach hold sway? I submit that the idea of compassionate presence may give some insight. In an envisioning of compassionate presence, the commonsense notion of compassion as a commodified object that is given or withheld needs to be reconsidered. In my imagining, environment does not grant compassion to her inhabitants, rather she herself awakens to compassion and inhabitants are mutually affected. Compassionate being for inhabitants becomes a possibility when their environment becomes compassionate. Similarly, inhabitants collectively do not grant compassion nor do they just act compassionately—they *are* compassion as the environment has become. In this compassionate being, the wound of eternal opposition, of divine and demonic is not cured but healed. The duality of *being* is realized for what it is—the gift of consciousness that entrusts humankind to reach for wholeness. But how does compassionate presence awaken in environment and concomitantly in inhabitants? While I've alluded to answering this question throughout, the question can be addressed more explicitly through Shin Buddhist thought considered in the next section.

Shin Buddhist Thought and Mutuality

Historically, Shin Buddhism arose in thirteenth-century Japan during the social upheaval in the country when Shinran Shonin, a Buddhist monk, gave up monastic life and found realization living amongst everyday people (Bloom, 2007, p. ix). His commentary on major Mahayana sutras became the guide for establishing Shin Pure Land Buddhism. Shin remains the major sect of

Buddhism in Japan, even today. In the discussion that follows it is important to keep in mind that Buddhism is not a theistic tradition. Buddha is not equivalent to a god; rather, Buddha is a way of naming *shinjin*, that is, non-duality or unity consciousness. The tradition does acknowledge a historical Buddha in the person of Sakyamuni Buddha (463–383 BCE). However, "Buddha" comes from the Sanskrit and simply means to awaken or an awakened person (Shigaraki, 2005, p. 7).

In a contemporary interpretation of Shinran's commentary on *nembutsu* (the chant, *Namo Amida Butsu*, "I seek refuge in the Buddha"), considered the defining chant in the Shin tradition, scholars Ueda and Hirota (1989) claim that Shinran removed *nembutsu* from the context of practice to one of realization—that is, of the presence of abiding wisdom and compassion. In this esoteric understanding, human being (self) and the divine (Other) are said to be in a co-constituting relationship. The formless absolute affected by the suffering (duality consciousness) of humankind is awakened to compassion and is thereby brought into *samsara* (that is, duality) and therefore into existence. The human self, affected by this abiding compassion, is transported and transcends its heretofore inescapable suffering (sacred wound). Rarely in religious traditions is human being thought to awaken the divine. However, in this interpretation of the *nembutsu*, Ueda and Hirota seem to suggest that divine becomes Buddha (the one awakened to compassion) even as human being realizes divine, abiding compassion. Thus in chanting *nembutsu* one calls to the divine as a small child calls to mother for assurance that she is there; that he, the child, can feel once again one with her. His vulnerability is thus sheltered by her all-encompassing attention. Mother in turn, as with the divine in human presence, is moved to compassion, is awakened by the precious vulnerability of the child.

The significance of *nembutsu* to this chapter is that it, too, is counter to commonsense understanding of subject and object. In chanting the *nembutsu*, I become an object to what has become compassionate subject (presence). In that presence, I experience a mutuality with all sentient beings—we are all objects to a larger presence and simultaneously subjects in a mutually constitutive relationship with this wholly other. In that mutuality my heart opens to all who suffer existence, making possible my own expression of compassion. In saying the *nembutsu*, the one who suffers and the one who knows compassion are one; they are reciprocal and mutual.

In Japanese, *kiku* means both to ask and to listen. Similarly, in nembutsu there is simultaneously caller and responder. In every moment one constitutes the other; without either there is neither. In nembutsu there is no I nor other. There is only the pervading, recursive dynamic of suffering-compassion that diffuses I-Other distinction. In this light, two who are one say the nembutsu even as the one and the other remain distinct. Again, as with the previous discourses, the duality of subject-object is blurred and thus duality itself. The conjuring of environment—of habitat and inhabitants—inspires a knowing of the many as One although paradoxically both habitat and inhabitants in their becoming, become more distinct from each other. Additionally significant to this chapter is the idea that compassion is awakened as a new pattern of mind when I attune and listen.

Reconsidering Environment as Learner

In the above image-evoking encounter with concepts from Jungian psychology, consciousness studies, and contemporary Shin thought, I consider how different discourses represent transpersonal, consciousness-forming realities. With each, the idea of *environment as learner* becomes more imaginable as the commonsense notion of subject-object duality is cast anew. The environment and human being evolve patterns accessible to mind. In keeping with the chapter's imaginative approach, I did not engage the abstract philosophical theorists who address being: for example, Kant, Husserl, Heidegger, Sartre, Ricoeur, and Derrida (Murray, 1986, pp. 18–22). Nor is systems theory's sense of emergence and complexity included. I chose instead to refer to ideas couched in ways that could be related more directly and imaginatively to the everyday process of learning.

I now use the language of the discourses just engaged to further illuminate the image of environment as learner and its relationship to contemplative pedagogy and to compassionate presence. I offer that when compassionate presence is archetypally available as environment's pattern of relating opposites, the possibility of engaging extreme polarities and traversing consciousness's inherent duality creatively, rather than reactively, becomes immanent. However, this begs the question: what is meant by compassionate presence and how is it evoked? Compassion is defined as "sorrow for the sufferings or trouble of another or others, accompanied by an urge to help. . . ." (*Webster's New World Dictionary of American English*, 1996). However, I suggest that compassion commonly considered in the logic of everyday English focuses on the helping action such that compassion may be thought of as a commodity as in a transaction—I give compassion by helping as it were. In the context of learning I, as instructor, can erroneously assume that I give these attributes of compassion to students or students give them to each other. This is not to say that the feelings of suffering are not the impetus for the giving, but rather a transactional mindset encourages thinking of compassion as a giving of what is in short supply; a fixing of a situation exclusively on the material plane. As important is an attuning to existential suffering so as to evoke a healing on the transpersonal, environmental plane. Thus, in the above story about the arousal of cultural complexes in an online class, if the instructor were merely to set a rule that everyone must be respectful and compassionate, she would be assuming that to be so is an entirely willed proposition and that students can give compassion and respect to each other. The tacit message is that one can give compassion without being compassionate. Most importantly to this chapter is the idea that to be compassionate is integrally tied with what is awakened in the ground of being, what is alive in the environment, and what feeds participants to become what they will.

Thus, what can be alternatively imagined when compassion is attributed to environment's learning rather than to the direct doing of individuals? First, with the image of environment as learner, we can consider more easily whether the pattern of compassionate relating is available to learners. The isomorphic relationship between whole and parts (habitat and inhabitants) discussed in consciousness studies comes to mind. Second, this alternative understanding of compassion as abiding in the environment helps to raise the question: who is the directing agent?

In my experience, utilitarian and popular understanding of meditation or quiet sitting or other contemplative pedagogies are about relaxing the body so that the mind can come to the learning undistracted by the noise of the every day. Similarly, contemplative practice may be thought of as a means to encourage inner calm so as to prevent overwhelm with topics certain to raise provocation. For others, the utility of contemplative practices may be a way to bolster learners' capacities to be more subjectively involved in learning that otherwise might remain disembodied and abstract. And for still others it may be to practice perfectly so that they may experience an altered state and reap the benefits. In a phrase, contemplation or meditation practice is thought of instrumentally, as a "spiritual technology" (Sharf, 1995, p. 259).

All of these intentions may find their positive consequence in learner capacities. However, these intentions presume an exclusive ego-level control that is primarily in relationship with itself with no regard to environment and to collective being—one meditates to calm one's emotions in order to engage more effectively in teaching and learning. What does not come readily to mind from this instrumental perspective is the understanding of contemplation as a mutual relationship with environment, as a listening-for and thus a being-of a whole-constituting presence; a preordained partnership of entity and surround. In realizing the limitations of human consciousness with its inherent duality and fragmenting propensity to polarize, contemplative practice may be thought of instead as a mutual listening. Were contemplation to be done in an attitude of listening for, rather than exclusively of doing to or getting from—what might shift?

Consider contemplative pedagogy as that which evokes compassionate presence in an enactment of listening for. Imagine compassionate presences as a certain patterning of the collective, meta mind of the constituting environment that calls instructors to design courses, facilitate discussion, and otherwise foster learning that is mutually inclusive. Contemplative pedagogy in this rendering would begin with the consciousness of the instructor who submits to possibility and calls to the environment of all-possibility, the ground of being. In turn the environment is awakened by the appeal. In a matter of speaking, environment attunes to the limits of its inhabitants and becomes compassionate. In that meeting of the one who calls and the one who responds I, as instructor, have available to me a different patterning of mind that enhances ways of relating.

Are we able to appreciate the irony? As good instructors, we may still yearn to be in perfect control of the subject matter even as more facilitative pedagogies come into vogue. However, the case this chapter furthers is that the "good" of teaching arises from temporarily suspending ego-control. The compassionate archetype, I assert, arises out of our imperfection, our of our Sisyphus wound. The environment "learns" compassion only when we, her inhabitants, submit to our limitations of being and call to her, if only in that imaginal moment that stirs our primal knowing of wholeness. In a profession that values us for our knowledge, for what we know, we submit to not knowing in order to make room for new depth.

A Case in Point—Another Page from My Teaching Experience

Thus, the assertion is that a different environmental personality arises from contemplative pedagogies that are initiated by an attitude of *listening-for* and *being-of*. Such an attitude evokes a compassionate presence that blurs subject-object dichotomies and in turn realizes a pattern of relating to the world that is whole-making, not at the expense of negation, but complementary to it. That said, the question remains: How does this change in available patterning transform the way teaching and learning manifest? What comes into being that heretofore remained unfulfilled? The answer to this question was somewhat expressed in the story about the arousal of the cultural complex. To further answer these questions within the limitations of this chapter, I discuss a course design element probably already familiar to many readers who think of themselves as facilitators of knowing rather than simply experts of knowledge. I am referring to ritual openings and closings that often take the form of a check-in and a check-out. I comment on how the intention for these can be of deeper significance than what is commonly imagined.

The course I use as an example is again one that is offered online. An online course is particularly suited to serve as an example as the instructor must be more deliberate in thinking about the virtual environment than she would about a physical classroom if only that the latter is too familiar to warrant notice. The name of the course is "Goodness, Evil, Politics and Change." Its topic, though naturally addressing the dualities of existence and their manifestations in the world, is not the focus here. Thus, the following discussion is applicable to courses across varying topics and disciplines.

In this graduate-level course, online learners engage in small, asynchronous study groups to discuss particular readings before they come together as a whole class to engage more directed and evocative questions from the instructor. Learners from different time zones over a long weekend are able to simulate a simultaneous coming together, which repeats on designated weekends throughout the semester. These gatherings are called weekend cafés. A typical café is structured online as four conference items that participants engage on successive assigned days. The first item calls learners to a ritual opening, so that they can prepare themselves to participate wholly. Typically, in this initiating space, learners post a greeting to their follow learners, and relay briefly what occupied them in the hours before and what they intend for the weekend. Two items follow, each with their own provocative question related to the readings. The fourth and final space allows for closing the weekend with a thoughtful reflection.

The structure of enclosing inquiry and discussion within demarcations of a ritual opening and closing is a common enough pedagogical element; however, with what attitude and with what intention do I enact this ritual practice? When I imagine environment as subject and as learner, how does this shift the significance of openings and closings for me? In an attitude of listening I do not simply construct the learning items. For in a listening attitude, I am of an environment where presence informs the doing. The ego that does is complemented by a self that is awake for being of. I am attuned to listen for what I do not know. In the listening attitude, I become aware of the needs of the community of learners. I intuit nuances from remembered previous postings. I feel learners' vulnerability as they face their unknowing in the process of inquiry. Thus, in a listening attitude, I can witness rather than merely judge learners and myself as we struggle with ideas that are not just adopted from the readings but are also informed by our embeddedness with the everyday of our existence. I can listen to learners as beings who are artfully knowing, and not just as objects, as minds cogitating. I can support learners in confronting assumptions and beliefs rather than being too ready to give disembodied critiques of what learners verbalize and attempt to share. In a word, I am moved to compassion by the knowing and the feeling that a whole embraces all of us.

Learning Fields and Relationship as Reality

The foregoing engagement with commentary on and concepts from Jungian psychology, consciousness studies, and Shin Buddhist thought, was offered to support the imaginal in conjuring environment as person-like. Before concluding, I offer this section as a brief pause to present two other relevant discourses that are explicit about the significance of the learning environment and the non-instrumental consciousness needed to evoke it. These are presented as further reading and potentially as further weight to what has already been introduced imaginally in this chapter.

Christopher Bache (2008) discusses the science of fields that supports the existence of collective fields ("learning fields" in the case of teaching) that transcend the time and space boundaries of ordinary consciousness. Bache, a college professor of 30 years, has also experienced the wisdom from the learning field that presents itself. He writes that in the mist of teaching, he sometimes experiences a small door opening in the back of his mind and a slip of paper coming through with an answer customized to the student for whom it is intended. To Bache, it does not feel like a stray thought of his own making; rather, he writes, "This was about cooperating with some mysterious process that brought out what was inside me in a way that was exceptionally fine-tuned to my audience" (p. 18). He merely needed to pay attention, to listen, as the door opened. Further, he needed to consider the messages coming through, to listen to them, even when they seemed "strangely off target."

De Quincey (2005) offers a radical philosophical discussion on intersubjectivity and relationship that brings to mind what I am calling *environment* or that "empty" space in which participants engage. He proposes that relationship is the underlying reality and selves (individual consciousnesses) are its expression. The insight de Quincey draws speaks to the significance of relationship, that is, environment as the ground of reality. The significance of environment prior to selves is profound. In this light he writes, "Whereas the ultimate ideal of objective knowledge is control, and the ultimate ideal of subjective knowledge is peace, the ultimate ideal of intersubjective knowledge is relationship—and, dare I say it, love" (p. 180). I take this sense of love to mean inclusiveness, a drawing into the wholeness of an abiding compassion.

Both Bache's learning fields and de Quincey's relationship as reality, speak to a constituting environment. As we instructors are of this environment, we are privy to her wisdom and compassion if we stop to listen and fall into the emptiness that is full.

Conclusion

In the foregoing, the blurring of real and imagined, metaphorical and substantiated, may have frustrated the reader who is more comfortable with firmer ground and clear-cut distinctions. I may also have lost the reader who needed to start with more theoretical and reasoned frameworks rather than organic scaffolding that emerges out of imaginings. For both of these readers, I hope they at least took away a seed that represents this question: What presence resides in my classroom or institution, what is my relationship to it, and how does it enable or thwart a depth in learning?

I hope readers who are practiced in any contemplative pedagogies, are nudged to find in themselves a listening-for and being-of attitude and are thus moved to cultivate these in learners so that they are as much embracing of their not knowing as much as they are exalted by their knowledge. I hope readers do not hesitate to imagine learning environment as alive and that they as learners are in a mutual, constitutive relationship with her. I hope all who have taken time with this chapter come away appreciating the ambiguity of the inner and outer, of the self and surround, and of the imagined and "real" that at once make learning possible and profound. And, finally, I hope that readers are reminded that enhancing knowing and knowledge requires, at some level, a surrendering to the original levels of wholeness, whether one believes that such engagement is with primal knowing, with the One, with the ground of being, with the collective unconscious, or with divine presence.

In summary, this chapter proposes that contemplative pedagogies that begin with a listening-for, being-of attitude awakens a compassionate patterning of mind in the collective, transpersonal order. A compassionate presence calls for mutuality in the face of ambiguity, complexity, and contention. With that, there is a further inquiry that I suggest readers may now consider, beyond the one that asks what presence is awakened by contemplative practice. Further inquiry might ask, "Is the presence in my classroom marked simply by an abiding calm or also by an active compassion?" For when the heretofore inferior archetypes stir in an allowing environment, is a calming presence enough to meet the complex-triggered flood of feeling? Is a calm presence adequate to foster learning or does it only temporarily diffuse provocation? I suggest that patterns of relating that engender listening-for mutuality, for wholeness, become most essential in times of irrational and overwhelming feeling. Learning into that which is overwhelming rather than neutralizing its charge, I submit, requires an active compassionate presence. Further, an attitude of listening-for and being-of for any contemplative practice compels the awakening of such a presence.

Notes

1. I refer to the environment as "she" in recognitions of the feminine archetype of birth and coming into being. Even when her archetypes are out of balance and the masculine is dominant, I still conceive of environment as she. She is still the ground of all ways of being whether their expression in the moment is predominately masculine or feminine or integrated.

2. John Heron (1992) presents a theory of the person with its implications for learning. His diagram of the modes of the psyche is shown below. He cautions, however, that the modes are separated only to better comprehend mind's dynamic. The modes should be thought of as interwoven.

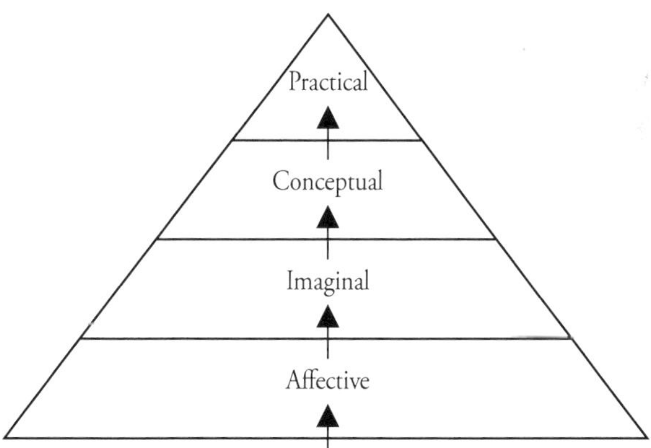

Figure 1. The Up-hierarchy of the Four Modes of the Human Psyche

Heron writes in part about the affective mode: "This is the domain of empathy, indwelling, participation, presence, resonance, and suchlike" (p. 16). Of the imaginal mode he writes, "This is the domain of intuitive grasp, holistic cognition, totalistic comprehension, metaphorical insight, immediate gnosis" (p. 17).

References

Bache, C. M. (2008). *The living classroom—Teaching and collective consciousness*. Albany, NY: State University of New York Press.

Benjamin, J. (1988). *The bonds of love—Psychoanalysis, feminism, and the problem of domination*. New York: Pantheon Books.

Bloom, A. (Ed.). (2007). *The essential Shinran*. Bloomington, IN: World Wisdom.

Buber, M. (1970). *I and Thou*. (Walter Kaufmann, Trans.). New York: Charles Scribner's Sons.

Combs, A. (2002). *The radiance of being* (2nd ed.). St. Paul, MN: Paragon Press.

de Rivera, J., & Sarbin, T. R. (Eds.). (1988). *Believed-in imaginings—The narrative construction of reality*. Washington DC: American Psychological Association.

de Quincey, C. (2005). *Radical knowing—Understanding consciousness through relationship*. Rochester, VT: Park Street Press.

Ferrer, J. N., & Sherman, J. H. (Eds.). (2008). *The participatory turn—Spirituality, Mysticism, Religious Studies*. Albany, NY: State University of New York Press.

Goodchild, V. (2001). *Eros and chaos—The sacred mysteries and dark shadows of love*. York Beach, ME: Nicolas-Hays, Inc.

Gozawa, J. (2000). Cosmic heroes, and the heart's desire—Transformative learning through conflict transformation. In C. A. Wiessner, S. R. Meyer, & D. A. Fuller (Eds.), *Challenges of practice: Transformative learning in action. Proceedings for the 3rd international conference on transformative learning*. Teachers College, Columbia University, New York.

Gozawa, J. (2009). The cultural complex and transformative learning environments. *Journal of Transformative Education, 7*, 114–145.

Heron, J. (1992). *Feeling and personhood—Psychology in another key*. Newbury Park, CA: Sage Publications.

Hobson, R. E. (1985). *Forms of feeling—The heart of psychotherapy*. London: Routledge.

Jones, R. A., Clarkson, A., Congram, S., & Stratton, N. (Eds.). (2008). *Education and imagination—Post-Jungian perspectives*. New York: Routledge.

Jung, C. G. (1959/1990). *The archetypes and the collective unconscious* (R. F. C. Hull, Trans.). Princeton, NJ: Princeton University Press.

Low, A. (2002). *Creating consciousness—A study of consciousness, creativity, evolution, and violence*. Ashland, OR: White Cloud Press.

Murray, E. L. (1986). *Imaginative thinking and human existence*. Pittsburgh, PA: Duquesne University Press.

Nisbett, R. E. (2003). *The geography of thought—How Asians and Westerners think differently . . . and why*. New York: The Free Press.

Romanyshyn, R. (2007). *The wounded researcher*. New Orleans, LA: Spring Journal.

Sharf, R. H. (1995). Buddhist modernism and the rhetoric of meditative experience. *Numen, 42*(3), 228–283.

Shigaraki, T. (2005). *A life of awakening: The heart of the Shin Buddhist path*. (D. Matusumoto, Trans.). Kyoto, Japan: Hozokan Publications.

Singer, T., & Kimbles, S. L. (Eds.). (2004). *The cultural complex—Contemporary Jungian perspectives on psyche and society.* New York: Brunner-Routledge.

Smith, K. K., & Berg, D. N. (Eds.). (1987). *Paradoxes of group life.* San Francisco: Jossey-Bass Publishers.

Ueda, Y., & Hirota, D. (1989). *Shinran—An introduction to his thought.* Kyoto, Japan: Hongwanji International Center.

Ulanov, A. B. (1996). *The functioning transcendent—A study in analytical psychology.* Wilmette, IL: Chiron Publications.

Webster's New World Dictionary of American English, (3rd College Edition). (1996). New York: Webster's New World.

21

What Next?

Contemplating the Future of Contemplative Education

Edward W. Sarath

The decade-plus that has passed since the American Council of Learned Societies (ACLS) launched its Contemplative Practice Fellowship Program, which might be seen as a landmark event in the modern-day contemplative studies movement, has seen a rising tide of publications, conferences, and curricular innovations that clearly suggest the field to be more than a passing fad.[1] In this essay, I reflect on this work through the lens of an emergent worldview called Integral Theory (Wilber, 2000, 2006). Mapping the interior and exterior dimensions of the human being and cosmos and recognizing the importance of diverse epistemologies, or ways of knowing, as central to inner-outer union, the integral vision cedes an important place for contemplative practices and related studies. It also brings into play an expanded slate of considerations that shed new light on current practices and possible future horizons for the contemplative education field. These include a more clearly defined conception of contemplative practice, delineation of a broader theoretical spectrum, and the situating of contemplative education within a non-dual perspective that, as posited by most all of the world's wisdom traditions, is predicated on the inextricable link between individual consciousness and the cosmic wholeness. Just as contemplative educators are able to step back and examine conventional education from an expanded and more critical perspective, consideration of contemplative education from the even more expansive integral vantage point further extends the critical framework through which the field might be viewed and thus able to progress.

Integral Overview

I begin with a brief overview of four key integral principles that are of relevance to the discussion. First is the identification of first-, second-, and third-person realms or perspectives within the inner-outer spectrum of reality (Esbjörn-Hargens, 2010; Wilber, 2006). First person is the interior, subjective domain of "I," second person the intersubjective "We" that can be seen as a kind of inner-outer bridge, and third person the objective, exterior "It" realm. Much of contemplative education may be seen as the addition of a first-person interior realm—with meditation being a key first-person methodology—to the largely third-person confinement lamented by a long legacy of educational thinkers (e.g., Bruner, 1960; Gardner, 1993; Maslow, 1971; Whitehead, 1929).

Integral education synthesizes all three realms, distinguishing itself both from conventional approaches and other alternatives such as "holistic" education (Gunnlaugson, 2010). Although appropriation of these principles to the arts has been limited, I argue elsewhere (Sarath, 2010, and 2013 in press) that jazz, due to its improvisatory core, exemplifies the capacity of the arts to bring a robust, creative/interactive, and thus second-person aspect, to the integral synthesis.

A second key integral feature is its emphasis on engagement with diverse epistemologies, or "Integral Methodological Pluralism," as means for achieving first-, second-, third-person synthesis. Contemplative practice is among the variety of methodologies that uphold both transformational and hermeneutic functions within the epistemological spectrum that comprises "Integral Life Practice" (Wilber, Leonard, Patton, & Morelli, 2008). In other words, transformational practice promotes expansion of inner experience, correlative to which are new interpretive insights.

A third facet pertains to the evolutionary trajectory that, proceeding from less-differentiated to more-differentiated wholeness, integral theorists locate in a variety of systems. Of particular relevance is the progression from pre-modern, modern, and postmodern to integral stages of sociocultural development (Wilber, 2006), the latter three most directly relating to the present analysis. Modernism is characterized by a split between first-person subjective/spiritual and third-person objective/scientific domains, as exemplified in the dualism commonly ascribed to the French philosopher Rene Descartes and which prevailed well into the twentieth century. Post-modernity involves the subordination of first-person interiors and the emergence of a second-person, intersubjective dimension; for example, the notion that reality and meaning are not rooted in transcendental or universal phenomena but rather are "culturally constructed" according to the relativistic factors of one's time and place. The integral stage involves the embrace of modern and postmodern insights in a first-, second-, third-person synthesis.

Fourth is the non-dual, integral worldview as an overarching conceptual framework that informs the broad variety of practices and premises that comprise integral contemplative education. Construed most robustly, non-duality—some expression of which is posited by most of the world's wisdom traditions—presumes that individual consciousness is inseparable from the cosmic intelligence that is the source of all creation, and that realization of this wholeness is the ultimate goal of contemplative development. Most traditions, in other words, posit some kind of cosmic narrative that, particularly from the standpoint of the mystical limbs of those traditions, situates human consciousness as a facet of the divine play of creation that sustains the entire cosmos: order is sustained. Although contemplative education is generally inspired by these traditions, with Buddhist influences arguably the most prominent, the field has been largely ambivalent regarding far-reaching questions of this nature. I will argue that aversion to this terrain, while on one hand understandable given the materialist backdrop within which contemplative educators must invoke often adept and courageous measures to advance this work (Sarath, 2003, 2006; also see the Denton chapter in this volume), is symptomatic of a broader "flatland" orientation (Wilber, 2006) whereby knowledge systems compromise interior and thus these kinds of broader issues and dimensions that are central to meaning and direction in human development. An understanding of how this orientation has manifested in the culture of contemplative education sheds light on prevailing curricular tendencies, thus laying groundwork for change.

We can begin to gain a clearer grasp of these points by viewing the evolution of contemplative education in terms of a four-stage sequence that proceeds from pre-curricular to early-curricular, mid-curricular, and integral stages.

Four Stages of Contemplative Education

In what might be called the "*pre-curricular*" stage, contemplative activity occurs outside of college and university classrooms in formats such as religious clubs and prayer and meditation groups. This stage correlates fairly readily with the modernist stage of sociocultural evolution, with interior engagement largely a tradition-specific endeavor (e.g., campus religious meetings) that, reflective of the centrality of the Cartesian partition (first-person/third-person split) to the purity of the scientific method, is kept far apart from classroom practice.

The above-mentioned ACLS initiative, in turn, signified the beginning of a second, "*early-curricular*" stage, involving the incorporation of meditation and related practices and studies in credit-bearing academic coursework (Bush, 2006). Characteristic of this stage-two approach, which defines the current focus of contemplative education, is that contemplative coursework is generally confined to isolated pockets—in single, elective courses rather than course clusters or programs. While at present having only begun to significantly broach the second-person domain (see chapters by Gozawa, Gunnlaugson, and Scott in this volume) that distinguishes the postmodern from the modern, this stage nonetheless exhibits strong postmodern tendencies in the extrication of contemplative practice from its tradition-specific settings and receptivity to diverse approaches to practice.

Stage three, which I call "*mid-curricular*," involves the design of concentrations or majors that enable students to delve more extensively into contemplative studies. In the Bachelor of Fine Arts in Jazz and Contemplative Studies (BFAJCS) curriculum at the University of Michigan, I have created what appears to be the first stage-three model at a mainstream university. Brown University Medical School's Contemplative Studies concentration (Roth, current volume) and Lesley University's Mindfulness Studies Program (Waring, current volume) are more recent examples of this kind of innovation. As I have discussed elsewhere (Sarath, 2003, 2006, 2010), students in the BFAJCS program take 20 to 25 credits of contemplative-oriented coursework, involving practice and theory, in addition to a full slate of jazz and overall musical studies, uniquely spanning the first-, second-, and third-person realms that, to be examined shortly, are central to the integral worldview. Inasmuch, however, as significant aspects of the curriculum, due to the constraints of the conventional academic setting in which it exists, fall short of integral approaches within their own boundaries, it must be considered as but preliminary headway toward a stage four, "*late-curricular*," or "*integral*" paradigm.

In the integral model, all coursework is designed around the interaction of interior and exterior epistemologies and content to harness the full range of intellectual, creative, interactive, and spiritual growth that characterize integral thought. By contrast, even while the BFACJS curriculum includes a significant contemplative component, it also depends considerably—as do most concentrations or majors—on coursework from a range of other areas, much of which will be approached conventionally rather contemplatively or integrally, across fields. Hence, the significant leap between stage 3 and 4 approaches.

The BFAJCS curriculum reflects not only more robust postmodern sensibilities in its strong second-person capacities—for example, interactive creativity, infusion of global influences—but also exemplifies integral features in its grounding of contemporary musical exploration in solid tradition-specific musical study. In other words, whereas the postmodern subordinates tradition, the integral celebrates both tradition and creative expansion of traditional boundaries. An examination of the "Integral Turn" that characterizes movement from stage 3 to stage 4 reveals how this trans-traditional/tradition-specific interplay manifests as well in a more broadly conceived approach to contemplative studies.

Stage 4 Contemplative Studies: The Integral Turn

What might an integral approach to contemplative education look like? Among the most prominent features are the inclusion of first-, second-, and third-person content and methodologies, albeit to varying distributions and emphases, in all coursework, clearly defined criteria for contemplative practice, organic linkages between practice and theory, both of which are approached from both tradition-specific and trans-traditional (Forman, 2004) perspectives, and the grounding of the model within a non-dual perspective. As we will see, the shift from stage 3 to stage 4 entails not only wholesale curricular reform, but a transformation in the cultural orientation of the learning environment. Accordingly, it might appear, for reasons cited above (the need for not only contemplative or integral course clusters but an entire curriculum that exemplifies these principles), that any such approach is unlikely in mainstream environments any time soon. However, it is not inconceivable that, short of an entire college or university shifting to an integral approach, a localized program might be established with this aim in an otherwise mainstream institution. Meanwhile, much is to be gained from a consideration of what such a program might look like as this sheds light on existing areas that might be readily modified for both immediate gains and longer-term, paradigmatic change.

Important insights may also be gleaned from the significant strides in an integral direction achieved over the past few decades at several alternative institutions. These include California Institute of Integral Studies (CIIS), JFK University, Maharishi University, and Naropa University, all of which were founded upon contemplative principles from the outset and are accredited at undergraduate and graduate levels.[2] As much as these institutions differ from their conventional counterparts, they also differ considerably from one another. Naropa University is Buddhist-inspired, CIIS and Maharishi University are inspired by Vedantic lineages, and while Naropa and CIIS foster more pluralistic cultures of practice, all students and faculty at Maharishi University engage in a uniform set of practices. Benefits in each orientation may be noted: pluralism allows for individuals to chart their own contemplative pathways, uniformity enables a kind of collective grounding and depth that, much like in an ashram or monastery where an entire community follows a shared routine would not be possible otherwise. Even if contemplative pathways in mainstream institutions will necessarily be forged according to the unique constraints encountered by faculty innovators, an awareness of the unique features of the alternative schools may significantly enhance these efforts.

Let us turn to the realm of first-person contemplative pedagogy to illuminate key distinctions between conventional and integral approaches and how an integrally informed core promotes the blossoming of key integral features in an educational environment.

An Integral View of First-Person Contemplative Pedagogy: Patterns and Possibilities

That essential questions regarding first-person pedagogy remain as elusive now as they were at the inception of this work suggests immediate gains may be had from an integral perspective.

What is contemplative practice? Inasmuch as a wide array of practices might be construed as contemplative, an equally viable question might be: What is *not* contemplative practice? Implicit in these questions are those related to integrity of practice: Might dimensions of contemplative experience and growth be compromised when practices are extricated from their traditional frameworks and integrated in college and university classrooms? Are all contemplative disciplines equally effective? Who decides? Who is qualified to offer instruction in such practices?

To be sure, these questions point to the highly complicated nature of introducing contemplative experience in an educational system not designed for such, and it is thus not surprising that contemplative pedagogues have resorted to a wide array of approaches according to their particular situations. On the positive side, this has resulted in a proclivity toward the idea of contemplation "writ large," characterized by receptivity to a broad swath of practices. At the same time, consistent with postmodern horizontal latitude that runs the risk of compromised vertical depth, it may also be susceptible to a kind of "anything goes" culture within a given institution and the field at large, which may ultimately detract from both individual student and faculty growth and advancement of this work.

Elsewhere (Sarath, 2006, 2010) I have proposed a framework that begins to address these concerns. Key is the conception of first-person experience in its most foundational form as the experience of pure consciousness (Alexander, 1990; Forman, 1990), or emptiness/shunyata (Govinda, 1969), in which one experiences only silent, radiant wakefulness, devoid of mental activity. Meditation, usually undertaken apart from ordinary mental, physical, sensory, or emotional engagement, is thus a primary means for first-person experience. In no way is this to confine first-person experience, or for that matter contemplative practice, to silent, sitting meditation, but rather to suggest that this particular practice (of which of course many varieties are to be found) might serve as a kind of anchor for a broader contemplative continuum that might include, among many possibilities, contemplative approaches to reading, writing, movement, nature communion, and creative arts. While it is important to recognize that everyone will walk a different pathway, I believe most individuals will benefit from some degree of silent meditation practice along with some degree of active contemplative engagement and thus do not believe it is unreasonable to regard this as a general precept for integral contemplative education.

In order to help students and faculty discover further direction within this wide range of options, I take an additional step and distinguish between "formal," "quasi-formal," and "non-formal" practices in order that students and faculty may gain a clearer sense of the benefits and limitations unique to the different approaches. By formal practice I mean engagement with the methodologies and conceptual resources of a contemplative lineage, thus enabling grounding not only in systematic instruction but also a theoretical and cultural context. Further benefits of formal practice frameworks include participation with communities of practitioners, availability of expert instruction, and access to the retreats or intensives that most serious practitioners attest are important to their growth.

Quasi-formal engagement involves learning meditation from books, or DVDs, or academic classrooms where practices are, almost necessarily to a significant degree, extricated from traditions. Non-formal engagement involves the broader array of practices that may be construed as contemplative, including sports, arts, and walks along the beach, but may not be necessarily approached with contemplative intention, nor generally involve contemplative-based theoretical models (e.g., models of mind, how transcendence is invoked within the discipline, and development over time). The point is not to privilege one approach over another, but rather to distinguish between the many possibilities available so that students and faculty can forge meaningful, diverse, and manageable pathways. And while engagement in some form of a formal/non-formal continuum is encouraged, this is not to deny the possibility that any given student may benefit significantly from quasi-formal practice. Nor is it to deny that institutions in vicinities where formal practice resources are not as readily available may need to rely more heavily on quasi-formal instruction, in which case instruction could nonetheless be inspired or informed by formal approaches. Most important is that students are exposed to as broad a vision of practice as possible, one that is both horizontally flexible in the individual choices it provides, yet vertically deep in its traditional grounding.

Let us examine the range of integral development that might extend from this approach.

Benefits of an Integral Approach to First-Person Pedagogy

Three general categories of benefits extend from the integral framework for first-person pedagogy presented above. The first has to do with what might be termed "integrity of practice." As noted above, engagement with a formal tradition promotes regularity of practice, interaction with a contemplative community, access to expert instruction and advanced programs. Also inherent in this framework is the cultivation of rich connections between first-person experience and third-person intellectual connections, what I have described as "integral threads" (Sarath, 2010), that are woven between inner experience and the various kinds of analyses—for example, mechanics of practice, nature of mind, cultural connections, developmental trajectories, etc.—available in many meditation lineages.

When this terrain is broached in the context of tradition-specific contemplative affiliation, there is an interior, organic link between direct, first-person transcendent experience, due to its richly meaningful and transformational nature, that instills entirely new kinds of third-person intellectual connections. When, in other words, students experience the noetic depth that Alfred Lord Tennyson describes as the "clearest of the clearest, the surest of the surest" (Alexander, 1990, p. 313), a powerful bond, and corresponding receptivity, is established with the many theoretical, cultural, and historical aspects of the framework within which that experience is invoked.

Here the importance of a conceptual foundation to contemplative development cannot be over-emphasized. Inner experience and outer understanding are not separate realms of growth, but co-evolutionary aspects of contemplative evolution. Wilber (2006) emphasizes that even though it is possible to invoke peak episodes—"states"—of higher levels of development, these will be understood only through the lens of one's present stage. States, then, are fleeting, temporary experiences in integral lexicon, while "stages" are enduring structures of growth. And while new conceptual insights unfold with new stages of development, grounding in a conceptual framework enables levels of meaning, clarity, and breadth of understanding that are not possible otherwise. It is one thing to invoke higher states from a conceptually neutral perspective, or, say, a materialist standpoint and interpret them as the result of particular kinds of neurological firing; it is quite another to understand them from a non-dual integral perspective as attunement with the ground of all Being, of all Creation. We will later consider empirical and theoretical support for the latter, integral interpretation. It is even possible that peak episodes without proper conceptual understanding may be confusing, as in the luminous perceptual phenomena that might accompany causal experience, or the extraordinary oneness of non-duality (Wilber, 2006).

A second kind of benefit stemming from integral first-person contemplative pedagogy has to do with enhanced abilities to navigate pathways across the contemporary spiritual landscape. Key here is the interplay of tradition-specific and trans-traditional grounding that is inherent in the above formal/quasi-formal/non-formal scheme. Tradition-specific entails engagement with a formal tradition as noted above. Trans-traditional (Forman, 2004) involves forging pathways that draw from diverse contemplative sources. While most individuals will combine the two approaches to some degree, the complicated nature of this process cannot be overemphasized. I believe preparing students for the challenges and opportunities inherent in this melding should be regarded as among the highest priorities for contemplative education, for it entails nothing less than cultivating what might be called a "twenty-first-century spiritual intelligence," for which several defining criteria might be noted.

One is the ability to apprehend the massive diversity of spiritual pathways and perspectives that increasingly characterizes our world with humility, respect, and discernment. One need not look far to find individuals who, cloistered within the confines of a single lineage, remain either largely oblivious to the broader spiritual mosaic, or perhaps prone toward denigrating views of traditions other than their own. At the opposite extreme are contemplative aspirants who succumb to a kind of "spiritual promiscuity," flitting about from one approach to another. Many shallow wells, a Zen proverb reminds us, do not yield water.

When tradition-specific and trans-traditional engagement coexists, a symbiotic framework enables practitioners to avail of both an interior anchor and exterior fluidity. Contemporary thinkers such as Elizabeth Lesser (1999), Robert Forman (2004), and Phillip Goldberg (2010) may offer timely wisdom in advocating grounding in a formal tradition as a basis for broader excursions. The complicated nature of these broader excursions cannot be overstated, however, and I believe it is important to distinguish between two approaches. One is the supplementation of a primary formal practice that is sustained in an intact form (e.g., as learned within a lineage) with one or more secondary practices as one is inclined. A second, and potentially more problematic approach, involves altering or combining practices into hybrid forms. My personal inclination is to regard methodologies for navigating interior realms as delicate, even sacred structures that have evolved over long periods of time and therefore are to be approached in their purest forms. Concerns about modifying these practices or melding them with others are perhaps something akin to those regarding genetic manipulation of the food supply, or other life forms, where exterior technological advances made without corresponding growth of interior awareness, and subsequent interior-exterior integration, enable meddling at foundational levels of the biosphere that may result in serious health and environmental consequences that are not immediately apparent.

A third benefit has to do with heightened critical faculties that are cultivated through a thoughtfully formed tradition-specific and trans-traditional interplay. These can be thought of in terms of interior and exterior tools. Regular experiences of pure consciousness/emptiness take awareness to a juncture transcendent of ordinary mental activity and thus step beyond, and directly witness the subtlest dimensions of mind in which the seeds for belief and ideology are planted and take hold. In no way does this ensure such practitioners will be free from conditioned attachments and possible dogmatic interpretations. However, when complemented with the outer tools inherent in trans-traditional exposure, the conditions for critical awareness are maximized, for now tradition-specific precepts are juxtaposed with their trans-traditional counterparts. As these bump up against one another, the fluidity of inner experience and the stability of reason work together to promote mindful scrutiny that, depending upon intention and commitment to critical discernment, may be directed equally to one's own tendencies as it is to outer phenomena.

The tradition-specific/trans-traditional interplay also has the capacity to contribute to the enrichment of the conceptual landscape. For example, students engaged in a Vedantic path and encountering its tradition-specific developmental scheme will find considerable compatibility between its higher-stage progression from *turyatit chetana* to *bhagavad chetana* to *brahmi chetana* and, respectively, the subtle, causal, and non-dual stages delineated in integral literature (Wilber, 2000, 2006) as manifesting across traditions. Elsewhere (Sarath, 2013) I suggest that this and other kinds of integral conceptual terrain may comprise the basis for a contemplative education core curriculum.

This core model need not succumb to the rigidity that plagues conventional approaches to core curricular requirements and, in fact, could boast formidable flexibility and currency while still covering baseline terrain for which, in my view, the integral synthesis excels as a primary source. And because this integral terrain would include a robust non-dual component, whatever exposure to this account of wholeness would be gained from formal engagement would be complemented, and reified, through the trans-traditional grounding accessed in the integral core. This would lend significant support to not only the expanded curricular pathways but also the new culture of contemplative education that characterize the integral stage.

Let us now turn to the realm of second-person contemplative pedagogy as a further gateway to the non-dual, integral spectrum.

Second-Person Contemplative Pedagogy: Gateway to an Integral Paradigm

Second-person reality is that which arises and is experienced through the interaction between individuals. This may pertain to two people in relationship, interactions within communities, social movements, and humanity at large. While second-person approaches have only recently begun to enter contemplative education discourse (Bache, 2008, also see Gunnlaugson and Gozawa in this volume), prominent among its practical applications include Bohmian dialogue (Bohm, 2004) and related modes of interpersonal communication that foster heightened listening and empathy skills and an alternative to conventional classroom discourse (Travers, 2010). The creative arts also offer promising formats for second-person engagement, with the collective improvisatory foundations of jazz—a key feature of the above-mentioned BFAJCS curriculum—a prime example. Inherent in this pedagogical model are both linear and nonlinear aspects of second-person experience. Linear interaction involves the often-intensive information exchange (e.g., musical ideas and responses) that comprises collective improvisation, nonlinear the experience improvisers often report of merging within a collective, intersubjective field. These modes of interaction are not confined to musical creativity and may manifest in any collective format.

The significance of the intersubjective domain to new pedagogical and conceptual horizons for contemplative education is underscored by both corresponding empirical research and theoretical work. Beginning with the empirical: While materialist accounts of consciousness as reducible (Churchland, 1998; Dennett, 1991) or epiphenomenal (Damasio, 2010; Searle, 1997) to a physical substrate tend to prevail in academic science and philosophy circles, intersubjectivity research, along with a broader slate of findings that strongly suggest the existence of physically transcendent and non-local dimensions of mind (Goswami,1993; Jahn & Dunne, 1987; Mason, 2007; Mayer, 2007; Nelson, 2002; Radin, 2006; Sharma & Clark, 1998), call for a far more expansive understanding. Among the more provocative of these findings are those that support the idea of rebirth, or reincarnation, and other manifestations of discarnate consciousness conducted at the Division of Perceptual Studies at the University of Virginia Medical School (Kelly, 2007), that mind and matter are interactive (Radin, 2006; Tiller, 2007), and of the existence of, and possibility to communicate, with spirit intelligences/entities by Gary Schwartz (2010) at the University of Arizona.

Of perhaps most immediate relevance to contemplatives and the emergent second-person aspect of contemplative education is the idea of a collective, field aspect of consciousness (MacTaggart, 2007; Sheldrake, 2009), and this field may be enlivened through collective meditation practice to promote harmonizing effects on the environment such as reductions in traffic accidents, violence, and hospital admissions (Mason, 2007; Sharma & Clarke, 1998). Lynn McTaggart (2007) has reported on research suggestive of links between intersubjective consciousness and weather patterns. While this kind of research is in its infancy, it is difficult to imagine a more promising or important contribution of contemplative studies—one that perhaps many contemplatives have scarcely imagined—than the possibility that meditation when practiced in large groups (the projects studied involved several thousand) can radiate coherence in a large metropolitan area and possibly beyond. The idea that students could be trained to participate in these groups would bring an entirely new dimension to the increasingly popular idea of "service learning," where students gain credit for community engagement as part of their education.

Theoretical work also suggests that the second-person realm may be an important gateway to new conceptual terrain. Christian de Quincey (2005), for example, argues that the collective dimension of mind is not epiphenomenal to individual consciousness, but in fact ontologically foundational to it. In other words, intersubjective mind is not strictly an emergent phenomenon, but a more differentiated stratum of cosmic intelligence that, while co-evolving with individual mind, underlies individuality in the broader scheme of creation. At which point, a contemporary vision of intersubjectivity aligns with, and thus yields connections to, traditional non-dual visions of wholeness.

An integral perspective promotes critical investigation of these ideas by not only scrutinizing them at face value but also by situating them and their competitors within their respective worldviews. While it is difficult to ignore the sheer volume of empirical findings that issue near-fatal challenges to materialism, I would suggest that of equal or greater concern regarding the materialist worldview are its narrow critical horizons, in which anomalous phenomena are either ignored or categorically dismissed (Bache, 2008; Radin, 2006). As Kuhn (1962) reminds us regarding the evolution of science, anomalies are often the primary catalysts for progress and innovation across fields. While the criteria mentioned above in support of a non-dual, integral worldview may stretch the horizons of many conventional educators, and even perhaps more than a few contemplative pedagogues, the point is not that this perspective be blindly embraced but rather mindfully and critically examined through the very openness to paradigmatically challenging possibilities that has always characterized cutting-edge breakthroughs. Here is where the above-mentioned critical tools inherent in the integral framework (integrity of practice and inner experience/self-awareness, tradition-specific/trans-traditional interplay, empirical findings, theoretical coherence) may enable a uniquely productive conversation to transpire in the twenty-first-century academy.

This kind of inquiry, moreover, need not be approached as a quest to delineate a single, static account that holds from here 'til eternity, but rather as the mindful, critical construction of a provisional conceptual platform from which current practices and assumptions are continually considered, and from which future explorations may also be launched. If the platform is scrutinized in an ongoing basis in terms of its coherence, richness, meaningfulness, as well as compatibility with as wide a range as possible of inner experience and outer perspectives (e.g., empirical grounding, theoretical support), then the prospects for dogmatic, exclusive interpretations are significantly reduced. One might argue, moreover, that evasion of this inquiry in deference to what at first glance appears to be a more neutral, or ambiguous worldview, may be as problematic as the blind acceptance of an explicit cosmic narrative. Both represent a form of clinging that poses limitations to contemplative growth. Given the extent to which contemplative education has been influenced by Buddhist thought, a primary and highly relevant example of this may be found in the pre-integral Buddhism, or what Wilber (2006) calls "Boomeritus Buddhism," that often prevails in contemporary spiritual circles.

Among the features of this orientation is an overarching subordination of conceptual understanding of the nature referred to above, within which a kind of default misinterpretation of the Buddhist doctrine of "annata," or no-self, is often presumed. Correctly construed, annata denotes the illusory nature of the egoic or personal self, an aspect of consciousness that rests atop a transcendent or eternal Self as does a wave atop an infinitely vast ocean (Dalal & Aurobindo, 2001; Govinda, 1969) and dissolves into that ocean through contemplative practice and growth. This notion is not unique to Buddhism and in fact is evident in much spiritual thought. Annata misunderstood, however, categorically rejects transcendent dimensions of consciousness, and thus reality, altogether. Correlations with materialist science, which as noted above also rejects notions of transcendent, interior dimensions of consciousness and reality, are readily invited through the erroneous understanding. Accordingly, proclamations as made by Sam Harris (2005) and Owen Flannagan (2002) to the effect that, among the world's religions, Buddhism is uniquely aligned with science in its disavowal of transcendent domains of consciousness in a single-stroke privilege not only a sadly impoverished account of Buddhism, but also an extremist account of science, or "scientism." With precisely this misguided perspective in mind, Wilber (2006) sets the record straight when he characterizes the correct and more expansive conception of consciousness as "no-self/Self" (p. 111), at once satisfying the emphasis on relativistic dissolution that is consistent with the narrower interpretation of annata while also situating it within the transcendent depth of the more expansive and authentic understanding.

In no way is this to question the richness of Buddhist thought and practice, but simply to suggest that, as any field, it is susceptible to paradigmatically divergent approaches, and if the field of contemplative education is to progress, these tendencies must be critically examined. It may be that, while Buddhist voices have been dominant in prior stages of contemplative education, those that assume prominence in coming years will be from a wider range of lineages, including those—such as Vedantic, Daoism, Abrahamic mystical paths (contemplative Christian, Islamic, Judaic), and indigenous traditions—with more explicit cosmic narratives prevailing in their respective discourses that give the notion of non-duality greater shape.

Closing Thoughts

Just as contemplative educators are able to examine the conventional educational paradigm, whose boundaries they extend with enhanced critical faculties, an integral perspective in turn extends the boundaries, and promotes enhanced critical examination, of contemplative education. Put another way, outreach—the attention devoted to advocating and forging pathways for this work to advance in the academy—must be complemented by "inreach," where contemplative pedagogues closely examine their own patterns and assumptions that guide this work, if the field is to progress. Evasion of core questions regarding the nature and integrity of practice, ill-defined theoretical terrain including default worldview and its farther reaches (e.g., cosmic narrative, purpose of existence, etc.), subordination of the second-person realm, and unexamined prominence of a pre-integral Buddhism are among the indicators of weak inreach, or self-critical inquiry, that I have considered in this chapter. An integral perspective not only helps identify these issues, but also reveals them to be part of an overarching matrix of related patterns that constrain contemplative education to a small portion of what it has to contribute.

Little elaboration is needed regarding the challenges that humanity confronts at this extraordinary juncture in history. Accordingly, education needs to be guided by the most expansive vision of the human being, human creative and spiritual potential, the individual-cosmos relationship, as well as the wide-ranging corresponding pedagogical innovations that stem from this vision. For this to happen, the notion of change must shift from horizontal expansion of conventional approaches—as earlier stages of contemplative education might be assessed—to vertical transformation of the paradigm from its conceptual and praxial foundations on up. The integral vision is unmatched as a blueprint to guide this evolutionary thrust.

Notes

1. The ACLS program has since terminated, with similar kinds of fellowships subsequently offered by the Center for the Contemplative Mind in Society, <www.contemplativemind.org>, which facilitated the ACLS project throughout its duration.

2. <www.ciis.edu>, <www.naropa.edu/>, <www.mum.edu/>, <www.jfku.edu/>.

References

Alexander, C., &. Langer, E. (Eds.). (1990). *Higher stages of human development.* New York: Oxford University Press.

Bache, C. (2008). The living classroom: teaching and collective consciousness. Albany, NY: State University of New York.

Bohm, D. (2004). *On Dialogue.* New York: Routledge.

Bruner, J. (1960). The process of education. Cambridge, MA: Harvard University Press.

Bush, M. (2006). Foreword. *Teachers College Record, 108*(9), 721–722.

Chalmers, D. J. (1996). *The Conscious mind: In search of a fundamental theory.* New York: Oxford University Press.

Churchland, P. (1998). Can neurobiology teach us anything about consciousness? In N. Block, O. Flanagan, & G. Guzelder (Eds.), *The nature of consciousness: Philosophical debates* (pp. 127–139). Cambridge, MA: MIT Press.

Dalal, A. S., & Sri Aurobindo (2001). *A greater psychology: The psychological thought of Sri Aurobindo.* New York:Tarcher/Putnam.

Damasio, A. (2010). *Self comes to mind: Constructing the conscious brain.* New York: Pantheon.

de Quincey, C. (2005). *Radical knowing: Understanding consciousness through relationship* Rochester, VT: Park Street.

Dennett, D. (1991). *Consciousness explained.* Boston: Back Bay.

Esbjörn-Hargens, S. (2010). Integral theory in service of enacting integral education: Illustrations from an on-line graduate rogram. In S. Esbjörn-Hargens,

J. Reams, & O. Gunnlaugon (Eds.), *Integral education: New directions for higher learning* (pp. 55–77). Albany, NY: State University of New York Press.

Flannagan, O. (2002). *The problem of the soul.* New York: Basic Books.

Forman, R. (Ed.). (1990). *The problem of pure consciousness.* New York: Oxford University Press.

Forman, R. (2004). *Grassroots spirituality.* Charlottesville, VA: Imprint Academic.

Gardner, H. (1993). *Multiple intelligences: The theory in practice.* New York: Basic Books.

Goldberg, P. (2010). *American Veda: How Indian spirituality changed the West.* New York: Harmony/Random House.

Govinda, Lama Anagorika. (1969). *Foundations of Tibetan Buddhism.* York Beach, ME: Samuel Weisner.

Goswami, Amit. (1993). *The self-aware universe: How consciousness creates the material world.* New York: Tarcher.

Gunnlaugson, O. 2010. Opening up the path of integral education: Reflections on a case study in changing from a holistic to integral college. In S. Esbjörn-Hargens, J. Reams, & O. Gunnlaugson (Eds.), *Integral education: New directions for higher learning* (pp. 303–316). Albany, NY: State University of New York Press.

Harris, S. (2005). *The end of faith: Religion, terror, and the end of reason.* New York: Norton.

Jahn, R., & Dunne, B. (1987). *The margins of reality.* San Diego, CA: Harcourt and Brace.

Kelly, E. F., Kelly, E. W., Crabtree, A., Gauld, A., Grosso, M., & Greyson, B. (2007). *Irreducible mind: Toward a psychology for the 21st century.* Lanham, MD: Rowman and Middlefield.

Kuhn, T. (1962). *The structure of scientific revolutions.* Chicago: University of Chicago.

Lesser, E. (1999). *The new American spirituality: A seeker's guide.* New York: Random House.

MacTaggart, L. (2007). *The intention experiment: Using your thoughts to change your life and the world.* New York: Free Press.

Maslow, A. (1971). *The farther reaches of human nature.* New York: Penguin.

Mason, L., Patterson, R. P., Radin, D., & Dean I. (2007). Exploratory study: The random number generator and group meditation. J*ournal of Scientific Exploration, 21*, 295–317.

Mayer, E. (2007). *Extraordinary knowing: Science, skepticism, and the inexplicable powers of the human mind.* New York: Bantam.

Nelson, R. D. (2002). Coherent consciousness and reduced randomness: Correlations on September 11, 2001. *Journal of Scientific Exploration. 16*(4), 549–570.

Radin, D. (2006). *Entangled minds: Extrasensory experiences in quantum reality.* New York: Paraview Pocket Books.

Sarath, E. W. (2003). Meditation in higher education: The next wave? *Innovative Higher Education.* (*27*), 215–34.

Sarath, E. W. (2006). Meditation, creativity, and consciousness: Charting future terrain within higher education. *Teachers College Record, 108*(9), 1816–1841.

Sarath, E. W. (2010b). Jazz, creativity, and consciousness: Blueprint for integral education. In S. Esbjörn-Hargens, J. Reams, & O. Gunnlaugson (Eds.), *Integral education: New directions for higher learning* (pp. 169–184). Albany, NY: State University of New York Press.

Sarath, E. W. (2013). *Improvisation, creativity, and consciousness: Jazz as integral template for music, education, and society*. Albany, NY: State University of New York Press.

Schwartz, G. (2010). *The sacred promise: How science is discovering spirit's collaboration with us in our daily lives*. New York: Simon and Schuster/Atria Books.

Searle, J. (1997). *The mystery of consciousness*. New York: The New York Review of Books.

Sharma, H., & Clark, C. (1998). *Contemporary Ayurveda*. Philadelphia, PA: Churchill Livingstone.

Sheldrake, R. (2009). *Morphic resonance: The nature of formative causation*. Bethel, ME: Park Street Press.

Tiller, W. (2007). Psychoenergetic Science: A second Copernican-scale revolution. Walnut Creek, CA: Pavior Publications.

Travis, M. (2010). "Council: Initiating a Contemplative Conversation in the Classroom." Talk delivered at Contemplative Education conference, Amherst College.

Whitehead, A. N. (1929). *The aims of education*. New York: Free Press.

Wilber, K. (2000). *The collected works of Ken Wilber, vol. 4: Integral psychology, transformation of consciousness, selected essays*. Boston: Shambala.

Wilber, K. (2006). *Integral spirituality: A startling new role for religion in the modern and postmodern world*. Boston: Integral Books/Shambala.

Wilber, K., Patten, T., Leonard, A., & Morelli, M. (2008). *Integral life practice: A 21st century blueprint for physical health, emotional balance, mental clarity, and spiritual awakening*. Boston: Integral Books/Shambhala.

22

An Inquiry into the Field Dynamics of Collective Learning

Chris Bache in conversation with Olen Gunnlaugson

OG: Through the process of editing our book, our editorial team discovered an unexpected contribution that we also happen to perceive to be quite significant as an emerging development within the greater field of contemplative studies. The unexpected element it turns out is deeply related to your work. Essentially we have identified the intersubjective dimension of contemplative practice in the classroom as a key emergent area of scholarship. Currently there are four chapters that build on this theme and when the dots joined for us, the next step was to connect with a scholar-practitioner in this area. So your name naturally came up.

Back in 2001 when I was working with dialogue groups at a progressive college in Sweden, I first encountered your work on morphic fields in the classroom in your book, *Dark Night, Early Dawn: Steps to a Deep Ecology of Mind* (Bache, 2000). Here's a passage from an article that you wrote called "High Octane Learning" (Bache, 2004/2005) that continues to resonate for me.

> *I believe that an important ingredient contributing to igniting these powerful transformational experiences has to do with the clarity, strength, and focus of the psychic field that surrounds and saturates the learning environment. This includes both the teacher's personal field (reflecting the depth of his or her spiritual practice) and the field created by all the students in the course. The stronger, clearer, and better focused the mental field of a given learning circle, the more likely it is that skillful*

> *inquiry will spark deep changes in people's lives. This is so true in my experience that I have become convinced that the intellectual exchange of ideas is but a vehicle for a more fundamental energetic exchange that takes place "underneath" the verbal dialogue.*
>
> *Everyone knows that words not supported by the energy of personal experience carry much less power to influence others than words which are. This happens, I think, not because the words themselves are different or are delivered with a different inflection, but because when people speak, they unleash a tangible but invisible power into the space around them. This power comes ultimately from our experience and from the energetic access that our experience has created in us. Our words float on this power, like a canoe floating on a rushing stream. Moreover, it is not just the speaker's power that is important here but the power of the mental-emotional-spiritual field of the entire group. . . . In the playful dance of course content and energetic resonance, ordinary learning sometimes crosses a threshold to become Great Learning. (pp. 35–36)*

As you've mentioned in your recent book *The Living Classroom: Teaching and Collective Consciousness* (Bache, 2008), it was chapter 7, "Teaching in the Sacred Mind" from *Dark Night*, that inspired you to go further into this subject.

I was wondering if you could begin our conversation today by sharing some of your more recent thoughts about this collective dimension of learning that you have been pursuing as a central aspect of your classroom teaching practice. And in doing this, can you say a bit more about your experiences with bringing classrooms across this threshold of Great Learning you speak of in the above passage.

CB: It is deeply encouraging that so many scholars are working in this field today. In *The Living Classroom* I am trying to understand two basic phenomena. The first is the powerful energetic resonance that sometimes springs up between teachers and students when we come together to learn—a direct energetic exchange that takes place at the "subtle level" of *ch'i* or *prana*. When we work with our students, what we *are* enters the circle, the subtle energetic self that lies beneath our conscious self. The deeper our spiritual practice—and we may be speaking of years or lifetimes here—the more likely it is that our presence will trigger a deeper response in our students. Our lives activate something in their lives through some form of energetic resonance.

This energetic exchange is always taking place whether we are lecturing, listening attentively, or simply walking into the room. But the effect becomes stronger, I think, if we meditate together, when we let the mental chatter and social face fall away and enter a state of present awareness. In or outside the context of meditation, this resonance occurs not because the instructor is *trying* to have a specific impact on their students but simply because it is a natural tendency of consciousness to establish these connections. As Steven Strogatz (2003) said in his book, *Sync: The Emerging Science of Spontaneous Order*, "For reasons we don't yet understand, the tendency to synchronize is one of the most pervasive drives in the universe, extending from atoms to animals, from people to planets" (p. 14). States of awareness are contagious. Clarity spontaneously triggers clarity. This can happen even if a student is unprepared for the influence, caught unaware by it, or even consciously resisting it.

The second phenomenon I'm exploring is *group fields*. From my perspective, collective fields of consciousness are formed whenever people work together in a focused manner on intellectually and emotionally engaging projects over a sustained period of time. They have nothing to do with meditation *per se*, but meditation seems to augment these fields. Usually these fields are so subtle that their influence goes undetected, but under certain circumstances they can become activated in ways that increase their influence in the room. It is as though after years of being dormant, they reach a critical threshold after which their presence begins to be felt.

My understanding is that in a supportive setting, which includes the use of skillful pedagogical strategies, these fields grow stronger year by year, and that they are more enduring than the individual students who contribute to them. They are true structures in the collective mind, standing whirlpools of energy within the local collective psyche that reflect our past collective actions and influence our present collective efforts.

For a simple metaphor, imagine that everyone in the classroom is standing in a large, calm swimming pool. Every motion each person makes sends ripples out that touch everyone else in the pool. Now imagine that everyone were to move in such a way that the ripples they created begin to reinforce each other. Instead of fragmenting and dissipating their energy, the waves begin to combine, become stronger, and generate stable patterns of influence. Those in the pool would begin to feel themselves gently rocked by the rhythmic energy of their collective collaboration.

The net effect of these two principles—*energetic resonance and group fields*—is that when an instructor works intensely with his or her students, especially if one does contemplative practice with them, there are many forces at play behind the scenes. The depth of the instructor's spiritual practice sometimes triggers a deeply felt transmission of insight underneath a verbal exchange. By "transmission" I mean something like the formal concept of *lung* in Tibetan Buddhism—the transfer of the energetic essence of an insight or experience. Second, the awakening of the individual is also influenced by the collective consciousness of the group field. I see this field as having at least two layers. The *class field* or *class mind* is the energetic field created by the students who are taking the course *this* semester. The larger *course field* is the energetic field that has been created by all the students who have ever taken this course with this particular instructor. The class field is like the outer cambium ring of a tree while the course field is the entire trunk integrating all the rings from previous years.

In the non-dual spiritual traditions, Mind is a preexisting reality that always and everywhere exists. Because it is the innate reality, the omnipresent nature of Mind can make itself felt at any point. The patterns of synergistic resonance and collective fields that emerge in a meditating classroom are surface ripples on the pond of Mind, more evidence of an underlying wholeness that lies beneath our conscious perception.

OG: Okay, stepping back again, I have a number of questions. I will likely return to some of these later on in the interview, but for now three main points come to mind. The first is this: can you say a bit more about how you might work with these classroom field dynamics of consciousness in the classes that you teach? The second place for inquiry is how do you relate this to the notion of instructor presence? In other words, if presence is tangible, felt, and can be cultivated and deepened, how do you work with this more conscious or experiential aspect? The third point for now that I'm curious about is this: have you experimented with meditating with your students in the fashion you describe to generate synergistic resonances? If so, can you share something about this experience? I'm curious how you accommodate, support, or encourage this particular emergence in your classroom.

CB: I haven't actually done a lot of contemplative practice with my students. I've meditated with them in a few of my courses—sometimes for one week and occasionally for an entire semester—but on the whole it hasn't been a major focus of my work as an academic. I've taught *about* contemplative practice much more than I've actually done it with my students. In this respect I represent someone whose career straddles the exciting transition we're making toward integrating contemplative practice more deeply into our curricula. Universities, especially state universities, were not as receptive to these initiatives when I began my career in 1978.

The story I tell in *The Living Classroom* is essentially the story of a conventional professor of religious studies who was doing very intense spiritual practice in his private life. I kept these two sides of my life separate, or I tried to, but as my spiritual practice deepened over the years, I found that my students were being affected by my practice without my intending it. Slowly I learned that when one opens to the ocean of consciousness, the *depth* and *breadth* of that ocean unfold together. The more completely I allowed myself to relax into the great depth of being, the more it appeared to activate an innate intelligence that lives in the great breadth of life, touching those around me in sometimes striking ways. Even now, after so many years, I find it difficult to find the words to express the delicacy, the subtlety, the power, and the extraordinary beauty of the process.

These are mysterious and deeply intimate dynamics that developed slowly and that cannot be distilled into a set of "techniques" to leverage change in the classroom. It took me years to acknowledge what was happening, years more to understand it, and still more to learn how to work with it. We do not control these dynamics. We are carried by them, led by them, drawn by them into unanticipated intimacies of soul. When we become transparent to the deeper currents of life, we are used by life in ways that evoke stunned respect and watchful humility.

My spiritual practice appeared to be changing my constitution in ways that made me into something of a lightning rod for my students, triggering a variety of psychological and spiritual openings in some of their lives. Again, I want to emphasize that it was not my intention to elicit these responses; in fact, I often worried about what was happening and sometimes tried to rein them in.

Underneath the cognitive exchange of ideas, a sometimes fierce but always compassionate energetic engagement was taking place spontaneously and without my conscious direction. A knowing sometimes came through my lectures that drew from the personal histories of my students, beyond anything "I" could possibly account for, and spoke to those histories. If I allowed myself to step aside, insights would sometimes rise that were composites of their psyches and mine. When we came together as older and younger learners, the life that lives in them and the life that lives in me, being ultimately the same life, seemed to draw together to awaken both of us to the deeper potential residing in our juxtaposition. Sparks of the kind that open destinies and ignite new vistas of understanding sometimes graced us.

As this process continued to evolve, I began to realize that it was being driven not just by my deepening spiritual practice but also by certain *collective* dynamics that were beginning to emerge in the room. Gradually I began to recognize that something like Rupert Sheldrake's morphic fields were involved, that my courses were generating *fields of consciousness* that were influencing how individual students were learning in them. These group fields were influencing how quickly students were understanding new concepts and how deeply these ideas were touching their lives. Moreover, as I already mentioned, these fields appeared to be growing stronger the longer I taught.

This represented such a radical shift in perspective that it was disorienting. To make sense of what I was witnessing in my classroom required that I rethink all my assumptions about how mind works in groups. It demanded a new starting point, a new model of consciousness, and a new set of pedagogical strategies.

OG: Can you say more about this model of consciousness and can you elaborate on the pedagogical strategies you're referring to here?

CB: I think we're witnessing a shift from what we might call the *paradigm of the private mind* to the *paradigm of the interconnected mind*. The psychology that emerged in the modern era under the influence of Newtonian physics was a deeply "atomistic psychology," by which I mean it emphasized individual consciousness. Newtonian physics saw the universe composed of fundamentally separate, irreducible bits—atoms—and psychology, with a few exceptions, similarly tended to view consciousness as composed of ontologically discrete bits—private minds. This followed seventeen hundred years of Christian theology emphasizing *individual* salvation, picturing souls as so many spiritual BBs rolling around on God's table.

Since the quantum revolution in the 1930s, however, an overarching theme of scientific discovery has been interconnectivity. Everywhere we turn, we are finding that systems we had previously thought were separate from each other are actually interconnected. The effects of quantum entanglement, once thought to be restricted to the subatomic realm, "scale up" into the macroscopic world. Chaos theory has shown us that the world we live in is awash with holographic patterns and fractal iteration. The recurring lessons seem to be that *life's parts cannot be meaningfully isolated from the systems in which they are embedded.* The postulate of existential separation is at odds with practically everything we are learning about how nature actually works.

Accordingly, we are beginning to shift psychological paradigms to what some have called a *quantum psychology* emphasizing nonlocal connectivity and fields of consciousness. Such a paradigm does not negate our individuality any more than quantum physics negates atomic reality, but it re-contextualizes it within the complementary truth of interdependence. We are recognizing more clearly the psyche's penchant for connectivity and the fractal, holographic quality of consciousness—the way that insights rise from collective depths, crystallizing in our individual minds but not necessarily originating there. *Consciousness is a collaborative affair from the very start*; our minds are always and continuously attuned to each other at subtle levels. These ideas are not new to spiritual thought, of course, but they are jarring to Newtonian-Cartesian thinking, which still constitutes the bedrock of academic thinking today.

In *The Living Classroom*, I outline a variety of strategies for working with fields of consciousness, dividing them into four categories: (1) preparing the field, (2) nourishing the field, (3) visualization exercises, and (4) closing the field. There is also a chapter on "café conversations" drawing from the work of Juanita Brown. These strategies do not "make sense" in the context of the old paradigm, but they make "perfect sense" inside the new paradigm of interconnectivity.

Because fields of consciousness are intentional fields, the strategies for working with them begin with refining and focusing intention—both the instructor's intention as convener of the course and the intention of the students who are taking it. Every stage of the course from drafting the syllabus, to "broadcasting" our goals for the course in meditation *before* the course begins, to negotiating the parry and thrust of authentic engagement once it begins, to skillfully closing the course at the semester's end is carried out with a shamanic-like recognition of the power of thought and appreciation of the underlying collective currents pulsing in the group. Visualization exercises can be crafted to support each phase of course field's development. Class discussions can be structured to more effectively mobilize the collective knowledge in the room, harvesting and cross-fertilizing student input to bring forward new levels of collective insight.

OG: In working with the fields of consciousness outside of classroom time, I'm wondering if you could elaborate on how this has affected your disposition as a lecturer or facilitator inside the classroom. In what ways has this approach shifted or changed the way you teach or lecture? For example, has your awareness of fields of consciousness altered the way in which you pay attention while lecturing or what you listen for when speaking and listening with your students? I'm not talking about strategies necessarily; rather, I'm curious about how this focus has influenced your way of being as an instructor or the way in which you pay attention to your students and the group field amidst a lecture or teaching session. Another way to think about this: as a meditator pays attention distinctively in meditation practice, based on meditative instructions, injunctions, training and practice, would you say this work has a kind of parallel in the classroom in terms of how you aspire to bring your classroom across the threshold of great learning?

CB: Yes, understanding fields of consciousness has deeply changed how I approach teaching. In addition to the specific strategies mentioned above, I find that I've adopted a different "inner gestalt" or inner posture.

As in meditation or shamanic practice when the shells of one's life fall away to reveal the inherent wholeness of life and the crystalline sinews that make that wholeness a living entity, the same thing happens in group settings. When one's mind stands naked before other minds, suspended in a moment in which all possibilities are present, there sometimes crackles the living pulse of a larger intelligence—attuned to this particular group of students but with roots extending back in time and out in space. When one has been touched by this intelligence even a few times, one naturally develops a respect for the awesome potential that is present wherever and whenever people gather in shared work. *It is as though by gathering together physically, we concentrate an extended network of energy, and once this network is concentrated, it comes alive in a more potent way.*

When I work with a group, therefore, I try to bring a sensitivity to this living intelligence that is everywhere bubbling underneath us, squeezing through the crevices and cracks created by people's needs or curiosity or angst. I try to listen attentively to "random" comments, to interrupt my normal patter to create the space to let a deeper inspiration come through. When a student asks a question, instead of giving the first answer that pops into my mind, I try to stop and hold the silence, waiting for a second or third answer to rise, an answer that often turns out to be more attuned to the hidden needs in the room, more informed by the histories no one has talked about.

I fail in this constantly, of course, for ego always thinks it knows best, especially the academic ego; but if I can remember to step aside and listen, the magic sometimes happens—the magic of a non-local intelligence tapping into hidden resources, siphoning off hidden pains.

To teach in this manner requires an inner as well as outer preparation. The outer preparation is the usual preparation of our course material. The inner preparation is more subtle and requires, I suspect, some practice of inner alignment—Yoga, Tai ch'i, or meditation—some centering practice. To teach in this manner is to teach *as* a spiritual practice, or as an extension of spiritual practice.

I hope this does not sound like a cliché; I don't know how else to describe it. Just as in meditation one pays attention to whatever rises in one's awareness, in this mode of teaching one creates openings to listen to what is rising from the depths of the moment. These openings may be brief, interrupting one's habitual thought stream when a student asks a question, or more systematic, as in collecting candid student feedback on an exercise.

At the center of everything one might "do" in specific situations is a certain posture—a *posture of collaboration* with unseen forces, of receptivity to an innate intelligence in the room, of respect for the larger whole one is *already* part of. It is a gestalt of remembering that however much preparation one has put into one's lectures, the living knowledge in the room is larger still. It is a posture of allowing oneself to become transparent (*sunyata*) to this deeper creativity.

The syllabus has called together a specific set of students to focus on a specific set of issues. In this scripted context, the unscripted can take the discussion in unanticipated directions, touch hearts in unanticipated ways, and set in motion unanticipated results. Thus, the "inner gestalt" is a delicate mix of careful preparation of content and surrender to the magic of circumstance.

OG: Returning to one of our overarching themes of the collective dimension of learning, I'm wondering if you could talk about how you view your students in the context of this experience. Are there ever moments where you approach them as co-participants in co-enacting these field dynamics? For instance, you mentioned the café conversations which you write about in *The Living Classroom*. I'm wondering to what extent these and possibly other processes you introduce encourage this more *intentional, group field-receptive, collectively intelligent* mode of participation.

I can't help but be curious what happens when your students start to become more attuned to this more profound order of collective learning that you are intending to bring forth? Do you ever have students ask you about this in or outside class? And if so, do you utilize some of the distinctions and language you write about in *The Living Classroom*? I can't help but imagine there being deciding moments arising from time to time in your lecture say, when there's an opportunity to open the learning field in the classroom for *a more participatory co-enactment* versus proceeding in a more monologic fashion? That said, I'm not simply talking about a break-out group or a lecture turning suddenly into a discussion. What's coming to mind is a kind of subtle shift in the group field that's felt in the room, one that prompts a deeper order quality of responses from you and your students.

CB: Again, I want to emphasize that these fields are not things that one can turn on or off with a strategy or technique. They are organic phenomena that develop slowly over time, a residual effect of the quality of engagement that has taken place around specific questions over months and years. I have always viewed my students as co-participants in these fields as it is primarily their learning that generates them. For a variety of reasons, however, I have been slow to invite them to *consciously* participate in facilitating them.

Most of the courses I taught at Youngstown State University [YSU] were not directly about consciousness, let alone something as subtle as the dynamics of collective consciousness. So for a long time I felt that I could not invite my students to participate in the deliberate empowering of their own fields.

This was simply not part of our course content. Even so, the effects of these fields were clearly being felt by students in the room. As one student I quote in *The Living Classroom* put it:

> All of us who have been in your classes feel a deep connection to one another. We don't know what it is. We only know that it is there. All that I know is that I have felt something binding us all together. I remember things going on around me in class with the other students. We were sensitive to each other's thoughts and feelings. . . . I always wondered if you knew what was going on because you never said a thing in class! Strange things were happening. The students closest to you expected them to happen. Were we crazy? "What the hell is going on?" we questioned. Imagine all of this taking place on a college campus. A college class that wasn't only a class, it was a community semester after semester. (Bache, 2008, p. 44)

After years of observing these fields and developing strategies for working with them privately in ways that did *not* require student participation, I published a chapter on them in *Dark Night, Early Dawn* (2000). Just as that book was coming out, I accepted a position as Director of Transformative Learning at the Institute of Noetic Studies from 2000 to 2002. It was here that I met Meg Wheatley and Juanita Brown and learned about the pioneering work being done in the dialogic community. This community uses skillful conversation to deliberately facilitate the emergence of the same collective intelligence that had been surfacing spontaneously in my classroom.

I was so taken with Juanita Brown's work with café conversations (later published in *The World Café*, 2005) that I collaborated with her to integrate café conversations into the Institute of Noetic Sciences's (IONS) 2001 national conference. At that conference twelve hundred participants went into small group conversations after each keynote speaker. It was an exciting protocol that elicited very creative responses from the floor.

When I returned to YSU in 2002, I began to incorporate some of Juanita's café protocols into my courses in what I called "Friday Cafés." (I describe these cafés in *The Living Classroom*, chapter 5.) I also began to discuss these collective dynamics more openly with my students and in some upper division courses began to invite them to participate in visualization exercises designed to consciously strengthen these fields, and then close them at the end of the semester. When *The Living Classroom* was published in 2008, I began offering seminars and workshops on this material. Fields had become the curriculum, allowing me to invite more public participation in the strategies I was exploring.

I currently view collective fields as a valuable and largely untapped resource for educators. The more we understand the subtle dynamics of group fields and the more we invite our students to consciously participate in these fields, the stronger and more empowered our teaching will become. Like the physicians who first washed their hands to reduce infections while most of their colleagues scoffed at the idea of "invisible germs," the teacher who consciously works with fields today is simply acknowledging something invisible but causally active in the room.

OG: To close our inquiry, I'm wondering if you could share a bit more of your post-TLC thinking on this subject. Has your thinking on this topic changed or shifted in any respect, even if in a subtle way?

CB: As I have been giving talks and workshops on *The Living Classroom*, I have been struck by how receptive people have been to these ideas and how deeply they resonate with their own life experience. Thousands of people around the country have been experiencing the same dynamics surfacing in their community groups, reading groups, and board meetings.

When I first struggled to articulate these concepts and speak about them publically in 1995, I felt like a heretic, barely able to say the words. Now, it seems that everywhere I go I am met by people who are coming to similar conclusions, either through their own experience or because of new trends in scientific research. There is a massive groundswell taking place around these ideas.

This groundswell is exactly what we would expect to observe when a paradigm shift takes place. This is not simply a new theory or pedagogical methodology. It is a new paradigm, a fundamentally new way of thinking about how the world works, in this case, a revision of our basic assumptions about how consciousness works.

The second observation I would make is more personal. In 2000 I made the decision to take my spiritual practice in a gentler direction. After twenty years of exploring the deep visionary states described in *Dark Night Early Dawn*, I shifted my practice more in the direction of meditation. The work became less shamanic and more contemplative, focused on the rhythms of daily awareness and the naked Presence alive in every moment. Rather than breaking through to new transpersonal domains, the work became the assimilation and integration of territory already explored. With this shift in practice, my energetic system also shifted. Over a period of five years, it slowed down and became calmer. You might say it found its new equilibrium, its new balance point in the world.

With this inner energetic shift, the dynamics of my classroom also shifted. The explosive lightning bolts of existentially attuned insight began to happen less frequently. Rather than spilling through me spontaneously, they now require a more conscious cooperation on my part to occur. The energy still crackles and arrows still hit unseen targets, but now there tends to be a more subtle dance taking place in the room. This shift seems to reflect the fact that the practices I am doing now are less cathartic and do not reach as aggressively into the deep collective psyche as my earlier practices did.

The fact that my classroom is responding to this shift in practice illustrates once again how *sensitive* the fabric of consciousness truly is. We live suspended in a living tissue that is exquisitely subtle and finely tuned. Changes in this tissue do not take place suddenly, but if we watch the shifting patterns that surround us, we can observe an ebb and flow that ultimately reflects our inner state.

I do not know how to balance the relative strength of the two factors we have been discussing: (1) energetic resonance generated by deep spiritual practice, and (2) fields of consciousness augmented through skillful pedagogical means. Both are important.

To use a simple analogy, I think of them as working together like a combustion engine. Fields of collective consciousness, when well choreographed, reach a critical state that is similar to the pressure that builds inside a cylinder. An instructor grounded in deep spiritual practice and transparent to the living intelligence in the room provides a spark that ignites the pressurized fuel. Less spark or less pressure, the result is less impressive. But when these two forces come together in a synergistic coupling, they can generate results that are life changing for our students. When this happens, Great Learning has entered the room.

References

Bache, C. (2000). *Dark night, early dawn: Steps to a deep ecology of mind.* Albany, NY: State University of New York Press.

Bache, C. (2004, November–2005, February). High octane learning. *Shift: At the Frontiers of Consciousness* (5), 35–36. Available at <http://media.noetic.org/uploads/files/s5_sensing.pdf>.

Bache, C. (2008). *The living classroom: Teaching and collective consciousness.* Albany, NY: State University of New York Press.

Strogatz, S. (2003). *Sync: The emerging science of spontaneous order.* New York: Hyperion Books.

Author Biographies

Mara Adelman PhD is an Associate Professor Asian Studies Program and Department of Communication at Seattle University. She teaches a wide range of social interaction courses; including interpersonal, cross-cultural, organizational, and introduction to communication theory. After years of writing about intimate, personal relationships combined with her alarm over the state of everyday distractions, techno-saturation, and pseudo-intimacy; Mara has focused her intellectual life on the study of restorative solitude. She offers her website, www.solitudecourse.com and faculty workshops in the hopes of addressing this neglected refuge in our everyday life.

Chris Bache PhD is *professor emeritus* in the department of Philosophy and Religious Studies at Youngstown State University where he taught for over thirty years in psychology of religion, transpersonal studies, Buddhism, and Eastern religions. He is also adjunct faculty at the California Institute of Integral Studies in San Francisco, and for two years was the Director of Transformative Learning at the Institute of Noetic Sciences in Petaluma, California. An award-winning teacher and international speaker, his work explores the philosophical implications of non-ordinary states of consciousness, especially psychedelic states. He has written a pioneering book in psychedelic philosophy and collective consciousness entitled *Dark Night, Early Dawn* (SUNY, 2000). In addition, he has written *Lifecycles: Reincarnation and the Web of Life*, a comprehensive study of reincarnation and karma in light of contemporary consciousness research. In his book *The Living Classroom* (SUNY, 2008), Chris presents his revolutionary ideas concerning the transpersonal dimensions of teaching. In addition to working with sacred medicines, Chris has been a Buddhist practitioner for many years.

Heesoon Bai PhD is a Professor in the Faculty of Education at Simon Fraser University. She has published widely in academic journals and edited volumes on topics including directions for philosophy of education, teacher education, ecology and environmental education, social responsibility and moral agency, and art education and Zen aesthetics. Professor Bai is active in the renewal and revitalization of Philosophy of Education in Canada and elsewhere. Following Raimondo Panikkar's lead, she understands philosophy's task for today's world to be "to know, to love, and to heal." She brings this "philosophy of philosophy" with her in her research contributions to a wide variety of fields in the area of education. Her most recent collaborative work experiments with a narrative inquiry and re-works one of the most important concepts in my philosophical work: biophilia. Her other research interests include Philosophy of Education, Applied and Comparative Epistemology, Ethics and Moral Education, Ecophilosophy & Ecopsychology, Consciousness Research, and Daoist and Buddhist Philosophies.

Daniel Barbezat PhD is a Professor of Economics at Amherst College. At Amherst he has taught a variety of courses but has specialized in economic history. In 2004, he won the Economic History Association's Jonathan T. Hughes Prize of Excellence in Teaching Economic History. Most recently, Prof. Barbezat has begun work on happiness and economics and the role of introspection and awareness in decision making.

John Eric Baugher is Associate Professor of Sociology at the University of Southern Maine. His areas of teaching and research include the Sociology of Death and Dying, Social Psychology, and Contemplative Pedagogy. He is currently writing a book on how routine encounters with dying persons shape the caring capacities of hospice volunteers in the United States and Germany, and how individuals integrate such experiences into their ongoing narratives of self. His recent publications include "The 'Quiet Revolution' in Care of the Dying" (2012), a chapter in *Inner Peace—Global Impact: Tibetan Buddhism, Leadership and Work*, and "When Grieving Adults Support Grieving Children: Tensions in a Peer Support Bereavement Programme" published in the British journal *Mortality* (2012). Professor Baugher serves on the editorial board for the newly launched *Journal of Contemplative Inquiry* and is an associate editor for *Leading with Spirit, Presence, and Authenticity*, which will be published on Jossey-Bass in 2014.

Richard C. Brown MA is Co-chair and founder of the Department of Contemplative Education at Naropa University. The department adapts wisdom, compassion, and skillful means drawn from Buddhist and holistic traditions to non-sectarian teacher education. After teaching public elementary school, Richard taught seven years at a Buddhist-inspired K–12 in Boulder, Colorado. He has been involved in the formation of several contemplative schools, has helped develop rites of passage programs, and has published a Buddhist view of child and adolescent spiritual development. Richard has written on various areas of contemplative teacher education including mindfulness, emotional awareness, and observation. He has consulted on three continents with educational organizations about how to bring mindfulness and contemplative education to teachers and schools. Most recently, Richard worked with the government of Bhutan as it launched the reform of the country's education system.

Avraham Cohen PhD is Senior Faculty at City University of Seattle (Vancouver, British Columbia site) in the Master's in Counselling Program and currently conducts a private counselling and psychotherapy practice in Vancouver. He has published widely, including peer reviewed journal articles, book chapters, and general articles, especially on the subject of Eastern philosophy and its practice applications in both psychotherapy and classroom settings. Dr. Cohen has presented his work at national as well as international conferences. Dr. Cohen received the 2007–2008 President's Award for Distinguished Contribution to the Discipline of Counselling from the BC Association of Clinical Counsellors. His 2008 article, co-authored with Dr. Heesoon Bai, "Suffering Loves and Needs Company: Buddhist and Daoist Perspectives on the Counsellor as Companion" was awarded the Professional Article of the Year Award by the Canadian Counselling and Psychotherapy Association.

Tom Culham PhD has been working with Heesoon Bai. He is an engineer with a 30-year business career. Currently, he teaches business courses at UBC and run a management consulting business. He believes virtue ethics is the strongest paradigm because it holds that cultivating virtue is a holistic, integrative process involving attention to perception, feeling, imagination, intuition, reasoning, and action. A focal point of his research is the Chinese conception of virtue, which refers to a substantive power that enables human beings to be moral agents enacting what is genuinely good. The research questions he is currently considering are: do studies within disciplines such as neuroscience and cognitive science provide empirical evidence supporting the Chinese Taoist conception of virtue as embodied, substantive, and inherent, and how might this inform virtue education design?

Diana Denton PhD is Associate Professor and Director of Communication, Leadership, and Social Innovation at the University of Waterloo. Diana integrates business and the arts in her work as professor, poet, and organizational consultant. Since 1980 she has maintained a private consulting practice specializing in training, coaching, and consulting in the areas of leadership development, interpersonal and team communication, conflict resolution, and performance management. Diana has facilitated numerous seminars for private, corporate, and educational groups. Her scholarship explores the intrapersonal, interpersonal, and organizational dimensions of communication through interpretive ethnographic and phenomenological inquiry. Diana is also a co-editor of three books: *Spirituality, Action & Pedagogy: Teaching From the Heart* (Peter Lang Publishing, 2004), *Holistic Learning and Spirituality in Education: Breaking New Ground* (SUNY Press, 2005), and *Spirituality, Ethnography, & Teaching: Stories From Within* (Peter Lang Publishing, 2006).

Joanne Gozawa PhD received her doctoral degree in Integral Studies with a concentration in Learning and Change in Human Systems from CIIS in 2000. She has taught at CIIS (Organic Inquiry), the Institute for Transpersonal Psychology, and at Presidio World College. Her experiences in transformative learning and sensitivity to cultural differences have focused her practice on evoking a field that is inclusive and nonjudgmental, *a field of mutuality* that gives groups of diverse participants the safety in which to question their deep assumptions. She has applied her approach to classes in transformative learning and to organizations interested in transforming conflict into collaboration. She hopes to broaden the theoretical ground of transformative learning with her work.

Olen Gunnlaugson PhD is an Assistant Professor in the Management Department at Université Laval. His research interests and teaching include Contemplative Theory and Practice, Complexity and Presencing, Approaches to Leadership, Consciousness Development, Development of Management Skills, Generative Dialogue and Collective Intelligence Approaches to Communication, and Leadership and Executive Coaching. His is an editor of *Integral Education: New Directions for Higher Learning*, published by SUNY Press.

David Kahane PhD is an Associate Professor of Political Science and Vargo Distinguished Teaching Chair at the University of Alberta. Aside from democratic theory and practice, he is interested in what moral and political theory can (and can"t) teach us about how we relate to the suffering of distant strangers.

Alfred W. Kaszniak PhD is a Professor in and head of the Department of Psychology, University of Arizona. His research program is aimed at increasing our understanding of human brain systems involved in both cognition and emotion. Specifically, his laboratory and clinic research currently involves four different, although related, domains of interest: (1) Neuropsychological aspects of aging, (2) Neuropsychological aspects of age-related disorders of the central nervous system, (3) the Neuropsychology of consciousness and self-awareness, and (4) Emotion. He is a Fellow of both the American Psychological Association and the American Psychological Society.

David Lee Keiser PhD is an Associate Professor in the Department of Curriculum and Teaching in the College of Education and Human Services at Montclair State University. He is interested in the ways in which the purposes of public education intersect with notions of democracy and social justice, how school/university partnerships work to provide the ethical and effective teachers to public schools, and how the nexus of mindfulness and teacher education can help navigate unchartered waters of the current high-stakes testing climate.

David M. Levy PhD is a Professor in the Information School at the University of Washington. For fifteen years (until December, 1999), he was a member of the Xerox Palo Alto Research Center (PARC) where his research focused on the nature of documents and on the tools and practices through which they are created and used. His current research focuses on information and the quality of life. His book, *Scrolling Forward: Making Sense of Documents in the Digital Age*, has just been published by Arcade Publishing.

John (Jack) P. Miller PhD has been working in the field of holistic education for over 30 years. He is author/editor of more than a dozen books on holistic learning and contemplative practices in education which include *Education and the Soul*, *The Holistic Curriculum*, and *Educating for Wisdom and Compassion*. His writing has been translated into eight languages. *The Holistic Curriculum* has provided the framework for the curriculum at the Whole Child School in Toronto where Jack has served on the Advisory Board. Jack has worked extensively with holistic educators in Japan and Korea for the past decade and has been visiting professor at two universities in Japan. Jack was one of 25 scholars invited to a UNESCO conference on cultural diversity and transversal values held in Kyoto and Tokyo in 2007. He teaches courses on holistic education and spirituality in education at the Ontario Institute for Studies in Education at the University of Toronto where he is Professor.

Deborah Orr PhD is in the Division of Humanities and the humanities graduate program and in the Graduate Program in Humanities, Religion, Values and Culture Field at York University. Her research and teaching bring a philosophical perspective to issues in the areas of gender, ethics, embodiment, spirituality, and pedagogy. Deborah has been active in organizing a series of conferences on holistic teaching and learning. She also teaches Iyengar Yoga, meditation, and philosophy.

Sean Park is a PhD candidate in Arts Education at Simon Fraser University, working with Heesoon Bai and Celeste Snowber. Sean is a Nei Gong and Tai Ch'i student of Sifu Lou Crockett at Blue Mountain Nei Gong, and musical director of Funk Depot Samba Orchestra. He is a staff member of the New Earth Institute. He offers training in Mindfulness-Based Stress Reduction.

Shahar Rabi is completing his PhD in Contemplative Education at Simon Fraser University in British Columbia, Canada and a Master's in Counselling Psychology at City University of Seattle (Vancouver campus). He is a Cofounder of the New Earth Institute, a non-profit research and education organization that offers integral education programs for youth and adults in Canada. Over the past fifteen years, Shahar has led workshops in Canada, Israel, India, and other countries about integral intelligence and well-being, taught philosophy in formal and informal education programs in high schools and universities, and worked as a dance teacher and choreographer. He is a Yoga and meditation teacher who lived in monasteries in India, Nepal, and Thailand, learned extensively from great teachers in the field of non-dual philosophy, and has been a part of communities engaged in the search for a unifying vision of a more holistic way of being.

Harold D. Roth PhD is Professor of Religious Studies and East Asian Studies and the Director of the Contemplative Studies Initiative at Brown University. Roth is a specialist in Early Chinese Religious Thought, Taoism, the History of East Asian Religions, the Comparative Study of Mysticism, and a pioneer in the developing field of Contemplative Studies. His publications include five books, *The Textual History of the Huai-nan Tzu* (Association for Asian Studies, 1992), *Original Tao: "Inward Training" and the Foundations of Taoist Mysticism* (Columbia University Press, 1999), *Daoist Identity: Cosmology. Lineage, and Ritual* (w/Livia Kohn) (University of Hawaii Press, 2002), *A Companion to Angus C. Graham's Chuang Tzu: the Inner Chapters* (Society for Asian and Comparative Philosophy, 2003), and *The Huainanzi: A Guide to the Theory and Practice of Government in Early Han China, by Liu An, King of Huainan* (w/ John S Major, Sarah Queen, and Andrew S. Meyer) (Columbia, 2009). He has also published more than three dozen articles on the early history and religious thought of the Taoist tradition, on the textual history and textual criticism of classical Chinese works, and on Contemplative Studies.

Saratid (Tong) Sakulkoo MS and MBA is a former monk, who has for five years tried to think about how to provide meditation techniques for his students, yet wonders if it is still useful. He teaches both graduate and undergraduate classes at Burapha University in Thailand.

Edward W. Sarath PhD is Professor of Music in the Department in Jazz and Contemporary Improvisation, of which he was the founding faculty member and chair (1987–2007), at the University of Michigan School of Music, Theatre, and Dance. As a leading innovator in the fields of improvised music, creativity and consciousness studies, and corresponding educational reform, he divides his time between performing, composing, teaching, and writing about these areas. He is the author of *Improvisation, Creativity, and Consciousness: Jazz as an Integral Template for Music, Education, and Society*, published by SUNY Press, and *Music Theory Through Improvisation: A New Approach to Musicianship Training*, published by Routledge. In addition to the above books, his writings appear in *Integral Education* (SUNY), *Innovative Higher Education, Journal of Music Theory, Handbook for Research on Music Education, International Journal for Music Education*, *Music Educators Journal*, *Jazz Research Papers*, *Jazz Educators Journal, Jazz Changes*, Harvard Law School's *Negotiation* journal, Columbia Teachers College's *Educational Record*, UCLA's *HERI* online journal, *Newsday*, and *Ultimate Reality and Meaning* journal. He is a fellow of the National Endowment for the Arts (three-time NEA fellow), the American Council of Learned Societies, the Ford Foundation, and the National Center for Institutional Diversity.

Charles Scott PhD is a teaching and administrative staff member at City University of Seattle and an Adjunct Professor at Simon Fraser University. His research and teaching interests include dialogue and its applications in education, contemplative practices in education, learning with international students, and the role of the arts in education. He received his PhD in Arts Education at Simon Fraser University; his dissertation examines Martin Buber's philosophy of dialogue as educational praxis.

Saskia Tait is a PhD student at Simon Fraser University under the supervision of Dr. Heesoon Bai. Her work has a focus on the application of integral theory and contemplative practice in different educational contexts. She is Cofounder and Executive Director of the New Earth Institute, a non-profit research and education organization that offers integral education programs for youth and adults in Canada. She is a published author, applying integral models and approaches to a variety of topics including education, sustainable development, and community development. She has also served as a Yoga psychology and philosophy teacher. She completed her 500-hour Yoga Alliance certified teachers training and has helped to teach advanced Yoga retreats and teacher training programs in Canada and India with World Conscious Yoga Family.

Daniel Vokey PhD is a Professor of Philosophy of Education in the Department of Educational Studies at the University of British Columbia. His current research interests include integrating Eastern and Western perspectives on the development of practical wisdom, focusing on the experiential side of the theory-practice dialectic through which intellectual and moral virtues are cultivated. In addressing this topic Daniel draws not only from his background in moral philosophy, but also from both his professional career in adventure-based experiential education (typified by Outward Bound) and his study and practice of Shambhala Buddhism.

Nancy W. Waring PhD is a Faculty Director of Lesley University's Mindfulness Studies Program. She developed the school's Advanced Graduate Certificate Program in Mindfulness Studies and the Mindfulness Specialization within Self-Designed Master's Degree Program. Under her direction, Lesley will launch a 36-credit Master's Degree Program in Mindfulness Studies in fall of 2014. Waring has presented on subjects in mindfulness and education at numerous conferences and special programs, including at the Mind & Life Symposium on Contemplative Studies in Denver, April, 2012. She has also presented at the Center for Mindfulness (CFM), the California Institute for Integral Studies, Harvard University, MIT, and the Center for Contemplative Mind in Society. She has given many workshops on mindfulness. She has completed the CFM's advanced teacher development training program in MBSR, and works with individual clients with chronic medical and other issues. She began her Vipassana training in 1982 with Jon Kabat-Zinn and her ongoing training in Insight Dialogue with Dr. Gregory Kramer in 2005. A long-time medical journalist and editor of *Hippocrates* magazine, Waring has written widely on allopathic and mind/body medicine.

Elise G. Young PhD is a Middle East historian and tenured faculty member in the History Department at Westfield State University. She has conducted research in Palestine, Israel, and Jordan, and has written extensively on women and modern nation-state building in those regions. She is author of *Keepers of the History, Women and the Israeli-Palestinian Conflict* (Teacher's College Press, 1992), an innovative feminist historiography of the war over Palestine.

Dr. Young's doctoral dissertation in Middle East history, based on research conducted in Palestinian refugee camps in Jordan in 1994/1995, is entitled: "Between Daya and Doctor: A history of the impact of modern nation state building on health east and west of the Jordan River."

Arthur Zajonc PhD is professor of physics at Amherst University, where he has taught since 1978. He has been visiting professor and research scientist at the Ecole Normale Superieure in Paris, the Max Planck Institute for Quantum Optics, and a Fulbright professor at the University of Innsbruck in Austria. Since 1997 he has served as scientific coordinator for the Mind and Life dialogue with H. H. the Dalai Lama whose meetings have been published as *The New Physics and Cosmology: Dialogues with the Dalai Lama* (Oxford 2004) and *The Dalai Lama at MIT* (Harvard UP, 2006). He currently directs the Academic Program of the Center for Contemplative Mind, which supports appropriate inclusion of contemplative practice in higher education. Out of this work and his long-standing meditative practice, Zajonc has authored *Meditation as Contemplative Inquiry: When Knowing Becomes Love.* He has co-authored a book with Parker Palmer, *The Heart of Higher Education: A Call to Renewal.* Zajonc blogs for *Psychology Today* on meditation. He has also been General Secretary of the Anthroposophical Society in America, a cofounder of the Kira Institute, president of the Lindisfarne Association, and a senior program director at the Fetzer Institute.

Index